THE KITCHENER ENIGMA

THE
KITCHEN
ARENA

THE KITCHENER ENIGMA

THE LIFE AND DEATH OF LORD KITCHENER OF KHARTOUM, 1850–1916

TREVOR ROYLE

The History Press

First published 1985 by Michael Joseph.
This revised edition published 2016 by The History Press.

The History Press
The Mill, Brimscombe Port
Stroud, Gloucestershire, GL5 2QG
www.thehistorypress.co.uk

© Trevor Royle, 1985, 2016

The right of Trevor Royle to be identified as the Author
of this work has been asserted in accordance with the
Copyright, Designs and Patents Act 1988.

All rights reserved. No part of this book may be reprinted
or reproduced or utilised in any form or by any electronic,
mechanical or other means, now known or hereafter invented,
including photocopying and recording, or in any information
storage or retrieval system, without the permission in writing
from the Publishers.

British Library Cataloguing in Publication Data.
A catalogue record for this book is available from the British Library.

ISBN 978 0 7509 6729 7

Typesetting and origination by The History Press
Printed and bound in Great Britain by TJ International Ltd

CONTENTS

	Preface and Acknowledgements	7
	Prologue	10
1	An Irish Boyhood	15
2	A Sapper in the Levant	29
3	Egypt: Riding the Desert Sands	50
4	Sudan: Planning for Victory	72
5	Omdurman: The Making of the Legend	95
6	Symbol of Empire	122
7	The Great Boer War	143
8	India: Commander-in-Chief	175
9	Egypt Again: Proconsul	202
10	War Lord: Raising the New Armies	227
11	The Need for Shells	257
12	Strategy on Three Fronts	281
13	Erosion of Power	312
14	An Unpitied Sacrifice	336
15	The Kitchener Legacy	366
	Notes	381
	Bibliography	395
	Index	402

PREFACE AND ACKNOWLEDGEMENTS

This book is being republished in 2016 to commemorate the centenary of the death of Field Marshal Earl Kitchener of Khartoum. It was first published in 1985 under the title *The Kitchener Enigma* and I have used the opportunity to make corrections, where necessary, to the original text. I have also reduced the length of the book and, more importantly, have recast the chapters dealing with Kitchener's role in the First World War to take advantage of the advances in scholarship that have taken place over the last thirty years. In this respect I am particularly grateful to have had sight of recent work undertaken by George H. Cassar, David French, Keith Neilson and Peter Simkins, whose *Kitchener's Army: The Raising of the New Armies 1914–1916* must be the definitive account of the formation of the largest British Army in history.

The suggestion to republish my book came from Michael Leventhal and I am grateful to him and the staff at The History Press for all their help and encouragement during the editing and recasting process.

Debts remain from the first edition and my first is to the members of the Kitchener family who provided me with access to previously unpublished letters and papers relating to Kitchener's private life. Mrs Anne Edgerly, Kitchener's great-niece, allowed me to borrow her collection of private letters written by Kitchener to his sister Millie between 1870 and 1899. The late Earl Kitchener lent me Sir George Arthur's notebooks and a selection of miscellaneous papers relating to his great-uncle. My thanks to him and to his sister, Lady Kenya Tatton-Brown, for their support and generous hospitality.

For help in researching Kitchener's childhood in Ireland, I must thank, first and foremost, my good friend the late Colonel Eoghan O Neill, to whom the original biography was dedicated. Through him I was introduced to three historians who gave freely of their time and experience to help me uncover some of the facts about the Kitchener family's residence in Ireland. They all have my thanks: Dáithi Ó hÓgáin, University College Dublin; Donall Ó Launaigh, National Library of Ireland; and Padraig Ó Snodaigh, National Museum of Ireland. Father J. Anthony Gaughan allowed me to use material from his extensive research into the local histories of Limerick and Kerry; Bryan MacMahon of Listowel and John Savage of Tralee helped in similar fashion, as did Seamus McConville, editor of *The Kerryman*. Dr K.P. Ferguson of the Military History Society of Ireland, and Irish labour historian Sean Hutton provided me with many useful leads in understanding Kitchener's attitudes to recruiting in Ireland during the First World War, and at a crucial stage in my examination of the Redmond Papers I was helped greatly by the insights provided by my good friend Owen Dudley Edwards, erstwhile Reader in Commonwealth and American History at the University of Edinburgh.

The late Sir Philip Magnus-Allcroft, a distinguished earlier biographer of Kitchener, commented on some of my findings and offered kindly encouragement, for which I am most grateful.

For their insights into the sinking of HMS *Hampshire* I owe thanks to John R. Breckenridge, who organised the underwater surveys of the wreck in 1977 and 1983, and to his associate Dr Larry McElroy, who gave me sight of his written research findings. Ex-Stoker F.L. Sims, the last living survivor of the *Hampshire*'s crew, allowed me to interview him: many of his comments on the disaster are contained in Chapter 14. He has my thanks.

Others who discussed with me aspects of Kitchener's life or who helped in other ways and to whom I owe thanks are: Derek Bowman, Dr Paul Dukes, Chris Graham, Callum Macdonald, Neil Mackay, Sorley

PREFACE AND ACKNOWLEDGEMENTS

MacLean, John Montgomery, Hayden Murphy, Walter Perrie, Lindsay Phillips, Dr Jill Stevenson and Francis Stuart. With the passing of the years some are no longer with us but their help and encouragement remain strong in the memory.

Libraries and their staffs must come high in the regard of any self-respecting author, and here I was not lacking support and helpful suggestions. Alan Taylor, formerly of the City of Edinburgh's library service and now a distinguished author, was always sympathetic and painstaking with my many requests for books and papers, and as ever the staff of the National Library of Scotland provided me with books and manuscripts in their customary professional way. I was equally well provided for at the Public Record Office, Kew (now the National Archives), which holds the principal Kitchener manuscript collection, as well as the Admiralty and War Office papers and other private collections quoted in the text. I should also like to thank the staffs of the libraries at the Imperial War Museum, the National Army Museum, the National Maritime Museum and Kirkwall Public Library, whose librarian, the late John L. Broom, provided me with useful newspaper cuttings relating to the loss of HMS *Hampshire*.

The author and publisher would like to thank the following for permission to reproduce their photographs in this volume: National Army Museum (pictures 1, 12, 13, 20, 23, 26 and 28), Illustrated London News Picture Library (2, 3, 5, 6, 8, 14, 15, 16, 21, 25, 30, 32, 33, 34, 36, 45, 46, 47 and 48), Mansell Collection (4, 7, 9, 22, 24, 29, 35 and 44), Imperial War Museum (10, 37, 38, 39, 40 and 41), BBC Hulton Picture Library (11, 19, 31, 42 and 43), Punch (17, 18, 27 and 49).

PROLOGUE

To most people, those who knew him by virtue of their service with him, or those who recognised him only by his beckoning finger and imperious wartime command to serve their country, Field Marshal Horatio Herbert Kitchener, 1st Earl of Khartoum and of Broome, was an enigma.

Given to being both anti-social and a stern taskmaster, he found it difficult to express his innermost feelings and frequently retreated behind a public persona consisting of cold unblinking eyes, a luxuriant moustache and a taciturnity that defied encroachment. Yet Brigadier-General Frank Maxwell, VC, whom Kitchener called 'The Brat' and who was his ADC and confidant from 1900 to 1906, was moved to write to his father that 'He [Kitchener] really feels nice things, but to put tongue to them, except in very intimate society, he would rather die.'[1]

Kitchener discouraged close acquaintance, even with those who served on his staff, yet he was given to sentimental gestures to those whom he admired or to those who had given him their loyalty. In August 1915, at a time when the nation was beginning to accustom itself to the big losses of the First World War following the Battles of Neuve Chapelle and Festubert, Kitchener lapsed into tearful silence on hearing the news of the death of Julian Grenfell, the much admired poet son of his friend Lord Desborough.

Kitchener was also a man who believed that he was defrauding the Almighty if he were not doing his full duty, but that belief in hard work

PROLOGUE

also carried with it the fear of failure. 'I wish you could tell me more what I'm doing wrong,' he asked Lord Derby, his Director-General of Recruiting in 1915. 'I feel there is something more I ought to do for the country. I am doing all that I can and yet I feel that I am still leaving much undone.'[2]

His ambition, which his detractors thought undisguised and vainglorious, took him to become Sirdar, or Commander-in-Chief, of the Egyptian Army; Governor-General of the Sudan; Commander of the British forces during the Boer War; Commander-in-Chief of the army in India; and British Agent and virtual ruler of Egypt. In turn he became one of the best-known symbols of Empire yet, when he was invited in August 1914, it took all the persuasion of his Prime Minister to make him Secretary of State for War.

In his private life he enjoyed collecting porcelain and antique furniture, practised flower-arranging, enjoyed inspecting a well-set dinner table, and amongst connoisseurs was considered an expert in *chinoiserie* and medieval armour. He turned his home at Broome Park in Kent into a personal monument to his many successes; nevertheless he shunned publicity and kept his personal life so private that only his sister Millie and a few chosen friends were privy to his innermost thoughts. Even his death was shrouded in mystery and rumour.

Given so many contradictions it is perhaps in the nature of this paradoxical man that it should have been someone who generally disliked him, David Lloyd George, who came closest to making the most pertinent remark about Kitchener when he compared him to 'one of those revolving lighthouses which radiate momentary gleams of revealing light far out into the surrounding gloom, and then relapse into complete darkness'.[3]

Even though Kitchener lacked the common touch of Field Marshal Lord Roberts, who was known by the homely soubriquet of 'Bobs', the British public worshipped him: yet all the hero-worship of earlier years was to pale into insignificance with the appearance of his famous recruiting poster during the early months of the First World War. Drawn by Alfred Leete, a self-taught artist from the West Country who had left school at the age of fifteen to pursue his chosen career, sign first appeared on the front cover of the magazine *London* on 15 September 1914.

It was a brilliant concept, and one of the simplest and most effective designs created by any artist of the war. It was quickly taken up by the Parliamentary Recruiting Committee, an all-party group headed by the Prime Minister, Herbert Asquith, Andrew Bonar Law, the Leader of the Opposition, and Arthur Henderson, the leader of the Labour Party. The committee first met on 31 August 1914 and was responsible for producing a series of recruiting posters designed to pull at the heartstrings of Britain's manhood. Other powerful posters with emotional slogans were 'Take up the Sword of Justice' depicting the loss of the *Lusitania*, and 'Daddy, what did YOU do in the Great War?' with its uneasy mix of domesticity and belligerence; but none had the simple directness or brought home the propaganda message more clearly than the creation of Kitchener as a messianic recruiting sergeant.

Later in 1914 the poster appeared in a number of guises but the centrepiece was always Leete's original interpretation, the pointing finger and behind it the bushy moustache. Their owner was not averse to being depicted in that way if it served the army's purpose, although he insisted on the addition of 'God save the King'. Since 1913 the War Office had employed the Caxton Advertising Agency to brighten up its recruiting campaigns and on the outbreak of war Sir Hedley Le Bas, Caxton's owner, was quick to recognise the value of Kitchener to the cause:

> I knew the solid advantages of that wonderful name and personality, with the power to move people and inspire them to patriotic effort. The right to use the name made the enormous task of finding a new army all the easier. We who managed details of the publicity campaign had a name to conjure with – a good will already created. So in all the appeals put out Lord Kitchener's name was our great asset and was never absent from them.[4]

And that good will counted for much. With the exception of Winston Churchill in 1940 no other British war leader has excited so much public enthusiasm for the country's call and in the early part of the First World War Kitchener was looked upon as the personification of the

PROLOGUE

nation's will to win. Later the Prime Minister's wife, Margot Asquith, who had once lionised Kitchener, remarked unkindly that he might not be a great man but at least he was a great poster.[5] Her throwaway remark was repeated gleefully by Kitchener's enemies and after his death in 1916 his recruiting poster seemed to mock its original intentions. When it was revived in the 1960s it was little more than a crude advertising symbol, also the motif of Carnaby Street and 'Swinging London'. With the cheapening of the poster Kitchener's star had also fallen and by the time his features were appearing on coffee mugs and badges, on T-shirts and posters, the famous moustache had become a joke, a relic of Britain's long lost past.[6]

Yet Leete's poster is also full of contradictions. The face is clearly Kitchener's, but Kitchener's crudely depicted as a younger man – in 1914 he was sixty-four, greying and heavy featured. Even the eyes are wrong, beetling and too closely set together, although Leete was careful to give them a cold arresting quality to increase the poster's impact. Only the moustache is Kitchener's, the instantly recognisable and bristling hallmark of the stern warrior. Any evaluation of the poster is bound to be unrewarding when it is compared to the photographs of the man himself. As a young man Kitchener was more than a little vain of his appearance and his photographs from that period show him to be handsome, if somewhat reserved. His eyes, piercingly blue and set far apart in a large face, were especially noticed. 'His head was finely shaped, and the eyes, blue as ice, were in early life of singular beauty,' wrote his colleague Lord Esher. 'Sandstorms and the Eastern sun ruined them in later years.'[7] Standing 2in over 6ft, Kitchener used his height to advantage to stare haughtily over the heads of those who stood before him. His large square frame, angular build and commanding presence set him apart from an early age and in later life his face was made distinctive by its high colour, the 'sunburnt and almost purple cheeks and jowl' making a 'vivid manifestation upon the senses' of the young Winston Churchill at the end of the campaign in the Sudan.[8]

None of us can escape the legacy of our appearance. From his youngest years Kitchener's looks attracted much comment: he was considered by many to have been almost too handsome for his own good in his youth, yet he allowed himself in later life to become a prisoner to his moustache. In the manner of the times Kitchener was invariably photographed looking fixed ahead, seeing only what he wanted to see, oblivious to all distractions. But there is a curious indecision and gentleness in the eyes. It is the face of a man who did not want to be forgotten.

1

AN IRISH BOYHOOD

Horatio Herbert Kitchener was born on 24 June 1850 at Gunsborough Villa, an unpretentious shooting lodge standing some 3 miles from Listowel in County Kerry in south-west Ireland. Later in life he was noticeably reticent about some of his family background, but whenever it was hinted that he came from Irish stock Kitchener would demur and repeat the Duke of Wellington's disclaimer of his own birth in Ireland that 'A man can be born in a stable and not be a horse'.

Like many other English families who settled in Ireland, the Kitcheners were always anxious to emphasise the purity of their English origins. These can be traced back to the reign of King William III when they were churchwardens of the Church of Holy Cross in the parish of Binsted on the Hampshire downs. In 1666 a Thomas Kitchener left Binsted to become an agent to Sir Nicholas Stuart of Hartley Maudit, whose estate was at Lakenheath in Suffolk. His grandson, also called Thomas, had three sons, the eldest of whom, William, became a successful tea merchant in London: this was a period when London was emerging as one of the world's great commercial centres and the city's merchants prospered accordingly. William also extended the family's fortunes by rising in society. He became a member of an ancient guild, the Clothmakers' Company, and his sister Elizabeth married a brother of the foreign editor of *The Times*, Henry Crabb Robinson, whose diary and correspondence threw much interesting light on the lives of his friends and fellow writers Wordsworth, Coleridge, Lamb and Hazlitt.

William Kitchener married twice, for the second time in 1797 to Emma Cripps, by whom he had three sons, the youngest being Henry Horatio Kitchener, the father of the future field marshal. He was born on 19 October 1805 at the family home at 8 Bunhill Row in Moorgate and he was named for Admiral Lord Horatio Nelson, whose death at the battle of Trafalgar took place two days later. The young Henry Horatio Kitchener was also to follow the profession of arms but he foreswore the navy for the army, being commissioned in 1830 into the 13th Light Dragoons. In 1845, as a captain, he married Frances Ann, the daughter of the Reverend John Chevallier of Aspall Hall in Suffolk.

If the Kitchener family was solidly and unprepossessingly English, by comparison the Chevalliers were glamorous and romantic. Of Huguenot stock, they had owned the handsomely proportioned Aspall Hall, near Stockmarket, since 1702 and down the years they also owned the living of Aspall, a benefice that allowed the eldest sons of the family to continue living in landed ease. Frances's grandfather, Temple Chevallier, was a scholar of Magdalene College, Cambridge; her uncle, Temple Fiske Chevallier, was a noted astronomer and a pioneer of science in education; and her own father, John, was a qualified physician who interested himself in agrarian improvement and the care of the mentally ill as part of his duties as the rector of Aspall. He married three times, his third wife, Elizabeth Cole of Bury (Lancashire), presenting him with five children, of whom Frances Ann, or Fanny, was the youngest. In their turn, five children were born to Henry Horatio and Fanny: Henry Elliott Chevallier (1846), Frances Emily (Millie) Jane (1848), Arthur (1852), Frederick Walter (1858). Horatio Herbert, being born in 1850, was therefore the third child and second son: from his father he borrowed Nelson's Christian name but throughout his life the family knew him as Herbert. In his adult years Kitchener was to be much taken with his Chevallier connection and the family followed his career closely. Whenever he could, he visited Aspall while on leave and when he came to be raised to the peerage in 1898 he took as part of his title the name of his mother's childhood home.

Shortly after their marriage Fanny accompanied her husband to India, where he reached the rank of lieutenant-colonel. However, shortly after

AN IRISH BOYHOOD

the birth of Chevallier, their first child, her health wilted and Colonel Kitchener decided to bring his family back to Britain where he transferred on half-pay to the 9th Regiment of Foot (later The Norfolk Regiment). Being put on half-pay was not an unusual experience for the Victorian army officer but it was a setback as it did not count towards an officer's career; also, if he remained on the half-pay list for more than two years compulsory retirement followed. After chasing appointments in Whitehall during the course of 1848, Colonel Kitchener finally decided to leave the army. He sold his commission early in the following year and determined to seek a more modest living elsewhere, in Ireland.

At the time, in 1849, Ireland was just coming to the end of the Great Famine, a disastrous four-year period that saw the failure of the potato crop, the staple foodstuff, bring huge distress to the rural population. To combat the effects of the subsequent evacuation of the rural areas and to infuse new capital into Ireland the government passed the Encumbered Estates Act of 1849 by which bankrupt estates could be sold to land speculators. On completion of a sale through the Encumbered Estates Court in Dublin the purchase money would be distributed amongst various claimants and the residue paid to the seller. Of the 7,200 petitions heard by the Encumbered Estates Court that year some 300 came from Britain: one of those successful was Colonel Kitchener.

Early in 1850 Colonel Kitchener bought the estate of Ballygoghlan, on the Kerry-Limerick border between Moyvane and Tarbert at the mouth of the River Shannon. The once thriving estate had been ruined by the famine, its village of the same name was deserted and the house itself was in such a condition of disrepair that the family could not immediately move in. While Colonel Kitchener busied himself with supervising the necessary alterations his wife stayed with a family friend at Gunsborough Villa, near Lisselton on the road from Listowel to Ballybunion, and it was while she was there that her third child, Horatio Herbert, was born during the early part of the summer of 1850. Three months later, on 22 September, he was baptised at the Protestant church of Aghavallen at Ballylongford. His godmother, Miss Mary Elliott, was the daughter of another English landowner at Tanavalla near Listowel. By the year's end the Kitcheners had moved into their new home and appointed a nurse for the children, Mrs Sharpe. Her memories paint a vivid picture of family life at Ballygoghlan.[1]

As was the case with the majority of the British speculators who bought land under the terms of the Encumbered Estates Act, Colonel Kitchener's presence caused a good deal of local resentment. Many bankrupt estates had been sold at the insistence of creditors and the new landlords were often only intent on getting a quick return on their capital outlay. They might have improved their properties and introduced new methods of agriculture but they were not always respecters of tenants' rights. As there was no law to protect the Irish peasant from rack-renting and eviction, the landlords used that freedom to coerce tenants into becoming little more than poorly-paid labourers and considered themselves free to evict those who failed to keep up with the increased rents.

It was not long before Colonel Kitchener exercised his rights in an attempt to make his estate quickly profitable. When one of his tenants who could not meet the new rents was evicted from his property the colonel ordered his bailiffs to set their dogs on any who disobeyed his orders. According to local tradition the tenant's family was also horse-whipped before the roof was burned off their cottage, thus making it no longer fit for human habitation. The incident may have been typical of many others perpetrated during those years but it created a good deal of outrage in the vicinity. Colonel Kitchener, like most of his class, underestimated the determination of the Irish peasants not to abandon land they took to be theirs by right of inheritance and his actions made him a hated figure.

Not long after that incident Colonel Kitchener evicted one Sean MacEniry, an articulate farmer who gained some measure of revenge by composing folk verses that lampooned his landlord.[2] The main thrust of his insults was MacEniry's claim that Colonel Kitchener suffered from bromhidrosis, an unfortunate malady characterised by a fetid stench from the body's sweat. Known in Irish as *boladh an tsionnaigh* (stench of the fox) or as *boladh an diabhail* (stench of the devil), the complaint is considered in the local folk traditions of Kerry and Limerick

AN IRISH BOYHOOD

to be 'the mark of utter depravity'.[3] Yet in carrying out evictions from his property and by behaving harshly towards his tenants, Colonel Kitchener was merely behaving like many other English landlords of the time. In their eyes, peasant-Ireland, tied to superstition and the Catholic Church, Gaelic-speaking and largely hostile to its landlords, represented a people who had to be brought within the 'civilising' influences of Victorian expansion and profit-making. Recent outbreaks of terrorism by various nationalist groups had only confirmed British distrust of the Irish and it was hard for the parliamentarians in London to grasp that the situation could only be retrieved by putting right fundamental grievances, especially those concerned with land tenure. The gulf between tenant and landlord was wide and Colonel Kitchener never made any attempt to bridge it: his children were brought up to look upon themselves as belonging to a superior race and from an early age his sons, noticeably Herbert, behaved in an imperious and arrogant way towards the Irish.[4]

However, Colonel Kitchener was determined to make his estate prosper and by 1857 he felt confident enough to extend his holdings by taking on Crotta House in Kerry, a seventeenth-century pile with an imposing front porch near Kilflynn, halfway between Listowel and Tralee. It had belonged to the Ponsonby family, which was part of the great house of Bessborough, and its acquisition was an outward sign of the colonel's continuing success. As a result, Herbert's childhood days were divided between the two houses but, although Crotta was the grander of the two with its large garden and views of the Slieve Mish mountains to the south-west, it was always regarded by the children as less homely than Ballygoghlan.

Family life was run on military lines and Mrs Sharpe, the governess, recounts how breakfast was served punctually each morning at eight o'clock and that even the maid serving breakfast to Mrs Kitchener in her bedroom had to wait outside the door until the clock in the hall struck the hour.[5] Punishment, too, was meted out on martial lines and the boys were encouraged to develop a sense of discipline based on a code of mutual honour. Tale-telling was frowned upon and stoicism of body and mind encouraged: when, for instance, at the age of ten

Herbert damaged his hand with a large stone he retired to his bedroom and would not allow his mother to be told of the injury. Before saying goodnight to her he hid his hand in his jacket sleeve behind his back so that she would not be alarmed. On another occasion he suffered without complaint the punishment of being pegged out for a minor offence – this involved him being spread-eagled beneath the summer sun on the front lawn with his hands and feet tied to croquet hoops.[6] And when he fell from his horse and injured his arm while hunting, his father ordered him to remount and continue the chase. This, too, he suffered without complaint.

Colonel Kitchener also employed his boys as additional hands to help in the improvement of his estates. According to Stephens, the colonel's steward, young Herbert was the equal of any man on the estate when it came to the cutting of turf and his father trusted him with the herding of cattle to market in Listowel although, in strict accordance with his instructions, the manager of the Listowel Arms Hotel was forbidden to serve the boy with breakfast until all the cattle had been sold.[7] As their father had a dislike of formal schooling, the boys' education did not pass beyond elementary instruction at the village school in Ballylongford: yet, on receiving a teacher's report that Herbert was a dullard the colonel flew into a rage and threatened to apprentice his son to a hatmaker. Consequently, private tutors were employed but this proved an unsatisfactory solution. Some years later, in 1867, when Herbert's learning was tested by his cousin Francis Elliot Kitchener, then a fellow of Trinity College, Cambridge, he was found to have only a rudimentary grasp of English and arithmetic and an almost complete absence of general knowledge.

Nevertheless, in his father's eyes, those drawbacks were not of any immediate concern as he believed that his boys should be practical first and academic second. So it was against a background of hard physical work and equally strict discipline that Herbert's childhood was spent. As a small boy he was pretty, fair and curly-haired, noticeable for his winning smile and arresting, sky-blue eyes.[8] Later, his hair turned dark and he quickly outgrew his brothers, to become a handsome, lanky boy who seemed in his teenage years to be too tall for his strength.

Nonetheless, he sat a horse well, and local tradition has it that, whenever he took cattle to market, he would delight in trying to chivvy them into a semblance of order. Certainly his erect military bearing was long remembered in the district.

Two anecdotes from his boyhood give a clue to the future man. One day his mother found him weeping inconsolably after coming across four dead fledglings in a felled tree: each bird had to be buried with great solemnity before he regained his composure. His mother worried about that side of his nature, fearing that he might repress his emotional instincts and so damage himself by his own self-discipline. Indeed, as he matured, Herbert tended to hide his sensitive side and adopt instead many of his father's mannerisms. Once, while watching estate workers felling trees, he struck a boy called Jamesy Sullivan across the knuckles with his riding crop. Stung by the assault, Sullivan turned on Kitchener and struck him from his horse, knocking him unconscious. Such an attack would have spelled immediate dismissal and ruin for the workers but, on coming round, Herbert refused to tell his father or to have the men punished. That degree of sensitivity, aggression and aloofness, when mixed with a sense of high moral purpose, was a powerful combination, and it turned Kitchener into a reserved and complicated young man. He preferred keeping himself to himself, and his family and friends noticed that, apart from the love he lavished on his frail, pretty mother, he disliked baring even the slightest emotion in public.

Although Colonel Kitchener was a stern father with an unpredictable temper, he lavished much care and attention on his wife and encouraged his children to adore her, too. The poor health that had attended her in India had followed her to Ireland and she became a prisoner to incipient tuberculosis. The south-west of their adopted country, with its temperate but damp climate, was not an ideal one for her condition, nor was it helped by the eccentricities of her husband's domestic arrangements. He hated to sleep beneath blankets, believing them to be unhygienic: instead, he preferred to cover their double bed with sheets of newspaper, specially sewn together, which could be varied in quantity according to the season of the year.[9] In that way, he argued, cleanliness could be allied to economy. While such a bizarre regime may have been suitable for a robust man such as the colonel, it was bound to have a deleterious effect on his wife.

On the whole, their time in Ireland had been unhappy for Fanny Kitchener. Her childhood and early years had been spent in comfort and ease at Aspall and she was used to a close and tightly-knit society that revolved around visits, musical evenings and gossip. Ballygoghlan was a gaunt and uncomfortable house, difficult to heat, and the winter evenings were long and cold. The houses of the surrounding English families lay far apart and it often took a whole day to make a visit. If she wanted to go further afield, it meant writing letters and staying the night. It was no place for a woman unless she shared with her husband the pleasures of the field, but Fanny had never been the outdoor type and gradually the circle of her existence narrowed to the two houses, her husband and the well-being of her children. As the years progressed she became increasingly unwell, and by 1863 she was virtually confined to her room.

The only remedy for tuberculosis known to the Victorians was treatment in the mountain air of Swiss health resorts. To have stayed on in Ireland would have spelled Fanny Kitchener's doom and so during the course of that winter of 1863 her husband put in hand the sale of his Irish estates. It was a good time to put them on the market. The population decline and the increase in the size and prosperity of agricultural holdings, together with his own improvement of his estates, made Ballygoghlan and Crotta attractive propositions that brought Colonel Kitchener a 'decent' return on his original investment of £3,000 when he came to sell them in the early part of 1864 (roughly £256,000 today). The family moved to Switzerland, first to Bex, then to Montreux.

Little now remains to remind the visitor of the Kitcheners' stay in the district. Ballygoghlan has long since disappeared but part of Crotta and Herbert's birthplace at Gunsborough still stand, the latter for many years in the possession of the O'Dowd family. In the tiny Church of Ireland chapel at Kilflynn, where the Kitcheners used to worship, a commemorative tablet was erected after the field marshal's death by a Mrs Tugham Hanbury, the wife of a naval surgeon. It gives his date of birth, wrongly, as 15 June 1850. Only once did Kitchener return to the south-west of Ireland, in the summer of 1910, when he made a motoring tour of Cork, Kerry and Limerick at the invitation of the Marquess of Lansdowne. He revisited some of the scenes of his childhood and, while in Tralee, was taken in a jaunting car to Crotta by the Savages, the family who had bought the estate and who continued to manage it. He astonished his hosts by remembering every field on the estate by its Irish name and he appeared to take great pleasure in walking through the house and its gardens recalling animatedly his boyhood days.[10]

After Ireland, Switzerland came as a rude shock. The town of Bex in the Canton Vaud was considered to be one of the best Swiss spas of the period. Its sulphur and brine baths were reputed to have qualities to dispel rheumatism and cure circulatory diseases, while the pure air of the mountains was supposed to work wonders for chest complaints. However, Fanny Kitchener's condition did not improve and during the summer of 1864 the family moved again, to Montreux on Lake Geneva. It was to no avail and by the end of the year Frances Kitchener was dead. Unable to find his bearings Colonel Kitchener decided to remain in Montreux and to bring up his children in Switzerland where his expenses would be much lower than they would have been had he followed his inclination to return to England. At the year's end, Herbert, Walter and Arthur were sent to school in Geneva before going on to boarding school at the gaunt Château du Grand Clos, at Rennaz near Villeneuve at the eastern end of Lake Geneva. By that stage Colonel Kitchener hoped that all his sons would pursue careers in the army.

Run by the chaplain to the English congregation in Montreux, Reverend Bennett, the school prided itself on its strict discipline and its ability to produce educated young gentlemen for the armed forces – those hoping to go to university were encouraged to return to England to be crammed by private tutors. The education at the Château du Grand Clos was well grounded, but elementary. Even so, Herbert found it a trial and as a result he worked hard to grasp the elements of grammar, science, mathematics and languages required to pass his entrance examination to Woolwich, the military academy at which cadets were trained for service in the Royal Engineers and Royal Artillery – against his father's wishes he had decided not to try for the cavalry and opted instead for the Engineers.

At this time he also became a proficient linguist, learning to speak German and French fluently. France in particular, the French people and all things French, were to be a lifetime's source of delight.

In 1866 there was further change when his father remarried, his second wife being his daughter's music mistress, Emma Green. The new domestic arrangements effectively broke up the family. The oldest brother, Chevallier, joined the army and married in 1877. Walter, too, became an army officer, being knighted and appointed a major-general before his death in 1912. Arthur became a scientist; but it was Frances Emily – 'Millie' to her brothers – who was Herbert's favourite, and he was godfather to her second child. From his time in Switzerland until his appointment as Sirdar of the Egyptian Army in 1892 he kept up an intimate correspondence with her from which a picture emerges of Kitchener that is very different from the stern taskmaster of later years. Millie, who married Harry Parker of Rothley Temple in Leicestershire in 1869, remained a constant source of encouragement to her brother and a confidante of many of his most private thoughts and innermost emotions.

In order to consolidate his financial affairs Colonel Kitchener now bought land in New Zealand, then in the final stages of the land rush and development of the South Island, and later in 1866 he visited his estate near Dunedin where his youngest daughter, Kawara, was born in 1867. On their return the Kitcheners settled in Brittany, at Dinan, while the boys continued at school in Switzerland.

Kitchener's strict diet of study and self-discipline at the Château du Grand Clos cured the academic inadequacies discovered earlier but they took their toll on his well-being. The cold and damp of the gloomy château did not help matters and it seems that the stress of working hard under those conditions helped to bring on a minor breakdown in the early spring of 1867. Alarmed, Colonel Kitchener ordered his son back to England to stay with his cousin, Francis Kitchener, in Cambridge. There he recovered his health and began a process of intense tuition for his entrance examination to Woolwich: for the final polish he went to London to study under a well-known army crammer, Reverend George Frost, whose home and study-centre was at 28 Kensington Court.

AN IRISH BOYHOOD

It was a fairly normal process for potential cadets to be given an extra course of study before the examination that would determine their futures, and Reverend Frost had an excellent reputation for 'cramming' his students for Woolwich – a glance at the results of the successful candidates confirms his status as London's most successful tutor.[11] Most of the boys in Herbert's group had been to English public schools and as a species they were quite alien to him; so much so that his time in Kensington would have been quite barren had it not been for the company of a fellow student, Claude Reignier Conder, who became his first close friend.

Two years older than Kitchener, Conder was the son of a civil engineer who also contributed essays to the *Edinburgh Review* and most of his childhood had been spent in Italy, where his education had been completed and refined by a series of tutors. Before going to Reverend Frost's he had spent some time at University College, London, where he laid the foundations of his later career as an archaeologist. Reserved and modest as a young man, Conder was a brilliant student who seemed to sail through the cramming course and when he first met him Kitchener stood in awe of his fluency and his urbane learning. In the examinations for Woolwich Conder gained a creditable ninth place in the entrance lists.

The Royal Military Academy at Woolwich had been founded by Royal Warrant on 30 April 1774 and for 200 years it was the cadet training establishment for most officers commissioned into the Artillery, the Engineers and, later, the Signals. Known as 'The Shop' – because its original home was in a workshop at the Royal Arsenal – during the 1860s it had been undergoing a process of rapid reform. Entrance examinations had been introduced, the harsher methods of discipline were being abolished and the buildings and barracks improved. By slow degrees the battle for professionalism in the army was being won and, although there had been cadet mutinies against conditions in 1861 and 1864, by 1868, the year of Kitchener's entry, Woolwich was a tough, down-to-earth institution whose lieutenant-governor (commandant), Major-General Sir Lintorn Simmons, an engineer, insisted on high standards of learning and discipline.

To get into the academy the successful cadet had to sit an entrance examination of no little complexity. Twelve subjects were on offer – mathematics, classics, English language and composition, English history, geography, French, German, geometrical drawing, freehand drawing, experimental sciences, natural sciences and Hindustani – and each candidate had to be examined in five, one of which, mathematics, was compulsory. A total of 2,500 marks was the minimum successful total, of which 700 had to be gained in mathematics. When Kitchener's time came – he was examined at the Royal Hospital, Chelsea between 2 and 11 January 1868 – he chose to be examined in mathematics, French, German, natural sciences and English history (he had already qualified in geometrical drawing) and from these he gained 3,753 marks, passing twenty-eighth in the list of fifty-six successful candidates. The highest mark of 6,452 was gained by an old Etonian, H.C. Chermside but, to put Kitchener's placing and marks into perspective, of the 116 original candidates sixty had failed to obtain the minimum marks and so failed the examination.

Fortunately for Kitchener, Conder was still at Woolwich and the friendship between the two young men deepened. At that time Conder was perfecting his knowledge of Hebrew and he introduced the language to his friend, thus implanting in Kitchener his first interest in the culture of the Levant, the area of the eastern Mediterranean now covered by Lebanon, Syria and Israel. That study led them back to the Bible and the two men became interested in Anglo-Catholicism, the High Church element in the Anglican Church that had been associated earlier in the century with the Oxford, or Tractarian Movement. Its adherents emphasised the Catholic, as distinct from the Protestant, character of the Church and paid strict attention to the rituals of the Christian calendar, commemorating feast days and observing fasts such as Lent.

However, for the young Kitchener at Woolwich, it was not all hard work and religious enthusiasm. To his sister Millie he reported during his first term in the spring of 1868 on the successful outcome of a sports day with flat races and steeplechases after a sumptuous luncheon in the gymnasium attended by the Prince of Wales and Prince Arthur of

Connaught. Kitchener entered his horse in three races but did not win anything, partly because he fell at the water jump, a monstrous affair 'about 20 feet square and five feet deep filled with water. Nobody being able to jump it every body went in. Some dived in and swam across. Others stumbled through it. In fact it was a most amusing sight for all except those that were in the water like me.' Not without a little pride though, he confided that she would be struck with awe by his 'military swagger' and by his 'giving the orders in a very imposing voice'.

In the summer of 1868, for his first break from Woolwich, he holidayed alone in the West Country, but instead of touring, as he had originally intended, he stayed for a few pleasurable weeks in Truro. Apart from walking with friends to The Lizard and to Land's End and delighting in the wild beauty of the Cornish coastline he had other more pressing reasons for enjoying his first real holiday. His vanity, he wrote again to Millie, had been greatly indulged as 'the few young ladies that Truro boasts of … see so very few young gentlemen that they are very different to les filles de Londres'. Four very pretty girls from the Chilcot family took his eye and with them there were picnics, expeditions, boating trips and croquet on the lawn. It was all very agreeable and on one never-to-be-forgotten evening there was dancing in their house by candlelight when he was the sole object of their attentions. As he wrote to Millie:

> Think of me with four young ladies, each longing for her swain. I really thought I should break a blood vessel or do something dangerous as they each caused great strain upon my legs. However I got over it and enjoyed it very much as the candle which lighted us was put out quite by accident and we got on very well without it.

He was eighteen, it was high summer and he had four pretty girls vying for his attention, the dream of any red-blooded young man. The next day he woke to ashes as the Chilcots ended their holiday and their dancing daughters passed out of his life.

There were other flirtations, too, while he was a cadet; one girl in particular, Eleanor Campbell of Thurmaston Hall in Leicestershire, took his fancy, but 'Nellie' was destined to marry in 1887 his future colleague in Egypt, Leslie Rundle. In his adult years, Kitchener kept a firmer check on his emotions but never again was he to feel quite as comfortable in female company. Even so, a sense of gallantry never deserted him and as a young man there is little doubt that he was well aware of and responsive to the attractions of girls.

Kitchener spent two years at Woolwich and passed out in December 1870, having missed one term in his second year due to illness and the stress of having to keep up with his colleagues. In spite of his hard work, his cadetship had been undistinguished: like many another man who achieved greatness in later life, Kitchener's early development was slow.

2

A SAPPER IN THE LEVANT

Kitchener's report on leaving Woolwich was not encouraging. Although his qualities as a linguist were noted and he was known to be a fine horseman, he was considered to be 'below rather than above the average standard of an R.E. officer'.[1] He was remembered by his fellow cadets particularly for his aloofness and also for his adherence to High Church rituals.

Before taking up his commission, which was granted to him on 4 January 1871, he travelled to Brittany to spend Christmas at Dinan. His relationship with his father had improved since Ballygoghlan days: the long absences had bound father and son together in a common understanding that grew stronger as the years went by. In all his later letters, Papa gave way to the more jocular endearment Governor. Like many another Victorian father who could not take to his offspring in their childhood days, the colonel began to admire his son's sturdy independence as he grew into manhood. For his part, Kitchener would have done anything to win his father's approval. Indeed it was his sense of filial respect that almost ended his career before it began.

The fact that Colonel Kitchener had never seen war service seems to have preyed on his mind, to the extent that he cherished the hope that his son would succeed where he had failed. As France, in that winter of 1870–71, was approaching the end of the disastrous Franco-Prussian War, what better opportunity would there be for his son to throw away the textbooks and see service in the field? Prussia's tactical superiority, and a complete breakdown in the French system of mobilisation, led to a series of inglorious French defeats culminating in the surrender of the Emperor Napoleon III at Sedan. Two French armies remained in the field, one on the Loire and the other on the Swiss border, but both were largely ineffective. By the beginning of 1871, in spite of spirited resistance in Paris, the war was as good as over – on 18 January Wilhelm I was proclaimed Emperor of Germany in the Hall of Mirrors at Versailles and by the Treaty of Versailles Alsace and eastern Lorraine were ceded to the new German Empire, thus sowing seeds of discontent that were to be harvested bitterly in the next century.

With his father's assistance, Kitchener made his way with a fellow cadet, Henry Lawson, to General Chanzy's army of the Loire, a makeshift force composed largely of reservists and conscripts of uncertain ability and enthusiasm. Earlier that month, on 10 January, it had been in action at Le Mans, an untidy defeat that had seen Chanzy's men being slaughtered by the new, revolutionary, rifled breech-loading Prussian artillery. Chanzy's army was attempting to relieve the siege of Paris but the extent of its advance was Laval, and it was there that Kitchener's war ended. He had been taught the first principles of ballooning at Woolwich and, anxious to put theory into practice, he ascended with an officer in a French artillery balloon without donning proper protective clothing. As a result of a chill caught in the cold upper air he developed pneumonia and pleurisy and Lawson anxiously sent for Colonel Kitchener, who brought him back to Dinan. Had Lawson not acted so judiciously Kitchener's life could have been lost as he had been placed in a cold and dirty billet long given up by the French. It took him a full year to recover from the effects of the illness.

Many of Kitchener's contemporaries would have given a year's promotion to have seen active service but his adventures also attracted the wrath of the War Office. Kitchener's commission had been granted to him when he was in the process of joining Chanzy's army and, as a serving officer, he had technically broken the strict neutrality maintained by the British government. Such a violation was open to punishment and, on his return to London, he was ordered to the War Office to answer for his actions to Field Marshal HRH the Duke of Cambridge, cousin to Queen Victoria and Commander-in-Chief of the British Army.

Cambridge was an autocrat who brooked no opposition and he was known to dislike officers who were 'clever'.[2] On this occasion, Kitchener had appeared to be too clever for his own good so, after throwing the rulebook at him, the Commander-in-Chief admonished him with a reprimand, an episode that Kitchener was able to turn to his own advantage later in life in conversation with Lord Esher:

> After the armistice and during the peace negotiations he returned to England, when he was sent for by the Duke of Cambridge, then Commander-in-Chief. 'He called me,' Lord K. said, 'every name he could lay his tongue to; said I was a deserter, and that I had disgraced the British Army. I never said a word; and then at the end, the Duke, with a funny sort of twinkle, added, "Well, anyhow, boy, go away, and don't do it again".[3]

Kitchener's first posting was to the School of Military Engineering at Chatham, which had been founded in 1812 to provide junior engineer officers with a course of practical training before they joined their units. The Royal Engineers is regarded as a corps d'élite within the British Army and in Kitchener's day it was generally understood to attract the more intelligent type of officer who, unlike their compatriots in the cavalry or infantry, did not have to purchase their commissions. Engineers had been an integral part of the army since the fifteenth century, when they had been responsible to a Board of Ordnance for the control of the King's Works and Ordnances. In 1716 an officer corps of engineers was established to command the Corps of Sappers and Miners, an arrangement that lasted until 1787 when the Corps of Royal Engineers was given its Royal Warrant. In 1855 the Board of Ordnance was abolished and the Royal Engineers and the Royal Artillery came under the control of the Army's Commander-in-Chief.

The courses at Chatham were very much suited to Kitchener as they were practical in nature. He learned the arts of field fortification surveying, submarine mining and estimating and building construction; he was introduced to new-fangled ideas such as electricity, photography and lithography, and he refined his knowledge of ballooning in field tactics. The school was the most advanced of its kind in Europe and the high standard of its courses gave a solid introduction to the role of the Royal Engineers within the British Army.[4]

Chatham was more to his taste than Woolwich had been, so Kitchener began to rise in the estimation of his instructors and to be noticed as a keen young officer of some promise: his records show a distinct improvement in his military performance. Somewhat to the amusement of his fellow officers he continued to observe High Church rituals, a phase in his life that lasted until 1874 when he joined the English Church Union, established to protect the interests of those churchmen who wanted to continue observing Anglo-Catholic practices within the Church of England. Although, for Kitchener, this was an important moral stance, he was not a bigot and his involvement in the defence of Anglo-Catholicism should be seen against the pattern of his times, the period in which the schism between the Anglo-Catholics and the evangelicals was at its widest in the Anglican Church. At Chatham he became friendly with one of his senior instructors, Captain H.R. Williams, an older man with High Church interests who, like Conder, became a friend and confidant. Kitchener's friendship with Williams was simple and trusting, based on a 'never to be forgotten brotherhood of keen Churchmanship' and, although his friend did not progress beyond the rank of colonel, in the days of his own fame and power Kitchener never forgot that early 'brotherhood', often sending Williams keepsakes from his visits abroad.[5]

Kitchener's promise brought him the reward of an appointment as ADC to Brigadier-General George Richards Greaves, a member of the War Office staff who had been invited to attend the manoeuvres of the Austrian Army during Easter 1873. Greaves had begun his career as an ensign in the 70th Regiment of Foot (later 2nd East Surrey Regiment) and came from a family with strong military traditions; he was a highly respected officer and Kitchener regarded the appointment as a feather in his cap. When Greaves fell ill on their arrival in Vienna Kitchener had to take his place during the manoeuvres and also at the official functions where, on more than one occasion, he found himself sitting next to the Emperor of Austria–Hungary, Franz-Josef, who as a young archduke had succeeded to the Hapsburg throne in 1848. Such attention rarely came the way of a junior officer but such was the impact that Kitchener made on his hosts that invitations to revisit Vienna were still coming to him in later years.[6]

His tour of Austria–Hungary ended with an inspection of military bridge-building on the Danube and, on his return to Britain, Kitchener was posted to a mounted troop of the Royal Engineers at Aldershot, which twenty years earlier had been designated the main training garrison in the south of England. Known to generations as 'The Camp' or as 'The Home of the British Army', it was a large area made up of barrack blocks, parade grounds and training ranges and it was there, in 'The Long Valley', that Kitchener put his men of 'C' troop through their paces to learn the use of field telegraphy during mock battles. It was there, too, that his knowledge of surveying was perfected to become the useful craft that gave him his first employment.

During the summer Kitchener holidayed in France with his father 'on the principle of economy' and while there was introduced to the art of photography, becoming an enthusiastic amateur photographer. He also took the opportunity to discuss his military career with his father. It was not at all certain what he would do next and he dreaded the thought of being sent to India. As he told Millie, he wanted a chance to see action and had therefore volunteered for Major-General Garnet Wolseley's expedition to the Gold Coast to fight the Ashanti in 1873:

> What an age it is since I have written to you and what an age since I have heard from you. You have quite forgotten your duty in not reporting to me the progress of my godson of whom you are in charge. I know you will say it is my fault, sobeit, forgive me. A great swell in a pulpit said, How charming it is to be sinned against because then you can forgive. Now *you* have the chance. Don't let it slip and you ought to thank me for it, but I am afraid you won't write me a line like a good girl to tell me how you are getting on and to show me that you have not quite forgotten you have such an encumbrance as a long-lost brother. Now for news. You know when I left Chatham I was posted to C troop RE. Since that I have been through Dartmoor manoeuvres where we were drenched with rain, then back here field day etc. Lots of work acting adjutant for some time, then the governor came down and paid me a visit which I think

he enjoyed. Since that, hunting and work. Saturday last we had a good run and in the evening I dined with Prince Arthur. Was not that grand? Today I rode the Colonel's horse and had a capital day. You must know I have volunteered for service on the Gold Coast. At least I have said if they order me I shall be glad to go. So the next thing you may hear will be my slaying niggers [sic] by the dozen ... Give my love to Harry. When are you coming home? Kiss my godson, he is not yours you know, for me.

The application to join Wolseley came to nothing but the time of inaction came to an end in November 1874. On Conder's recommendation Kitchener was seconded to the service of the Palestine Exploration Fund, which had been founded, on 22 June 1865, with the object of accomplishing 'the systematic and scientific research in all the branches of inquiry connected with the Holy Land, and the principal reason alleged for conducting this inquiry [being] the illustration of the Bible'.[7] There had been a considerable number of quasi-religious bodies founded earlier in the century to conduct similar inquiries but their objectives had been to challenge, on a biblical basis, the various scientific claims that had been made concerning man's evolution. The Palestine Exploration Fund, the last of its number, was the most successful largely because its founding committee had determined that its findings should be based on scientific principles and that the claims of religion should not override material or worldly considerations. To this end it had been suggested and accepted that the main part of the work should be undertaken by officers of the Corps of Royal Engineers. Their tasks were the detailed survey of Palestine, the drawing of an accurate map, the investigation of biblical sites and the study of Palestinian place names.

Conder had joined the Fund in 1872. Since that time he had been conducting the survey of west Palestine and it was the death of his assistant, Charles Tyrwhitt-Drake, in June 1874 that had opened the way to Kitchener's appointment. He owed his preferment to a remarkable man, Sir Walter Besant, who had been secretary of the Fund since 1868 and who held that post for eighteen years. As fundraiser, administrator, mentor and transcriber of the scholarly transactions, he brought manifold talents to the work of the Fund and was the driving force behind its success. Today, he is perhaps best remembered for being a founding father of the Society of Authors in 1884 but his appointment to the Fund was instrumental in laying the foundations of his career as a man of letters. 'The salary was sufficient for bread and cheese, the hours were not excessive, leaving plenty of time for my own work,' he wrote in his *Autobiography*, 'and the associations were eminently respectable.'[8] Besant was particularly fond of Conder and assisted him greatly with his own publications, but he warmed to Kitchener too. For the next ten years he was to be an important correspondent and Kitchener's letters to him from the Middle East reveal a deep love for and commitment to the desert and its peoples.

It had been tacitly agreed by the War Office and the Palestine Exploration Fund that a condition of the Engineer officers' employment was that they would be free to undertake military intelligence work, an understanding that continued until the outbreak of the First World War. During the last quarter of the century the British government was still wrestling with the 'Eastern Question', which had arisen in 1822 with the Greek revolt against the Turks and which had continued with the gradual break-up of the Ottoman Empire in the Balkans. This shaky edifice, which stretched from the Persian Gulf in the south to Budapest in the north, and from the Caspian Sea in the east to Algeria in the west, was falling slowly apart due to an absence of administration and funding and intrigue at the court of Constantinople. Matters had come to a head in 1853 when Britain had sided with the Turks over Russian claims to sovereignty over the holy places in Jerusalem. The resulting Crimean War had ended in stalemate and solved nothing, and for the next half century the peoples of the Balkans were united in their hatred of Turkish rule. Those patriotic sentiments had been enflamed by Russian promises of support, and it was against a background of continuing unrest in the Balkans and the Near East as a whole that Kitchener met up with Conder on 19 November 1874 in the Plain of Philistia.

He had journeyed out by train to Venice before hurrying on to Trieste to catch the ship that took him by way of Corfu to Alexandria and thence to Jaffa. During this pleasant voyage he flirted so outrageously with a pretty American girl that her husband felt forced to remonstrate with him about his behaviour. (Apparently they had been caught together 'on the deck by the light of the moon [singing] Yankee Doodle and such like'; Kitchener told Millie that her husband was 'a nonentity his wife very much the reverse'.) At Alexandria he had his first view of what the Victorians called the Near East and he was captivated immediately. A curious dance by black Nubians on the quayside caught his eye and he stood there spellbound for two hours. The next day he continued his journey and, after a night at sea, he woke early on the Sunday morning of 15 November to watch the sun rise over the Holy Land. He wrote to Millie:

> It was glorious more from associations than anything else seeing for the first time that land which must be the most interesting for any Christian. The sun rose in a golden halo behind the hills and we rushed towards it through the deep blue sea ... all around the town are orange plantations surrounded by cactus fences. It is the greenest place I have seen in Palestine.

From the outset Kitchener threw himself into everything he tackled. Surveying, photography and copying inscriptions formed the main thrust of his work and by the following year his name was appearing prominently and regularly in the Fund's quarterly statements. This was work to Kitchener's liking: it demanded infinite patience, a mind tuned to practical details and a regard for economy, and he rose to all three challenges. It taught him to work alone with the minimum of supervision, to rely solely on his instincts and it also brought him into contact with the open spaces of the desert and its peoples, his appreciation of which would gain in strength as the years went by.

At Christmas Kitchener fell ill with fever and was ordered to rest in Jerusalem, where he busied himself with the orderly presentation of Conder's notes and studying Arabic. By Easter he was back again in the field near Gaza where he was involved in a minor adventure saving Conder from drowning in the Mediterranean at Ascalon. 'A strong suck-back of the waves carried me out into the broken waters,' wrote Conder, 'whence I was rescued by Lieutenant Kitchener.'[9] The incident occurred on 5 April and three months later Kitchener was again to be a saviour when he was prominent in repelling an attack by a group of Muslim dissidents in Upper Galilee. Conder's party had arrived in the village of Safed and pitched camp in an olive grove when they became the object of abuse and catcalls from a group of Arabs led by an elderly sheikh called Ali Agha Alan. Conder remonstrated and knocked the sheikh down when he attempted to draw a weapon – his report of the affray gives a good account not so much of the predicament in which the officers found themselves, but of their attitudes towards it:

> They addressed me with many curses, and the old man thrust the battle-axe against my ribs; but it was a wonderful instance of the influence which a European may always possess over Arabs, that they allowed me to take them by the arms and turn them round, and that on my telling them to go home, with a slight push in that direction, they actually retreated some little way.[10]

However, Conder's action only raised the temperature. A hail of stones followed and he was forced to order the release of the Arab, who had been tied up with ropes after being knocked to the ground. It was a dangerous moment: Conder was hit over the head by an Arab wielding a huge club and would have been finished off had not Kitchener 'parried another blow which smashed his hunting crop, and maimed his arm; we both recovered together and repelled their blows with our steel-headed whips'.[11] The order was then given to retire to a neighbouring hill where help arrived in the shape of a platoon of Turkish troops accompanied by the British consular agent.

The crowd dispersed and Conder ordered his party to leave the area for Haifa where they could recuperate in safety: his own injury left him permanently scarred, Kitchener's thigh had been badly bruised, and as both men were suffering from fever there was no option but to suspend the survey. Throughout the incident Kitchener had displayed great resolution in coming to his friend's aid and Conder was quick to underline the part played by his second-in-command, reporting to the Fund that he 'must inevitably have been murdered but for the cool and prompt assistance of Lieutenant Kitchener, who managed to get to me and engaged one of the club-men, covering my retreat'.[12]

Conder's wound meant that he could take no further part in the field work and although he spent another term working for the Fund in the 1880s he retired to live in Cheltenham, where he died in 1910. After spending fifteen months in London working on the notes and the map, Kitchener returned to Palestine in February 1877 in charge of the survey. Before leaving Britain for the Middle East, Kitchener visited his father in Dinan and also prepared for press his only book publication, *Lieutenant Kitchener's Guinea Book of Photographs of Biblical Sites,* which was published by the Fund. It contained a dozen photographs taken by Kitchener in Palestine together with an accompanying text. Although it was handsomely produced its sales were minimal, no doubt because its selling price was considered to be too high. Walter Besant handled the publication of the book and had to endure several letters from the fledgling author, who wanted the book to be cheaper and to contain more photographs, and in the event the only interested purchasers of the book were supporters of the Fund.

On returning to Palestine Kitchener began to relish his first command and threw himself into the task of completing the survey of Galilee. In his reports to the Fund in London he displayed a growing confidence and he began to make political suggestions based on the intelligence reports he was completing in tandem with the survey – he was adamant, for example, that British interests in Palestine should be reinforced by the appointment of a consul in Haifa. The outbreak of war between Russia and Turkey presented him daily with the delicate task of negotiating his party's progress with local officials and sheikhs, thereby laying the foundations of diplomacy with Arab peoples that stood him in good stead in later life. As a military officer he was fascinated by the strategic situation that was unfolding around him and also by the country's responses to it. Revolts against Turkish rule in Bulgaria had attracted Russian support and after months of meaningless negotiation had brought Russian troops to the walls of Constantinople.

In spite of the dangers, the picture that Kitchener presents of his work in Palestine is a pleasant one. Rising early, he and his companions would devote themselves to whatever task called them that day – surveying a valley perhaps, or investigating the site of a holy well – before the fierce midday sun drove them to siesta. Forgetting lunch they would gather in the cool of evening to eat together in front of a smoking fire, a 'babel of grunting camels and shouting servants' acting as a familiar chorus. On other days there would be dreary rides across the desert, which he found not to be 'flat as people think but one mass of hills, all brown and looks from a distance like a brown petrified sea'. There were religious festivals to be observed – 'it is the oddest sight possible to see these solemn-looking creatures in dressing gowns with large felt hats rushing around in a ring like mad and shouting to the music of the fife and drum badly played. They were crowded in the tomb like sardines and did not smell so fresh.' And then there was leave in the Mediterranean cool of Beirut where he could relax over long dinners with Levantine friends. His many letters to Millie, who was then living in New Zealand, are illuminated by the energy and devotion he put into his work in Palestine – 'every day, from morning to night, I enjoy life amazingly'.

By working his men hard Kitchener completed his work in Galilee on time and at the end of November he sent his survey team back to Britain while he, acting on the spur of the moment and assisted by the standing he enjoyed amongst Turkish officials, took himself off to view the war on the Turkish–Russian front at Kamerleh in Bulgaria. He went by rail from Constantinople to Adrianople and then on to the front by way of Tatar Bazardjik, and during the course of that journey he kept a diary that formed the basis for his first article in *Blackwood's Magazine* (one of his first literary efforts, an anonymous article on the reorganisation of Asiatic Turkey, had appeared in the *Pall Mall Gazette* the previous summer).

Kitchener's article opens with a spirited description of the landscape, a bare and uncultivated plain with absurd contours followed by the railway that crossed it, but the essay was not merely a military appraisal of the situation. It took a side-swipe at the Liberal leader W.E. Gladstone, whom he detested, and expressed disquiet at the gallows he frequently saw on the lamp-posts in the Turkish-held town of Tatar Bazardjik.

> Our impression of the Bulgarians was not favourable. They seem to be a most despicable race. Morally they appear to be at the lowest ebb; and if some of those

> who agitated about the Bulgarian atrocities [committed by the Turks] really saw and talked to the people, they would, I feel sure, modify their opinion.[13]

At Kamerleh he also met, for the first time, Valentine Baker whose career offers a bizarre footnote to Victorian military history. Three years earlier Baker, a well thought-of army officer with an unsurpassed knowledge of Middle Eastern affairs, had brought disgrace upon his head while serving as assistant quartermaster-general in Aldershot. On 17 May 1875, he took the train from Liphook to Waterloo and found himself sharing a first class compartment with a young girl called Rebecca 'Kate' Dickinson. Some minutes later, while the train was at full speed, the driver was disconcerted to see a girl clinging on to an open carriage door. On stopping the train the driver and his guard heard Miss Dickinson claim that she had been sexually assaulted by Baker. In spite of his social connections and his friendship with the Prince of Wales, Baker was committed to trial on a charge of assault and attempted rape, and amidst a public outcry was fined and sent to prison for a year. This he bore with considerable fortitude but his career in Britain was at an end. Fortunately, though, for his military instincts, Baker's actions did not attract opprobrium in the Ottoman Empire and on being released he was appointed a major-general and pasha in the Turkish Army. In 1877 he had won universal acclaim for his conduct in leading the Turkish forces at the Battle of Taskhessan and beating off a superior Russian force by the skilful deployment of his cavalry. 'Allah has smitten the English with such blindness that they allow a man like him to leave their army,' remarked a Turkish artillery officer who witnessed the affray and Baker's handling of it.[14] Most British army officers who met him warmed to Baker in spite of his disgrace and Kitchener was no exception: he became an ardent champion of his leadership abilities when he returned to Britain.

On Christmas Day, after lunching with his medical compatriots – 'the attempted plum pudding more resembled a poultice' – Kitchener returned to Constantinople by the simple expedient of hiding beneath the seat in a first-class carriage when officials told him that no seats were available. At the beginning of January 1878 he was in London again, where he took up residence with his father in a flat at 18 Albert Mansions in Victoria Street. The colonel had separated from his second wife and in 1878 was attempting a legal settlement, a state of domestic discord that did not appeal to Kitchener. Each day he would leave the flat and take himself off to Kensington Gore to work in the map-room of the Royal Geographical Society – he had been elected a Fellow in the previous year. By the summer's end he and Conder had finished the preparation of the 1 in survey of some 6,000 sq. miles of Palestinian territory, reduced map, twenty-six volumes of 'memoirs' or notes, six of which bore Kitchener's name, and a number of detailed plans of archaeological sites, such as the groundplan of the crusading castle at Râs el 'Ain. The committee of the Fund was impressed. 'It may in short be fairly claimed for the survey of West Palestine,' wrote Besant, 'that nothing has ever been done for the illustration and right understanding of the historical portions of the Old and New Testament, since the translation in the vulgar tongue, which may be compared with this great work.'[15]

Kitchener worked again, briefly, for the Palestine Exploration Fund in the summer of 1884 on the survey of southern Palestine – but the first four years' work in Palestine had set him up sufficiently to give him a reasonable idea of his own capabilities. For one whose academic record had been poor he had proved to be a painstaking scholar. He had been introduced to the craft of administration by being plunged into it in the field and he had bowed to the expediency of a strict economy. His military horizons had widened too; exposure to a country under Ottoman rule had introduced him to Arab aspirations and to the means employed by the Turks to keep them in check. Not the least of that understanding was his first-hand knowledge of the decaying Ottoman Empire and the threat its dissolution posed in the Balkans and the Levant and to Britain's imperial trade routes through Egypt. He had also come to respect the desert and with the sense of awe came a liking for living in warmer climes – between 1877 and 1914 he was not to spend a winter in England. So strong was that feeling of identification with the Levant that he grew a beard and spent his private hours clad in Arab dress, dispensing mint tea and burning incense.

His brother, Walter, was amazed to find Kitchener, attired thus, sitting cross-legged in the Victoria Street flat where cushions and heavy drapes had replaced more conventional furniture. Finally, his work for the Fund had so marked him as a coming man that, in 1915, Professor Samuel Daiches of the Jewish College in London, himself no mean Palestinian scholar, could claim at a public lecture that the years in the Levant had laid the foundation for Kitchener's future career:

> No recorded period in the life of Kitchener gives us such an insight into the mentality of Kitchener and into his ways of work, reveals to us the mind, heart and character of Kitchener, as well as the four years' work he spent in Palestine and in Palestine work. His indomitable energy, his unequalled thoroughness, his hunger for work, his mastery of detail, his preparedness, his economy in men and material, his making sure of success, his sense of duty, his ability to inspire others with zeal for work and his clear and crisp style: all these characteristics of Kitchener of today we find in Kitchener nearly forty years ago when he was doing his Palestine exploration work.[16]

High praise, but it was justified. Between them, Kitchener and Conder had extended present knowledge of known sites – the synagogue at Capernaum and Jacob's Well at Nablus, for example – the natural features of the country had also been delineated in great detail and, as a result, the events of the Bible would be better understood by scholars in the future. A number of new sites had been surveyed and in many places received scholarship had been questioned and revised, Kitchener remarking somewhat tartly that he had been able to correct those 'who looked more for what ought to be in the country than what is'.[17] Not the least of Kitchener's virtues was that he had directed the latter part of the survey under trying conditions and yet he had managed to keep within the budget allotted to him.

In August he travelled to Dublin to lecture to the meeting of the British Association on The Survey of Palestine, the only occasion he lectured in public; he was applauded for his passionate plea for the preservation of the Capernaum synagogue and for his remarks, delivered in an off-hand way, that his party had collected 2,770 names for the map, in so doing displaying a knowledge that put to shame the official guides. On 10 September 1878 he delivered his final report and on the same day he accepted a new appointment, the survey of the island of Cyprus.

Cyprus had been transferred to British control at the Congress of Berlin in 1878, which attempted to bring stability to the Near East. As a result the island was to remain under Turkish suzerainty but it would be administered by Britain and a first essential was the provision of a decent map. Kitchener's work in Palestine had been noticed in Whitehall and it was a natural progression that he should be seconded again, this time into the service of the Foreign Office to whom he would report.

When Kitchener arrived on the island on 15 September 1878 he was more than a little surprised at what he found. The governor's residence was a tented village 2 miles outside Nicosia, a large number of men belonging to the six battalions of the garrison had succumbed to fever and lay ill in makeshift hospitals, dozens of bars had opened in Larnaca and everywhere there was filth and pestilence. The High Commissioner, Lieutenant-General Sir Garnet Wolseley, had arrived two months earlier and his initial buoyancy had given way to a well-disguised despair at the task that faced him. He had made a name for himself with a mixture of military appointments: as an administrative officer he had been Edward Cardwell's mentor during his military reforms of 1871, and he had also led a number of small-scale imperial military expeditions such as the Red River Expedition in Canada of 1869–70 and the first Ashanti War of 1873–74. So concerned was he with innovation and the niceties of correct military administration that the phrase 'All Sir Garnet' had passed into the language as representing the acme of military efficiency. A thoughtful and progressive soldier, he was the author of several books on military subjects, and ambitious junior officers vied for his attention. During the Ashanti War Wolseley had attracted to his staff a tightly-knit group of officers whose careers were subsequently marked for greatness by reason of their association with him. The 'Wolseley Ring', as it was known, included Redvers Buller, Evelyn Wood, George Colley, George Richard Greaves and Baker Russell, all of whom reached high rank and played important roles in Britain's military history. To attract Wolseley's attention was to hasten the career of any enterprising young officer, but, unfortunately for Lieutenant Kitchener that did not happen to him.

One reason was that Kitchener was an outsider and Wolseley was suspicious of the reasons for his appointment and his connection to the Foreign Office. Wolseley also looked on his own posting as being something of a sidestep in his career and, as reports reached him of his contemporaries furthering their careers in Afghanistan, he was beginning to grow restive. 'All our thoughts here are now turned to the Afghan frontier,' he wrote to his wife in November, 'and I long to be in the saddle leading our men through those passes which former wars have made so familiar to us in history.'[18]

Realising that he could only maintain his reputation by making a success of his administration in Cyprus, Wolseley set about his work with a will. His first task was to reorganise the island's taxation system, which was based on land ownership. So corrupt had been the Ottoman administration that he was forced to begin all over again to ascertain the ownership of most of the land on the island. A land commission was established and Wolseley also instituted a number of agrarian reforms to improve usable land and to prepare it for the British government's planned colonisation of Cyprus by Maltese farmers. For this task he needed a serviceable map and it was on this point that he came into conflict with Kitchener, who wanted to repeat his success in Palestine by producing a map based on the proper principles of triangulation, one that would be of permanent use to scholars and archaeologists. Wolseley thought otherwise. His immediate need was for a roughly accurate map that could be used to determine property boundaries and which would meet the requirements of his land commission. Kitchener's grandiose and scholarly ideals did not appeal to him and, when he wrote to Whitehall requesting clarification back came the reply that a revenue survey would be sufficient. Kitchener was spared any further unpleasant confrontation when Wolseley was appointed to command the army in South Africa.

The man who saved Kitchener from Cyprus was another Engineer, Colonel Charles Wilson. He had been born in Liverpool in 1836, educated in Bonn and had made a name for himself with his survey of Jerusalem in 1866 and with his ordnance surveys of Scotland in 1866 and Ireland ten years later. In 1865 he had been employed by the Palestine Exploration Fund, surveying the countryside between Beirut and Hebron. Wilson had known of Kitchener's work and on learning of his predicament in Cyprus he was only too happy to offer his fellow sapper employment of a diplomatic kind.

On 26 June Kitchener took up a new post as military vice-consul in the town of Kastamonu in northern Turkey, where he spent the winter but, as he told Millie, it may have been a grand thing to be in the position to be welcomed into the presence of high-ranking Ottoman officials but the Anatolian climate left much to be desired:

> It is horribly cold here. We were wrapped in winter garb of snow a few days back and it still remains on the hills all around. I don't know what I should do without the fur coat I took from you. By the by there are a number of sables here. The export amounts to 3000 skins. They are rather dear but if you have grand envie de faire la Russe [sic] let me know. A new pasha has arrived. Great firing of cannon and commotion in the town but as it snowed the whole time the entry was a failure. We have interchanged official visits and I don't think much of him. He is a great swell with Mushier and Vizier but is a regular Turk of the old school. I am established in a large house of which I only occupy two rooms. There was no other to be got in the town. My house is all windows and consequently all draughts. It is impossible to warm it so you must excuse this writing as my hands are frozen. I hate the cold – this will be the first winter I have had for a good many years. It is certainly going to be something to remember.

Cold or no cold, Kitchener had been charged with a task and from his reports to the British ambassador in Constantinople, a detailed picture emerges of the difficulties he had to encounter.[19] Kitchener was appalled by the brutish nature of Turkish rule and he was quick to underline the oppression, starvation and cruelties that were the lot of the local population. Bribery, corruption and torture were practised on a universal scale and Kitchener's reports resound with moral indignation. It was to no avail, of course. Britain had no intention of offending the Turkish government whose officials saw no reason to mend their ways on account of British squeamishness. The following year, 1880, saw Benjamin Disraeli fall from office and Gladstone's Liberal administration sweep in on a tide of morality and justice that would not brook the presence of British officers serving the needs of such a barbarous despotism as the Ottoman Empire.

By that time Kitchener had returned to Cyprus at the request of the new High Commissioner, Major-General Sir Robert Biddulph, who had succeeded Wolseley after a spell as military secretary in Constantinople. Another Engineer and a member of the Wolseley Ring, Biddulph was an accomplished administrator and he was destined to bring order to the government of Cyprus by revising the system of taxation and by instituting a programme of public works. He was a great friend and admirer of Wolseley – they had met at Lucknow during the Indian Mutiny – but he refused to bow to him over the matter of the survey of the island. After persuading the Foreign Office to fund a survey based on correct ordnance principles, he wrote to Kitchener offering him the post of Director of the Survey at a salary of £672 a year, with an additional sum to be paid for the new registration of lands. It was a handsome offer but Kitchener at first demurred, feeling that his future might lie in the diplomatic line under Wilson's patronage; on consideration, however, he accepted, even though as he told Millie, now that winter was over, he had come to be very fond of Anatolia:

> I was sorry to leave Anatolia with its lovely scenery and the glorious feeling of being the biggest swell in the country to return to hum drum work again, but that is wrong. This is not hum drum work and surveying is always interesting. Still I miss the crowds to see me arrive and the governors of districts here do not back out of my presence. I suppose I shall get used to being an ordinary mortal again before long. I have a jolly house and garden here if you could send me any seeds of plants it would be jolly as though I have a large garden I have no flowers.

On his return to Cyprus in March 1880 Kitchener set up house in Nicosia, sharing the accommodation with a young Scottish aristocrat, Lord

John Kennedy, the sixth son of the Marquis of Ailsa, one of Scotland's wealthiest landowners. A subaltern in the Royal Scots Fusiliers, Lord John Kennedy was nine years Kitchener's junior and during their brief friendship he encouraged a very different Kitchener to emerge. Far from being the reserved lieutenant who had bridled against Wolseley's authority, Kitchener revelled in his new freedom. Apart from the problems he encountered in the mountainous south-west of the island the survey presented little difficulty to Kitchener and his assistant Lieutenant S.G. Grant, although on two occasions they were shot at by bandits. Their 1 in map was eventually published in 1885 and was much praised in military and civilian circles, confirming Kitchener's reputation as an accurate cartographer.

With time on his hands Kitchener allowed his horse-riding talents to shine by twice winning the steeplechase at the Nicosia racecourse and by acting as whip to the local hunt. More daringly, egged on by his high-spirited companion, he kept as a pet a bear cub that had been sent to him from Anatolia and he became known as something of a gadabout. A first moustache began to adorn his upper lip but he kept its growth within proportions. It was to be another two years before it reached the luxuriance that became his hallmark.

Another taste that he developed in Cyprus was collecting porcelain and this became a lifelong passion. He took a leading part in founding the Cyprus Museum and acted as its honorary secretary and curator. It had come into being by virtue of British enforcement of an Ottoman law of 1874 that insisted the government of Cyprus receive a third part of any finds from archaeological excavations on the island. Although Biddulph was happy enough to see the law being enforced he made it clear that no public funds would be forthcoming for the museum, which in Kitchener's time was little more than a crudely catalogued collection of antiquities kept in the outhouses of the Commissioner's Office in Nicosia. Nevertheless, Kitchener took his duties very seriously and reported his finds faithfully to the Trustees of the British Museum, who were so impressed that in 1881 they offered him the command of an archaeological expedition to Assyria and Babylonia. Biddulph refused permission, but Kitchener put up a characteristically stout defence, arguing that he could combine the excavation with diplomatic and intelligence work by applying to the Foreign Office to appoint him consul at Mosul in the valley of the River Tigris.

Cyprus was a happy interlude for Kitchener. It still retained the atmosphere of a frontier town and had not yet acquired any social niceties – an attempt at a 'season' in the winter of 1879–80 had failed when Lady Wolseley and the wives of other officers had found the extremes of temperature not to their liking. As a result, there were few parties or official receptions, and the British officers turned to sporting activities in their spare time. The club, as in other parts of the Empire, became the social fulcrum. Kitchener enjoyed that vigorous all-male society and diverted himself with its pursuits: he may have considered Cyprus a poor enough billet when he first arrived but he came to enjoy the simple pleasures it offered. Never again in his life was he to be so carefree:

> We have had some very decent sport lately [he wrote to Millie in January 1882] with our Harriers. Not much lepping but plenty of galloping over rocks. I have not much news to tell you since last week. Office every day until about 5 p.m. and then a ride if I can get one. I am doing some excavations amongst the old tombs at Salamis and have found a good lot of things. Only one gold ear ring in the precious metals but plenty of pots, pans, glass, alabaster and statuettes more or less broke. I have a grand pig with something inside that rattles. Would amuse the children only it is very precious, almost too utterly. I daresay you will see them all some day in the South Kensington Museum.

The government of Cyprus also introduced him to the 'wheel of Empire' and he came to appreciate the niceties of imperial administration. A memo he wrote for the Foreign Office two years after he left bears the signature of the late Victorian Empire-builder. It shows that Kitchener favoured a firm administration, a just system of taxation based on land ownership and a network of district officers to enforce the law. There is no mention of Turkish rule or of the aspirations of the Greek Cypriots for *enosis*, the renewal of their historic links with Greece. Although conditions had improved on the island, he lamented the fact that 'the late Liberal administration unfortunately thought it necessary to give the Cypriots elective self-government before they were prepared for it' and he believed that the effectiveness of British rule should be held up as a shining example for the Turks to emulate.[20] It is an assured document and in its confident phrases can be felt the respect that its author had for the value of duty to Empire.

3

EGYPT: RIDING THE DESERT SANDS

Despite the pleasures of living in Cyprus, Kitchener soon began to grow restless. The return to power of Gladstone as Prime Minister in 1880 had ended British involvement in the affairs of Turkey and, for the moment at least, it seemed that the Eastern Question had been solved. Gladstone's appeals to the finer points of British morality in his international dealings also meant that the country's imperial ambitions might be stilled temporarily and, as a consequence, there might be fewer opportunities for the ambitious officer. Kitchener had made a name for himself as an administrator, archaeologist and cartographer, but like any other enterprising soldier he knew that rapid promotion would only come his way once he had proved himself on the field of battle. Ironically, but fortunately for Kitchener, it was Gladstone, a staunch opponent of imperial aggression, who was forced by circumstance in 1882 to take a hand in the affairs of a country – Egypt – where British interests were threatened.

These centred on the Suez Canal, which had opened in 1869 to link the Mediterranean and the Red Sea and had become a vital artery on the sea route to India. Although the canal had been built largely with French capital Egypt was in dire financial straits due to the folly of its nominal ruler Khedive Ismail Pasha, who owed allegiance to the Sultan of Turkey. When he succeeded his uncle in 1863 Egypt was a relatively prosperous country made wealthy by the sharp rise in the price of cotton caused by the American Civil War, but Ismail had expensive tastes and this led to a massive deficit and expensive borrowing overseas. By 1875, almost insolvent, he was in dire need of £4 million to pay off overdue interest charges at several foreign banks. Then Britain played her hand. Acting independently, Benjamin Disraeli, the Prime Minister, persuaded the British merchant bankers Rothschild to find the money on the country's behalf. In return Britain acquired half the share in the Suez Canal Company and so became drawn directly into Egyptian affairs. The following year saw the bankruptcy of Egypt and the establishment of a British-French control commission that governed the country's finances and much else besides. When it became obvious to Britain and France that Ismail was unable to mend his ways, pressure was put on the Sultan of Turkey to bring his unruly vassal into line and he was deposed in favour of his eldest son, Tewfik, whom the control commission soon found easier to control.

However malleable Tewfik might have been in the hands of his Franco-British masters, his subservience was abhorred by Egypt's religious leaders, who resented a powerful Christian presence in their country. It was also resented by Tewfik's military leaders, who felt humiliated by the economic restrictions that had been placed on their army. Throughout the summer of 1881 tensions grew in the country. Europeans were assaulted in the streets and, with the army in a state of near mutiny, Tewfik capitulated and agreed to the formation of a national government with a charismatic officer, Colonel Arabi, as secretary of state for war. That winter saw nationalist fervour expressed in the streets of Cairo and Alexandria, and Arabi's slogan, 'Egypt for the Egyptians', appeared everywhere as the rallying point for a broadly-based popular nationalist movement. As Arabs ran through the streets shouting death to the Christians, Britain found herself having to act alone, France having decided that military intervention in Egypt could leave her exposed to German intrigue in Europe.

Much though it offended his principles, Gladstone was forced to take the path that had been so effective in the past: the Mediterranean fleet was despatched to Alexandria in a show of strength and also to uplift British subjects. On 10 July 1882 its commander, Admiral Sir Beauchamp Seymour, informed the Egyptian garrison that he would open fire the following morning unless the shore batteries were dismantled.

During those tension-filled days Kitchener sent off a series of telegrams in an attempt to find employment in Egypt, but because the Foreign Office had a lien on his appointment in Cyprus his requests fell on deaf ears. Kitchener was not to be denied, however. He asked for, and was granted, a week's leave and crossed quickly over to Alexandria, where he boarded Seymour's flagship and presented himself for service. The military liaison officer aboard HMS *Inflexible*, Lieutenant-Colonel A.B. Tulloch, was content to turn a blind eye when he realised that Kitchener, a fluent Arabic speaker, would make a useful addition to his intelligence capabilities. Tulloch was anxious to discover the deployment of the army that the Egyptians had drawn up to forestall a possible British invasion and, with Kitchener as his companion, the two men slipped ashore disguised as Arabs. There, they were able to take notes and draw sketch maps of the lie of the land and, after an adventurous twenty-four hours, they were picked up by rowing boat and taken back to *Inflexible*. The reconnaissance whetted Kitchener's appetite for action and he was determined not to bow out when fighting looked imminent. He watched Seymour's bombardment of Alexandria but his requests for a temporary secondment were ignored in Cyprus, where Biddulph demanded his immediate return to duty. While Kitchener was explaining his absence an expeditionary force, under the command of Sir Garnet Wolseley, landed in Egypt on 21 August and three weeks later it annihilated Arabi's army at the Battle of Tel-el-Kebir. At one stroke Britain found herself in single occupation of Egypt.

It was not a position that the government relished, and Gladstone's Foreign Secretary Lord Granville quickly promised that Britain would quit Egypt in 1888 once the country's civil and military houses had been put in order. To complicate matters, however, intervention in Egypt meant that Britain had also to contend with neighbouring Sudan – a vast country one-third the size of the United States of America – which formed part of the Khedive's realm and which, by 1883, was in the grip of a Pan-Islamic revolt led by the messianic Mahdi. This powerful personality, born Mohammed Ibn Al-Sayd Abdullah near Dongola in 1844, claimed to be the Mahdi, the 'expected one', descendant of the prophet Mohammed, and it was his intention to raise a holy war or *jihad* to rid the country of the hated infidel. Soon news began to filter out of Sudan of the fall of Egyptian garrisons and the wholesale slaughter of communities opposed to Mahdist principles. As Gladstone was anxious to keep Britain out of any further imperial adventuring it fell to the authorities in Egypt to deal with the problem but their hopes of a military solution evaporated in November 1883 when an ill-equipped and demoralised force commanded by Colonel William Hicks was destroyed by the Mahdists at El Obeid. The disaster signalled the end of British ambitions along the Nile and it was agreed that the country should be evacuated, the Mahdists left to their own devices and the Egyptian-Sudanese border sealed.

Early in that momentous year Kitchener arrived back in Cairo, having finally secured a transfer to a posting that would give him a chance to prove himself on active service. Typically, he had chosen a pragmatic solution to his problem. Under General Sir Evelyn Wood the Egyptian Army was being trained to standards that would allow the government to keep order internally and to guard the border with Sudan; Wood had called for this new force to be staffed by twenty-six British officers and it was there that Kitchener saw his chance. At the same time Sir Evelyn Baring had been appointed British agent and consul-general and, for the next twenty-four years, latterly as Lord Cromer, he was to be the effective ruler of Egypt, known to everybody simply as 'The Lord'.

Kitchener was gazetted a captain on 4 January 1883 but, along with the other officers in Wood's army, he enjoyed the benefits of a local posting one higher in rank; so it was as a major or 'bimbashi' that he joined the only Egyptian cavalry regiment as second-in-command to Lieutenant-Colonel Taylor of the 19th Hussars. The British officers were well paid and enjoyed good conditions of service, but the Egyptian Army as a potential fighting force was considered by most British officers a dubious proposition. Years of defeat had crushed the spirit of the men; paucity of equipment and an alien officer class had done the rest, for prior to the British occupation of Egypt, the army had been officered by Turks and Circassians.

There was no shortage of Egyptian volunteers for the new cavalry regiments but they were of uncertain quality. Kitchener's methods of selection were therefore simple but effective. Recruits had to mount their horses and ride around, Indian file, in a wide circle while he stood in the centre with a long whip in his hand, looking like a circus ringmaster. 'Neither audible nor visible sign did he give of any feeling aroused by him by a spectacle mostly disappointing and sometimes ridiculous,' commented one observer. 'His hands buried in his trouser pockets he quietly watched the emergence of the least unfit.' Taylor took a different attitude, suppressed his laughter and left well alone, but Kitchener scowled and muttered, 'We'll just have to drive into these fellows.'[1] Once selected, Kitchener's cavalry troopers were soon able to ride in formation and to carry out elementary battlefield exercises. Kitchener emerged as an inspiring leader and Taylor was forced to admit that his taciturn second-in-command may have been quiet and clever but he was a good officer, for 'that's his way'.

As the Egyptian regiments were essentially fresh units Wood ordered that they should have new uniforms and each commanding officer was given six months' grace to produce suitable designs. Most of the infantry plumped for dark jackets, khaki pantaloons and fezes topped with red hackles, but Taylor thought that the cavalry should have something grander. The task fell to Kitchener, who chose a uniform pattern based on that worn by the 19th Hussars. Unfortunately, his brother officers found his proposals too modest and contributed their own ideas, some of which were so gaudy that Kitchener wrote in exasperation to Millie – who had volunteered to provide the material – that they would 'turn out like rather over-coloured rainbows. I for one strongly object'. Eventually Taylor's regiment settled for a light blue uniform that Kitchener thought to be too loud and out of keeping in Wood's economy-conscious army.

When the cavalry first appeared on parade in July wearing their new uniforms they provoked a good deal of derision, and Kitchener was mortified by the mockery, which he took personally. The fact that

Kitchener's drilling of his regiment had been singled out by Wood for praise did not help matters and another point of annoyance was that he had advanced his claims for a medal for his part in the 1882 campaign. Earlier he had told Taylor and others that he had lobbied Lord Alcester, the naval secretary, for what he believed was his just reward in Tulloch's reconnaissance and this had not made a good impression. As was to become a pattern in future years whenever he felt slighted, Kitchener sulked and took to spending much of his free time in the barracks at Abassyeh. Soon he was seen less frequently at the smart Khedival Club and as a result people began to think of him as a cold and ruthless man who spent too much time pursuing his own career. 'We all hated the sight of him in Cairo,' was a typical comment from a jealous brother officer.[2]

That was unfair. Before the matter of the uniform had caused him to withdraw Kitchener had enjoyed socialising with his brother officers. 'The Colonel and I have determined to give an evening party with dancing,' he told Millie. 'The Grotto will have to be lit up with about 1000 lamps and floors laid down for dancing besides arrangements for supper. We expect about 100 people. I have to make all the arrangements.'

Kitchener also went out of his way to meet several wealthy Egyptians who intrigued him and he liked Cairo for its easy mixture of cultures, part Levantine, part Muslim, part African, part French and part British imperial. One Egyptian who became a particular friend, and who offered him generous hospitality, was Nubar Pasha, the prime minister, much admired for his political and intellectual tastes. From him Kitchener learned something of the background to the problem of Egypt's involvement in Sudan and he mastered, too, some of the arts of eastern diplomacy.

Kitchener also met up with Samuel White Baker, who was holidaying on a river boat, the *Osprey*, on the Nile with his wife Florence and daughters Agnes and Ethel. He was in Egypt to visit his brother Valentine Baker, who had been appointed by the Khedive to command the Gendarmerie, a para-military force formed to keep internal order and to back up the army in its military operations. Baker was supposed to have been given the command of the Egyptian Army but Queen

Victoria had not forgotten his conviction for assault and so Wood had become Sirdar in his place, Baker being demoted to command a 'rubbishy lot of worthless ex-soldiers who were to be called gendarmerie'.[3] Kitchener enjoyed the Bakers' company; he admired the brothers for embarking on adventurous journeys of exploration and for their manly virtues. He also admired Valentine's eldest daughter, Hermione, an attractive, but sickly, sixteen-year-old. Certainly there seems to have been sufficient attraction for the Bakers to believe that an engagement might be imminent, and Valentine's wife made it clear to her friends that Major Kitchener was going to marry her daughter.[4] Hermione's death from typhoid fever on 21 January 1885, while Kitchener was at Korti, extinguished those hopes and his own memento of their relationship was a gold locket given to him by Valentine and which he wore for many years around his neck.

Kitchener had been much amused earlier by the manner in which his brother officers had lined up in order of rank to pay court to even the plainest women in Abbasyeh. 'There are only 2 ladies here,' he wrote to Millie, 'and they are followed about by a long train of generals and colonels so that there is no chance of speaking to them hardly. As they are both ugly this is not so much to be regretted.' Consequently his involvement with Hermione Baker was thought to have been a feather in his cap. The only other female company he had kept had been in March when his troop was guarding the Khedival harem. 'Very pleasant,' he wrote home, 'as some of the Egyptian princesses are very pretty and amiable. How would you like a dusky sister-in-law?' Such escapades were a far cry from the Kitchener of later years who could appear gauche in the company of young women and whose 'taste in womankind [tended] rather to the motherly and "unsmart".'[5]

In November 1883 Kitchener spent his leave assisting the Palestine Exploration Fund in its survey of the Arabah Valley, the long glen that leads south from the Red Sea at the Gulf of Aqaba. It was little more than a token survey of the desert of Exodus; but the expedition presented Kitchener with a further opportunity for pushing his name into the limelight. At the year's end he received a message from Wood announcing the news of the disaster that had overtaken Hicks and warning of the domino effect it might have on the loyalties of the Arabs in their vicinity. Kitchener realised that if the scent of action was in the air, his proper place was in Cairo; so, leaving the expedition to return to Egypt by way of Gaza, he set off with four servants across 200 miles of the inhospitable Sinai Desert. His little party often had to travel at night and, to parry any trouble from the local tribes, Kitchener passed himself off as an Egyptian official called Abdullah Bey. Only his crystal-clear blue eyes betrayed his disguise but at night, around the campfire, the Arab tribesmen warmed to this tall erect stranger who seemed to understand them and their customs. 'I was everywhere well received,' he told Besant on his return to Cairo, where his journey across the Sinai, with its aura of adventure and derring-do, was admired greatly even by those who had come to dislike him.[6]

The enterprising action commended itself to Wood and drew Kitchener into the Sirdar's plans for improving British knowledge of Sudan. In March 1884 he was attached to the intelligence group that included Major Reginald Wingate, whose star was then rising as the one British officer able to comprehend the need for accurate information about Sudan and the mood of its peoples under Mahdism. The failure of the Hicks expedition burst the dam that had previously kept the Mahdi's adherents in check and an ensuing defeat of Baker's gendarmerie at Suakin left the remaining garrisons in a desperate position. Khartoum, the centre of administration, was now threatened and, to complete Baring's problems, ranged alongside the Mahdi as an ally was a ruthless Turkish-Sudanese slave trader, Osman Digna, who held most of the Red Sea coast. In Britain the moves in Sudan had divided public opinion. Those who agreed with Gladstone wanted to leave well alone, but others regarded the Mahdi as just another native rebel who had to be brought under control and that action had to be taken to secure the country. As happened so often when Victorian Britain faced an extremity, the public called for a hero.

They found one in General Charles Gordon, a man who generated wildly differing emotions. To the public he was a hero who had made his name as the fearless leader of irregular troops fighting Taiping rebels in China, and a Christian who upheld the most solemn virtues of his creed. To Baring he appeared 'half-cracked' but many others admired him and he enjoyed a powerful following in British political life. His mystical belief that God had revealed His will to him and his published ramblings about the site of Old Testament stories, including that of the Garden of Eden, make him a somewhat unlikely hero. However, his service in China and Sudan, where he was governor in 1877 and where he worked tirelessly against the slave trade, had earned him universal respect. Accordingly, his supporters set about promoting his cause, the most prominent being W.T. Stead, the editor of the *Pall Mall Gazette*, who advocated that Gordon be sent 'with full powers to Khartoum to assume absolute control of the territory, to relieve the garrisons, and do what he can to save what can be saved in the Sudan'.[7]

With public hysteria mounting and with Gordon's name on everyone's lips, Gladstone was forced to act. Gordon was appointed to go to Khartoum to report on the situation, to oversee the evacuation of the civilian population and single-handedly restore order. His story is soon told. On 18 February Gordon entered Khartoum, where his arrival was met with universal acclaim: the inhabitants lived in mortal fear of the Mahdists and they expected Gordon to save them from fates worse than death. To begin with, Gordon threw himself with enthusiasm into organising the city's administration and its defences but the initial euphoria evaporated when a 30,000-strong Mahdist army surrounded Khartoum and a long siege began. Throughout the spring a series of contradictory and increasingly anguished messages from Gordon arrived in London – some stated that all was well, others, to the Liberals' horror, asked for help 'to smash up the Mahdi' – and he made it quite plain that he would not abandon the city. In London his attitude and his plight set alarm bells ringing and by midsummer the public was baying for an expedition to relieve their knight-errant hero.

As those cries were reaching their shrillest, Kitchener had been caught up, too, in the inexorable march of events in Sudan. His attachment to the intelligence group found him useful employment gathering information in the Berber region on the Nile below the Fifth Cataract, where he was also instructed to maintain contact with Gordon. His assistant was Major Leslie Rundle and the two young men set about

EGYPT: RIDING THE DESERT SANDS

creating an irregular force of Arab tribesmen who, it was hoped, would relieve Berber by opening the way to Suakin on the coast. Not for the first time in Britain's dealings with the Arabs, emissaries were sent into the desert, dressed in loose, comfortable Arab dress and armed with money to bribe the neutral sheikhs into becoming loyal subjects. Kitchener relished those new-found responsibilities and, by June, he was working on his own in the desert establishing the necessary outposts to complete the collection of sound intelligence. He was beyond the writ of Egyptian help or influence but, as he told Besant, he loved the work. 'Just got back from 17 days desert ride and rather exciting hunt of one of the Mahdi's emirs.'[8]

In June he was in Korosko attempting to encourage the Kababish tribe to assist a rescue attempt into Khartoum. The following month saw him in Dongola on his most dangerous mission yet, to contact the Mudir, a wily Circassian who, handled correctly, could have been a useful ally. Initially Kitchener was mightily impressed by the Mudir's offer of help, but on 19 August he was reporting back to Cairo that the potentate 'has already tried to deceive me and is an intense intriguer'.[9] Never a man to invest any first meeting with friendship or cordiality, Kitchener was learning his trade fast: that to play the intelligence game, the successful agent had to possess a bottomless supply of patience, to sift through any amount of seemingly useless information and to delight in interpreting the subtle manoeuvrings of his opponents.

He also took pleasure in the romance afforded by his role. Wearing Arab clothes and surrounded by a group of twenty faithful Arab tribesmen dressed in white and sworn to him by the rites of blood brotherhood, he moved quickly over the desert wastes. At night it was bitterly cold, during the day a scorching sun beat down from a cloudless sky and the desert itself, rocky in places, scrub and soft sand in others, sapped the energy of all but the most hardy. Flies and insects of insatiable curiosity were further torments. Life was cheap. 'The Sudan is a man eater — red-gorged but still insatiable,' wrote G.W. Steevens, correspondent of the *Daily Mail* and one of the new journalists whom Kitchener admired. 'Turn your pony's head and canter out a mile; we are at the cemetery. No need to dismount, or even to read the names

– see merely how full it is. Each white cross is an Englishman devoured by the Sudan.'[10]

And yet for all its hardships, men such as Kitchener fell in love with the place, for its clear desert air, the long gallops over the featureless sand and the friendship and fierce loyalty of the desert tribes. The austerity of life that had encouraged its people to embrace the puritanism of Islam also bred a fanaticism that can scarcely be comprehended by those who have not stared out over its seemingly monotonous but ever-changing wastes. Once he had experienced both the solitude of the desert and the camaraderie of its denizens, Kitchener was a changed man. From his companions he learned to assert himself, to value himself and to believe in the divine right of his mission, and by the year's end he was confiding to Cairo that he 'would not mind' governing the province of Dongola. Soon Kitchener's efforts were being appreciated in high places in Cairo. 'This is an excellent officer in every respect,' noted Wood, 'a good Arabic linguist – a fine horseman – great determination and courage.'[11] And in Khartoum Gordon noted in his journal that he liked 'Baker's description of Kitchener – the man I have always placed my hopes upon, Major Kitchener, R.E., who is one of the very few superior British officers with a hard constitution, combined with untiring energy'.[12]

By the summer's end Kitchener was in direct contact with Gordon. The general's dangerous position and the determination with which he maintained his solemn duty to remain in Khartoum had a deep effect on Kitchener, who began to fret that nothing was being done to relieve Gordon. 'My opinion is, decidedly, send up your troops,' he signalled to Baring. 'There is no difficulty, and one good fight close to Khartoum will see the matter through.'[13] Earlier that summer he had confided his worst fears to Millie: 'if we go on much longer in this way Gordon's blood will be on the G.O.M.'s head [Grand Old Man, i.e. Gladstone]. How the English people can stand it I cannot understand.'

In August Gladstone – who believed Gordon to be pulling Britain in the direction of a war of conquest against the Mahdi – bowed to public pressure and ordered a British relief force to march to Gordon's rescue. It was commanded by Wolseley, who returned to Egypt on

10 September with the intention of making a cautious progress up the Nile towards Khartoum; he was determined not to fall into the same trap as Hicks by over-extending his lines of communication. To this force Kitchener was assigned as intelligence officer under Colonel Charles Wilson, the Royal Engineer who had given him his earlier chance in Anatolia. By the end of September Kitchener was the only link with Gordon and it was from his temporary headquarters at Ed Debba that he organised the chain of messages into Gordon's camp.

In Khartoum events were moving towards a climax. On 5 September Gordon lost almost 1,000 men in an ill-advised skirmish with the dervishes, as the soldiers in the Mahdist army were known. As a result the peasants stopped bringing in fresh produce and supplies began to run low. It was at this point that Gordon decided to make a last stand. In circumstances that are difficult to understand fully he allowed his able second-in-command, Colonel Stewart, to leave Khartoum in the steamer *Abbas*. His party, including the three consuls, took with it sundry despatches, letters, the cypher book, and a reproachful letter to Baring that accused him of sleeping in a comfortable bed while Gordon and his fellow citizens contemplated an awful death.

On receiving a message that the *Abbas* had left Khartoum, Kitchener asked Wolseley to be allowed to take an armed steamer – which was available at Dongola – to escort Stewart's party but his request was refused. Instead, an impatient Kitchener sent a runner to intercept Stewart at Berber, telling him to leave the steamer there and to take the overland desert route to Dongola. The message never arrived. After passing Berber, Stewart's steamer entered hostile territory and all its occupants were murdered by Arab tribesmen after it struck a rock and Stewart and his party were unwittingly ensnared by the hospitality offered by a local sheikh. The news of the betrayal of Stewart and his death enraged Kitchener and it brought home to Wolseley the need to get into a higher gear. Sadly, the loss was much grimmer than anyone could have supposed. Had Stewart managed to reach Kitchener, Gordon's plight would have been more easily understood by Wolseley on the line of march, by Baring in Cairo and by Gladstone in London. As it was, the general opinion was that he could hold out.

The increased interest in Sudan and the part played in the rescue attempt by Kitchener brought his name into the public eye and, as *The Times* said in an editorial, Kitchener's word was to be trusted:

> What adds to the importance of a story in itself coherent and probable is that its most important details come from Major Kitchener at Debbeh. He is no doubt dependent for information upon natives coming across the desert, and in that circumstance we may find a ray of hope. But he comes into direct contact with these natives, he has some experience in testing and examining their statements, and he would not transmit such serious news unless he had good reason for believing it to be true.[14]

Other newspapers were equally fulsome in their praise. As Wolseley's army made its way up the Nile, Kitchener seemed to be the only soldier actually doing something useful. His father and Baker stirred up eulogies in other quarters, in London clubs and in the provincial press, and the name of Major Kitchener began to take on a ring all of its own. Publicity of this kind was exactly what Kitchener had been seeking when he went on active service and he revelled in his role as Gordon's only link with the outside world, the army's forward listening post in the vastness of the desert.

However, if Kitchener was the darling of the British public his relationship with Gordon was a pendulum of wildly fluctuating emotions. His message that a relief force was en route to Khartoum prompted a 101-gun salute and signalled general rejoicing in the city but very soon Gordon's moods were again at their blackest. Throughout the siege he kept a journal, an extraordinary stream of consciousness, a mixture of schoolboy jokes and wild surmising about his fate, which became a kind of sacred text for the late Victorians. In it he pondered everything from the mysteries of the hawk on the wing and the antics of the mouse that kept him company to the awful warning from Herodotus about the desert swallowing up Cambyses and his army. Most of all, however, he reserved his opprobrium for Baring, Gladstone and, in the circumstances unfairly, for Kitchener. 'I never saw such a poor lot as these outsiders [Kitchener's intelligence network]. Even if they had to

EGYPT: RIDING THE DESERT SANDS

pay £20 out of their own pockets, one might have expected them to do it, considering the circumstances they might have been paid back. I never saw such a feeble lot in all my life.'[15] That was unfair. Not only did Kitchener not know the direction that Wolseley might take during his final approach to Khartoum, he was even being reprimanded for wanting to take a native force to Berber to seek news of Stewart. Throughout this period Kitchener behaved most honourably and his concern for Gordon was all the more earnest for his being the only man in direct contact with him. At other times, though, Gordon would acknowledge that help, and would hint that Kitchener had a messianic quality about him, prophesying that he would become in time the undisputed ruler of the Sudan. 'Whoever comes up here had better appoint Major Kitchener Governor-General, for it is certain, after what has passed, I am impossible. (What a comfort.)'[16] It was an extraordinary piece of divination and for the last months of his life Gordon became obsessed with the notion that Kitchener should be his successor, perhaps sensing in him a kindred spirit.

The news that Stewart's expedition had failed was announced to Gordon by the Mahdi in a long letter of 22 October, which also invited him to surrender. It contained sufficient evidence taken from Stewart's journal, the cypher book and the despatches about the conditions in Khartoum to convince Gordon that his enemies knew the parlous state of his defences. The final stage of the siege had now begun. By the second week of November the city was under shell-fire and the falling River Nile began to open up a possible route through Khartoum's defences. Panic began to set in as supplies became almost impossible to obtain and the dead lay unburied in the streets. On 15 December Gordon played his last hand when he sent a desperate message by the steamer *Bordein*: 'NOW MARK THIS, if the Expeditionary Force, and I ask no more than two hundred men, does not come in ten days, the town may fall; and I have done my best for the honour of my country. Goodbye. C.G. Gordon.' 'You send me no information, though you have lots of money. C.G.G.'"[17]

This was not an inaccurate summary, but two weeks later a runner arrived at Korti with the contradictory message that 'Khartoum is all right. Could hold out for years.' This was presumably penned in order to confuse the Mahdi should the messenger fall captive, but in the event it only served to sow further muddle in the minds of his friends. Wolseley's plan involved his army following the course of the Nile – Canadian voyageurs had been employed to navigate the river boats over the treacherous cataracts until it reached Korti, where the great river begins its long bend eastwards. There, a desert column composed of 1,100 men of the Camel Corps and the Royal Sussex Regiment, under the command of Sir Herbert Stewart (no relation of the murdered Stewart), would strike off across the Bayuda Desert to Metemma above Khartoum. This was Kitchener's territory and he was seconded to the column as its intelligence officer when it began its long march on 30 December. The going was hard. Wilson had not purchased sufficient camels so the beasts were over-burdened and many dropped in their tracks before they reached their destination. Worst of all, according to the recollections of Count Gleichen, a Grenadier Guards officer attached to the Camel Corps, there were flies everywhere. 'How flies and insects manage to exist in the Desert was always a puzzle to me. I always imagined that insects required a certain amount of dampness, but no – the common or garden fly was as much at home on the driest slopes of the Bayuda Desert as in a lodging house kitchen in England.'[18] In the company of six Arab scouts Kitchener went on ahead of the desert column and set up a forward camp at Jakdul but he was fated to go no farther. Stewart, having returned to Korti to collect the remainder of his force, then ordered Kitchener to return there too while he set off for Metemma. Kitchener was not pleased. He had always imagined that the nature of his work guaranteed him a place in the vanguard of any relief force. In a letter to Millie dated 12 December 1884 he wrote:

> My Lord Wolseley has not forgotten or forgiven and has just given me a gentle reminder. When Colville was sent to Merowi while I was at Debbeh I was told I was to go with Stewart across the desert to Khartoum so I was delighted yesterday. Wilson wires so sorry but Lord W wishes you not to go with Stewart so I have been nicely done. I suppose Colville will go. It is a great thing in these days

to be a guardsman. I fancied I had little claim to get on to Khartoum. However if it does Gordon no harm I do not care much how it would be but unfortunately believed Lord W for a month … at present I am puzzling my head how to get rations for 1000 men and camels moved 5 miles without transport. I have also to lay a telegraph line without any assistance. I am in the grand position of being head and tail of every department.

Stewart's order to stay behind with the administrative and logistical sections, however much it may have irked him, probably saved Kitchener's life. He missed the first engagement with the dervishes on 17 January 1885 at Abu Klea where Colonel Fred Burnaby of The Blues, one of the most experienced soldiers in the column, lost his life. The following day Stewart was mortally wounded during a skirmish near Metemma and the command devolved to Wilson.

Three days later the column met the *Bodein* carrying Gordon's fateful last letter announcing the imminent fall of Khartoum but Wilson was inclined to delay because Gordon also said that Khartoum 'could hold out for years'. This reaction later helped to cast him in the role of villain of the piece. Had he thrust on, argued his critics, Gordon would surely have been saved but his decision to spend three days reorganising his troops and repairing the steamers sealed the general's fate. With hindsight, though, it is clear that, in the circumstances, Wilson did the right thing. His reinforcements were still a long way downriver, his men had taken part in two fierce engagements and were exhausted, and he realised that the defeat at Abu Klea would only have encouraged the Mahdists. Besides, he had orders only to make contact with Gordon and not to engage the enemy until the arrival of the main force. Later, when he was being vilified as the man who failed to save Gordon, Kitchener stood by Wilson and his official report on the fall of Khartoum is generous: had Wilson saved Gordon he would have been the hero of the hour; had he tried and failed he would have fallen foul of his military bosses.

With a small party of men drawn from the Royal Sussex and the Sudanese troops, Wilson set off in the *Bodein* on 24 January. Another steamer followed behind towing a barge laden with supplies. Their voyage was punctuated by rifle fire from the banks, which increased in ferocity as the city came into view four days later on 28 January. For the previous twenty-four hours Arabs had called out from their hiding places along the river that Gordon was dead: now the ruined buildings, the onslaught of artillery fire and the absence of Gordon's flag from the palace roof confirmed their worst fears. Khartoum had fallen and Gordon was indeed dead.

On the morning of 26 January, realising that the relief force would soon be within fighting distance, the Mahdi had ordered the taking of Khartoum. For six horrible hours the dervishes murdered, raped and destroyed and it was during that maelstrom that Gordon fell within his palace grounds. In the eyes of an adoring public he was nothing less than a martyr of Empire, sacrificed on the obduracy of Gladstone's Cabinet. The reality was probably different. Gordon was far too committed a soldier and Christian to have gone to his death so meekly, and most eyewitness accounts argue that he died fighting. Later, his head was cut off and taken to the Mahdi, who was mightily displeased: he had thought to save Gordon and to convert him to Islam.

There was little for Wilson to achieve by remaining in the vicinity so the little flotilla turned around amidst a hail of shell and rifle fire and began the long journey back to Metemma, which it reached on 4 February. The following day the news of Gordon's death reached London and its announcement prompted a nationwide outburst of dismay and anger directed at Gladstone's government. London was swept by 'a mood of hysteria which lasted for about three weeks, drew crowds every day to Downing Street in the hope that they might have a chance to hoot and jeer at the Prime Minister'.[19]

When Wilson reached Jakdul the air of gloom and despondency was increased first by the absence of supplies, and then by the arrival of replacement boots that turned out to be of such small sizes that most of the men could hardly get their feet into them. 'They were as hard as bricks,' remembered Gleichen, 'there was no grease to soften them and the only way of using them was to slit them open at the end, and shove your toes through.'[20]

Kitchener, meanwhile, had been detailed to accompany a new commander for the desert column, Redvers Buller, an experienced soldier whose task was to restore discipline to Wilson's demoralised troops. With Kitchener he arrived on 11 February after taking the long route over the desert from Korti and both men were quick to note the dispiriting effect that Gordon's death had had on the men. Buller's orders were to join up with the rest of the army, the river column that had followed the course of the Nile to Berber, but that force, too, had had its troubles. At Kirbekan they had clashed with the dervishes, lost their commander and been forced to retreat. Buller had no option but to lead his weakened forces back to safer quarters at Korti. At Abu Klea they set about defending the wells against attack before Kitchener and the other officers begged Buller to allow them to be filled in to hinder the dervish pursuit. At first Buller refused permission, stating that such an action was contrary to the rules of war, but Kitchener took a harder line. He realised that the absence of water at Abu Klea would be a serious blow to Mahdist hopes. Buller eventually agreed to the filling in of the largest well, an order that Kitchener felt free to interpret in his own way. Leaving two officers to deal with the principal well he told them that he would 'go and see about the rest'.[21]

However inhumane it might have seemed, Kitchener had lived in the desert long enough to know that its harshness made the tribesmen look on kindness as weakness, on gratitude as stupidity. Since witnessing a spy being put to death at Dongola with expert cruelty, he had carried with him a bottle of cyanide of potassium for use had he been captured during his intelligence work. 'Death at their hands I did not fear,' he told a friend, 'in fact I expected it. But such a death!' Friends he might have been with many Arabs who were loyal to the British but he knew, too, that the tribesmen of the desert could be unforgiving enemies, indifferent to pain and suffering.

On reaching Korti, Kitchener found a letter from Gordon awaiting his arrival. Written on 26 November 1884, it rambled over several subjects – the lack of cypher book, his fears for Stewart's safety, a request for thanks to be sent to the king of the Belgians, and even his apologies to Kitchener for speaking ill of him in his journal – but it was the postscript that tugged at Kitchener's heartstrings. Again Gordon played the role of John the Baptist: 'If you would take the post up here of Governor-General, with a subsidy of £500,000 a year – for you will get no taxes – it would be well for the people, and you would have no difficulty that you could not master. D.V.' [22] So moved was Kitchener by the appeal that, on 17 March 1885, he forwarded the letter to his father for safe-keeping:

> I enclose a letter from Gordon to me, which came down in his steamer. It is the best reward that I shall get for a good many months' hard work; so please keep it most carefully for me. I feel that, now he is dead, the heart and soul of the Expedition is gone. The shock of the news was dreadful, and I can hardly realise it yet. I also send you a bond for money signed by Gordon; hundreds of thousands [pounds worth] passed as money in Khartum, showing how much he was trusted by the people. I also send his decoration for the defence of Khartum. [23]

Gordon's death had a lasting effect on Kitchener. Having been the last man to remain in contact with him Kitchener felt that he had enjoyed a special relationship. Gordon's prophetic words had inspired him, too, and from this time he began to see himself as someone whose role it was to avenge him. It was a part that came naturally to him for there were many points of similarity between the two men. Both were officers of the Royal Engineers, single-minded to a fault, both believed that he travelled fastest who travelled alone and never married, both were completely loyal, almost fanatical in their attention to duty, and both hid their innermost feelings behind masks of public inscrutability. It was hardly surprising that Kitchener, whose beliefs had been hardened by the quasi-ascetic nature of his work in the desert, should have felt himself drawn to an oracular soldier such as Gordon:

> Thank Harry [he wrote to Millie on 25 April 1884] very much for his Gordon's life [Hake]. I read it with some pleasure but did not think it did justice to the subject. Some day we shall have the real life written but his character will hardly ever be really understood for it had no smallness in it and there is so much of that in the world. I suppose some time or other we shall withdraw from here and abandon all the advantages we have gained by the dear purchase of many

valuable lives and I feel convinced it will only be to come back again later to pour out more blood for the defence of Egypt.

At home in London Gladstone made bellicose noises in the House of Commons about the need to defeat the Mahdi but they were uttered more to appease public opinion than to involve Britain in any fighting. He had no intention of annexing Sudan and, at the end of March, when Russian ambitions on the Afghan border seemed to be threatening British interests in India, the events in Khartoum gradually lost their immediacy. However, Gladstone misunderstood the strength of feeling that Gordon's death had aroused. Misguided he may have appeared, and an insubordinate trouble-maker who refused to abandon Khartoum, but for many he enjoyed a god-like status. Forthright Buller disagreed and said that Gordon was not worth the camels but most officers shared Wolseley's thoughts as he expressed them to Kitchener on 30 January, that 'God must be very angry with England when he sends back Mr Gladstone to us as First Minister ... Nothing is talked of or cared for at this moment but this appalling calamity that has fallen upon England.'[24]

By midsummer Sudan had been evacuated; only the port of Suakin on the Red Sea coast was retained, while the largest army garrison was at Wadi Halfa on the border with Egypt. It was a situation that spelled doom for the remaining outposts of Egyptian authority within the country. 'But the English,' noted Alexander Mackay, a Scottish missionary based at that time in Buganda, 'to the amazement of all the Arabs, and the bitter disappointment of all the Europeans and Egyptians, turned tail, no man knows why, and ran home leaving all the garrisons to the mercy of the murderers. Now the great provinces of Bahr-el-Ghazal and the Equator are merely a prey to the slave raids of the Dervishes of the Mahdi party. This desertion of the great Negro land, which Gordon governed once in the most humane manner, has been called in England "the leaving alone of a brave people to enjoy their freedom". Certainly the Dervishes have thus been left alone to devastate the fairest part of Central Africa, that, too, by the English, who once said they were determined to stop the slave-trade there.'[25]

If an astute member of the Church Missionary Society such as Mackay could pour such scorn on Gladstone's policy of 'scuttle' then it was felt much worse within the army. Kitchener's chance to express his keen sense of personal dismay came in August when, at Wolseley's request, he completed a report on the fall of Khartoum. It is an admirable document that demonstrated Kitchener's grasp of the situation; it is also the most eloquent account of 'The memorable siege of Khartoum', which:

> ... lasted 17 days, and it is not too much to say that such a noble resistance was due to the indomitable resolution and resource of one Englishman.
> Never was a garrison so nearly rescued, never was a Commander so sincerely lamented.[26]

That was not Kitchener's last word on the affair, however. He also drew up a memorandum for Buller on the current situation in the Sudan and, like his earlier paper, it reveals his sound and untrammelled way of thinking.[27] Intelligence had shown that many tribesmen were disappointed by the shortage of booty in Khartoum and that their disaffection had been nurtured by an outbreak of typhus fever and by the customary feuding between the different tribes. The possession of the wealthy province of Dongola would, however, bolster the Mahdi's prestige and so Kitchener proposed that the British, under the Egyptian flag, should hold Dongola by re-organising control under a new Mudir and three subordinates or 'vakils'. It is a classical statement of late Victorian British imperialism: establish a protectorate with a strong local man at the helm who in turn is dependent upon imperial power for his survival. Kitchener's call to 'unmuzzle Egypt' is a characteristic example of his own thinking on the subject allied to a vigorous prose style:

> If ... the English taxpayer does not like paying for putting down a false prophet and protecting Egypt, then I should take off the muzzle, and let Egypt act energetically for herself and her own preservation. Send up six Egyptian battalions to take the place of the English troops withdrawn, leaving three English battalions here. Reform the Egyptian cavalry and artillery. Let every post along the frontier be made as strong as possible by fortifications and guns.[28]

Later, many of the ideas in Kitchener's paper were put into action but, with the withdrawal of the British-Egyptian forces, Baring's response was cautious. Major-General Sir Francis Grenfell succeeded Wood as Sirdar and, on 21 April, Parliament agreed that offensives against the Mahdists should cease forthwith and Dongola should be abandoned. Kitchener was ordered to proceed with his intelligence work along the frontier but his heart was no longer in his work: as long as there had been a possibility of engaging with the Mahdist army and the chance of saving Gordon he had been content to negotiate with hostile tribesmen and to infiltrate their numbers, duties that required tact, skill and courage. Now that the heart had gone out of Wolseley's army Kitchener felt that his task in the Sudan had reached an impasse, and the last picture we have of him is sitting beside his chief during interrogation sessions with the local sheikhs during which he acted as translator as well as interpreter of events. It was a far cry from an earlier occasion when, dressed as a Bedouin, he was stoned by a British soldier who caught him prowling round the camp at Korti looking like a 'blooming nigger [sic]'.[29]

In June Kitchener was gazetted a brevet lieutenant-colonel in the British Army, a temporary promotion that allowed a major to be an acting rank higher. The promotion was much prized and it gave him considerable satisfaction: 'I am most grateful to you for my brevet,' he wrote to the Sirdar, 'and especially pleased as it shows me you approve of my work.'[30] He was also awarded the Khedive's Star but his time in Sudan was temporarily at an end; he resigned his commission in the Egyptian Army and on 3 July returned to Britain, where he was one of the officers presented to Queen Victoria at Osborne. However disastrous or badly managed the Gordon relief expedition may have been, one officer had made his name. Within the army Kitchener's exploits in the desert now gave him the ear of senior officers, and by the public he was known as the man who had kept in touch with Gordon until the very end. Above all, he now had a name and that counted for much during the reign of Queen Victoria when soldiers who were successful became the objects of great popular interest.

4

SUDAN: PLANNING FOR VICTORY

In the same month that Kitchener received his brevet, the Mahdi died and was succeeded by another equally charismatic figure, Abdullahi Ibn Muhammed, known as the Khalifa, or 'the successor'. But whereas the Mahdi had seen himself as the epicentre of a religious revolt, the Khalifa, a member of the Baggara tribe, was only interested in exercising power. During his despotic rule those who offended him became all too familiar with the vocabulary of mass murder, rape and savagery; and drought and plagues of biblical intensity added to the despair that was the lot of most of his subjects. Several Europeans, including Rudolf Slatin, Joseph Ohrwalder and Charles Neufeld, survived imprisonment by the Khalifa, and their accounts, although biased, are grim testimony to the barbarity of his rule.[1] When they were published in the 1890s they raised an outcry in Britain, re-awakening the public's desire to avenge Gordon. By that time, just as Kitchener had predicted, the Egyptian Army was in a position to put itself into the field as a committed and disciplined force.

When Kitchener arrived back in London in the summer of 1885 he found himself in the unaccustomed position of social lion: suddenly hostesses began vying for his company, anxious to entertain the tall and youthful colonel. Until this time, Kitchener had had little experience of society but he knew that if his career were to prosper, then invitations for weekend house parties should not be turned down. In this respect he received guidance and advice from Pandeli Ralli, whom he had first met in Cyprus. This colourful figure had just finished a five-year period as Liberal MP for Wallingford and was embarking on a social career. A small, dapper man of great personal wealth, he was devoted to society, entertainment and travel, and into his orbit swam many of the most fashionable figures of the day. His sister, Janie, was married to Sir Richard Moreton, Queen Victoria's Master of Ceremonies, while Lady Moreton was Lady of the Bedchamber to the Duchess of Albany: through these family alliances Ralli had access to the court and that connection, together with his genius for hospitality, made his London residence at 17 Belgrave Square one of the best-known centres of gossip and social intrigue in the capital.

Ralli was quick to seek out Kitchener's company and to renew his acquaintance with the man whose name seemed to be on everyone's lips. Thus began a lifelong intimacy between the two men. Ralli asked Kitchener to look on his Belgrave Square house as his own home and for many years it was to be Kitchener's social headquarters when in London.[2] His new friend was also able to offer him advice about which invitations to accept and which to turn down tactfully. Such counsel was invaluable, for Kitchener was not only finding his way in society but also determined to make it pay for his ambitions. It was not just social climbing that drew Kitchener to Ralli. Both men had a liking for Levantine civilisation and an admiration for things French: in the years to come Ralli was one of the few men who knew Kitchener intimately, but like those others he kept their friendship extremely private.

In August 1885 Kitchener accepted an invitation to visit Taplow Court in Berkshire, the seat of William Henry Grenfell (later Lord Desborough), one of the great amateur sportsmen of his day. At Oxford he had been a distinguished athlete and oarsman and after leaving he had rowed an eight across the English Channel. He swam Niagara twice, his interest in big-game hunting took him to India and Africa, and he climbed in the Rockies and in the Alps. A tall, muscular man who encouraged weekend guests to spend some of their time punting on the River Thames, Grenfell immediately took to Kitchener and they became firm friends. In 1887 Grenfell married Ettie Fane, a granddaughter of the Earl of Westmorland, and Kitchener became godfather to their youngest daughter, Imogen. In the company of friends such as Ralli and Grenfell, Kitchener relaxed: close friendships and loyalties of that kind were important to him, although he showed the knack, too, of engineering them with people of influence.

Through his friendship with Grenfell, Kitchener received his first experience of country house parties – social events attended by political insiders, ostensibly for relaxation, field sports and the like, but also as venues for sounding out political ideas and for making and breaking reputations. The gentlemen spent their days on the river or in the field but, after dinner, when the ladies had retired, they moved to the smoking room for drinks, cigars and gossip: there, amidst the smoke and bonhomie, Kitchener was able to lay the foundations of his future career by cultivating the patrician families of England, who still played a major part in British politics. He was also careful to nurture the friendship of aristocratic ladies, who for their part were intrigued by the aura of reserve with which Kitchener surrounded himself.

Kitchener's new connections came to his aid in November when he was posted to rejoin the Royal Engineers in Ireland to assist in the design of new barracks in Cork. As such an appointment would have taken him out of the limelight and back to routine military chores Kitchener did all in his power to have the order rescinded and his efforts were rewarded when the Foreign Office again asked for his services. This time it was as the British member of the Zanzibar Boundary Commission, which had been established to ascertain the territorial limits of the Sultan of Zanzibar. It was a good job on two scores. Kitchener became financially better off as the post carried a salary of £1,000 in addition to his pay as a lieutenant-colonel and his promotion prospects were not harmed as his reports would go direct to the Prime Minister. Nevertheless, Kitchener did worry about the appointment. 'I have dined with a good many people,' he told Millie before Christmas, 'and no doubt ought to be happy, but being of a discontented nature Zanzibar is not the place to satisfy this craving. I am always looking to Cairo and should like to know how things get on there.' The island was not to his liking either: Zanzibar boasted few amenities, it seemed to rain every day and, with no big game hunting by way of sport, a disconsolate Kitchener reported that his activities were confined to swatting enormous mosquitoes.

Fortunately there was work to be done. Britain's involvement in the affairs of Zanzibar dated from mid-century and it had been strengthened in the 1870s when it was thought the opening of the Suez Canal would help to create new trading stations along the east African coast. Those hopes had not materialised, but the coastal strips remained important as staging posts for the exploration of the hinterland – a vast area that had been left alone by the great powers until Britain and France began to jockey for position along the Upper Nile. Britain had established friendly communication with the Sultan Barghash through its forceful consul-general, Sir John Kirk, but Zanzibar was slow to feature in British aspirations. It was left to Germany to begin the colonisation of east Africa when Karl Peters of the German Colonisation Society entered into several agreements with various inland tribal chiefs, thus giving Germany a lead in securing a sphere of influence in the Zanzibar hinterland. Most of those agreements were specious enough, for the chiefs did not understand the import of signing away possession of their lands, but British governments, in spite of Kirk's vociferous protest, were inclined to leave well alone and to favour German interests. France, mindful of the frailty of her eastern border on the Rhine, and anxious to maintain her own hold on the Upper Nile and in central Africa in the face of British ambitions, also kept quiet. The final German coup came in August 1885 when a German naval squadron arrived off Zanzibar and demanded the immediate ratification of Peters's treaties: it was then that Britain and France joined with Germany to go through the motions of international peace-keeping by establishing the Boundary Commission.

At the beginning of 1886 the three Commission members attempted to work out the limits of the Sultan's authority, which Kitchener and the French member took to be up to 40 miles inland from the coast. These computations were not to Peters's liking and when he clashed with Kitchener a sharp rebuke arrived from Berlin accusing the British member of favouring the French – this may have been true from an emotional point of view but the Commission's papers confirm Kitchener's impartiality.³ Lord Rosebery, Gladstone's new Foreign Secretary, cautioned Kitchener officially about the German complaint, but, as an alarmed Millie discovered, the Foreign Secretary was not slow in offering private support to her brother:

> I must say [Kitchener wrote on 6 June 1886] Ld Rosebery has done me very well. He sticks up to the Germans like fun. I admire him. I gave him a hint of a dirty trick the Germans were playing and he positively almost frightened me by the persistence which he rubbed it in at Berlin. The ambassador wrote to Ld R 'they seem rather sore about it' so he wrote out to me for any more details which I have sent in plenty.

Despite those efforts to curb the Germans the talks dragged on through the summer until, in an effort to demonstrate their neutrality in the area, the governments acted together over the heads of the Commission and agreed that the Sultan's territory should consist of a 600-mile coastal strip, together with the islands of Zanzibar, Pemba and Mafia. The great east African hinterland was declared open and, as spheres of interest, Britain was granted present-day Kenya and Germany present-day Tanzania, while France was granted the neighbouring Comoro Islands off the coast of Madagascar.

For his role in the negotiations Kitchener was awarded the CMG and he also received the thanks of Lord Rosebery in a letter of 27 March 1886: 'It seems to me that you have steered your course with great skill and impartiality amid circumstances of difficulty.'⁴ In September 1886 Kitchener returned to Britain but had only reached Suez when his fortunes took another turn. There, a message awaited him appointing him Governor-General of Eastern Sudan and the Red Sea Littoral, and ordering him to Suakin, its capital, which had been under more or less constant siege since the policy of 'scuttle' had begun. By 1886 it was a fortified town holding out against the surrounding hostile forces led by Osman Digna and his Hadendowa tribesmen.

SUDAN: PLANNING FOR VICTORY

Thus, when Kitchener arrived in Suakin he discovered that, despite his awesome title, his authority extended only a few miles inland. Nothing daunted, however, he was determined to add as much lustre as possible to his appointment. He enjoyed being addressed as 'your excellency', he had the services of an ADC, a young subaltern of engineers named W.S. 'Monkey' Gordon, a nephew of the martyr of Khartoum, and with him Kitchener quickly turned the Governor's tumbledown residence into a 'swagger establishment'. It was refurbished in style with new drapes and furniture and, from London, a grand new dinner service was selected by Millie so Kitchener could entertain regularly and graciously. Kitchener took a great deal of interest in these arrangements, selecting the menus and organising the place settings himself. Although he admitted to Millie that his duties as host made him nervous, he put on a great show when the new Sirdar (Grenfell) visited him in December 1887, and he was rewarded by his guest's fulsome praise for the new-look residency. Kitchener's anxieties had been exacerbated by the lack of a wife to help him with his entertaining, and so Millie came out to Suakin in the spring of 1887 to help him. She arrived bringing with her a stock of bed linen, towels and other necessities for the residency. Millie was an extrovert who rode well and who smoked cigars in public: men who met her were frequently taken aback by her plain speaking and by the strength of her personality. But it was a happy time, with boating expeditions in Kitchener's personal yacht, *Jaffarieh*, hunting for deer and gazelle, and a round of parties that Millie remembered as being notable for the native brass band, which played raucously throughout. When she returned home at the summer's end Kitchener missed her company and bombarded her with requests to repeat the visit both for his sake and for the sake of her admirers in Suakin.

Kitchener's orders were to keep what he held, a task made easier for him by 'the irrepressible Osman Digna' whose forays were now, at worst, only a nuisance. By the end of 1886 the garrison had been reduced to one regular battalion (Xth Sudanese Regiment) and a mixed force of irregulars and gendarmerie. To begin with, therefore, Kitchener's policy had to be one of retrenchment. From his intelligence sources he noted that Osman Digna's power was on the wane, that not a few tribes were tiring of the Khalifa's oppressive rule and that trade had been disrupted severely during the three or four years of skirmishing. Under the circumstances he reasoned that his best option would be the creation of new alliances with the disaffected tribes in the area. To ease that policy Kitchener had been given large sums of money to disburse as subsidies or bribes, but he had not lost his touch in dealing with desert chiefs and during his term of office one of his delights was pitting his wits against theirs during the lengthy negotiations.

From them he learned that the Mahdists were threatening to invade Egypt – which they did in the following year – and acting on knowledge that the enemy was planning to purchase modern arms he placed a ban on trade with the interior. His policies brought an immediate rebuke from Baring and for his pains Kitchener was not only attacked as a bully in the British radical press, but also in the correspondence columns of *The Times*. Such hostility was music to his ears: it meant that his work was controversial enough to warrant attention in Britain. Nothing would have been worse for his prospects than silence.

At the beginning of 1888 he wrote a patient and well-argued letter to *The Times*, putting his strategy into perspective and answering those critics who thought he had been adopting too aggressive a policy. In trade, said those who disapproved of his rule, lay peace; withdraw it, and the peaceful process of orderly colonisation ground to a halt. Kitchener countered that his policy of refusing to trade with any but the friendly tribes who entered into alliances with him was the better one:

> I have written upon the gate of Suakin, 'Peace to those who enter and leave the place', and I have strictly carried out those principles. I have promised to all Arabs who have come in that they shall not be re-taxed as formerly, and that all that is required of them is that they should live in peace and use this place as a market.[5]

The letter not only silenced his critics but brought him praise from his peers. Wolseley wrote to him, lending him support, and Kitchener began to think about adopting a more aggressive policy against the surrounding tribes. His chance came early in 1888 when Osman Digna, tiring of Kitchener's repressive tactics, decided to lay siege to Suakin;

no easy task, as Kitchener had ordered the construction of an intricate pattern of fortifications and ditches. Unable to storm them directly, Osman Digna's army took up position 15 miles to the north at Handub, a village scarcely capable of offering any defence itself but one that threatened Suakin's harbour directly. Realising how frail was the enemy position, Kitchener asked Grenfell for permission to attack it with his regular battalion but the request was refused – the last thing Grenfell or Baring wanted to risk was another Gordon-type rescue operation.

Kitchener opted to act on his own initiative and ignore Grenfell's order. In so doing he displayed both courage and an understanding of the position but unfortunately, as it turned out, his tactics were not the equal of his initiative. On the early morning of 17 January he led a mixed force of irregulars, and gendarmerie, stiffened by members of the Xth Sudanese, towards Handub. The infantry was ordered forward to engage the enemy while Kitchener waited in the rear with the cavalry. It was a common enough stratagem – the infantry's first assault would be followed up by a sweeping cavalry movement – but at Handub it went almost disastrously awry. The infantry charged quickly through the village, killing as they went, but in so doing they failed to cover their rear and the reorganised enemy took full advantage of their plight.

At that point, realising that his advantage was slipping away, Kitchener engaged his cavalry to cover the hasty retreat back to Suakin, and while under heavy fire a bullet hit him in the face, breaking his jaw. He was rushed back into the town while the cavalry spread across the field to cover the retreat and also to mop up isolated pockets of resistance. Osman Digna was also wounded, and during his flight a large number of slaves fell into the cavalry's hands to be taken back to Suakin and freedom. The skirmish had not been altogether successful but what mattered most was that a victory had been gained at little cost to the British-Egyptian army. Two hundred of Osman Digna's men lay dead while Kitchener's force lost only nineteen casualties and twice as many wounded. The news was hailed in the press in Britain and changed the tune of many of those who had attacked Kitchener's policy; it also added to the belief that Kitchener was indeed the coming man in the army. *The Times* wrote:

> No one desires anything but peace and the restoration of commerce with the tribes of the interior. There may be different methods of pursuing that object, but there is no difference of opinion as to the object to be pursued. The policy of Colonel Kitchener has been severely criticised and its results have certainly not been entirely satisfactory, but it is only fair to consider that his position is a very difficult one and the whole situation is full of uncertainty and obscurity. It is clear at any rate that Suakin and those who rely upon its garrison for protection must be secured from attack. This is a matter of plain duty, into which no disputed questions of policy can enter. Hostile tribes and predatory bands, whether 'rebels' or not, must be taught to respect the Egyptian flag and the territory and property it covers. They will be let alone so long as they refrain from aggression. If they attack, the attack will be repelled, and they will be attacked in their turn, as they were attacked at Handub yesterday.[6]

That was a fair reflection of British policy and of Kitchener's difficulties in interpreting it. Egypt had to be seen to be the nominal ruler in the area. No matter how much the charade was bolstered by British arms and money, Sudan had to be left alone for the time being unless its population proved to be too troublesome. What appealed to a large proportion of the population in Britain, especially to those of martial disposition, was that Kitchener had secured a victory over the dervishes using Egyptian troops. It gave a real fillip to a public avid for tales of derring-do, although all it served in reality was to throw the Suakin area into turmoil as previously friendly tribes turned to Osman Digna.

Baring's initial reaction was one of alarm. He complained to the new Prime Minister, the Marquess of Salisbury, that Kitchener was only interested in gaining 'the maximum amount of glory' but by the beginning of the following year he generously agreed that Kitchener's policies towards the Arabs had been correct and that 'no one possesses so much influence with the heads of tribes as Colonel Kitchener'.[7] Salisbury, in his turn, had been as impressed by Kitchener as Baring had been chary. 'I was much grieved to hear of Kitchener's wound,' he wrote to Baring. 'Though I do not think I have ever met him, I have been familiar with his name for many years, and feel as if I know him well. He is a very gallant officer – though a headstrong subordinate.'[8]

Kitchener was well rewarded for his adventure at Suakin. Queen Victoria made him one of her aides-de-camp and requested that news of his recovery should regularly be made available to her; he was promoted brevet-colonel and the Khedive made him a Pasha. His wound made headline news and daily bulletins were issued from the Cairo Citadel Hospital whence he had been transferred the day after the battle on board the frigate HMS *Starling*.

On arrival Kitchener's condition was pronounced to be 'very serious' and the doctors set about trying to find the offending bullet, which was thought to be lodged in his jaw. Kitchener had been wounded on the right-hand side of his face at the joint of his jaw and the bullet had caused a comminuted fracture of his jawbone, that is, the bone had splintered, leaving a gaping wound. It was a painful injury, made worse by infection and, with the throat and tonsils inflamed, breathing and swallowing became difficult for him. The bullet could not be found by doctors and two days later, seeing that it had not turned septic, the doctors gave up the search and sewed up the wound. Later, Kitchener claimed that the bullet had found its way into the throat, almost causing him to choke to death, but added that he had saved himself by the simplest of means – 'with a desperate effort he swallowed the bullet and nature did the rest'.[9] Given the type of wound he had suffered, this seems unlikely, but it was typical of the kind of grim humour Kitchener used to bring to personal anecdotes. Certainly, the wound left little visible evidence and did not spoil his looks.

A month later his wound had healed sufficiently for him to return to his post at Suakin, where he was met by 'a most cordial reception from the people who all turned out when I landed and illuminated the town in the evening'. He bombarded Baring immediately with memoranda stressing the importance of his stronghold as a jumping-off point for any move against Sudan. Like most officers who served in the Egyptian Army, Kitchener saw invasion and the revenge of Gordon as the long-term objective and he fought consistently against the official attitude that a British presence in Suakin existed only to protect the Red Sea littoral and to discourage slaving in the immediate area.

That summer of 1888 he returned to England on leave and set about reinforcing his ambitions; Salisbury, who had already remarked on Kitchener's gallant behaviour at Suakin, invited him to stay at Hatfield, his country seat. The Cecils had been involved in English politics since Elizabethan times, and in 1888 Salisbury, the third marquess, was enjoying his second term as Prime Minister. An intellectual who was a Fellow of All Souls, Oxford, his personal interest lay in scientific invention, particularly in the fields of electricity and telegraphy, and he was possessed of a high moral outlook, each day beginning with prayers in the family chapel. Both he and Kitchener agreed that Britain's security lay in ensuring that its colonies were safe and its trade routes guarded. As regards Sudan, Kitchener wanted to avenge Gordon, but good-housekeeping told him that reserves had to be built up, that time had to be bought. Salisbury went along with that, telling Baring that the Mahdists 'were created for the purpose of keeping the bed warm for you', but he also took a wider view of events.[10] The 'scramble' for central Africa had begun and Salisbury had to balance British interests: Italy had to be kept in check in Ethiopia, German involvement in east Africa had to advance in step with British claims, and there was the ever-present danger from French colonial ambitions in the Upper Nile through the hinterland of the French Congo. For centuries Egypt's security had depended on possession of the flood waters of the Nile and Baring worried incessantly about Italian incursions at Kassala towards the Atbara and French challenges on the Upper Nile. Salisbury's solution was to seal off the approaches to the Nile Valley, a policy that would require the eventual recapture of Sudan. He also told Kitchener that he would be promoted to the rank of adjutant-general to Sir Francis Grenfell.

Kitchener returned to Cairo on 13 September and a week later he was in action again. To ease the situation at Suakin, Grenfell moved two brigades into the area, one under Kitchener's command and the other under the direction of Colonel Charles Holled Smith, the new governor-general of the town. In a spirited skirmish outside the fortifications, near the fort of Gemaizeh, a large Mahdist force was beaten off and Kitchener's brigade played a prominent part in the action. For the

SUDAN: PLANNING FOR VICTORY

first time Sudanese battalions were given a leading role, an experiment that Grenfell admitted after the battle was fully justified:

> The Soudanese soldiers behaved not only with gallantry, but steadiness. They advanced 300 yards under fire without firing a shot; and even when the trenches were reached they did not entirely lose their formation. Led by British officers, the Black Brigade will become a powerful engine. The black not only hates the Dervish, but despises him, and has not the slightest hesitation in attacking him, even when in superior numbers. This confidence in themselves and in their British officers is of enormous value in savage warfare.[11]

One of the battalion commanders in Kitchener's brigade was Captain Hector Macdonald of the Gordon Highlanders – Kitchener had first come across him in 1885 when Macdonald was second-in-command to Valentine Baker in the Egyptian gendarmerie. Three years younger than Kitchener, 'Fighting Mac', as he came to be known, had risen through the ranks – unusual in Victorian times – and he was an experienced soldier with eighteen years of active service behind him. As a former colour sergeant who believed in the virtues of drilling as a means of instilling discipline he was ideally suited to train the unruly, though brave, Sudanese troops and he was to become an important cog in Kitchener's wheel of reform in Cairo. The Sudanese troops were to prove their worth throughout the campaigns against the dervishes in spite of their tendency towards over-zealousness in battle. At the Battle of Toski, fought on 3 August the following year, Macdonald was astonished to discover that his Sudanese had taken his shouted orders to be a sign of fear; instead of obeying his commands to get into their lines as the dervishes approached, his troops crowded round him, saying, 'Don't be afraid, we are here, and we shall protect you. Have no fear, it is all right.'[12] Minutes later they were in the thick of the battle.

It was at Toski that the Khalifa's ambitions in Egypt finally came to an end. A force of almost 6,000 dervishes, small by Mahdist standards, under Wad-el-Nejumi, one of their most able leaders, had advanced beyond Wadi Halfa into an area north of the Sudan border that was governed by Colonel Josceline Wodehouse, an artilleryman and an outstanding field commander. By harrying the dervish army with his horsemen and sending a flying column to cut off the advance, Wodehouse was able to forestall Wad-el-Nejumi's forward progress until Grenfell could arrive with reinforcements. Cut off from his own supply route, the dervish leader then had no option but to fight or to retire south again under Grenfell's offer of surrender. No self-respecting dervish leader could ever take the latter course. Having seen his offer refused and realising his enemy's limitations, Grenfell decided to attack immediately before his British brigade arrived. (By then it was only at Aswan.) Kitchener, who was in charge of the cavalry, was ordered ahead of the army to reconnoitre the area. Having sighted the enemy and noted that they were attempting to move to the north-west, away from Grenfell's main force, he engaged the Mahdists, drawing from them heated fire before he withdrew his men prudently behind a group of small hills. His action both headed off Wad-el-Nejumi's army and lured it to destruction. Near the village of Toski, halfway between Wadi Halfa and Korosko, Grenfell and Wodehouse brought up their infantry and, as the dervishes charged from the safety of their defensive positions, they were shot down by withering and disciplined rifle fire and by an equally intensive artillery barrage. The result was a punishing defeat: Wad-el-Nejumi was killed and the remnants of his force fled back over the border to Sudan. There were fewer than 200 casualties in Grenfell's army but six times that number in the dervish force; 4,000 prisoners were taken.

Kitchener had played a vital role in the battle, his cavalry action both beginning the action and acting as decoy – when he withdrew his men, he ordered his squadron of Camel Corps riders to dismount and line the ridge to give Wad-el-Nejumi a false impression of the size of Grenfell's army. For his services he was mentioned in Grenfell's despatches and awarded the CB (Companion of the Order of the Bath). When he told Millie, he was rightly exultant at his success, but in his description of the battle there is a sense of the almost religious purpose that he brought to his mission against the dervishes who had slain Gordon:

SUDAN: PLANNING FOR VICTORY

> What a change it was only 13 days from London gaieties organising a force here with the heat at 110 in the shade. Our enemy kindly waits for us and are from all accounts most fanatically inclined – they have brought all their women and children with them and have no food for them so they leave them to starve. The poor creatures come into us in the most ghastly state, mere walking skeletons. I shall be glad when we get at the brutes who have brought about all this suffering.

The victories at Tokar and Toski marked a watershed in Egyptian policy towards Sudan and, from 1891, it was generally understood that it was only a matter of time before the country would be annexed. Having proved that its men could face up to the dervish tactics of the headlong charge that had previously so terrified the Egyptian soldiers, the army felt more confident, especially as money was now slowly accumulating in Egypt's exchequer.

For the time being, though, Baring was determined that Egyptian affairs should have priority. He wanted to complete the construction of the great reservoir at Aswan and to extend communications south by pushing the railway and the telegraph to the border at Wadi Halfa. The Egyptian Army had also to be re-equipped, re-armed and reorganised. For the first time Kitchener came into contact with military administration on the grand scale, a task that he found to be entirely to his liking. In the autumn of 1889 he used his leave to visit India for the first time, his brother Walter being stationed there with the West Yorkshire Regiment. On his return to Egypt Baring offered him the post of inspector-general of police, which he could combine with his military duties, and he posed the invitation in terms that suggested official disapproval if Kitchener refused. Although Kitchener was far from popular in Cairo, Grenfell had found him to be an ideal second-in-command and Kitchener had good reason to believe that his name was starred for even higher promotion: to Millie he wrote in January 1891 that Grenfell 'seemed as permanent as ever, no sign of moving for years, so I go on waiting. It is a poor game but perhaps it is worth it'. Remembering the difficulties Baker had faced with that 'rubbishy lot of worthless ex-soldiers' he must have asked himself if the move was worthwhile but presumably Baring had told him privately that far from spoiling his chances it might enhance them, for Kitchener occupied the police post for the whole of 1890 and part of 1891.[13]

The year 1892 proved to be a momentous one for Egypt and for the two men most closely associated with the country's fortunes. In June Baring was raised to the peerage as Lord Cromer and on 13 April Kitchener was appointed Sirdar in place of Grenfell, who returned to the British Army and was later promoted field marshal. Kitchener's appointment with the local rank of brigadier-general owed much to Baring's support. He had pointed out to Salisbury that he was an efficient officer, that he had executed his police duties soundly and that he was the man on the spot who had experience of Egypt and was known and trusted. Salisbury's backing was crucial as the post of Sirdar, although a military appointment, owed its patronage to the Foreign Office and not to the War Office. Given Kitchener's friendship with Salisbury, that support was offered in the strongest possible terms.

All the same reasons that had accompanied Kitchener's previous promotion were used again to justify his latest preferment, but they could not soften the blow amongst the British civilian and military community in Cairo, whose choice would have been Wodehouse, the victor of Toski. During his years in Egypt Kitchener still preferred the privacy of his own home or his office to the club or the mess, and he continued politely to turn down invitations to parties and picnics. Yet it had not gone unnoticed that he took pleasure in the company of wealthy Turks, Jews and Arabs and that his own quarters had been embellished in a most un-British fashion with oriental tapestries and ostentatious displays of porcelain. Even Salisbury's son, Lord Edward Cecil, Kitchener's future ADC, was moved to admit that he did not take to his chief at that time, finding him to be 'uncouth and uncivilised' and '*cassant* [abrupt] and rude'.[14]

Fortunately for Kitchener however, Cromer, his boss, admired him and he proved to be a faithful ally during the six years of planning that would be needed for the reconquest of Sudan. Like all relationships, theirs was frequently put under some strain and it was said of Kitchener that he was congenial to Cromer's head but not to his heart. Cromer had known all along, however, that any campaign would have to be paid for by the Egyptian exchequer, that economy was the watchword and that plans would have to be laid carefully to transport the army into the Sudanese heartland and back again. Sound administration was to be preferred to élan in battle, and sixteen years later Cromer admitted that, given the circumstances, Kitchener had been the ideal choice:

> Young, energetic, ardently and exclusively devoted to his profession, and, as the honourable scars on his face testified, experienced in Soudanese warfare, Sir Herbert Kitchener possessed all the qualities necessary to bring the campaign to a successful issue. Like many another military commander, the bonds which united him and his subordinates were those of stern discipline on the one side, and, on the other, the respect due to superior talent and the confidence felt in the resourcefulness of a strong and masterful spirit, rather than the affectionate obedience yielded to the behests of a genial chief … A first-rate military administrator, every detail of the machine, with which he had to work, received adequate attention. Before any decisive movement was made, each portion of the machine was adapted, so far as human foresight could provide, to perform its allotted task. Sir Herbert Kitchener also possessed another quality which is rare among soldiers, and which was of special value under the circumstances then existing. He did not think that extravagance was the necessary handmaid of efficiency. On the contrary, he was a rigid economist, and, whilst making adequate provision for all essential and necessary expenditure, suppressed with a firm hand any tendency towards waste and extravagance.[15]

This was no bad encomium but Cromer's support was regarded as yet another example of Kitchener's sycophancy. Faced by that bad feeling, the new Sirdar began to collect around him a staff of young officers who would owe him total loyalty and who would take no heed of snide remarks. These men would form his administrative staff and would also command the Egyptian and Sudanese battalions, with more experienced officers being given the command of brigades. Kitchener's aloofness, and his almost obsessional regard for his personal privacy, only reinforced prejudices against him and, after his appointment as Sirdar, the legend grew that Kitchener was more of a machine than a man, a cold and humourless automaton more concerned with efficiency than with human affection. But while the legend certainly had a kernel of truth – as Kitchener had admitted to Millie, he was ambitious – it can also be claimed that it was the very opposition to him and his aspirations that forced him into the position of having to maintain a stern and unbending public presence. To Millie, now living more or less permanently with her family in New Zealand, he confessed the isolation that he felt in his new position and looked, as ever, for her support, especially in his social affairs:

> You have now got a full blown Sirdar and a Brigadier General for your brother and I think you should seriously consider your duty to him and make up your mind to pay him a visit and help in the entertaining of the outside crowd ... I have moved into the Sirdar's house as it is larger and better for entertaining ... If you do not do something in the way of helping me in the entertaining I shall be driven into some rash alliance of a matrimonial nature, so you have your warning and better look out.

He also admitted to Millie in an earlier letter that, although his house needed looking after and he thought that a woman would be 'quite necessary', it had been 'too difficult to find one to marry'. Quite simply, Kitchener had spent so much time furthering his own career that he had not allowed himself the time to attempt a suitable match.

His public demeanour can also be explained by the fact he had reached high rank at a comparatively early age – he was forty-one when he was appointed Sirdar – and he was determined to hold what he had. Any slip in private behaviour, any rumour, however unfounded, would have been accepted by his enemies as a means of dislodging him. Earlier, during his first posting to Egypt, he had seen one fellow officer attempt suicide and another succeed in killing himself when they each discovered that their wives had gone off with other men. Cairo had been scandalised and the surviving officer had lived only to see his career end in ruins. Kitchener could not afford distractions of that kind. He already had a compact family circle and a powerful group of friends in England; he could see no reason to bend to any over-familiarity in Egypt.

SUDAN: PLANNING FOR VICTORY

The staff that Kitchener now built up around him in Cairo was young in years but greatly experienced in Egyptian and Sudanese affairs. Leslie Rundle became his adjutant-general and moved into Kitchener's old house, and Reginald Wingate, a superb intelligence officer, was appointed Director of Military Intelligence, charged with being the Sirdar's eyes and ears in the territory south of the border below Wadi Halfa. Wingate, one of a new breed of officer, whose own career became as closely identified with Egypt as was Kitchener's was one of the few senior officers to whom Kitchener could confide his thoughts and feelings. Wingate, for his part, liked him too, remembering later that, in spite of the cold face he showed to the world, Kitchener 'had one of the kindest of hearts, and under his cold exterior, there was a fund of real sympathy and even affection'.[16]

With two such loyal lieutenants in Rundle and Wingate, and enjoying a good relationship with Cromer, Kitchener had laid the foundations for a successful period of office: his next move was to build a protective wall of sound middle-ranking officers. These men, young subalterns or captains in the British Army, were appointed to the service of the Khedive in the rank of major (bimbashi); they were paid £450 a year and were contracted for a minimum period of two years, whereupon their record would be reviewed by Kitchener himself. Anyone who failed to come up to his expectations could expect to have his contract terminated and be sent home on the next ship. From the outset Kitchener told prospective candidates that his operation had no room for passengers and that faint hearts need not apply. Conditions would be tough, he warned, and they could expect to work long hours in difficult terrain, often with obdurate troops under their command. Kitchener also told them that he did not expect married officers to apply for such posts. There were two main reasons for this. First, bachelors did not have to be paid a married man's allowance and that was an important consideration to Kitchener who was working on a fixed budget. Secondly, he reckoned that married officers might not give him 100 per cent effort if they had to worry about their wives left behind in England or in Cairo where they might be prey to the 'society racket', as Kitchener called it. There was also a school of thought within the army that believed young officers might hold themselves back in action for fear of making their wives widows and that, in any case, men working under difficult conditions should think of their service first and their own needs second. As officers remembered after the campaign was over, Kitchener had not underestimated the difficulties of the campaign:

> One notices how beastly the food is, how monotonous and dreary the country, how hard it is to amuse oneself; one longs for the sight of fresh green vegetables, fresh butter, to find one's things are not smothered in sands, to get out of the sight and smell of a camel, to see a real green field; or with the many who are living entirely, or almost, by themselves on the line of communications there is a strong desire to walk into a mess again, and hear several fellows chaffing one another, to go into a theatre where one will forget ammunition, equipment, camels, water-supply, food arrangements, boats, railways, angarebs, natives, drill, baggage, etc. etc.[17]

Each year, from 1892 to 1898, Kitchener would use the Junior United Service Club to interview those young men who met his exacting conditions of service. Very soon he had surrounded himself with an admirable set of subordinates who in return for Kitchener's patronage gave him nothing but fierce loyalty no matter how hard their work or how severe the tenor of their service. They came to be known as 'Kitchener's Band of Boys'. Amongst their number were Archibald Hunter (later lieutenant-general) and Hector Macdonald ('Fighting Mac') who concealed his own marriage to remain in Egyptian service. At the height of his fame after Omdurman, Macdonald always maintained that the success of the campaign was due entirely to Kitchener's 'wisdom, his foresight and his indomitable energy'.[18]

Kitchener then set about reforming the Egyptian Army. As early as 1884 he had admitted to friends that he thought little of British involvement in Egypt and to Millie he had suggested that Britain's best course would be to disband the Khedive's army and replace it with British regiments, who would soon put paid to the Khalifa and his rule in Sudan. In that way the country would come within the British sphere of influence and the headwaters of the Nile would be protected from foreign interference. Privately he thought it would be in everyone's interests if Britain ended the charade of the protectorate and turned Egypt, along with Sudan, into a British colony. Others, such as Alfred Milner, at that time Under-Secretary in the Ministry of Finance, agreed with him: 'Scott [John Scott, Judicial Adviser] is now practically Minister of Justice and Kitchener Minister of the Interior', he noted in his diary early in 1892.[19] Annexation of Egypt, though, would have alienated France and, although successive British administrations agreed with Cromer's estimation that the incapacity of the Egyptian ruling class to rule excluded any British withdrawal, no government was prepared to extend British influence in Cairo until the time was ripe.

Under those circumstances Kitchener was forced to comply with the official British line that the security of Egypt was the responsibility of the Egyptian Army, that British regiments, other than those on garrison duty, would not be based in Egypt and that those British officers under his command would think of themselves as owning their first allegiance to the Khedive. At his disposal he had fourteen battalions of infantry, eight of which were Egyptian and six Sudanese; he also had three batteries of light artillery, four squadrons of cavalry and a transport section that was later entrusted to the command of his brother Walter. In all, he commanded an army limited by treaty to 18,000 men. There were some Egyptian officers under his command but none could rise above the rank of lieutenant-colonel: the British officers, under an agreement reached in 1886, were regarded as 'temporary Egyptians', they took Egyptian forms of rank and wore the uniform of the Egyptian Army. Under Wood and Grenfell the Egyptian soldiers had been transformed into a reasonably efficient fighting force and the actions along the frontier had convinced the men that they could stand and fight against the headlong dervish charge.

Kitchener's method of working during his first years as Sirdar was simplicity itself. His subordinates were ordered to instil discipline and a sense of pride into their battalions and this they did with the help of white NCOs by dint of constant drilling. The Sirdar himself paid little attention to those niceties, preferring to delegate the responsibility for fighting arrangements to those who had actual experience of warfare. Instead, he turned to administration and, with Rundle, worked out a system of strict economies to keep the Egyptian Army within budget.

Establishment costs were kept to a minimum, nothing was allowed to be wasted, and although the men were well armed and well fed, the army's commissariat pared back on uniforms, boots and other less essential equipment to such an extent that the Egyptian battalions on manoeuvres often looked like rag, tag and bobtail outfits instead of fighting soldiers. In most of his dealings with his subordinates Kitchener avoided paperwork and preferred to delegate by spoken command once his mind was made up, frequently making his battalion commanders guess the extent of his wishes. His office was chaotic; ADCs used to remember how papers and maps with tiny flags, signifying dispositions and possible manoeuvres, were strewn over the floor and that the filing system was non-existent, yet Kitchener could usually recall the import of any command without referring to his daily orders.

At the forefront of his mind, always, was the burning sense of mission to avenge Gordon and retake Khartoum: hardly a day passed without Kitchener reminding himself of the nature of his personal crusade. To his father, he wrote early in 1893 suggesting that now was the time to stir up a commotion in the press and in the London clubs for the reconquest of Sudan, and this Colonel Kitchener was happy to do in spite of increasing frailty. In fact, he died in the following year and his death broke up what unity his family had managed to preserve over the years after leaving Switzerland. 'What gadabouts we all are to scatter ourselves across the world!' Kitchener had said to Millie in October 1890. He himself was not destined to live again in England for any length of time until 1914, Millie stayed on in New Zealand, where Arthur also lived for a time before his death in Sicily in 1907, and Walter, after a successful army career, went on to become Governor of Bermuda.

Although Kitchener was admired by Cromer for the forceful way in which he had set about perfecting the Egyptian Army, he had qualms about Kitchener's 'mania for economy', which had caused a great deal of resentment among British and Egyptian officers who believed they could not maintain the efficiency of their battalions without additional equipment. Those requests Kitchener tartly ignored, pointing out to his officers that all a good soldier required was a steady aim and the ability to stand firm when the dervishes charged. Kitchener had given his word that the Egyptian Army's expenditure would not go over budget and he was determined to keep it.

Only one shadow fell across his career in Egypt during those years. The year 1892 saw the succession of a new Khedive, Abbas Hilmi II, a self-possessed, articulate and proud eighteen-year-old whose education had been completed in Vienna and who knew something of European politics. In Cromer's eyes the new ruler was too sophisticated for his own good and he immediately set himself the task of acting as mentor to his charge by impressing upon him the benefits of Empire and constitutional monarchy in the British understanding of that concept. Unfortunately for Cromer the new Khedive was not prepared to listen as he was a cultured, if headstrong, young man who took a good deal of pride in his sense of nationality. Supported by an enclave of ministers with nationalist beliefs he began increasingly to question Cromer's policies, so much so that the British agent informed the Foreign Office that the sooner the Khedive received a short sharp shock the better it would be for all concerned. It fell to Kitchener to administer that medicine.

In January 1894 the Khedive, accompanied by his Under-Secretary at the War Ministry, Maher Pasha, went on a tour of inspection of the Egyptian Army units stationed along the frontier with Sudan. There, he took the opportunity to criticise the officers who commanded them. The drill was not to his liking, he was critical of the march-past, complained that the troops were not well turned out and told Kitchener that he was mortified to have such an inefficient army at his disposal. Kitchener was incensed and a furious telegram was sent to Cromer in Cairo and copied to Major-General Sir Frederick Walker, the officer commanding the British garrison, hinting that mutiny was in the air. 'I pointed out that the position of English officers in the country would become almost untenable if they were so publicly rebuked and that it would be impossible for me to obtain the services of good officers in the Egyptian Army if this continued.'[20]

Curtly, Kitchener tendered his resignation and, with his senior officers, withdrew to the headquarters camp. The following day Cromer telegraphed his support and moves were put in hand to clip the Khedive's wings. Rosebery was informed of the 'frontier incident' as it came to be known, and chose to back Cromer. If the Khedive did not agree to dismiss Maher Pasha (whose influence may have lain behind the incident) and apologise to Kitchener in public, the army would be put under British command. Rosebery added that he would 'also at once publish the various instances of insults which have occurred of late so that the country may realise the situation'.[21] The inference was clear: Abbas Hilmi had to back down or face humiliation and possible abdication.

Cromer had chosen his moment well. He knew that Kitchener would not brook any insults, real or imagined; in rising to the Khedive's bait he had precipitated a crisis that allowed Cromer to flush out several leading nationalists and to bring Egypt more directly under his control. The Khedive duly apologised in an Order of the Day, Maher Pasha was exiled to the governorship of Port Said, and the now aged Nubar Pasha was reinstated as prime minister and Cromer's puppet. Kitchener himself was knighted, Rosebery telling him in his letter announcing the award of the KCMG that:

> It would be idle to deny that I have chosen this particular moment for the recommendation in order to make it clear to all whom it may concern that I feel the warmest sympathy with you in the very difficult circumstances in which you have been placed for some time past, and which have recently come to a head … I hope this may encourage you to persevere with patience and dignity in your present course.[22]

As for Abbas Hilmi, he never forgave Cromer and never forgot the humiliation he had received at Kitchener's hands. Kitchener himself was equally uncompromising – he told Queen Victoria during this first visit to Windsor in 1896 that Abbas Hilmi was 'wicked, cruel and weak'.[23] In time, that also came to be the accepted view of the Foreign Office.

5

OMDURMAN: THE MAKING OF THE LEGEND

In 1894 Lord Rosebery assured Cromer that 'no instructions will come from this country for a reconquest of Sudan ... even if I received an urgent request from the Egyptian Government for a Sudan expedition I could not bring the present Government to agree to it.'[1] In other words, Britain continued to pay lip service to the notion that the recapture of Sudan was a matter for the Egyptians themselves to decide and that under Cromer's firm guidance civil reforms had to be completed before military adventures could be contemplated. A few months later the Conservatives returned to power with Salisbury as Prime Minister, the last to sit in the House of Lords. In many observers eyes the Tories, having attacked Gladstone for inaction over Sudan, could hardly refuse to move now that they held the reins of power.

Salisbury was not the man to be moved by hysterical demands for rapid imperial expansion but he knew, too, that when he chose to act he could count on a large measure of public support. 'How long are we going to tolerate this absurd political farce?' asked Edward Bennett, Fellow of Hertford College, Oxford, and a typical New Imperialist. 'When will a British government have the courage to inform the world that we officially recognise what is already a fait accompli and intend to remain in sole and permanent possession of a country for which we have done so much?'[2] Others joined in, the most prominent being Alfred Milner, who argued that Britain was justified in the course of action she had adopted for the country:

> The truth is that the idea of a definite date for the conclusion of our work in Egypt is wholly misleading. The withdrawal of Great Britain, if it is not to end in disaster, can only be a gradual process. An intangible influence made up of many elements, like that of England in Egypt, cannot be withdrawn, any more than it can be created, at a certain hour, or by a single act.[3]

The calls for Britain to take an initiative were music to Kitchener's ears, especially when his name was associated with them. While on leave in England in the summer of 1895 Kitchener emerged as one of the great imperial symbols of the age, the man upon whose broad shoulders rested the hopes of Britain and her people. His growing stature also attracted the attention of the court. Ever since his exploits at Suakin Kitchener had been a favourite of the Queen's and when he visited her at Windsor he was encouraged to develop his ideas for the future. At dinner Kitchener's abruptness disconcerted members of the Royal household such as Marie Mallet, a maid of honour who thought him a resolute, 'cruel man', adding that 'later under the influence of whisky and tobacco he thawed ... he hates the Turks, the Sultan most of all, and openly asked why we do not assassinate the Sultan. He simply longs for murder and execution would be his greatest joy if he were to have his own way in Cairo.'[4] How the other guests reacted Marie Mallet does not record, but Ian Hamilton, later his chief of staff in South Africa, recalled that his chief was much given to thinking aloud, often using the most disconcerting phrases and causing alarm to those unused to his manner of speaking.[5]

At the summer's end, after making arrangements for Millie's daughter Frances to enter Newnham College, Cambridge, at his expense, Kitchener returned to Egypt to continue preparing his army for the day when it would be asked to put principle into practice. Kitchener began to enjoy life in Cairo and entertained frequently, invitations to his residency being much prized. If at times he appeared withdrawn, his new ADC, Lord Edward Cecil, could draw him into a good mood and his conversation would range over his interests, horse-breeding, porcelain and Egyptian antiquities, displaying a reserved charm that delighted his guests. 'I had a big fantasia for all the Egyptian officers,' he told Millie, 'and it went off very well. Everything was eaten and drunk that I had in the house.' The Prince of Wales stayed with him, Pandeli Ralli was a guest in the winter of 1895–96 and his brother-in-law, Harry Parker, Millie's husband, dropped in regularly to see him en route from New Zealand to Britain. Kitchener paid careful attention to his family. When his nephew, Arthur Chevallier Parker, wanted to join the army he helped ease his way to a commission in the Royal Sussex Regiment but told Millie that her son would have to serve four years in India before he would offer him employment in Egypt. Kitchener was not a man to offer privilege without responsibility.

During the summer of 1896 Kitchener told Millie that the reconquest of Sudan 'must come soon' and that, in his opinion, it would be as a result of the activities of the Italians in Ethiopia. 'I have been and am very busy about the Kassala advances of the Italians,' he had told her on 27 July 1894. His intuition was remarkably sage. Although the Italian ambitions in Ethiopia had seemed to Cairo to threaten British interests, it had not been an easy passage. In January 1896 their main base at Kassala, the object of Kitchener's interest two years earlier, was under threat and two months later they were defeated at Adowa. Suakin was put in danger by the defeat and the British in Egypt were faced by the spectre of a European nation being humiliated by the dervishes. Clearly something would have to be done, but Salisbury chose to act not so much as to avoid problems in the eastern Sudan as to shore up the Triple Alliance that had been created in 1882 to embrace Germany, Austria–Hungary and Italy. On 10 March the Italian ambassador in London requested that Britain make a demonstration along the Nile into Sudan to ease the Italian position, and at a Cabinet meeting two days later approval was given for an Egyptian advance to the village of Akasha some 60 miles into Sudan and for a display of force across the desert towards Abu Hamed. A telegram announcing the decision was sent to Cairo during the early hours of the morning of 13 March. Two officers, Lord Athlumney and Major Watson, decoded it and immediately took it to Kitchener's residence. The Sirdar appeared at a window, lantern in hand, and after much persuasion opened his door to the nocturnal visitors. Watson gave him the message and Athlumney entered to find 'the delightful tableau of the Sirdar pyjama'd with a lamp in one hand and the precious telegram in the other, dancing a wild fandango around the hall, with his ADC holding him by the elbows'.[6]

To begin with there was some confusion as to what should happen once the advance was made; Cromer and Kitchener were agreed that any forward movement should retake the whole province of Dongola and do so in the name of Egypt. Cromer was unyielding on this point as a War Office telegram had been simultaneously despatched to Major-General C.B. Knowles, GOC Egypt, informing him of the move and implying that British troops might be needed. On 14 March Cromer told Salisbury that he would not permit War Office interference and that henceforth the matter would have to be put in his hands. 'Unless the business is worked through me the utmost confusion will arise.'[7] This was a vital point, for it was already being suggested in the War Office that Kitchener was not the man to lead the expedition. His enemies recalled his lack of fighting experience and his behaviour at the time of the 'frontier incident' involving Abbas Hilmi. Now Commander-in-Chief in succession to Cambridge, Wolseley was caught in a dilemma. He had come to respect Kitchener but he also had to listen to the claims of more senior officers and for a time he thought that Grenfell, the previous Sirdar, would make a good compromise and would be responsible to him at the War Office and not, as Kitchener was, to the Foreign Office. This intelligence alarmed Kitchener as he knew that without Cromer's support his position would be jeopardised and that Cromer had threatened Salisbury with resignation over the Cabinet's clumsy handling of the affair.

Fortunately for both men Salisbury made amends at a meeting of the Cabinet on 15 March when it was agreed that Cromer should make the arrangements for the expedition and that he should take his instructions from the Foreign Office and not the War Office, thus ensuring that Kitchener would remain as Sirdar. On the same day Cromer telegraphed to Salisbury his complete confidence in Kitchener, whom he had found to be 'cool and sensible and [who] knows his job thoroughly and is not at all inclined to be rash'.[8]

OMDURMAN: THE MAKING OF THE LEGEND

Everything was to be done according to the book. As Cromer was concerned that British soldiers might be needed to strengthen the Egyptian Army, Kitchener agreed to a battalion of the North Staffordshire Regiment being held in readiness at Wadi Halfa. He also requested that Suakin be strengthened by an Indian Army battalion so that its garrison could join his seven Egyptian and five Sudanese battalions as his army began the haul south to its first objective of Akasha. The desert village was taken easily, allowing Kitchener to ponder his next move. Some of his more fiery battalion commanders wanted to press home the advantage of surprise and to attack the dervishes at their next stronghold, the village of Firket to the south, but Kitchener's lines of communication were already extended, he had to move up supplies, men and ammunition, and he had to ensure that these were protected from attack while in transit. Any assault on his supply lines would be disastrous – this was the fear of the British Cabinet – but Kitchener was alive to the danger and at every stage of the expedition he moved forward only when his rear was fully protected. To keep his army supplied Kitchener had made arrangements for 5,000 camels to be bought for his transport department, a purchase that made Salisbury suspect that Kitchener planned a lightning strike south. But Kitchener was too cautious a commander to risk a rash forward strategy and, besides, 5,000 camels would have been insufficient for such an enterprise as each beast could only carry 300lb of provisions and required themselves 100lb of provender en route. The camels and the transport department were put under the command of the newly arrived Walter Kitchener, who expressed both alarm and admiration for the autocratic way in which his brother exercised supreme command.[9] To supplement those supply requirements river steamers belonging to the travel firm of Thomas Cook and Sons were commandeered. These elegant, white-painted craft with their polished brass, tasteful staterooms and impressive paddle-wheels now performed sterling service of another kind, ferrying troops and provisions up the Nile; but when the water was low they could only be used on the lower reaches and a means of hauling them over the cataracts had to be devised.

Kitchener then turned his attention to the old railway line that ran from Egypt into Sudan but stopped short at Sarras north of Akasha.

Despite its broken-down track and antique rolling stock Kitchener realised that it could play an important role in his plans. Egypt was scoured for men who had worked on the railways and a motley collection of ex-firemen, ticket collectors and plate-layers was formed hurriedly into a makeshift railway battalion to repair the line south to Akasha. Equipment was hard to come by but somehow it was found and gradually a railway line took shape: if a locomotive fell off the rails it was manhandled back on to the track; if the line was swept away it was rebuilt; and always at the centre of such operations was the Sirdar himself. Kitchener's early training as a military engineer made such work congenial to him; throughout the campaign he led by example, often taking a hand himself at driving in the spikes and cursing those who were less willing to labour in temperatures that often rose above 100°F. He was inspired, and the men admired Kitchener for the grit he showed in pushing himself as well as those he commanded. This was not a campaign calling for tactical flair; rather it would be won by perseverance and attention to detail, virtues that Kitchener possessed aplenty. If, however, he had been killed, said one of his staff, the whole operation would have ground to a halt since Kitchener's mind was the sole repository of the concept of the campaign.

Having secured his lines of communication by the end of May, Kitchener felt ready to advance on Firket. In a simply executed action the cavalry feinted across the desert while three brigades of infantry, after a night march, made a surprise dawn attack on the fortified village. The dervishes were overwhelmed by the ferocity and the suddenness of the onslaught; they suffered about 1,000 casualties together with 600 men taken prisoner, but the great bulk of the force fled south into the desert to fight another day. It was an inexpensive victory, Kitchener's army only losing twenty-three dead and eighty-three wounded. Cromer received the news with no little satisfaction and, although he told Salisbury that the battle had been won in spite of War Office interference, he also rubbed home the point that the Egyptian Army had not been found wanting under fire: 'the fellahin can undergo fatigue and march well and Kitchener has a fair degree of confidence in their fighting qualities when commanded by British officers'.[10]

OMDURMAN: THE MAKING OF THE LEGEND

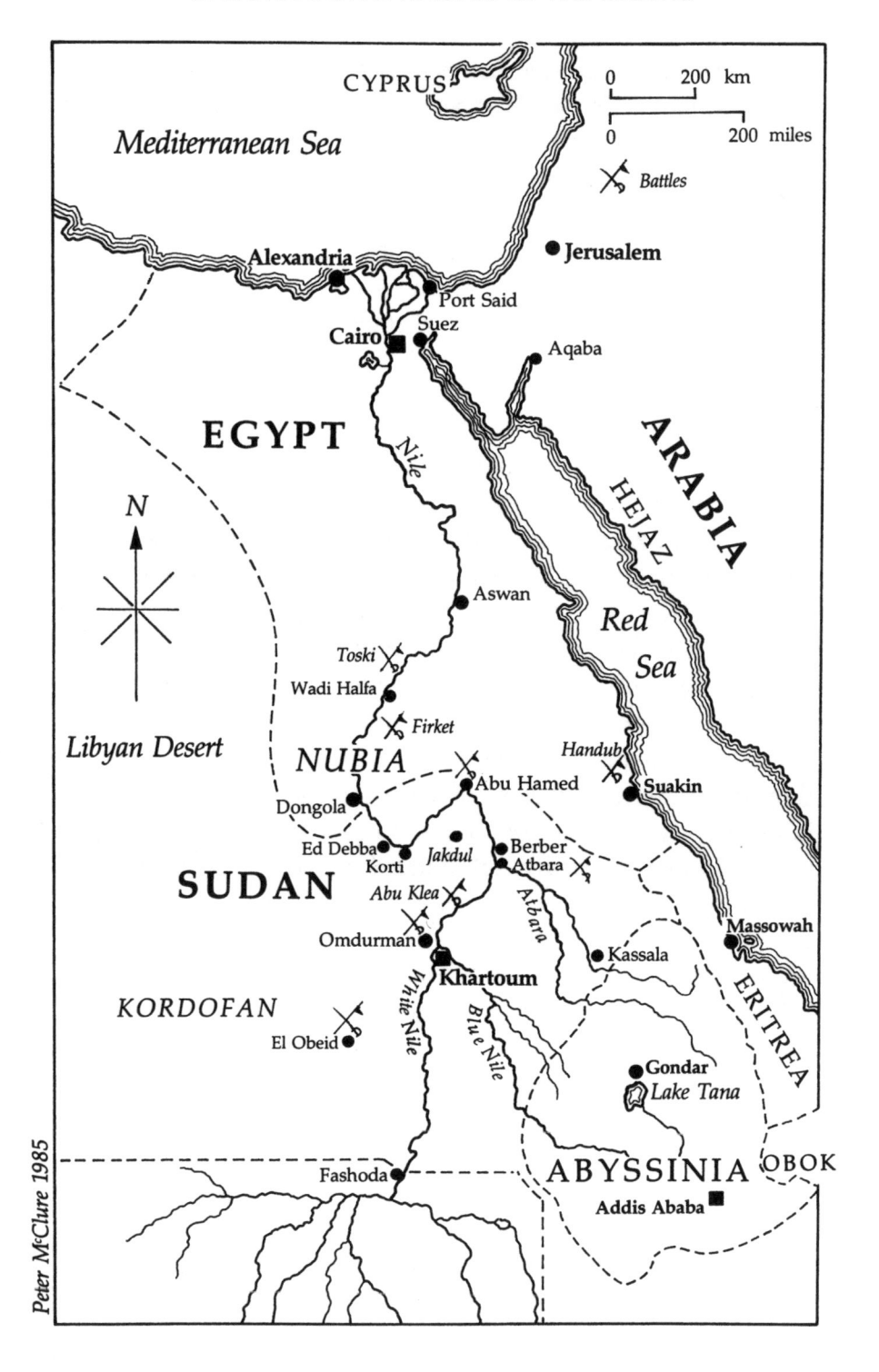

Although pursuit into the desert was again an alluring bait, Kitchener refused to take it, Cromer having vetoed any further advance beyond Dongola before he left for his annual leave in Britain. Instead, Kitchener was ordered to flush out pockets of resistance in the province and he began by moving his base to Sukkot, where he awaited the arrival of a new class of gunboat that would be assembled at Kosheh and used to make safe the waterway and river banks.

The defeat of the dervishes at Firket did much to raise the morale of the Egyptian Army. In the days that followed, while Hunter and Macdonald kept their men finely tuned with daily drills and weapons practices, Kitchener turned his attention to the logistical situation. Battle techniques did not interest him, which was why his 'band of boys' contained so many men who had proved their worth in previous campaigns; what taxed his mind more was how to make the most of his gains. Ahead lay the next enemy stronghold of Kerma, 86 miles away across the desert or 127 miles up the River Nile, with all its problems of navigation and danger of attack from the banks. During previous campaigns the dervishes had always chosen to attack at the point where the enemy line was most extended and Kitchener was determined not to play into their hands. It would have been easy to send the 2nd Brigade with three battalions of Sudanese under Macdonald ahead of the main force to take on the dervishes at Kerma, but it would be difficult to keep them supplied or to bring up reinforcements before the arrival of the main force. Kitchener decided that the best solution would be to take and hold the river route with the gunboats that were taking shape at Kosheh.

These were largely antique in design or hastily converted river steamers but there was one modern class of vessel built in sections in England and transported to Kitchener's forward post on the Nile. Known as the *Zafir* class, they had been designed by Kitchener and they were formidable craft – each was 140ft long, armour plated and armed with one twelve-pounder, two six-pounders and four Maxim guns; additional refinements included searchlights and ammunition hoists but their greatest asset was that they had a draft of only 39in, allowing them to operate in the shallowest of waters. The officers in the accompanying Naval Brigade were no less efficient and numbered three men destined to become admirals – Stanley Colville, H.L.A. Hood and Colin Keppel – as well as a future Admiral of the Fleet in young Lieutenant David Beatty, RN.

Unfortunately the flotilla would not be ready until September and in the intervening months the fates seemed to conspire against Kitchener. Water was in short supply and the troops tended to drink any liquid they came across in the desert, however turgid or unwholesome it first appeared. Often the brackish water caused little more than stomach upsets, but at Firket the water had been contaminated by decomposing bodies buried hastily in shallow graves and a wave of cholera swept through the camp. Twenty British officers died and an even larger number of Egyptian and Sudanese soldiers. It was also one of the hottest summers on record but in 1896 the weather defied logic and the province of Dongola was hit by violent storms that caused flash floods and the consequent disruption of the railway line and the camel routes. Many officers had to be sent home unfit for further service and by the year's end deaths from disease and hardship were six times as high as casualties in battle.

On 12 September the advance eventually began and Kitchener bent his mind to moving the 12,000-strong army south to Kerma – two battalions, the 5th and 6th Egyptians, remained behind as a rearguard. A week later, after a cautious route march along the east bank of the river, the force reached Kerma to find it deserted. The town offered a good position with well-constructed fortifications but no sooner had Kitchener taken it than Wingate brought him the disturbing news that the dervish force had taken up an even more commanding position a few miles away on the opposite bank of the river, thus blocking Kitchener's progress to Dongola. It was under the command of Emir Wad Bishara, one of the more able dervish leaders, who had read the situation well. Faced by an army twice the size of his, he had decided not to hold his ground at fortified Kerma but to move to higher ground on the opposite bank where his elderly cannon would command both the river and the route south along the east bank. This action surprised Kitchener, who had not expected the dervishes to show such good tactical sense – Wad Bishara had deployed his meagre forces with an eye both for the terrain and for Kitchener's future intentions. As his infantry could not cross the river to engage the enemy due to the dervishes' superior position, Kitchener ordered up his gunboats, Colville taking them into action between a hail of cannon and rifle fire from an enemy who realised that they were defending the last line of defence for Dongola.

As a result, Wad Bishara was wounded by a shell that fell near his tent and his injury, together with the heavy concentration of shell-fire, demoralised the dervish army. At midnight he called a council of war: he ordered that the defence continue but his emirs thought otherwise, arguing that, just as a merchant involved in a trading enterprise who discovers that he is losing money should withdraw, so should a general retire from a battle in the face of defeat. During the early hours of the morning the dervish army melted away into the desert, allowing Kitchener free access to the Dongola and the virtual repossession of Dongola province beyond the third cataract.[11]

The gunboats then raced ahead and on 23 September Kitchener entered Dongola to find it, like Firket, deserted. Ahead lay the strategic towns of Ed Debba and Merowe, both of which were taken without any opposition, thus adding 450 miles of the River Nile to Egyptian territory. The first stage of the reconquest of Sudan was over.

For his part in the Dongola campaign Kitchener was promoted to the substantive rank of major-general in the British Army; his despatches recorded 'the high qualities, endurance and bravery of the Egyptian troops' and several other officers also received rewards from a grateful British government. The best news of all as far as the Sirdar was concerned was that Cromer now seemed to be willing to countenance an advance beyond Merowe towards Abu Hames in the following year, without involving British troops. The only problem was finance. Egypt's budget was controlled by the Caisse de la Dette administered by an international board of directors representing Britain, Austria, Germany, Italy, France and Russia, and all additional expenditure had to be sanctioned by this body. The refusal of the French and Russian Commissioners to allow Egypt to borrow a sum of £500,000 from the reserves to cover the cost of the expedition had been referred to the courts, which had subsequently found in their favour.

The money, therefore, would have to come from Britain's exchequer and Kitchener hurried back to London at the end of the year to pursue his cause amongst the leading politicians. He was convinced that the dervishes could be beaten by his Egyptian troops and that any check on his campaign would eventually cost more money than a rapid advance south. He dined with Salisbury and the Duke of Cambridge and on 12 November wrote a tactful yet forthright letter to Sir Michael Hicks-Beach, the Chancellor of the Exchequer, making the case for additional expenditure on Sudan's military railway, the construction of three more gunboats and £55,000 worth of ammunition. It was a sensible plea, made more forceful by his argument that time wasted on discussions in London could return the upper hand to the Khalifa, who might at that moment be coercing wavering Arabs to join his forces. Hicks-Beach, who until then had stood out against unnecessary expenditure on colonial ventures, was impressed enough by Kitchener's proposals to authorise the additional payments out of the British exchequer.

Salisbury wrote to Cromer congratulating him on the completeness of Kitchener's success and on the mood of optimism in the Cabinet that the campaign would shortly reach a fruitful conclusion. Kitchener returned to Sudan at the beginning of December 1896 and took stock of his position. The Nile was his lifeline but in places it was unnavigable or only navigable at high water, necessitating a system of alternative transport; and the great bend of the river eastwards from Wadi Halfa back to Abu Hamed caused endless delays that Kitchener would have to avoid if his lines of communication were to be kept intact. A railway would change all that, but a railway that followed the obvious route, the path of the Nile from the terminus at Kosheh, would be both prohibitively expensive and time consuming to build. Any other route – Suakin to Berber and Korti to Metemma were also considered – would involve the taking of a dervish stronghold. The solution, argued Kitchener, was to throw the line over the Nubian Desert from Wadi Halfa to Abu Hamed. On the map it looks easy enough, 235 miles across a flat desert, but at that time the terrain was unmapped and thought to be waterless. The climate was known to be extreme and there was the added danger of attacks by dervish raiding parties.

The railway battalion would have to carry its own equipment and supplies and water would have to be found: in the event two wells were discovered by Lieutenant Cator of the Royal Engineers, both at equal intervals into the desert from Wadi Halfa. How fortunate these finds were can be gauged from the fact that no other wells have ever been found in that desert – this 'miracle' came to be known by those who doubted him as 'Kitchener's Luck'.

The railway battalion was augmented by the addition of specialist track-layers from Britain commanded by a group of Royal Engineer officers. The story of their achievement is one of the most remarkable of the whole campaign, for they had to face a difficult terrain racked by a pitiless sun and sudden, terrifying sandstorms; their equipment was often antiquated and they had to work within the confines of a tightly limited budget.[12] They had every reason to hate the man who had ordered the railway's construction and yet between them and Kitchener there grew a fierce loyalty. After the war Kitchener was criticised for putting his men through unnecessary hardships in the desert, but he shared their dangers and their discomfort, frequently riding a locomotive to inspect the work, offering advice here, a command there. In this work Kitchener was fortunate in his officers. He owed much to Cator, who died of fever before the line was finished. However, his greatest debt was to the man who planned and oversaw the enterprise, Lieutenant Percy Girouard, RE, a French-Canadian who had worked previously on the Canadian-Pacific Railway. Girouard was an expert engineer and surveyor and he was also one of the few men prepared to stand up to Kitchener. Other officers waiting for the expected explosion after Girouard had held his ground in argument would be amazed to see Kitchener smile grimly and then concede the point.

By mid-July the railway, which had been constructed at the sensational rate of 2 or 3 miles a day, was in striking distance of Abu Hamed, which Kitchener then ordered Hunter to storm. The brunt of the fighting was undertaken by Macdonald's Sudanese troops and the town was taken easily, the dervishes deciding to fall back towards Khartoum. A month later Wingate reported that Berber had been abandoned and Kitchener ordered his men and his flotilla of gunboats south again – by the beginning of September they were within 200 miles of Khartoum, too far forward to withdraw and yet far enough south to make a rapid strike on the Khalifa's forces. Kitchener's rapid advance threw Cromer into a panic. In October he informed Salisbury that the capture of Khartoum was both unnecessary and beyond the financial means of the Egyptian exchequer, and that 'in moments of retrospection I tear my hair over the hurried decision of 1896. It had upset all my calculations and introduced an entirely new element into Egyptian politics.'[13] Cromer became convinced, too, that Kitchener was working in collusion with the War Office to burnish his own image and that the appointment of Sir Francis Grenfell as GOC, British troops in Egypt, was the harbinger of more interference. He also rejected the idea that France wanted to win control of the Upper Nile valley and, in a startling reversal of policy, told Salisbury that he was no longer concerned about the possibility of another power controlling the headwaters of the Nile. By the end of the year he was using every argument at his disposal to put off a further advance towards Khartoum. Cromer's coolness over the expenditure of further sums in Sudan communicated itself to his staff and his financial adviser, Sir Elwin Palmer, began to take a tighter hold of the reins of the Egyptian budget.

In the desert, with his army stretched down a long and perilous line from Wadi Halfa to Berber, Kitchener worried himself to the point of nervous collapse. Cromer's indifference and his tightness over money led Kitchener to quarrel with Palmer, who refused to sanction funds for the British occupation of Kassala that Kitchener thought necessary to protect his army's eastern flank. Kitchener also realised that, as his army's lines of communication were overstretched, he could hardly move towards Khartoum without reinforcements, preferably a British infantry brigade. But if that were granted, he knew, too, that he might be superseded in command and the arrival of Grenfell, far from being the signal for Kitchener and the War Office to work in tandem, as Cromer had suspected, only served to make Kitchener feel that command was about to be wrested from him now that victory was in sight. Kitchener had always liked Grenfell and on 14 October he wrote to him explaining that as he had to deal with Cromer over political and financial matters he hoped that he would be excused copying all correspondence to him. He was also diplomatic enough to offer his allegiance to a soldier senior to him in years and experience, 'I hope you will never imagine that I desire to work off my own bat and not loyally serve under you.'[14] It was Kitchener's greatest fear that his army might be overcome by a superior dervish force and that British troops would be deployed by the War Office, leading to his disgrace and loss of command.

Four days after writing that conciliatory letter to Grenfell, Kitchener exploded. The stress created by the 1897 campaign – the building of the railway, maintaining the lines of communication, the financial anxieties – finally broke him and on 18 October he sent a furious telegram to Cairo, tendering his resignation. It was a threat that bore no terror for Cromer: he knew the strength of Kitchener's ambitions and the pressures under which his Sirdar had been working. Salisbury was informed that Kitchener had temporarily lost his nerve but that there was no need to make any precipitate move involving British troops. It was an awkward situation. The War Office counselled a rapid advance south backed by British troops under Grenfell; the Foreign Office insisted that Cromer must have the last word while supporting Kitchener as commander of the Egyptian Army, which they maintained must be the spearhead of any move made against the Khalifa.

The deadlock was broken by Wingate, who brought sensational news out of the desert in December that the Khalifa was planning to move against Kitchener with an army 100,000 strong. To the suspicious the timing seemed to suggest a plot dreamt up by Wingate and Kitchener; but to Cromer in Cairo and to Salisbury in London it portended ruin and a possible repeat of the events of 1884. Wingate's information was, in fact, inaccurate but it created the desired effect. A British brigade was despatched to Sudan under Major-General W.F. Gatacre, an efficient and industrious officer who matched the Sirdar in his single-mindedness. Kitchener was confirmed as Commander-in-Chief, the British exchequer agreed to fund the remainder of the campaign and a 'two flags' policy was agreed upon. It would be an Egyptian campaign backed by Britain: Cromer's insistence on this point was to have an important bearing on events once the campaign had drawn to its conclusion.

The arrival of Gatacre's brigade – composed of 1st Battalion Royal Warwickshire Regiment, 1st Battalion Lincolnshire Regiment, 1st Battalion Seaforth Highlanders and 1st Battalion Cameron Highlanders – strengthened Kitchener's options significantly. He enjoyed complete dominance of the Nile through his flotilla, which had also been reinforced by the arrival of a new model of gunboat, even larger and more heavily armed than those of the *Zafir* class. His army was being increased, too, by deserters from the Khalifa's forces and, above all, Wingate and Slatin were able to provide him with a continuous supply of accurate information from their network of spies around Khartoum. As if that superiority were not enough, Kitchener's army was equipped with the latest weapons. Each soldier, British, Egyptian or Sudanese, carried a Lee Metford Mark II rifle with a bolt and magazine action for loading eight bullets: this was particularly effective for use behind stockades and its rapid fire gave Kitchener's soldiers a three to one superiority over the best weapons of the Khalifa's troops. The artillery had been bolstered by the arrival of further numbers of the Maxim machine gun. There was also a battery of 5.5 Howitzers capable of firing the new lyddite high-explosive shells, whose 'man killing' abilities were reported to be very good. Finally, since it was commonly believed by the British troops that the standard issue .303 bullet was incapable of killing the dervishes in the full flight of their charge, Gatacre's men were ordered to make dum-dum bullets, which exploded on impact, by flattening the heads of their rifle ammunition.

Against those innovations the dervishes were armed at best with ageing Martini-Henry breech loaders and home-made ammunition; at worst with antique elephant guns, or swords, daggers and lances – weapons that had been in use since the days of the crusades. Their tactics, too, belonged to another age, having been honed to the simplicity of attacking in wave after wave along a broad front.

In Khartoum the Khalifa had been watching Kitchener's advance with mounting curiosity and concern. He showed particular interest in the coming of the railway; having never seen one before in his life he was anxious that his generals should do their utmost to capture it so he could see it at close quarters. However, he was not yet ready to fight, for the Mahdi had come to him in a dream to tell him that victory would be his on the plains of Kerreri outside Omdurman and that the Sirdar and his army would therefore have to come to him. Until that happened he ordered Osman Digna to harry the advancing army, causing it more irritation than punishment, until it could be engaged by the main dervish force under the command of a young emir called Mahmud. In late February that force streamed across the Nile at Metemma and disappeared eastwards into the desert in order to outpace Kitchener and to lure him to Berber and the new railhead. This movement mystified Kitchener, who had been expecting a pitched battle farther south, on the river, but Wingate was able to read Mahmud's intentions and warned that Berber would have to be protected. Alive to the danger, Gatacre hastened south with his brigade, covering some 130 miles in just over six days, an astonishing feat considering the conditions and the fact that his men had just finished an arduous route march. Having reached the place where the River Atbara joins the Nile, Gatacre, now joined by Kitchener and his army, found Mahmud encamped behind a formidable zeriba – a stockade constructed from thorn bushes. With a dry river bed behind his army Mahmud had ordered his men to dig in and wait.

The delaying tactics forced Kitchener to reconsider his position: he held the advantage in terms of military superiority but Mahmud's position could only be held at the expense of a pitched battle. For a fortnight there was stalemate, Gatacre pushing for an attack, Hunter counselling caution: unable to make up his mind Kitchener even asked Cromer for his opinion about which course he should take. Cromer, having taken advice from Grenfell, was disposed to think that no attack should take place for the present but he left the matter in the hands of his Sirdar. On 3 April, Hunter, having spent several days reconnoitring the dervish positions, changed his mind and it was agreed that Mahmud's zeriba should be stormed a week later, on the morning of Good Friday.

By dawn on 8 April, after a hazardous night march, Kitchener's 14,000-strong army had marched to a ridge within 1½ miles of

Mahmud's camp, where they deployed with Maxwell's brigade on the right, Gatacre's on the left and Macdonald's Sudanese in the centre. As the sun began to light up the scene the artillery set up a tremendous bombardment, abetted by rocket projectiles from the naval division, and when it died down after about ten minutes the advance began along a broad front. In the van were the men of the Camerons, who marched into battle with bagpipes playing and excited shouts of 'Remember Gordon!' Their bravery was not to be doubted but the dervishes exacted a dreadful toll and several officers fell as the Highlanders made the first penetration of the zeriba. Behind them came the remainder of the British brigade and Macdonald's 2nd Sudanese brigade, with its XIth battalion especially seeing fierce hand-to-hand fighting. After half an hour it was all over, the zeriba had been overrun, 3,000 dervishes lay dead and Mahmud was captured. 'The scene in the zareba [sic] after the battle was horrifying,' noted one eyewitness. 'The trenches were filled with the slain Dervishes in every position that the agony of death could assume. Many were mangled into mere fragments of humanity far beyond recognition'.[15]

After the battle Kitchener allowed himself a moment's relaxation, his colleagues marvelling to see him smile and speak gently to the men of the Camerons as they buried their dead. But that display of generosity could not hide the fact that the Atbara had been won at a terrible cost – 600 casualties, mainly from the Camerons and the Seaforths. The sadness at the losses, though, was mingled with profound satisfaction that a crushing blow had been dealt against the Khalifa and the knowledge that the day of reckoning could not now be far away. At home in Britain the victory was met by jubilant public excitement with Kitchener playing the role of hero of the hour. 'I assure you', wrote Lord Roberts, 'that the skill and prudence you displayed are thoroughly appreciated by civilians as well as by soldiers.' And from Wolseley came equally heartfelt congratulations: 'The whole conception and execution has been without fault and reflects the greatest credit upon all concerned, but beyond all others, upon you, the able commander in the field.'[16]

However, there were also critical voices. Kitchener's tactical sense seemed to be crude and had also caused unnecessary casualties.

There were also rumours that no prisoners had been taken and that the wounded dervishes had been shot on the orders of the Sirdar; the medical services had been so meagrely equipped, as a result of Kitchener's economies, that many wounded men died who might otherwise have been saved. The final barbarism seemed to be Kitchener's treatment of the captured Emir Mahmud, who was put in chains and led in triumph behind Kitchener during the victory parade in Berber on 14 April. He was destined to languish for many years in an Egyptian jail.

In his hour of glory Kitchener paid little heed to his critics. If he had used bludgeoning tactics at the Atbara, then they were justified as he was fighting a poorly armed force that had been virtually destroyed by his superior firepower. He also claimed that the tactics had been worked out by his brigade commanders: having brought his army safely and cheaply into the desert, he said, it was their duty to do the fighting for him. (This was true: Hunter, having carried out the final reconnaissance, decided the method of attack, although the ultimate decision was left to Kitchener.) As far as the wounded were concerned, Kitchener countered his critics by telling them that in warfare, especially in battles fought in hostile climates, there were bound to be casualties in spite of the presence of clearing stations and military field hospitals and that these had been as well provided for as in any other Victorian colonial campaign. The information that the victorious soldiers had killed off many wounded dervishes was unfortunately shown to be correct but there is no evidence that Kitchener actually ordered the atrocities.

With the news of the victory came fresh demands from the British public for more information about the campaign, with the result that an army of war correspondents was hurriedly formed to cover the final stages of the war. Some of them, including Bennet Burleigh of the *Daily Telegraph* and Fred Villiers of the *Illustrated London News*, were experienced journalists; others had little or no experience, such as Edward Bennett or Harry Cross of the *Manchester Guardian*, whose only qualification was that he was a schoolmaster and a rowing Blue. Others such as Frankie Rhodes of *The Times*, the brother of Cecil Rhodes, were ex-soldiers, but experienced or not, Kitchener was contemptuous of the entire press corps and did his best to confine them far from the front at Abu Hamed. Only two were granted favour – Hubert Howard, another correspondent of *The Times*, and G.W. Steevens of the *Daily Mail*. It was only after representations had been made by the proprietors of *The Times*, arguing that the Khalifa did not read London newspapers, that Kitchener was forced, against his judgement, to give facilities to war correspondents. As Bennett reported, Kitchener did this with ill-concealed grace:

> I did not enjoy the interview which was as barren of results as it was humiliating. The only parallel to it which I can think of is that of a row of curates before a brusque and autocratic bishop. During the brief commonplaces which passed between us, the general impression conveyed to me was the immeasurable condescension of our chief in even deigning to address the representatives of a Press which has never failed to extol even to the verge of exaggeration the achievements of the Anglo-Egyptian army and its leader.[17]

In earlier years Kitchener had been quick to exploit the press to further his own aims, but in time of war he could see no reason why the public should be told his every move and he added insult to injury by keeping an expectant press corps waiting in the hot sun outside his tent before sweeping past with an imperious command, 'Get out of my way, you drunken swabs!'[18]

Another influential war correspondent was the young Winston Churchill of the *Morning Post*, who went into battle as a fighting soldier, seconded to the 21st Lancers. He owed this unique position entirely to his family connections and to the machinations of his mother, who put pressure on Kitchener to accept her son into his army. Balfour, Salisbury and even the Prince of Wales were but a few of the country's leaders whom she had badgered and the story of her doggedness in the face of the Sirdar's opposition is one of the more interesting social sidelights of the Sudan campaign.[19] When Lady Randolph visited Cairo to try her luck with Cromer, Kitchener again demurred but he was foiled by the Adjutant-General, Sir Evelyn Wood, who used the opportunity to second Churchill from his regiment, the 4th Hussars, to the 21st Lancers when Kitchener requested additional cavalry cover. Kitchener was infuriated by Wood's wiliness, considering Churchill owed everything to political influence and nothing to personal ability. In this estimation he was mistaken as Churchill went on to display considerable gallantry and he repaid his debt to those who had helped him by writing the best account of Kitchener's campaign in his book *The River War*, even though he told his mother that Kitchener 'may be a general – but never a gentleman'.[20]

The quickening pace of Kitchener's campaign also caused pulses to race within the British Army. War meant casualties and casualties meant promotion: the War Office was flooded with applications to join the 2nd British Brigade, which had been ordered to Sudan during the summer to strengthen Kitchener's army for the final push. It consisted of the 1st Battalion Grenadier Guards, 1st Battalion Northumberland Fusiliers, 2nd Battalion Lancashire Fusiliers and 2nd Battalion The Rifle Brigade. On its arrival at Fort Atbara, Gatacre assumed command of the newly created British Division with his brigade commanders being Andrew Wauchope of The Black Watch and the Hon. N.G. Lyttelton of The Rifle Brigade. Other notable arrivals were the Hon. Edward Montagu-Stuart-Wortley, who had command of the 'Friendlies', an irregular native cavalry force, and a smart young cavalry captain called Douglas Haig, who had been attached to the Egyptian cavalry in February 1898 and had made his presence felt quickly among his fellow officers.

Kitchener immediately appointed Haig a squadron commander in the Egyptian Cavalry division, commanded by Lieutenant-Colonel G.R. Broadwood. At staff college Haig had distinguished himself more through his thoroughness and attention to detail than through any hint of brilliance, and he had subsequently come to the attention of Sir Evelyn Wood. Those attributes, intense concentration and single-minded purpose, attracted Kitchener and he gave much encouragement to a younger man who seemed to him to mirror many of his own characteristics. For his part, Haig was equally impressed by Kitchener and by the sense of purpose he had brought to the whole campaign; his first letters to his sister Henrietta reflect the admiration he felt for his chief and his style of command:

> I see that you imagine that I am with the Sirdar [he wrote on 1 April]. He is the one man that does everything himself and has no HeadQr Staff at all! Indeed General Hunter who has hitherto commanded the troops in the field cannot get the Sirdar to tell him what his position in the army is! In addition the Sirdar is most silent and no one has even the slightest notion what is going to be done until he gives his orders! He has two aides-de-camp who have a hardish time but beyond them he employs no staff at all. Sometimes it might be better for the comfort of the troops if he had a staff, but on the whole things get along very well and the Cavalry get a pretty free hand.[21]

In later correspondence with Wood, Haig's hint of censure about the lack of a staff was to grow into a full-blooded criticism of Kitchener's tactical deficiencies. After the Atbara battle he reported that the artillery fire had been insufficient to break down the dervish fortifications, that the British infantry advance had faltered through inaccurate small-arms firepower, that an enfilade of concentrated machine gun fire would have obviated the need for cavalry operations and that the high casualty rate subsequently could have been avoided by working out the tactics beforehand instead of on the field of battle. As an exercise in reporting battle tactics, Haig's letter to Wood of 12 April is a useful corrective to the more popular accounts of the battle, some of which compared it to the Battle of Waterloo. In one other respect, Haig and Kitchener were in complete agreement: both heartily disliked the accompanying press corps, a species whom Haig described to Henrietta as being, '... most degrading. They can't tell the whole truth even if they want to. The British public likes to read sensational news, and the best war correspondent is he who can tell the most thrilling lies.'[22]

During the summer break from operations Kitchener went on leave for a month in Cairo while his army took final shape in encampments between the River Atbara and Berber in preparation for the march to Omdurman. Kitchener was so confident of success that he told Cromer his army might be 'inconveniently large', an assessment that was not far off the mark. When it assembled at Wad Hamed on 21 August for inspection by Kitchener, the 25,000-strong force stretched out for 3 miles in the desert.

It was an imposing spectacle, just as Kitchener intended that it should be. Dervish scouts were taking a close interest in the advancing army – Haig noted in his diary that much of his squadron's time was spent in seeing them off – while the Khalifa pondered his next move. To have given up Omdurman and to have moved south into the desert areas, as sense dictated, would have meant the abnegation of Mahdist power; to stay put heralded imminent destruction from Kitchener's superior army. Only one course seemed to lie open to him – to put his trust in his dream of victory at Kerreri and to put in hand such measures as building a series of forts outside Omdurman and mining the river to prevent the gunboats closing in to shell the city. From Slatin's intelligence, Kitchener knew that the Khalifa would never abandon Omdurman; all that was required was to march south and defeat the enemy as quickly and as economically as possible.

On 23 August, from the top of a hill called Jebel Royan, 7 miles south of Wad Hamed, 'Monkey' Gordon gazed through his telescope towards the horizon and through the haze of the desert heat he caught the army's first glimpse of Omdurman 40 miles away, with the white dome of the Mahdi's tomb visible clearly above the houses of the town. To Kitchener it seemed a good omen that the first sighting should have been made by Gordon's nephew. But moving the vast army towards its final goal was no easy task and for the next five days it lay like an uncoiled snake along the banks of the Nile. Haig and other officers fulminated in private at the apparent crudity of Kitchener's thinking – the line was over-extended and, apart from the meagre mounted troops, largely unguarded; an attack at that vulnerable point in the campaign would have spelled disaster. To those fears, though, Kitchener appeared oblivious. From Slatin's intelligence reports he knew that the Khalifa had withdrawn all his forces to Omdurman and that it was his intention to lure the British-Egyptian army into a wasteful attack on its fortifications.

On 30 August, after his cavalry had reached and scouted the Kerreri hills, Kitchener sent an ultimatum to the Khalifa, calling on him to surrender. If he refused, Kitchener continued, then at least he should evacuate women and children from Omdurman prior to an artillery bombardment and 'the punishment prepared for you by the praised God'. The Khalifa disdained to reply.

Two days later, on the morning of 1 September, the gunboats, which had sailed to within range of Omdurman, and the artillery drawn up on the east bank of the river, opened up a fierce barrage on the town. Not only did the falling shells cause carnage and structural damage but the gunners had been taking bets on which gun-crew could score the first hit on the Mahdi's tomb. Soon its range was found and to the consternation of the city's inhabitants it received a number of direct hits. To Kitchener and his army assembled on the Kerreri ridge it was a terrible sound as the 5in howitzers' shells roared through the air and, although they could not see the devastation, many thought that no army could survive such a pounding. Some of the more thrusting British officers even began to fret that the dervishes might be in no fit state for a proper fight.

Kitchener was under no such illusion. Realising that the Khalifa would remove his army, now 50,000 strong, from Omdurman on to the Kerreri plain, Kitchener ordered his men down from the ridge to take up position near the village of El Egeiga at a bend in the Nile between the hills and the river. There, a rough zeriba was hurriedly thrown up and shallow trenches dug, a difficult task for an army that had spent most of the day beneath the glare of the sun and with no food since breakfast. Tempers began to fray as the brigades wheeled and marched into their positions, the officers shouting commands while their men stumbled over the rough and stony ground. Such was Kitchener's incapacity for delegation that none of his brigade commanders knew the overall plan. ADCs and other messengers merely galloped with orders from Kitchener to the individual commanders, who were left to carry them out as best they could. After a good deal of cursing, the rank and file of Kitchener's army finally got themselves into position by mid-afternoon, in a wide arc with the river behind them: the plain was a perfect place to do battle, an amphitheatre with the Kerreri ridge to the north and the hills of Jebel Surgam to the south.

As he expected the first attack to come from the south-west Kitchener had ordered Gatacre's British Division to take up the left of the line, backed by Maxims and three batteries of artillery. Maxwell's 2nd Egyptians were in the centre while the right was held by Macdonald's Sudanese, covering the weaker and untried Egyptians on the extreme right of the line commanded by Lieutenant-Colonel D.F. Lewis. As the threat of an immediate dervish attack began to recede – by then the Khalifa had drawn up his army in a large mass to the west – the soldiers were ordered to redeploy into a wider arc to give themselves more room to fight, and the day came to an end with both sides lined up in battle order, each waiting for the other to make the first move. Previously, during the reign of the Mahdi, most dervish victories had been won at night or in the early hours of the morning when men's resolve was at its weakest, and Kitchener feared that the Khalifa would repeat such tactics at Kerreri, especially against his nervous Egyptian troops. To minimise that danger, Wingate sent spies into the dervish camp, posing as deserters, to pass the word that it was Kitchener who was planning the night attack. It was a calculated risk, as the Khalifa had also considered a night attack only for his emirs to convince him that the best chance of victory would be to attack Kitchener's army and then to lure him into an attack on Omdurman. Then, when his lines were extended, it could be assaulted and defeated.

At dawn the first phase of the dervish plan was put into operation when a force led by Sheikh ed Din, the Khalifa's son, feinted across the plain to the north where they engaged Broadwood's cavalry and came under the fire of the gunboats. This diversion allowed the main dervish force under Osman Azrak to cross the plain in a frontal attack on Kitchener's lines at 6.30 a.m. while the Khalifa and Yakub waited in reserve behind Jebel Surgam. To the waiting British troops this presented an awe-inspiring spectacle: line after seemingly irresistible line of dervishes making their way forward in tight battle order, a wave of humanity pressing on to break on the concentrated fire of the British and Egyptian infantry. 'They came very fast,' reported Steevens, 'and they came very straight, and they presently came no further.'[23] When the excitement of that first charge died down and the smoke cleared, some 2,000 dervishes lay dead in front of the British lines and many more broken bodies were left to crawl away painfully from the field of carnage. The massacre was almost over and it was only 8.30 a.m.

Throughout the first charge Kitchener had taken up position in the centre behind the Camerons and from a small knoll he had organised his defences rather as a conductor might lead his orchestra. Each division in the wide arc of the fortified zeriba stood ready to fight but the timing and interpretation were in the hands of the Sirdar. From his vantage point, Kitchener sent messengers to the different sections of the field in response to the changing tempo of the battle – when he perceived that the Rifle Brigade and the Lancashire Fusiliers were ill-placed on the left, they were hurriedly ordered to support the Camerons and the Seaforths where the fighting was at its hottest. For Kitchener it was a virtuoso performance but, since he lacked any overall picture of his opponent's intentions, it almost brought about his downfall. Having sent off the main force, his intention was to take Omdurman before it could be occupied by the Khalifa: the order was given for the army to move, division by division, from its defensive arc into a line of march, a ponderous process that temporarily put the army at risk. The 21st Lancers were ordered ahead to reconnoitre the ground between Kerreri and Omdurman and it was at this point in the battle that the regiment made its celebrated charge on a dervish position, an action that in the public's mind epitomised the glory of Kitchener's victory. As a result of the action the 21st Lancers, which had never before gained a battle honour, won three Victoria Crosses.

At this point in the battle it is not difficult to see where Kitchener went wrong. The desire to take Omdurman quickly, and without recourse to street fighting, was undoubtedly strong but Kitchener had misread the dervish positions. He was unaware of the strength of the force that had regrouped to the north of the Kerreri ridge under Yakub, the Khalifa's son. As the great army began to swing south, Macdonald's brigade was left to bring up the rear without any cover – Lewis's Egyptians had been moved into the safety of the centre – and with an expanse of ground between it and the main force, which was in jubilant mood and eager to be the first to enter Omdurman.

It was a dire moment for Kitchener, one which could have lost him the battle, but Macdonald was alive to the danger. Harry Pritchard, his ADC, was sent galloping to the Sirdar but was told that Macdonald was not to engage but to continue his march on Omdurman. Macdonald, however, was already under fire and before Pritchard could gallop back the sound of that gunfire could be heard across the plain. 'Hello, that must be Mac!' said Kitchener and immediately made preparations to move Maxwell's brigade across Jebel Surgam to cover Macdonald's flank. Kitchener's reaction to the sudden emergency was typical of the pragmatic way he had conducted the battle – he was able to meet each new exigency with a solution that worked.

Back at Macdonald's lines the sight of the approaching dervishes had worked the Sudanese into a frenzy and they were blasting off their rifles without thought of aim nor, more importantly, of ammunition. Alive to the danger, Macdonald grabbed Pritchard and walked in front of his men, knocking up their rifles with his swagger stick so that, as the dervishes approached the lines, they met not random firing but a withering curtain of bullets that sent them reeling. No sooner had that attack been repelled, however, than a fresh problem faced Macdonald. A Camel Corps officer arrived at the front with the news that a new and formidable force, numbering perhaps 20,000, was about to strike and that, on Hunter's instructions, he was to withdraw. Macdonald's response was that he would see the dervishes damned first. He called his battalion commanders together and hurriedly sketched out in the sand a new plan of defence – they were to move their men battalion by battalion into a new line of battle, beginning with the XIth.

Having wheeled his brigade Madconald then had the task of meeting that last fanatical attack, and at one point it seemed as if their suicidal tactics might win the day. On some parts of the front the Sudanese were engaged in fierce hand-to-hand fighting, their ammunition having been exhausted, and the Xth were already taking the brunt of the onslaught with fixed bayonets. 'The valiant blacks', reported Churchill, 'prepared themselves with delight to meet the shock, notwithstanding the overwhelming numbers of the enemy.'[24] At that point the pressure on their lines began to slacken as, on Kitchener's orders, Wauchope's 1st British Brigade attacked the remnants of Yakub's force and the Lincolnshire Regiment arrived to strengthen Macdonald's right. The combined rapid fire of the two brigades soon dispersed this final onslaught and the enemy began to retire to the safety of the Kerreri ridge with Macdonald's Sudanese in pursuit.

The battle was over and the British-Egyptian lines secure but even though Kitchener was heard to remark as he watched the chase, 'I think we've given them a good dusting, gentlemen', he had little cause for satisfaction. Defeat had almost been snatched from the jaws of victory and through his own tactical inexperience he had placed Macdonald's brigade in a position of the utmost danger. In the circumstances it is not difficult to disagree with Haig's analysis:

> The Sirdar's left should have been thrown forward to his hill [Khor Shambat] and gradually drawing in his right and extending his left south-westwards, he might have cut the enemy off from Omdurman and really annihilated the thousands and thousands of dervishes. In place of this, altho' in possession of full information, and able to see with his own eyes the whole field, he spreads out his force, thereby risking the destruction of a brigade. He seemed to have had no plan, or tactical idea, for beating the enemy beyond allowing the latter to attack the camp.[25]

No such considerations troubled Kitchener as he made his stately way towards Omdurman riding on his white charger in the midst of the two Highland regiments, in his own mind at least the equal of any Khalifa. The Kitchener legend had now been created.[26]

6

SYMBOL OF EMPIRE

The race was now on for the glory of first entering Omdurman and it was Macdonald's Xth Sudanese who claimed that right by thrusting through Maxwell's advance guard, brooking no opposition from the British ranks, not even from the Grenadier Guards, who found Sudanese bullets whistling over their heads when they stood their ground. In spite of those antics there was good humour amongst the ranks, which lasted until they reached the outskirts of the town.

There, the sight that met them was that of a charnel house. Broken bodies lay in pools of blood, their crushed limbs and spilled intestines grim testimony to the efficiency of the weapons of modern warfare. Some of the wounded betrayed the helpless stoicism of those about to die; others had decided to take an infidel or two with them before departing this life, and the advancing British-Egyptian army was often obliged to kill or be killed as wounded dervishes made final despairing attacks on their ranks. Killing the wounded became a necessary measure, but the action gave rise to stories similar to those repeated after the Atbara campaign and Winston Churchill was amongst several observers who put the blame on the Sirdar. 'I shall merely say', he wrote to his mother, 'that the victory of Omdurman was disgraced by the inhuman slaughter of the wounded and that Kitchener was responsible for this.'[1]

Edward Bennett followed Churchill's lead in the *Contemporary Review*, claiming that it had been common practice for Kitchener's army to kill off the enemy wounded during the last days of the Sudan campaign. His comments caused much offence but no evidence remains of any orders having been given to kill wounded dervishes – as Bennett had claimed. Kitchener was too cautious a commander to be soiled by such an order, although he may well have turned a blind eye to what was happening.

As they made their way through the dirty streets of the town, the soldiers may have wondered why they had come so far to win so little – a collection of sprawling shacks with poor, wide-eyed inhabitants beginning to suffer from the worst effects of privation and staring at their victors as if they had arrived from another planet. At the Mahdi's tomb, symbol of Gordon's death and the holy grail of the long march south, Lieutenant-Colonel Horace Smith-Dorrien led in his XIIIth Sudanese to deliver the final indignity: the desecration of a place sacred to those who worshipped Allah. It was perhaps at that point, with the Khalifa long fled into the desert, the people of Omdurman realised they were well and truly beaten. Indeed, many of the dervish ranks now chose to turn coat and throw in their lot with men who only a few hours previously had been their enemies.

Throughout the remainder of the day Kitchener seemed impervious to the mayhem that surrounded his army. He watched the release of the Khalifa's prisoners, including the German merchant Charles Neufeld, giving him a slap on the shoulder with a cheery 'out you go!' He visited the Mahdi's tomb, which was destroyed a few days later by a party of Royal Engineers under the command of 'Monkey' Gordon: Kitchener, too, knew the value of making symbolic gestures.

It was at the Mahdi's tomb that he almost lost his life when a stray shell fell near him, a narrow escape for, as he moved away with the comment that 'it would be a pity to lose our ticket when the day is won', another shell exploded nearby, killing the war correspondent Hubert Howard. Later, in a place of safety, he gave an evening press conference and dictated telegrams to Salisbury and to the Queen, but in the midst of the excitement that gripped the captured town, Kitchener, like most of his men, found it difficult to rest. Finally persuaded by his staff to lie down and sleep, he gave thanks for the victory that had been so cheaply won. Kitchener was the architect of that victory, it had been due to his tireless energy that the expeditionary force had reached its objective, and it had cost the British taxpayer little – later he was to remind Cromer that he had brought Sudan into the Empire for the paltry cost of £2 2s 6d per square mile or £1 3s 6d per head of population.[2] Above all, he had completed a messianic task. 'Surely he [Gordon] is avenged!' Queen Victoria noted in her journal on receiving news of the victory.[3] A stain of dishonour had been wiped from the annals of British history. Outside the walls of the town, on the Kerreri plain, lay some 10,000–12,000 dervish dead. The losses in Kitchener's army amounted to forty-eight dead and 434 wounded.

The following day, 4 September, the large and unlovely gunboats *Abu Klea* and *Melik* slipped their moorings and negotiated the narrows of the Nile by the swamp-ridden Tuti Island that separates Omdurman from the city of Khartoum. Shortly before ten o'clock they moored at the tumbledown stone quay that fronted the river by the Governor's Palace and, slowly and silently, some 500 selected troops disembarked down the high gangplanks and lined up in open square with their backs to the river. Among their number were kilted Highlanders, men from the English counties, guardsmen and riflemen, men of the Camel Corps, fellahin soldiers of Egypt and Sudanese troops resplendent under white fezes topped by red hackles. Britain's imperial might had come to pay its last respects to the memory of a perfect Victorian hero: in the centre of the serried ranks, head and shoulders above his brother officers, stood the erect figure of the Sirdar.

In front of the silent troops, the ruins of General Gordon's last residence seemed to mock their ambitions. The upper storey had fallen down, the windows were still blocked by the bricks that Gordon had installed for his last defence and beside the steps where he had met his end lay an unruly pile of broken stones and woodwork. Only the wilderness of the gardens, with an acacia tree spreading like a weeping willow and the sweet smell of pomegranate, reminded the onlookers that this had once been the centre of influence in Sudan, a city which for all of them had become a place of personal pilgrimage:

> Compared with treeless, brown, arid Omdurmam, Khartoum wore an air of romance and loveliness that well became such historic ground. An odour

of blossom and fruit was wafted from the wild and spacious Mission and Government House gardens, which even the dervishes had not been able to wreck totally.[4]

On the roof, above the spot where Gordon had fallen, stood two flagpoles. At a signal from Kitchener the Union flag sprang free into the breeze, to be followed, after a salute from the *Melik* and the playing of God Save the Queen, by the breaking of the Egyptian flag on the other. This was no idle gesture to British-Egyptian solidarity; on the contrary, it signalled the direction arranged by the politicians for the future of Sudan. 'At Khartoum, when it was captured,' Salisbury had instructed Cromer, 'the British and Egyptian flags would fly side by side as a symbol of the juridical regularity of the two conquerors who would jointly claim possession of the Mahdi state from Halfa to Weadelai by right of conquest.'[5] And so it was that, on that hot September's day, Sudan was brought by Kitchener into the British Empire, to become a British-Egyptian condominium, an arrangement whereby Britain was allowed to rule the country in the name of Egypt. Another piece of red had been added to the map of Africa, and Sudan was to remain in that colour until it gained independence in 1956.

A twenty-one gun salute thundered out from the *Melik* to mark the occasion – live ammunition was used as there were no blanks available and the shells whistled eerily over the heads of the onlookers towards the distant desert. After cheers had been called for Queen Victoria and the Khedive, General Wauchope stepped forward and called for three cheers for Kitchener, which were loyally given. There followed a simple service of thanksgiving. The band of the Grenadier Guards played 'The Dead March' from Handel's *Saul* and the Presbyterian chaplain, Reverend Wilkins, read the Fifteenth Psalm; the Lord's Prayer was led by the Anglican chaplain, Reverend Watson, and to complete the ecumenical circle benediction was said by the Catholic padre, Father Brindle. He was the most popular man of God among the troops in the Sirdar's army since he had opted for the lot of the ordinary soldier during the long march south.

Pipers from the two Highland regiments struck up a lament and, as they did so, a handful of Sudanese spectators broke into a high-pitched wailing, the two sounds, according to those who were present, perfectly complementing each other in a coronach for the dead Gordon. 'As the last wail died over the water,' remembered the Methodist chaplain, Reverend O.S. Watkins, 'the Soudanese band commenced playing Gordon's favourite hymn, Abide with me. A strange sound that, to hear black Mohammedans playing a Christian hymn!'[16] For many of the soldiers present it was a moving experience and, most surprisingly of all, even the Sirdar was affected. Unable to control his emotions, Kitchener turned to Hunter and asked him to dismiss the parade. Before the gunboats returned to Omdurman half an hour was allowed for the men to wander through the gardens and take stock of their achievement.

Much moved by the scene, Kitchener walked apart from his senior officers and kept his own counsel, a moment of grace before he bent his shoulder again to the wheel of duty. To instil awe of British rule, and to break whatever might remain of the Mahdi's power, Kitchener decided to destroy the massive tomb that dominated the town of Omdurman. Later, his action caused an uproar in Britain and questions were asked in the House of Commons, but Kitchener was able to parry them by arguing that the tomb, already damaged by artillery fire, was in a dangerous state, and secondly, that as a symbol of the rule of the Mahdi, it had to be removed. Both were convincing reasons but what followed next was less easy to excuse. The embalmed corpse of Mohammed Ibn Al-Sayd Abdullah was disinterred and, on Kitchener's instructions, tossed into the Nile. Only the shapely skull was spared: it was presented to the Sirdar, who thought to mount it as an ornament, the final insult being Kitchener's action in keeping it in an old kerosene tin before deciding its future. When the story was leaked to the press it occasioned feelings of disgust that threatened Kitchener's newly won popularity. John Morley, the Liberal MP and pacifist, later attempted to block Kitchener's rewards from a grateful House of Commons and C.P. Scott, the editor of the *Manchester Guardian*, waged a long press campaign against Kitchener, describing his action as being worthy of the Huns and Vandals; even Queen Victoria was moved to rap his knuckles, reminding her favourite general that the Mahdi, despite all his cruelties, was after all 'a man of certain importance'. Kitchener tried to cover his tracks by explaining that he had wanted to present the skull to the Royal College of Surgeons but the damage had been done and, although the skull was buried in secret at a Muslim cemetery at Wadi Halfa, the story lived on in liberal minds as another example of Kitchener's insensitivity and leanings towards barbarity.

Having dealt summarily with the immediate problems of policing and supervising Omdurman — his army had to be quartered and arrangements made for returning the British brigades to Egypt — Kitchener turned his attention to the greater matter of continuing British policy in east and central Africa. During his leave in Cairo in August he had received from Cromer sealed orders that had to be opened and acted upon once the Khalifa's power had been smashed. They came from the Foreign Office and commanded Kitchener to mount an expedition to forestall an anticipated annexation of the territory to the south by the French under the command of Captain Marchand. By what means Kitchener was to achieve that end was left unclear although the orders impressed upon him the necessity not to acknowledge any French claims. Two days later, the steamer *Tewfikiah* arrived in Omdurman carrying a story that its crew had been fired upon by a strange force of Europeans at the old Egyptian fort of Fashoda and that several of the crew had been killed. To Kitchener the news meant only one thing: a French force had overrun the upper reaches of the Nile and had staked a claim, thereby threatening the fruits of his victory at Omdurman. Not knowing the size of the French force, Kitchener fully expected that the hard-won campaign would count for naught and a prospect of further battling opened up before him. Five days later Kitchener left Omdurman to investigate the position, taking with him Wingate, a flotilla of five steamers, two battalions of Sudanese (XIth and XIIIth), two companies of Cameron Highlanders, a battery of artillery and four Maxim guns, a force strong enough to display British intentions and yet nimble enough to escape should the French be at Fashoda in strength.

In the event Kitchener's fears were groundless. After a heroic journey of two years that had taken them from the Atlantic coast across Africa,

Marchand and his party were in dire straits. They had been in Fashoda since July but were now short of supplies and ammunition and the entire party of 120 Senegalese soldiers and seven French officers was dispirited by the non-appearance of a corresponding French party from Somaliland that was supposed to have met up with them in southern Sudan. Weakened by fever and exhausted by their 3,000-mile trek, they had also been attacked by dervishes and would surely have been overwhelmed later had not Kitchener won his decisive victory. In spite of all these vicissitudes Marchand believed he could maintain his claim on the upper reaches of the Nile and thus provide France with an east-west belt of influence across central Africa. Known to his fellow officers as 'John the Baptist', Marchand was remarkably similar in temperament to Kitchener: he commanded respect among those he led, he was totally committed to the task in hand and he was driven by an iron will. Also, he was scornful of Britain's policies in Africa, believing them to have been designed solely to frustrate French ambitions. He was about to face a man who was equally single-minded and such was the delicacy of their position that one false move could have precipitated a crisis.

Kitchener's flotilla reached Fashoda in the early morning of 19 September. It was immediately clear that his force greatly outnumbered the French. Nevertheless, both commanders were determined to go through the diplomatic formalities; letters were exchanged, compliments offered, guards of honour mounted and a formal meeting arranged to discuss the position. It was all very amicable. Kitchener came to Fashoda knowing that he held the trump card of a superior force, but his handling of Marchand was sympathetic and businesslike. For one thing, Kitchener liked the French and spoke the language well; for another, he was sensitive enough to recognise that Marchand was driven by a patriotism and sense of duty similar to his own. Patiently, he explained to Marchand – whom he appears to have liked at first sight – that he had come to claim the area of the upper Nile in the name of the Khedive by right of re-conquest and hinted that he was in a strong enough position to enforce those rights. To this Marchand replied that he had already entered into treaties bringing Fashoda and the surrounding Bahr-el-Ghazal into French protection and that he had strict orders to hold on to his acquisitions and, if necessary, to fight to the last man.

It was a difficult moment, but Kitchener was equal to it, suggesting a compromise whereby the Khedival flag of Egypt should fly alongside the tricolour of France until the respective governments had come to a fresh position about the future of the area. Indeed, so determined was Kitchener not to upset French pride that he had worn Egyptian uniform and kept the Union flag and other trappings of British authority well in the background. Marchand would have preferred to refuse the offer but he recognised, too, that his position was impossible: after a momentary diplomatic pause he agreed to Kitchener's suggestion and with due pomp and ceremony both flags were raised beside the fort.

Having secured a temporary solution to the problem Kitchener left a small garrison at Fashoda and retired to Omdurman before returning to Cairo on 6 October. The Fashoda Incident, as it came to be known, showed Kitchener working at his most pragmatic. Denied access to the British Cabinet's view on the matter, Kitchener had to live off his wits. His professional relationship to Cromer had made him privy to British concern about the French presence in central Africa but, having been out of contact with Cairo for a fortnight, he was unaware of the current state of play – in fact, of his party, only the Sirdar knew that the force at Fashoda was French. Taking neither of his accompanying senior officers, Wingate and Smith-Dorrien, into his confidence Kitchener seemed to have reached a compromise almost off the top of his head – Smith-Dorrien recalled seeing the two men remonstrating angrily with each other on the deck of the gunboat *Dal* before 'glasses … full of golden liquid were soon being clinked together by the two central figures, who until that moment I had believed engaged in a deadly dispute.'[7] But the diplomacy was not just a sudden flash of inspiration. Later, Lord Edward Cecil remembered that Kitchener displayed a good understanding of Marchand's psychological make-up, especially of his pride in France and her army, and that the turning point came when Kitchener casually let slip the news about the Dreyfus Affair, the scandal that was then crucifying the French Army, and its scandals about treason and anti-Semitism.[8] As a Parthian shot he left the tiny French garrison with newspapers detailing the case and he also took steps to ensure that it could not communicate with the outside world, thus deepening its sense of isolation from what was happening in Paris.

Kitchener's handling of the Fashoda Incident was all the more praiseworthy when one takes into consideration the background against which it took place. In Britain the press was up in arms about what was presented as a French trick to cheat Britain out of the rightful spoils of victory and some newspapers began to wildly preach war. In France, public hysteria about 'Perfidious Albion' also reached new heights, although most politicians knew that any conflict with Britain was out of the question. Not only was France in disarray with the army torn apart by the Dreyfus Affair but there was also the knowledge that Russia, her ally, would not help and that in any conflict British naval superiority would be a decisive factor. Bellicose noises continued to be made on both sides of the Channel until November when France, aware that Britain meant to stand firm over her position, backed down and ordered Marchand – whom Salisbury described discreetly as 'an explorer in distress' – to retire to Ethiopia, leaving Sudan in British-Egyptian control. In deference to French pride, Fashoda was expunged from the map and the place of Marchand's last stand was renamed Kodok.

Kitchener arrived back in Britain on 27 October when the Fashoda Incident was still occupying the headlines, but his return signalled a change of focus in public opinion. He sailed from Calais to Dover on the cross-channel steamer *Empress* of the London, Chatham and Dover Line in the company of a small staff, but to the disappointment of the huge crowd gathered on the Admiralty Pier, Kitchener was not wearing the expected uniform but a grey suit. For a few minutes there was some confusion as to the identity of the great man, but when the Mayor of Dover stepped forward to greet Kitchener a loud cheer went up from the surrounding spectators, hats were thrown in the air and handkerchiefs waved from the trains in the nearby railway station.

A special train had been detailed to take him to Victoria Station, which he reached at seven o'clock that evening. If the welcome at Dover had been rapturous then the atmosphere that awaited him in London bordered on hysteria. Among the official welcoming party on the platform were Wolseley, Wood and Lord Roberts, whom he was to meet for the first time, but their attempts at providing a courtly reception were dashed by a large crowd determined to offer their own greeting. Barriers had been erected at the point where Kitchener's carriage would halt near the exit to the station yard but these were trampled underfoot as the crowd surged forward, leaving The Times to deplore the fact 'that adequate measures were not taken to preserve that decorum and good order without which enthusiasm quickly degenerates into something unpleasantly like anarchy'.[9] The ceremonies had quickly to be curtailed. Kitchener was spirited out of the station to Belgrave Square, where he was the guest again of Pandeli Ralli, but even then the crowds refused to disperse completely, almost as if to leave would destroy the spell of Kitchener's homecoming. It was a foretaste of what lay in store for him over the next few days. After short respites at Hatfield, where Salisbury appointed him Governor-General of Sudan, thus fulfilling Gordon's prophecy, and at Balmoral, Kitchener set off on a nationwide tour. The universities of Cambridge and Edinburgh awarded him honorary degrees, London made him a Freeman, as did many other British cities, and at a state banquet in the Mansion House in London on 4 November the great men of his country, including the Prime Minister, assembled to pay their respects to the hero of the hour.

His luxuriant moustache now seemed to be the symbol of all that was good and virile about the British Empire, and his portrait began to appear on biscuit tins, tea caddies, buttons, trays, badges, postcards, anywhere there was marketable space. Every schoolboy knew of his feats and there was a tremendous public excitement when it was announced that he had been raised to the peerage, taking the title Viscount Kitchener of Khartoum and Aspall. When informed of the elevation, Kitchener had wanted to be known as Lord Khartoum of Aspall, telling a friend that 'Kitchener is too horrible a name to put a "Lord" in front of', but he was finally persuaded to keep his surname in the title.[10] There was, in fact, a particularly satisfying ring to the title he eventually chose. Kitchener had become a household name and a national property; Khartoum, for so long a city linked with Gordon's martyrdom, had become a symbol of vengeance and British prowess at arms; and Aspall, for Kitchener at least, stood for all that was good and gentle about his native England. The quiet country house in Suffolk, the home of the Chevalliers that he visited frequently when on leave, had become an important sanctum, a memory, as he told Millie, that he had cherished during the long days in Sudan.

There was a dichotomy of attitude also in Kitchener's acceptance of his numerous public honours. During the Sudan campaign he had waged a war of economy as fierce as any battle fought against the dervishes – officers remembered his anguish at seeing ammunition being wasted once the Battle of Omdurman had been won and his rage at brigadiers whom he thought to be treating their men too lavishly – but back home in Britain he gave acquisitiveness full rein. The City of London had presented him with a costly though ugly sword of honour. When other cities attempted to follow suit, with equally expensive though undoubtedly equally tasteless, gifts, Kitchener let it be known that, if the cities of Britain wanted to honour him, they should do so with gold plate and furniture. A reward of £30,000 from Parliament had given Kitchener his first tangible wealth and he began to dream of an English country house that would be a stylish and suitable residence for him in retirement. Such a house would obviously have to be filled with furnishings to match the grandeur of his owner's ambitions. So the general who had made a virtue of regarding personal comfort as beneath consideration suddenly made a *volte-face* when it came to the amassing of personal possessions.

To the astonishment of close friends he now demonstrated another habit that was to stay with him for the rest of his life: he began to display a proprietorial interest in other people's possessions. If a piece of porcelain or other small and costly object took his fancy, he would admire it and then expect it to be presented to him; that 'courtesy' not being forthcoming, he would simply pocket it, no matter whose home or official residence he happened to be visiting. Wingate's son, Ronald, recollected how family treasures had to be hidden away before Kitchener paid a visit and Nancy Astor told Maurice Collis that when she saw Kitchener eyeing her belongings, she told him flatly, 'I won't give you anything.'[11] So imperious did Kitchener become that he expected his wishes to be fulfilled and, unlike Nancy Astor, few hostesses had the temerity to stand up to him. By 1898, too, Kitchener had collected magpie-like a large amount of booty, which he stored in Cairo: his hoard included carpets, jewellery and furnishings as well as the detritus of the battlefield such as scimitars, old guns and armour. When, in the following year, he rebuilt Gordon's palace in Khartoum for his own use, his means of furnishing it were brutally simple. 'Loot like blazes!' he told members of staff, who long ago had become accustomed themselves to a life of frugality. Added to the rancour aroused by the newspapers over his treatment of the Mahdi's skull, these revelations caused many to think him unattractive and coarse but the majority regarded him with approval, agreeing with G.W. Steevens that the figure of Kitchener 'ought to be patented and shown with pride at the Paris International Exhibition, Exhibit no. 1, hors concours, the Sudan machine'.[12]

On 7 December, the round of receptions, banquets and presentations came to an end and Kitchener left Britain for Cairo to be briefed by Cromer before taking up his post of Governor-General of Sudan. For fifteen years his name had been associated with that country: first as the romantic major spying the desert's wastes and keeping in constant contact with the doomed Gordon; second, as the firm-handed governor of Suakin; finally as the leader of the army that had saved the country from the Khalifa. He was also an administrator of proven ability, a noted Arabist and he knew the country well. That Kitchener was the right man for the job there could be no question, but another reason may have prompted Salisbury's decision to appoint him. At the age of forty-eight Kitchener was still a relatively young officer and in the Army List of that year, 1898, his name stood at 41st in the list of major-generals of the British Army; above him in rank there were many officers of greater experience and many of them were still jealous of Kitchener's rapid rise to power and prestige. After the excitements of Omdurman and the glory that accompanied his homecoming, it might have been difficult to find a suitable niche for him at home or abroad. Sudan was, however, a suitable posting allowing, as it did, the War Office to be freed of a potentially thorny problem and Kitchener himself to be accorded a suitably sonorous gubernatorial post.

Under the terms of the condominium agreement that was signed on 19 January 1899, the Governor-General of Sudan would be appointed by the Khedive on the recommendation of the British government; Sudan was therefore to be governed in name by Egypt but in practice by Britain, and successive governor-generals would introduce a system of rule through district officers similar to that employed in Britain's other great imperial holding, India. Under Kitchener's guidance the Sudan Civil Service soon took shape and he took care to ensure that it worked: his district officers had to accustom themselves to the possibility that their chief might arrive suddenly in one of the villages under their charge, both to check up on their work and to give impromptu audiences to local men of authority. Not only did such visitations help to keep the staff on their toes but they demonstrated that the Governor-General cared.

Before taking up his appointment in Khartoum, Kitchener had laid down the precise conditions of his service. At his insistence two articles of the condominium agreement, numbers IV and VI, had been altered to allow the Governor-General to have full control over the fiscal and financial aspects of the government of Sudan, although he still had to work within a budget of £350,000 agreed by Cairo. With his long experience of Kitchener's prickly attitude, Cromer kept aloof from day-to-day financial dealings and left it to his financial adviser, Sir Eldon Gorst. To begin with, Kitchener kept up a pretence of concurring with the regulations but he soon reverted to the system that had served him so well in the past, namely that the man on the spot had a better grasp of the situation than had civil servants in offices hundreds of miles away. Improvisation, he argued, was 100 times more useful than plans and budgets that did not take local conditions into account. Money was diverted from one budget to another to serve the needs of the service and, when requested by Gorst to account for his actions, Kitchener simply refused to give reasons for his decisions. Soon Cromer was telling Salisbury that Kitchener's method of government was 'perhaps a little more masterful and peremptory than is usual in dealing with civil affairs', but in truth Kitchener had his hands full dealing with the problems facing Sudan and his means were both expedient and justified.[13]

SYMBOL OF EMPIRE

After many years of autocratic rule by the Mahdi and the Khalifa Sudan required, first and foremost, a bureaucracy – supplied by Kitchener's governors and district officers – and a set of regulations by which the country might be run. By and large only Britons were allowed to assume the administrative roles although Kitchener recognised that minor secretarial posts would later have to be filled by the Sudanese themselves. Accordingly, a programme of rudimentary education was instituted: one of the fruits of Kitchener's prestige had been his ability to persuade leading financiers to contribute £111,000 towards the establishment of a Gordon Memorial College in Khartoum, Cromer laying the foundation stone on 4 January 1899. Communications were improved and railroad and steamer services regularised to make way for that newly established imperial phenomenon, tourism; also, a system of taxation was instituted that would take into account the special needs of the impoverished Sudanese. As had been the case in other parts of the Empire, local civil laws, in this case those belonging to the Islamic code, were to be respected where they seemed to make sense but the penal code was based on the successful model that had been evolved in British India, administered in the main by the local district officers. This was all in keeping with the principles of British imperialism. Kitchener wanted to introduce British civilisation but, like other Empire builders, he recognised that local customs had to be respected, especially those pertaining to religion, and he gave orders that Islam was to be accorded full dignity. Above all, Kitchener realised that Sudan needed a centre and he threw himself with enthusiasm into the reconstruction of Khartoum as the capital of the new country. Accordingly a new city began to rise above the ruins, designed in accordance with imperial fashion, with the administrative offices and European quarters neatly laid out and separated from the native areas in a logical network of rectangular districts intersected and joined together by diagonal streets radiating from the centre. For his work in creating the new Khartoum, Kitchener was made an honorary fellow of the Royal Institute of British Architects and he added his touch to a style of architecture commonly known as imperial gothic. His nephew, Alfred Chevallier Parker ('Wallier'), joined his staff and was put up in the Khalifa's old house in

Omdurman until more suitable quarters could be found in Khartoum but, as Kitchener told Millie on 23 September 1899 after his summer's leave, his attention was again being turned to more warlike activities:

> I am full of work as you can guess, all sorts of questions to settle. I hope soon to get into comfortable quarters in Khartoum but the place is not yet finished and before it is I shall have to be off after the Khalifa again. 450 miles up the White Nile is a long way.

Although he had smashed Mahdist rule at Omdurman, the Khalifa's flight and his continued presence in southern Sudan was a source of irritation. Kitchener's brother, Walter, had been despatched with a punitive expedition in January but had failed to find him and was now being sent to South Africa where war between the Boers and Britain seemed imminent. To friends in England Kitchener had boasted that he alone could find and destroy the Khalifa, but the scrub and jungles of Kordofan combined to frustrate his task force when they ventured south in October and it was left to Wingate to catch up with the Khalifa and his remaining cohorts near Gedid Wells, south of El Obeid. There, on 18 November, the dervishes made their customarily brave full-frontal attack on the British guns and the Khalifa, realising that all was lost, sat down in their midst facing Mecca to await his fate.

For Kitchener the Khalifa's death was a particularly satisfying moment. He was not the kind of man to allow loose ends to interfere in his scheme of things, and its timing was also appropriate since, towards the end of that year, the joys of Empire building were beginning to pall. At that stage in his career, so soon after the long stretch of the Sudan campaign, Kitchener was in no mood to concentrate his entire attention on the needs of the Sudanese people. Although he had looked on the post of Governor-General as his by right of conquest he recognised that it would do little to further his career. During his summer leave he had travelled to Dublin to discuss his military future with Lord Roberts, and to his now ever-widening circle of influential friends he had dropped hints about an appointment in India. In particular the exalted post of Commander-in-Chief had swum into his sights:

Kitchener was acutely aware that he had been branded in the army's eyes as an 'Egyptian' and that Egypt's army, in spite of its resounding successes in Sudan, was still regarded in some quarters as inferior. India, though, 'perhaps the army's true home', was a different matter[14] and 'Indian' soldiers had risen high in the Victorian army's command structure: Roberts, who was to succeed Wolseley as Commander-in-Chief in 1900, had begun his army career as a subaltern in the East India Company's artillery and other near-contemporaries of Kitchener's who furthered their careers in India included Haig and William Birdwood, both of whom became field marshals.

As in the past, Kitchener used his influence to obtain his wishes. He became a close friend of the Duke of York and at Panshanger, the home of Lord and Lady Cowper, he was able to state his case to his fellow guests, politicians including Arthur Balfour and St John Brodrick, soon to become Secretary of State for War. Other guests of the Cowpers were George Curzon, now Viceroy of India, and the imperial pro-consul Alfred Milner, and it was during this leave that Kitchener chose as his confidante Lady Cranborne, the elegant wife of Salisbury's eldest son Viscount Cranborne (later 4th Marquess of Salisbury). The second daughter of the Earl of Arran, Cicely Alice Gore was a brilliant hostess who turned the family seat at Hatfield into a centre of social and political excellence and whose sparkling personality was widely recognised as a great asset to her somewhat diffident husband. Like many other society hostesses, she was fascinated by Kitchener's taciturnity and by his forbidding exterior, believing it to be nothing more than a mask hiding feelings that ran deeper than the surface gaiety of his more socially adept contemporaries. His stern impassive face, still handsome despite the ravages of the desert sun, his erect bearing and the knowledge that he kept women at a distance, combined to excite her interest in Kitchener. At house parties she and other society ladies competed for his attention and were charmed by his hesitant though courtly responses.

Surprisingly, perhaps, that unbending gallantry was carried over to his more discreet and unpublicised friendships with such well-known courtesans as the ageing Catherine Walters who, as 'Skittles', had been Lord Hartington's mistress but was then a society lady living in some style in Mayfair. The celebrated singer Nellie Melba also sought out Kitchener's company as did the actress Sarah Bernhardt, and one revealing scene of Kitchener during this period of his life shows him gravely walking besides Skittle's bathchair in Hyde Park – one of the greatest soldiers of his generation in conversation with one of the greatest harlots of hers. All of Kitchener's women friends remained loyal to him to the end and one of the last letters he received was a delightful response from Sarah Bernhardt in 1916 when Kitchener had gently refused her permission to return to France in a troopship after a performance in London because of the danger of submarine attack. 'Mais alors!' was her reaction. 'It would be a matter of dying with our soldiers. *Quelle gloire!*'[15] At the time Kitchener was Secretary of State for War, the embodiment of Allied hopes for victory, and his secretary Sir George Arthur remembered how he was bombarded by highly perfumed letters from admirers that had to be removed discreetly from the presence of War Office staff.

The instrument that ended Kitchener's term as Governor-General of Sudan was not found in the drawing rooms of Panshanger or Hatfield but came from the outbreak of the Boer War in 1899. Before Kitchener had gone on leave that same year Cromer had advised him not to think in terms of a return to Khartoum, for the sorry truth was that his Governor-General's methods, although successful in the beginning, had quickly turned sour. Kitchener had proved to be too impatient and too great a believer in autocracy to bend to the imperial will and his financial procedures in particular were causing havoc in the country. He had withheld local allowances from his Egyptian officers with the result that sections of the army were in a state of near mutiny, and his decision to keep the south of Khartoum as a military district had brought considerable hardship to its people. An outbreak of plague and Kitchener's insistence on maintaining trade restrictions had added to their misery, and parts of the country that had not yet benefited from the beginnings of civil authority were in a depressed state. This was, in fact, achieved by Kitchener's successor, Reginald Wingate.

The effects of Kitchener's indifference to the feelings of his men in Sudan led the XIVth Sudanese to mutiny early in 1900 when it was rumoured that they were to be sent to fight in South Africa. Their uncharacteristic action was effectively halted by Wingate. He knew that there was no truth in the story but British prestige had been dragged down to such depths by Boer victories at Magerfontein, Colenso and Stormberg during the so-called 'Black Week' early in December 1899 that it was feared in 1900 that Boer successes would spread disaffection towards British authority in safer areas such as Sudan. By the time of the mutiny, though, Kitchener was in South Africa where, at Salisbury's request, he had been appointed Chief of Staff to Lord Roberts. He, in turn, had been appointed to succeed as Commander-in-Chief in South Africa General Sir Redvers Buller VC, the scapegoat for 'Black Week' with whom Kitchener had served in Sudan.

Lord Roberts was one of Britain's most renowned soldiers and, depending on whose side you were – the best-loved field marshal in the British Army. 'The greatest and most loveable man I have ever known', wrote Sir Henry Rawlinson, later Commander-in-Chief in India. 'A scheming little Indian', a self-promoting adventurer hungry for glory, was the less kindly view of those army officers who belonged to Garnet Wolseley's rival Ashanti ring. For years there had been intense rivalry between the two men that had culminated in Wolseley's appointment as Commander-in-Chief, yet Roberts remained – in the public's mind, at least – the more illustrious figure. His winning of a Victoria Cross during the Indian Mutiny and his celebrated march from Kabul to Kandahar during the Second Afghan War had given him a veneer of glamour, so much so that following the disasters in South Africa he was the people's choice for command and for the restitution of British arms. When it was announced that Kitchener was to be his second-in-command, thus bringing together two of the best-known soldiers of the day, public satisfaction was only tempered by the news that Roberts's son, Freddy, had been killed at the Battle of Colenso.

The two men had only met briefly twice before and to observers such as Major-General Sir George Younghusband of the Indian Army and a convinced Roberts supporter they seemed to have little in common:

> Lord Roberts was the modern Bayard, chevalier sans peur et sans reproche. Lord Kitchener was fashioned more on the lines of Bismarck. Both were born British, but one developed into the highest type of English gentleman, the other acquired more Teutonic characteristics. It would therefore be somewhat difficult for an honest admirer of Lord Roberts to be an equally honest admirer of Lord Kitchener.[16]

But that comparison is not the whole story. Differences there were between the two men. Roberts was a small man little over 5ft in height, Kitchener a foot taller; Roberts enjoyed the reputation of a humanitarian who cared about the welfare of his men, Kitchener had scarcely been known to so much as address a private soldier; Roberts had demonstrated in Afghanistan in 1879 that emotional intuition in battle which characterises the great field commander, a quality that was absent in Kitchener's psychological make-up; Roberts was genial and liked company, Kitchener was reserved and aloof; seventeen years separated them, yet there was sufficient affinity to make them an effective team in South Africa.

Both men sensed that an aptitude for politics was an essential ingredient in successful soldiering and Roberts had cultivated his career as assiduously as had Kitchener. He knew how to use the press to his own advantage and over the years he had advanced his claims amongst society and political wives, where his diplomacy and forceful open character were especially admired. Throughout the autumn of 1899 he had been using those attributes to persuade the Secretary for War Lord Lansdowne that his rightful place was in command in South Africa; besieging him with a stream of telegrams and letters as he kept a close watch on the official signals emanating from Buller in South Africa. Kitchener, too, had been busy. That September he had written to Lady Cranborne in forceful terms, 'If you see the chance I hope you will put in a word as if the Cape war comes off it will be a big thing and they might give me some billet.' Her father-in-law, Lord Salisbury, insisted on Kitchener's appointment three months later.[17]

On 17 December Roberts had been granted his wish and the following day Kitchener was appointed Roberts's Chief of Staff, a position that amounted to second-in-command of the British Army in South Africa. His duties amounted mainly to executing Roberts's overall plan. In other areas, such as supply and communications, he was to be given a more or less free hand. Once again, Kitchener's appointment over the heads of officers senior to him caused great resentment – many officers in the field were local lieutenant-generals or generals – but this dislike was mitigated by the total trust invested in him by Roberts, who later said that his number two's self-possession, appetite for strenuous work and loyalty were 'beyond all praise'. On Boxing Day 1899 Kitchener arrived in Gibraltar from Alexandria on board the cruiser HMS *Isis* to find Roberts waiting for him on the *Dunottar Castle*, the same liner that had taken Buller to South Africa two and a half months earlier. The two men immediately sat down to make sense of the military situation and to draw up a plan that would claw back victory from defeat.

Britain had been at loggerheads with the Boers – Dutch immigrants who had settled in Cape Colony – for most of the century. Even when the Boers began trekking north to establish Transvaal and the Orange Free State in 1837 the confrontation continued and broke out into open war in 1880 as a result of non-payment of taxes. Following the defeat of a British force at Majuba Hill an uneasy peace was restored, with the Boers operating self-government under British suzerainty, but it was a powder keg awaiting the spark. The fuse was provided by the discovery of seemingly limitless supplies of gold in 1886 in Witwatersrand – the 'Rand' south of Pretoria. The lure of untold riches attracted speculators from Britain and all over Europe and before long the Boers were outnumbered by foreigners or *uitlanders*, who threatened their traditional conservative way of life. To protect his fellow Boers in the Transvaal, President Kruger passed stringent laws excluding non-Boers from participation in political life while retaining the right to tax them.

Such a state of affairs was bound to cause trouble but when it came in 1895 it proved to be a botched business. Acting in the belief that an *uitlander* uprising was imminent, the British imperial adventurer Cecil Rhodes encouraged his associate Dr Starr Jameson to lead a raid into the Transvaal to bring down Kruger's government. It was an abject failure but it had far-reaching consequences. Rhodes was disgraced and Britain was made a laughing stock. To make matters worse, the subsequent negotiations to retrieve the situation settled nothing. Each new concession was met with further demands and gradually a full-scale war became inevitable. In 1899 Britain despatched 10,000 troops to South Africa while the Transvaal, now backed by the Orange Free State, made plans for mobilisation. War was declared on 12 October after Kruger's demands that Britain remove her troops from the frontier were ignored contemptuously in London and within a week Buller was on his way to South Africa to take command of the imperial forces in what everyone hoped would be a short sharp war.

It turned out to be nothing of the sort. Defeat followed defeat, Buller was sacked and a puzzled nation began to ask why the British Army had fallen so quickly from grace. On board the *Dunottar Castle* Kitchener had been quick to spot some of the reasons, writing to Pandeli Ralli from Madeira that it seemed to him that the army's transport was in a shambles and that the artillery was incapable of supporting the infantry. 'My God!' he wrote. 'I can scarcely credit their taking the fearful responsibility of sending us into the field practically unarmed with artillery.'[18] There was a job to be done and from his early letters to his friends at home Kitchener claimed that he was the only man capable of doing it. All his thoughts and energies for the coming twenty-nine months were now to be turned once again to the business of waging and winning a war.

7

THE GREAT BOER WAR

The military situation confronting Roberts and Kitchener when they arrived in Cape Town on 10 January 1900 was not encouraging. The Boers, anxious to press home their numerical advantage in October 1899, had attacked on two fronts: in north-eastern Natal to possess Dundee and Ladysmith before sweeping on towards Durban and the coast; and in the west across the frontier of the Orange Free State to take Mafeking and Kimberley before pushing south into Cape Colony. In both cases it was expected that the Afrikaners of both colonies would rise in their support, and in the event some 10,000 did so. It was a sensible plan – to overrun Natal and Cape Colony before the arrival of British reinforcements and then dictate terms – and it might have been successful had the Boers not been diverted by time-consuming sieges at Kimberley, Ladysmith and Mafeking.

Having arrived in South Africa at the end of October Buller's first instinct had been to raise the three sieges and to push into the Orange Free State, where a bridgehead could be established before the invasion of the Transvaal. The strategy could not be faulted but Buller was unfortunate in his commanders and in the preparedness of their men. Lieutenant-General Lord Methuen was sent to relieve Kimberley; the redoubtable Gatacre, who had fought alongside Kitchener at Omdurman, was despatched to stem the Boer tide in Cape Colony, while Buller himself marched north-east into Natal to relieve General Sir George White, who was cooped up in Ladysmith. Within a few weeks Methuen had

THE KITCHENER ENIGMA

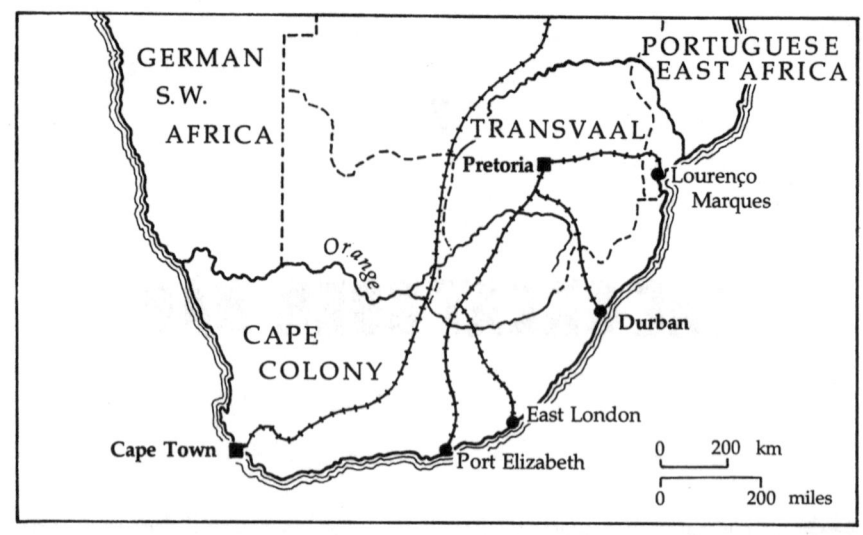

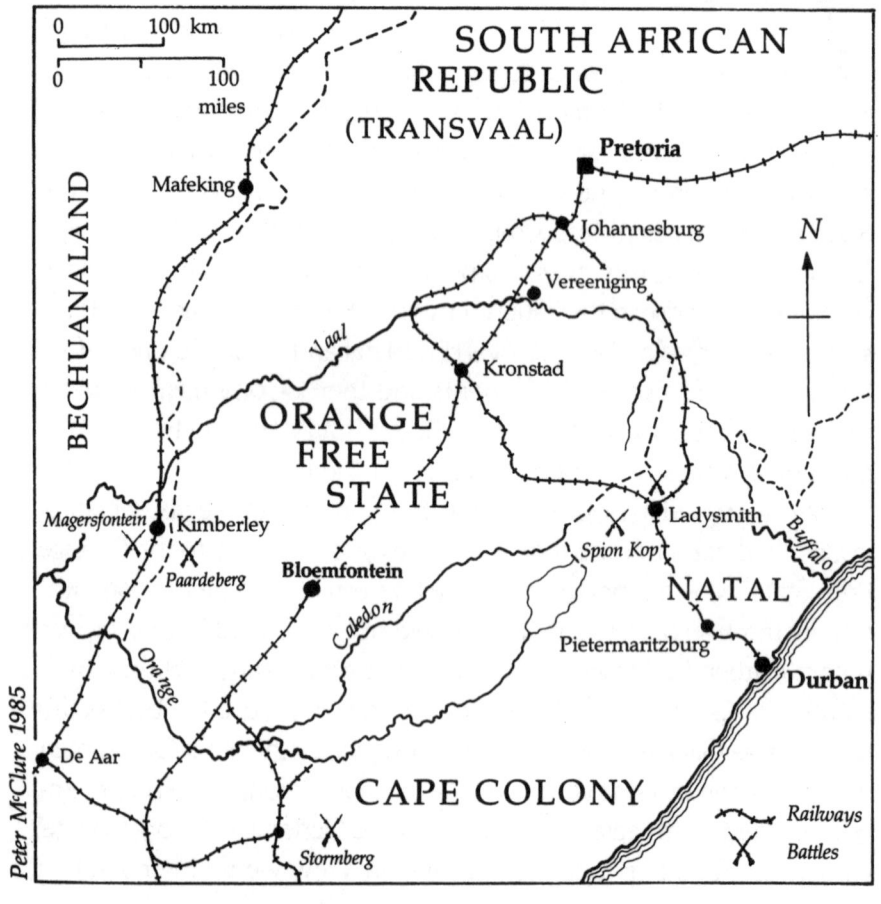

been bloodily repulsed and the Highland Brigade smashed at the Battle of Magersfontein where its well-liked commander Andrew Wauchope had been killed; Gatacre was defeated at Stormberg, and Buller's own force was embarrassingly overrun at Colenso, where he also lost his guns to the enemy. The army had been thoroughly humiliated and it was little wonder that so much was expected of the two new commanders, Roberts and Kitchener.

The British Army's failings had been cruelly exposed by a Boer force whose physical make-up was ideally suited to the prevailing conditions. Over the generations the Boers had become accustomed to fighting as a natural fact of life and they were soon able to put a 50,000-strong force into the field. Apart from units of artillery and armed police it was less a regular army than a citizens' militia. It was a democratic army with very few ranks of office that relied not upon drilling but on knowledge of basic tactics and on the mobility and marksmanship of its men. Each Boer soldier was expected to possess a pony and each commando or basic field unit made its own arrangements for transport and provisions. Tactics were worked out beforehand so that each man knew what was expected of him and in return the state provided a Mauser rifle, which was superior to the British Lee-Enfield or Lee-Metford. It was more accurate over a longer range and to those attributes the Boers brought their own skills; years of self-sufficiency had turned them into expert hunters, able to judge distance, read landscape and use cover. Above all they were more mobile and showed a disconcerting ability to melt away into the surrounding countryside once a battle or skirmish was over. The British hated those tactics: Kitchener wrote to Willy Grenfell's sons complaining that, unlike the Sudanese, the Boers refused to stand up and fight like men.[1]

Given such a mobile and efficient enemy, and a country whose topography enforced long lines of communication, Kitchener and Roberts set about instituting a series of reforms in the army in South Africa. Transport was the first problem, for if the British Army Service Corps kept to the railway system, the one sure means of transportation, then their movements immediately became known to the Boer commanders: if they wanted to move cross-country then a workable method of transport had to be found. The existing system was that each brigade had a supply column that provided the food and ammunition for the battalions. Each battalion had its own transport officer and a suitable number of wagons and carts. This system had been worked out by Wolseley and it was found suitable for campaigns in which brigades frequently had to operate at long distances from their base. However, to Kitchener's eyes, it smacked of waste. Having accustomed himself in Sudan to regard his army as an indivisible unit, he could see no sense in allowing each battalion to possess its own transport – if it was not on the move, he argued, its wagons, carts, mules and oxen would be lying idle. Kitchener therefore centralised the organisation, creating a pool, or 'supply park', of ox wagons and mule carts that would be made available to the entire army, but its introduction in the middle of a campaign was the signal for chaos. In place of the experienced Army Service Corps men the new system was given over to officers who had often shown that they were unsuited to other tasks.

Kitchener's scheme was sound enough, but it paid little attention to the logistical situation facing Roberts's army. To make matters worse, Kitchener forced the reforms through, accepting no advice and brooking no opposition. 'I am afraid I rather disgust the old red-tape heads of departments,' he told Ralli. 'They are very polite, and after a bit present me with a volume of their printed regulations generally dated about 1879 and intended for Aldershot manoeuvres, and are quite hurt when I do not agree to follow their printed rot.'[2] But Kitchener was wrong. The new system was not an improvement: many men went hungry or ran out of ammunition on the advance to Bloemfontein and gradually the old system was brought back into operation. Some of Kitchener's colleagues never forgave him and General Lyttelton, another veteran of Sudan, told his wife that in future Kitchener would be known as 'K[itchener] of Chaos'.[3] Partly the problem lay in the fact that Kitchener had no real experience of the organisation of the modern British Army – he had last served as a practising soldier in its ranks in Aldershot in 1874 – and he wanted to employ the tactics that had served him well in Sudan; partly, too, he wanted to stamp his authority in South Africa but, in spite of the reputation he had built up as the organiser of victory,

Kitchener was not a good all-round administrator. Whereas it had been comparatively simple to hold within his head the strategy and the needs of his 25,000-strong army as it made its way down the Nile, Kitchener found it difficult to adapt to the new conditions in South Africa, and in 1903 the official *Report of His Majesty's Commissioners on the War in South Africa* was critical of the transport arrangements made during the course of the war.[4] One area, however, in which he was successful, was in creating a force of 15,000 Mounted Infantrymen (MI), which was used in conjunction with the cavalry and whose genesis owed much to the success of the Boers' tactics.

If Kitchener's behaviour was disliked by many of the field commanders in South Africa, Kitchener himself had equally small regard for the army he found there. 'I must say,' he told Lady Cranborne, 'I like having the whole thing cut and dried and worked out; but people here do not seem to look upon the war sufficiently seriously. It is considered too much like a game of polo with intervals for afternoon tea.'[5] As a result Kitchener was ruthless in recommending changes to Roberts when he felt that an officer had been incompetent. During the first half of 1900 Gatacre was sacked, as was Lieutenant-General Sir Henry Colvile, the commander of the 9th Division. Although they were dismissed in Roberts's name it was common knowledge that the recommendations had been made by Kitchener, who was anxious to build up his own team and many of those new commands went to men who had been in the 'band of boys' in Sudan. Douglas Haig was made Chief of Staff to John French's cavalry division, the command of the 2nd Cavalry Brigade was given to Broadwood, now a major-general, the ravaged Highland Brigade was revitalised by the appointment of Hector Macdonald as its commander, and Horace Smith-Dorrien was given the 19th Brigade. Henry Rawlinson also joined Kitchener's staff, Percy Girouard went to work on the South African railway system and, later in the year, Kitchener appointed a new ADC, Captain Frank Maxwell who was given the unusual and unlikely distinction of being allowed to play court jester to his chief's entourage.[6] Within days of his appointment he received a new nickname: Kitchener would only call him 'The Brat' and so he was styled for the remaining years of his appointment, until 1906 when he married.

Born in Guildford in 1871 of Scots ancestry, Francis Aylmer Maxwell had been commissioned into the Royal Sussex Regiment in 1891 and his first posting was to the regiment's 2nd battalion in India. He served with the Chitral Relief Force in 1895, the year that Kitchener's nephew, Millie's son 'Wallier', joined the regiment. In the following year he transferred to the 18th Bengal Lancers where, by further coincidence, his brother subalterns included R.J. Marker and Oswald FitzGerald, both of whom were later to serve as ADCs to Kitchener. By 1899 he was in South Africa attached to a new detachment, Roberts' Horse, and he went on to win the Victoria Cross on 31 March 1900 for saving the guns of the Royal Horse Artillery at Sanna's Post. Known throughout the army for his bravery and striking looks, Maxwell regarded the Boer War as something of a lark, a view he expressed in his letters home to his father, which abound with sporting phrases and spirited allusions to 'Johnny Boer' really being 'a pretty good chap'.[7] Many thought him shallow but very few failed to be charmed by his unselfconscious gaiety and his schoolboyish enthusiasm. After the dry humour and tendency towards melancholia of Lord Edward Cecil it might seem odd that Kitchener turned to a seemingly foppish young man but there was a reason for his choice.

In the first place, Kitchener had heard good reports of Maxwell from 'Wallier' and he valued family opinion in such matters. Now aged fifty, Kitchener was not prepared to break new ground in his friendships, everyone close to him had to have the ring of familiarity. Apart from his friendships with powerful politicians and socialites, and his close relationship to Millie and his brothers – Walter was in South Africa in command of the 5th Brigade – Kitchener kept only a small and loyal group of close friends. There was another side to Maxwell's preferment, however. Kitchener's exalted position had made him more unbending and austere than ever before and, contrarily, for that reason he seems to have been drawn to 'The Brat's' youthfulness and infectious gaiety. There were enemies who suggested that it was an unnatural relationship, that Maxwell was acting Patroclus to Kitchener's Achilles. However, both men lived together at Command Headquarters, where any scandal would have been detected easily. Rather, their strange fellowship appears to have been paternal in origin, Kitchener allowing 'The Brat' indulgences that would have brought immediate retribution had they been perpetrated by others, and treating him almost as the son he knew he would never have. Ian Hamilton remembered that, whenever Kitchener sat down to dinner with his staff and treated them to a display of taciturn contempt, Maxwell would make a point of telling jokes or irreverently pulling his chief's leg. As the assembled company waited in trepidation for the expected thunderbolt, Kitchener would smile grimly, the clouds would lift and a semblance of good humour returned to the dinner table.

It was part of Kitchener's policy to surround himself with a circle of efficient subordinates but he proved himself to be a loyal second-in-command to Roberts. The tactics worked out by the two men were similar to Buller's and had all the merits of simplicity; but whereas Buller had allowed himself to be overcome by doubts, Roberts had a greater sense of purpose, a bigger army and an energetic chief of staff known for his ability to get things done in the next stage of the war. Instead of sacking Buller, Roberts had demoted him to command the army in Natal, where he continued his attempts to relieve Ladysmith. The key to the raising of the siege lay along the Tugela River, which bisects Natal, and it was along its banks that he was twice bloodily repulsed in January at the battle of Spion Kop and Vaal Krantz. Undeterred by those setbacks, Roberts ordered Buller to maintain his position in Natal while he began a flanking movement towards Bloemfontein with the intention of taking the Orange Free State, engaging General Cronje's army that was then holed up at Magersfontein, and relieving Kimberley. General Piet Cronje was the leader of the Transvaal commandos, and such a move, if successful, would have cut him off from his line of retreat north and forced him to move eastwards towards Bloemfontein, where he could be engaged by Roberts's army. In conditions of utmost secrecy a 40,000-strong British force and a mass of transport had assembled at Methuen's camp on the Modder River. Having given hints that he intended to push north along the eastern route of the railway through Naauwpoort and Colesberg, Roberts travelled incognito with Kitchener by ordinary mail train on the evening of 6 February 1900, their destination being the headquarters of the army on the Modder.

Five days later, leaving Methuen to bombard Cronje's laager, the huge army swung southwards in a feinting movement towards Ramdam, a motley collection of farmsteads inside the borders of the Orange Free State and south of the Modder and Riet rivers, the two natural obstacles that lay between it and Kimberley. Headed by French's Cavalry Division – which contained two brigades of Mounted Infantry under Colonel O.C. Hannay and Colonel C.P. Ridley – it was an impressive sight and its sheer size was the wonder of all who beheld it.

The 17-mile march south was a simple trick designed to confuse Cronje and the halt at Ramdan was but a prelude to the operation of Roberts's flank movement. Shortly after arriving there Kitchener took French and Haig to one side and, telling them that the Empire's future well-being rested upon their shoulders, ordered the cavalry to strike across the Riet at De Kiel's Drift before riding north to relieve Kimberley. French and his men accomplished the first river crossing easily enough but ran into difficulties at Klip Drift on the Modder, where they were confronted by a strong Boer force. Showing good tactical sense and a great deal of élan, French found a gap in the defences and rode his cavalry at speed through it. It was one of the few successful cavalry actions of the war and later that day, 15 February, Kimberley was relieved. One of the reasons for French's success was his insistence that his division retain its own transport, but despite that advantage his men had become hopelessly entangled with Tucker's ponderous bullock wagons while crossing the Riet. Within two days of the march from Ramdam the centralised transport system was lagging behind the rest of the army, unarmed, and the bulk of the animals were exhausted: to make matters worse, Christian De Wet, the outstanding Boer guerrilla leader, succeeded in capturing 200 British wagons at Waterval Drift, thereby putting Roberts's army on short rations.

The success of French's cavalry dash to Kimberley and the inexorable march north of Roberts's army were enough to persuade Cronje that he was in danger of being marooned and that his defensive position at Magersfontein, which had withstood so many assaults, was now vulnerable to a frontal attack. His best hope was to retire along the Modder towards Bloemfontein and by employing his superior mobility – he was outnumbered eight to one – to cut free of Roberts's army and join up with Boer reinforcements. Later that night, 15 February, Cronje's soldiers, their ponies, their wagons and their wives, began an orderly and restrained procession out of their laager, and, astonishingly, it was completed without drawing any attention from Lieutenant-General Thomas Kelly-Kenny's 6th Division camped a few miles away to the south. Two days later, harassed by Mounted Infantry units alerted to their escape, Cronje and his army found themselves digging in to a new defensive position on the Modder, at a place called Paardeberg. Cutting off their planned route were 1,500 men of the Cavalry Division under French who had ridden that morning, at Kitchener's behest, from Kimberley and had completed the ride in a mere six hours, a creditable time considering their exertions thirty-six hours earlier at Klip Drift. Even at that point Cronje could have escaped by brushing aside French's small force and running for Bloemfontein, but the unexpected nature of French's appearance and a desire to save his men's wagons seems to have persuaded Cronje to stand and fight.

Throughout those two momentous days – which had seen the triumph of Kimberley and the despair of Cronje's escape – Kitchener had attached himself to Hannay's Mounted Infantry and it had been largely due to his foresight in ordering up French that Cronje had been forced into a defensive position. Meanwhile, Kelly-Kenny's division had arrived on the scene and he set about surveying the position with Kitchener, who was in a state of excitement now that the scent of battle was in the air. But what they saw when they surveyed Cronje's laager from a hill to the west did not offer them much comfort.

The Boers were dug in on the north side of the river, flanked by high rocky ground, and the defence of the laager had been made easier by the presence of ravines running down to the river (natural trenches) and thick scrub (natural fortifications): it was a position that seemed to deny the possibility of a frontal attack and Kelly-Kenny, accordingly, worked out a plan to suit the terrain and the strength of Cronje's position. Early next morning he would bombard the laager with his artillery while his infantry encircled it; by sitting tight and putting the Boers under pressure he would besiege Cronje and wait for his surrender.

These tactics, though unadventurous, were sensible: Kelly-Kenny's men were exhausted and on short rations. There was nowhere for Cronje to go, and any expected relief force headed by De Wet could be beaten off with some ease. Unfortunately for Kelly-Kenny he was accompanied by Kitchener who, after surveying the position, had other ideas: engage the enemy and smash him ruthlessly before he had time to complete his defences.

Such tactics had worked at the Atbara when Kitchener's army had steamrollered its way into Mahmoud's zeriba; there seemed to be no reason why they should not work here. But Kelly-Kenny opposed those plans, arguing that a frontal assault would spell ruin to his tired and hungry men. It was to no avail; Kitchener was determined to have his way and when his arguments failed he pulled rank. Earlier Kitchener had submitted to Kelly-Kenny's superior rank of local lieutenant-general even though he himself was higher in the Army List, but on 17 February with battle imminent a galloper was sent to Roberts, lying in bed with a chill at Jacobsdal, asking who was to command. The reply was that Kelly-Kenny should regard Kitchener's orders as coming from himself. 'I will submit to even humiliation rather than raise any matter connected with my command,' was Kelly-Kenny's indignant response.[8] After all, reasoned the Irishman, he had been fighting in China while Kitchener was still a boy and now he had been humiliated publicly by Roberts who had chosen to disregard his local superior rank – he was a lieutenant-general and Kitchener a major-general.

The decision was popular among the rank and file, who began to show considerable enthusiasm for engaging Cronje's Boers. At dawn on the following day, 18 February, Kitchener made a rudimentary reconnaissance of the south side of the river and from some high ground surveyed the Boer laager. 'It is now seven o'clock,' he said, looking at his watch. 'We shall be in the laager by half past ten.'[9] How he would carry out that threat was another matter as, during the course of the battle, it became obvious that Kitchener had little clear idea of how to put his tactics into action. He abhorred giving written orders and, when the battle was at its hottest, insisted on riding furiously from position to position giving shouted commands that seemed to those who received them to be devoid of logic. Frequently orders were given to individual units without reference being made to senior officers. Kelly-Kenny thought Kitchener insane, and Smith-Dorrien, who was ordered to take his 19th Brigade across the Modder at a place where the river was in flood, admitted later that there was neither rhyme nor reason to the command and that throughout the day he was 'in a complete fog, and knew nothing of the situation either of our own troops, or of the Boers, beyond what I could see, or infer, myself'.[10]

The first assault on the laager was made by the 6th Division from the south bank, while Smith-Dorrien and Macdonald made a right hook on the Boers upstream with Hannay's Mounted Infantry and the 18th Brigade completing the encircling movement on the Boers' left flank. Following a massive artillery bombardment the infantry swarmed into action in an attempt to cross the river, but the awkward terrain, the strength of the Boer defences and the accuracy of the Mausers held off the British assault and by midday no unit had managed to get within 300 yards of the Boer trenches.

Early on in the battle a confident Kitchener had telegraphed triumphantly to Roberts that the attack had been so successful that 'it must be a case of complete surrender'. In this he was deceived by the success of his artillery barrage; by the day's end the forces were at stalemate. Kitchener's troops surrounded the laager but they had failed to make any impression on its defences. There had been about 1,200 British casualties to the Boers' 300 and to make matters worse the exhausted British troops to the south found themselves under fire from De Wet's guerrillas on a nearby hill or kopje, ignored by Kitchener as a defensive position. All attempts to retake it had failed and little remained but to dig in for the night to see what the following day would bring.

Kitchener's last despatch to Roberts spoke of a more determined assault being made the following day. When Roberts arrived at ten o'clock that, too, was his first inclination but the presence of De Wet and the sight of the British wounded unnerved him: he was facing many of the difficulties that had confronted Buller, opposition from a determined enemy and an unacceptably high number of casualties. Having spoken to the commanders Roberts baulked at sending more men to useless deaths and on 20 February all frontal attacks came to an end. When Cronje refused to surrender to the encircling British army Roberts ordered the artillery to bombard the laager into submission; two days later De Wet's men melted away from their kopje and the battle was won. Tactfully, Roberts ordered Kitchener away from Paardeberg on 21 February to repair railway lines and bridges in the Colesberg area with the result that his chief of staff was not present when Cronje surrendered on 27 February, the nineteenth anniversary of Majuba.

Britain had won its first major battle of the war, thus paving the way for the capture of the Orange Free State, but it had come at a cost. After the war arguments raged about the choice of tactics. The *Official History* attacked Kitchener for his methods and praised Roberts for bringing some much-needed sense to the battlefield, but L.S Amery, the war correspondent of *The Times*, thought that Kitchener's tactics should have prevailed, that the infantry had already gained a moral victory and should have been allowed to press home their advantage, whatever the cost, on the second day. As it was, Cronje was the real loser as his fellow countrymen never forgave him for surrendering on Majuba Day and in 1904 his fall was made complete when he took part in a re-enactment of the battle at a trade fair in the United States. Roberts's reputation was further enhanced by the victory but within certain sections of the army Kitchener was decried for the brutality of his tactics. To those charges Kitchener paid little heed, telling Lady Cranborne that, 'War means risks, and you cannot play the game and always win; and the sooner those in authority realise this, the better.'[11]

The capitulation of Cronje's army opened the way to Bloemfontein, which fell on 13 March, and suddenly the end of the war seemed to be in sight. Ladysmith had at last been relieved by Buller; Mafeking, to universal rejoicing throughout the Empire, had ended its 217-day siege on 16 May; Johannesburg capitulated a fortnight later, Pretoria on 5 June. With all the important centres falling this should have signalled the end of the hostilities. Joubert, the Boer Commandant-General, had died and Kruger was in flight – eventually he would escape to Holland – but the wavering determination of the Boer war council had been strengthened by the strategy put forward by Christian De Wet. Instead of fighting pitched battles complete with wagons and womenfolk, he argued that smaller numbers of men should be used to harry the British and destroy their lines of communication.

The Boer war council was now dominated by De Wet, Jan Smuts, a Cambridge-educated lawyer, and Louis Botha, who had so bedevilled Buller's advances on Ladysmith. These new men had the utmost confidence in their tactics and in July and August De Wet achieved some outstanding success in the eastern Orange Free State attacking British positions and blowing up railway lines while outwitting the pincer movements set up to capture him. During this stage of the campaign Kitchener failed to engage the Boer commandos and allowed De Wet to escape at Olifant's Nek on 13 August after a chase lasting nine days. A few days later Roberts pulled him out of the field and ordered him to return to administrative duties in Pretoria.

While Kitchener cooled his heels with staff work in the Transvaal capital, Roberts and Buller combined their forces on 25 August at Belfast to hunt down the Boer forces remaining in the field. Two days later Botha's army was defeated at Bergendal and his fragmented army retreated towards the Mozambique border. With the Boers in disarray and each day bringing news of the capture of their guns and large numbers of prisoners, Roberts judged the war to be over apart from the necessary mopping up operations. On 25 October he announced the annexation of the Transvaal and began the arrangements for Kitchener to take over as the British Army's commander while he returned to London to become Commander-in-Chief in succession to Wolseley in 1901. For his services Roberts was made an earl and appointed a Knight of the Garter.

It was now left to Kitchener to solve the problem of defeating a Boer force that Roberts had described as consisting of 'a few marauding bands' and whose capture seemed to be more the business of the police than the army. So great was Salisbury's confidence that a victory had been won that he called an election in September and, carrying all before him on a wave of public enthusiasm, saw his Conservative administration returned with a slightly increased majority. It was against that background that Kitchener took over the command of the army on 29 November but, as he quickly discovered, his job was not so much a simple matter of polishing off a few stragglers as fighting a full-scale guerrilla war. In claiming that the war was practically over Roberts had failed to understand the strength of Boer resistance. Not only were there at least 30,000 guerrillas still in the field but no account had been taken of their feelings. Those men who stayed on to fight cared little that their major cities had fallen; their loss did not signal the end of nationhood. As long as they had rifles and ammunition and their sense of loyalty to the Boer cause they pledged themselves to continue the fight. They knew that the overwhelming superiority of the British Army made outright victory impossible but they took heart from its over-stretched lines of communication and from Roberts's decision to supply only jury-rigged garrisons to each new district as it fell into his hands. Most of the veldt was still free and the guerrillas made it their home, using deception, speed and marksmanship in place of fortifications and artillery. Some areas, such as the western Transvaal and Zoutspanberg to the north, were never occupied.

Many of Kitchener's divisional commanders were exhausted by the strain of continuous warfare and dispirited by their inability to deliver a crushing blow to the unseen enemy; others, in Kitchener's words, had become loafers and loungers. Several established favourites, such as Rawlinson, French and Broadwood, were still in the field and new blood and been introduced with the arrival of Leslie Rundle, John Maxwell and Julian Byng, but others had to go. The Highland Brigade was disbanded and Hector Macdonald returned to his pre-war posting in India; Archibald Hunter retired injured after obtaining the surrender of the Boer General Prinsloo; Buller returned to his job at Aldershot training troops, taking with him Kelly-Kenny, who became adjutant-general. Hunter's relationship with Kitchener, begun in Sudan, later continued in India. In 1910 he married the widow of a Scottish shipping magnate and Kitchener was his best man.

The fates awaiting the other senior officers were less kind. Macdonald became Commander-in-Chief in Ceylon, where he fell from grace in a scandal involving young boys. To save his, and the army's, name he committed suicide in Paris rather than face a court martial. Buller was sacked by the War Office. An anonymous letter to *The Times* (written by Amery) had accused him of trying to persuade White to surrender Ladysmith: the War Office refused Buller right of reply but in an attempt to clear his name he did so at a public dinner at which Amery was present. He retired to his West Country estates and died there in 1908.

According to Sir George Arthur, Kitchener was completely impartial in the appointment or sacking of senior officers and the records confirm this.[12] There is no evidence of personal malice in Kitchener's system of appointments but, lacking a kindly touch, many of his decisions were passed on to the officer concerned in a brusque and unfeeling manner. If a man was tired or stale, he simply had to go. The same strictures applied to the men. The army that Kitchener inherited from Roberts was exhausted and its lines over-stretched; consequently it was not suited to the business of dealing with guerrilla warfare. Roberts, too, had insisted on fighting on a broad front, thus allowing the Boers to swarm into the rear and cause havoc, just as De Wet had succeeded in doing in July and August. To help the army out of this predicament Kitchener renewed his faith in the Mounted Infantry: at Roberts's prompting, the Cabinet made available additional funds to increase the Mounted Infantry strength to 80,000 men by May 1901. Many of these units consisted of colonial irregulars, excellent horsemen who could ride as hard and shoot as accurately as their Boer counterparts. However, despite the improvements wrought by the increased numbers of mounted infantrymen, Kitchener harboured doubts about the army's effectiveness and, as the guerrillas continued to inflict irritating blows during the early part of 1901, he admitted to Milner, now High Commissioner, that his constant worry was that his troops, many of them raw and untried, would surrender if they found themselves in a tight spot. In his opinion two solutions presented themselves for finishing the war quickly: to enter into peace negotiations with the Boers, or to drive their guerrillas into the open and destroy them.

Kitchener had good reason to want the war ended. The recent election had returned his friend St John Brodrick to the War Office as

Secretary for War and to him Kitchener confided, as he had to Roberts, that an ambition for India burned in his mind. The spark had been lit in the summer of 1900 by George Curzon, who had been Viceroy of India since 1898 and who was determined to add to the splendour of his post by the appointment of Britain's most illustrious soldier as his army's commander. His enthusiasm, however, was not shared by others. Brodrick would have preferred to see him go to the War Office to reorganise the army once the war in South Africa had finally come to an end. Lord Lansdowne, now Foreign Secretary, distrusted Kitchener's abilities in administration, while the feline Lord Esher, shortly to head a commission to consider how the army might be reorganised, thought Kitchener too uncouth and ruthless for the post. Curzon, though, continued loyally to support Kitchener's claims. Nor was Kitchener willing to be put off course by a handful of politicians, and during the winter of 1900–1901 he kept up a barrage of correspondence not only with Brodrick but with Lady Cranborne, to whom he admitted that he would rather sweep a crossing than accept the War Office. Eventually Brodrick relented. In March 1901 he promised Kitchener the post of Commander-in-Chief in India once the war in South Africa had come to a successful conclusion.

In addition to operations in the Orange Free State and the Transvaal, Boer guerrillas made sporadic attacks into Natal and Cape Colony in an attempt to persuade Cape Afrikaners to rise in their support. These largely unsuccessful actions resulted in the declaration of martial law and the war entered a new phase of insurgency and counter-insurgency operations. Early in Roberts's reign as Commander-in-Chief it had been British policy to treat Boer farmers caught up in the war leniently and, as far as it was possible, to prevent unnecessary casualties. Kitchener agreed with this course, telling Salisbury in March 1900 that the Boer farmers should be reassured that their land would not be taken away from them. But as Boer resistance became more difficult to crack, so did British attitudes harden.

British columns chasing Boer units began to burn down farms suspected of harbouring guerrillas. Crops, too, were destroyed, but far from deterring the Boers and the farmers, the new tactics only served to strengthen their resolve. Had the Boer leaders been adept or sophisticated enough to present their case to the international press, the spectacle of British soldiers burning down farmsteads and turning out innocent women and children on to the open veldt would have made a telling propaganda point. As it was, the activities went largely unreported and it was left to the British press to present their own side of the story, a good example being a pre-election editorial in *The Times* that expressed the view that Britain was being too lenient in its treatment of the Boers. The press wanted the war ended quickly. Kitchener, it was generally agreed, would soon put an end to this sorry state of affairs.[13]

With his army stretched out along the main lines of communication, Kitchener decided to turn the position to his own advantage. He began by ordering a series of drives across the country to sweep the Boers out of their hiding places. Everything in the path of the advancing infantry had to be destroyed, with the result that Kitchener found himself facing large marauding gangs of farmers, plus their women and children, swarming over the blackened remains of a ruined countryside. His solution to the problem was to house the dispossessed, and the families of Boers who had surrendered, in protected camps alongside the main railway lines until the hostilities came to an end. These would be run on military lines: basic rations and accommodation would be provided and, as a consequence, the civilians would be kept clear of the main war zones. Brodrick was alarmed by the appearance of these internment, or concentration, camps but Kitchener claimed that the problem of a rootless population had been solved. The unfortunate truth was that Kitchener paid little heed to the proper provision of the camps; people were herded together in harsh conditions, rations were basic and medical supplies almost non-existent. The introduction of the camps became a source of great bitterness in the years to come.

Like many of Kitchener's ideas, the policy of drives worked better on paper than it did in practice. It was a simple enough proposition to sweep across country and to describe success in terms of 'Boers in the bag', but the terrain militated against the British methods. In return for several days' effort British columns would capture, on average, 100 Boers, but they were more than compensated for that lean bag by the huge numbers of oxen, cattle and sheep taken at the same time. At that rate the countryside would be quickly denuded while it would take years to capture all the fighting Boers still in the field. So confident, though, was Kitchener that the Boers would not stand for his scorched earth methods that in August 1901 he issued a proclamation saying that all Boer leaders would be banished and their land confiscated unless they surrendered by a certain date. By way of reply the Boer guerrillas stepped up their campaign and units under Smuts began to make deep incursions into Cape Colony. Clearly, other tactics had to be tried. Frustrated British soldiers became more bloodthirsty in their treatment of prisoners and Kitchener began a policy of executing Cape Colony rebels who had thrown in their lot with the guerrillas – thirty-three were executed while 500 more were sentenced to death but had their sentences commuted.[14] Other captured Boers were imprisoned and Kitchener even suggested that captured Boers should be deported to the Dutch East Indies, Fiji and Madagascar. This outburst was ignored by the Cabinet who, as 1901 dragged on, began to wonder if Kitchener was capable of inflicting defeat on the Boers. Their disquiet increased when a column commanded by Methuen was surprised by the Boers at Tweebosch and the general captured – on this occasion Kitchener's nerve failed him and he had to take to his bed for thirty-six hours. The annihilation of another mounted column commanded by Colonel G.E. Benson, one of his best commanders, also caused Kitchener to panic and to lose his appetite both for his food and for his involvement in the war. In a fit of despair he wrote to Roberts in November 1901, 'Who would have thought when you left Johannesburg that I should be a year in command with the war still going on?'[15]

To add to those difficulties Kitchener was becoming involved in an increasingly acrimonious argument with Milner over the correct policy for South Africa; at the same time he was also being pressed by the Cabinet to keep the costs of the war down to a reasonable level. His solution to running the war economically was the blockhouse, an ugly, though effective, cylindrical mini-fort made of corrugated iron and concrete, surrounded by ditches and barbed wire. Each one cost the British taxpayer a mere £16 and they proved to be good value.

The system had been begun with the fortified posts that protected the main railway routes; using them as a baseline Kitchener divided up large chunks of the Orange River Colony (as it was now called) and the Transvaal into areas and the blockhouses were built at strategic points on the grid. Each blockhouse was garrisoned by a platoon and linked to its neighbour by telegraph and by a massive hedge of barbed wire. Although it was primarily a defensive measure to prevent Boer movements, the blockhouse and barbed wire system could be also used as a net into which Boers could be channelled by infantry drives or Mounted Infantry sweeps. It proved to be a highly efficient method and by the war's end the country had been festooned with some 8,000 blockhouses over an area covering almost 4,000 miles.

To Kitchener's delight the 'bag' from the mounted columns had quadrupled by the beginning of 1902 but no leading generals were ever captured, leaving Kitchener to complain to Brodrick that 'as long as De Wet is out, I can see no end to the war'.[16] Partly the reason for this lay in the success of the Boers' own hit-and-run tactics, but they were aided, too, by the inability of the British to co-ordinate the sweeps. In an attempt to remedy that shortcoming Roberts sent his Military Secretary, Lieutenant-General Sir Ian Hamilton, out to South Africa at the end of 1901 as Kitchener's chief of staff.

Hamilton's arrival proved to be a godsend. By 1902 the sweep and drive system and the network of the blockhouses had been extended into the western Transvaal, where thirteen columns of Mounted Infantry were in the field. Their success rate had been reasonably high but time and again they had been outwitted and, in spite of their superior numbers and equipment, the morale of the British soldiers was in danger of cracking. Hamilton helped to change all that when Kitchener allowed him to take over the job of co-ordinating the movements of the columns. Instead of working in isolation, as they had tended to do, the columns in 1902 worked to a pre-arranged plan. When they rode out on to the veldt each column knew what the other was doing; by co-operating with one another during their sweeps they were able to engage the Boers and, as a result, to take more prisoners. The weekly 'bag' began to look more encouraging. In mid-October the previous year Kitchener had admitted wearily to Brodrick that 'it [the war] is not like the Sudan and disappointments are frequent'.[17] By the following April he was able to tell Lady Cranborne that peace was in the offing and that he hoped to see the Boer leaders in King Edward VII's coronation procession. The real reason for Kitchener's optimism, however, was that by April the Boers were showing a willingness to enter into peace negotiations.

The earliest attempts to broker a peace settlement had been made by Kitchener in February 1901 when he contacted Botha through the Boer general's wife and the two men had met at Middelburg in the eastern Transvaal. Although Kitchener had ascertained from London that the independence of the Orange Free State and the Transvaal was not negotiable, he was anxious to be lenient and his proposals centred on four objectives that he felt could form the basis of a lasting peace: a general amnesty for all Boers and Cape and Natal rebels; an assurance that the Boers would have a say in their own affairs; the continued predominance of a white race in South Africa; compensation for war damage.

As the two senior generals in the field Botha and Kitchener made the first tentative moves. Both men liked one another, but both had to report back to the politicians. When the main points of the peace plan were worked out on paper Kitchener's proposals began to look less than water-tight. Milner, as High Commissioner for South Africa, did not intend to see the implementation of a peace treaty that would leave the Boers undefeated and ready to press their claims again in the future. He was unwilling to compromise and refused to grant a general amnesty, a point on which he was backed by the Cabinet. The other proposals were watered down to make further negotiation impossible and when Milner's plan was forwarded to the Boers on 7 March it was rejected out of hand nine days later.

Kitchener was infuriated by this outcome and felt strongly that Milner's obstinacy over the amnesty was the cause of the breach in his dealings with Botha. He told Brodrick that, although he had done all in his power to try to make Milner change his mind, the High Commissioner had chosen to be vindictive. 'We are now carrying on the war to be able to put 200–300 Dutchmen in prison at the end of it. It seems to me to be absurd, and I wonder the Chancellor of the Exchequer did not have a fit.'[18]

In Britain the news of the failure of the talks was met with disappointment, although the majority view remained that the war could only be ended through a military victory or by the unconditional surrender of the Boers. Only the anti-war faction was outraged enough to continue the argument in the press and at political meetings: Lloyd George placed the blame firmly on the shoulders of the government, who had lacked the vision shown by its army commander: 'There was a soldier, who knew what war meant; he strove to make peace. There was another man, who strolled among his orchids, 6000 miles from the deadly bark of the Mauser rifle. He stopped Kitchener's peace!'[19] It had been no idle gesture on Kitchener's part. He did want the war to end and he did want to appear magnanimous in dealings with the Boers to achieve his ends. Also, if the war were prolonged, he might lose the Indian appointment. Besides, he disliked the kind of war that he had been forced to fight – the burning of farms, the imprisonment of Boer families, the chasing after bands of guerrillas who could run rings around his own army. In his heart of hearts he probably realised that, without the defeat of the Boers, ultimate victory would bring him little credit and that any failure would damage the reputation he had so carefully created.

Unfortunately for Kitchener, Milner believed in unconditional surrender and in the consequent creation of a new South African Crown Colony over which he would rule as an imperial pro-consul as grand as Cromer in Egypt or Curzon in India. Initially, relations between Kitchener and Milner had been cordial enough. There had been some friction between them when they had served together in Egypt but the breach had been healed at Hatfield in December 1898 when the two men had talked far into the night, long after the rest of the Salisbury's guests had gone to bed. 'Kitchener!' exclaimed Milner to Lady Edward Cecil on 29 October 1900. 'It is fortunate that I admire him in many ways so much, and admiring, am prepared to stand a lot and never take offence … I am determined to get on with him, and I think he likes me and has some respect for me, if he has for anybody. But shall I be able to manage this strong, self-willed man "in a hurry" (for he is dying to be off in time to take India) and turn his enormous power into the right channel?'[20]

As the period of their service in South Africa wore on, however, Milner came to distrust Kitchener and to suspect him of trying to make a hasty and ill-advised peace to further his own career.'I do not know what Lord Kitchener's plans are,' he told the Colonial Secretary Joseph Chamberlain on 17 January 1901.'He keeps them, quite rightly, entirely to himself, and he is unquestionably a man of great ability, unconventional mind and strong will.'[21] His suspicions had been given some substance at the Middelburg conference when he had complained that Kitchener gave too many vague promises and unnecessary concessions to the Boers. Stories of differences between the two men had begun to percolate back to London, although Milner was always quick to quash them and to praise Kitchener as a '*homme sérieux*, practising himself, and enforcing upon others, the highest standards of workmanlike strenuousness, indefatigable industry and iron perseverance'.[22]

The difficulty was that both men not only held different views about negotiating peace, they also disagreed about how the war should be run. Milner thought that Kitchener's strategy of treating the whole of South Africa as enemy territory was fundamentally wrong and that it should be possible to secure each territory before dealing with the next. Milner did not like the Boers and refused to trust them: once he had met their leaders Kitchener had come to respect the Boers and a bluff soldierly solidarity sprang up between him and Botha. (Other soldiers responded to that feeling – Hamilton now called the Boer leaders 'the best men in South Africa'.) Milner also felt that the only way to end the war was by winning it: Kitchener saw that the continuing war of attrition was damaging the army's morale, in spite of the success of Hamilton's big sweeps, that the country's exchequer was being drained, and that the British Army was being made to look ridiculous. Milner wanted to see the Boers defeated and negotiations made with those who had surrendered: Kitchener knew that the only realisable negotiations would be those carried on with the Boer generals still in the field. With both men holding such opposed points of view, a clash became inevitable. When the moves for peace began in April 1902 they were as much about whose views, Milner's or Kitchener's, would predominate, as they were about ending the war.

The talks, when they came, had an odd genesis. On 7 March Kitchener sent Botha and Schalk Burger, the acting president of the Transvaal, copies of correspondence he had received from the Foreign Office dealing with an offer from the Netherlands government to act as the mediator in any peace negotiations with the Boers. Lansdowne had turned down the offer, adding a rider that, 'The quickest and most satisfactory means of arranging a settlement would be by direct communication between the leaders of the Boer Forces in South Africa and the Commander-in-Chief of His Majesty's Forces.' The Boer leaders now understood that the British were prepared to negotiate with them and not with the Boers who had surrendered, and that the initial point of contact was to be Kitchener and not Milner, whom they disliked. Two weeks later Burger responded by asking for safe conduct through the British lines so that he could discuss the matter with his colleagues; this was agreed by Kitchener and a meeting was arranged for 12 April to be held in Melrose House, Kitchener's headquarters in Pretoria. To begin with the negotiations seemed to go well but it soon emerged that the Boers would not recognise any annexation of their republics, nor would they budge on the question of independence. An impasse seemed inevitable until Kitchener asked for a breathing space to discuss the proposals with his political masters: now the nature of the proceedings would be more akin to a peace conference than a negotiation of terms of surrender and Milner was brought into the discussions. Alert to the new conditions, he cabled Chamberlain for instructions, warning him at the same time that Kitchener 'does not care what he gives away', and received the reply that the Middelburg terms were to form the basis of the negotiations, with the important provisos that no date was to be fixed for Boer self-government but that the amnesty was now negotiable.

The Boers asked for a truce so they could discuss the proposal with their leadership. This was refused by Kitchener but he did offer a 'go-slow' so that the leaders could be given safe-conduct passes while still being kept aware of the might of his mailed fist – throughout the uncertain days of negotiation Hamilton kept up his Mounted Infantry sweeps in the western Transvaal. Kitchener's tactics worked. By 15 May the Boers had conferred and their sixty delegates had assembled at the agreed meeting place of Vereeniging on the banks of the Vaal, straddling the border of the Transvaal and the Orange Free State. Kitchener had done everything within his power to treat the Boers with honour: a huge marquee had been erected to house the meetings of the Boer delegates and it was there that they reviewed their position.

The picture that began to emerge in the first meetings was far from conclusive. While many of the Boers were dispirited, hungry and bereft of transport and other comforts, a hard core of militants believed that the guerrilla war could, and should, be continued. Others felt that the war should be ended for the sake of the women and children in the concentration camps; the hardliners argued that it was because of the future welfare of their families that the victory should be sought in the field and not around the negotiating table. Eventually, after much heated and passionate discussion, it was the spectre of a ruined homeland and of the people divided by civil war that tipped the balance. Koos De La Rey and De Wet, the undefeated generals, opted for compromise and with their fellow elected negotiators – Botha, Smuts and Judge Barry Hertzog – travelled to Pretoria on 19 May to put their case to the British.

They had been permitted by the delegates to offer a number of concessions, including the Rand, in return for the republics being left as self-governing countries under a British protectorate, a proposal that was anathema to Milner. Sensing in advance the British reaction, their second line of discussion was to reopen the Middelburg proposals, but when Milner introduced a draft that implied a declaration of surrender, it was the Boers turn to explode. De Wet angrily threatened to withdraw from the meeting, and at that crucial moment Kitchener, without consulting Milner, played his hand. Turning to Jan Smuts, the lawyer, he suggested that General De Wet should see the proposals worked out on paper before he came to any decision. To this De Wet agreed and the Boer lawyers, Smuts and Hertzog, sat down with Milner and the Attorney-General of Cape Colony, Sir Richard Solomon, to draft the peace terms. Kitchener had shown considerable dexterity in handling the Boers and the tact and diplomacy he brought to the negotiations was superior to that displayed by Milner. He knew when to lower the temperature and, just as he had refused to upset Marchand's sense of honour at Fashoda, so was he careful not to dent Boer pride at Vereeniging. For his pains he received little thanks from Milner, who to the last complained to Chamberlain that he felt that he had to negotiate with Kitchener while the Boers looked on. 'Kitchener is a strong man,' he thundered, 'but all he is doing is to paralyse me.'[23] Milner, with his new 'kindergarten' of aides, young Oxford-educated administrators, wanted to reorganise the country along British lines: Kitchener, the pragmatist, knew that peace would only come when the Boers realised that self-government was theirs for the asking, whatever the politicians said.

During the course of the negotiations he took Smuts to one side and said, 'I can only give it to you as my opinion, but my opinion is that in two years time a Liberal Government will be in power, and if a Liberal Government comes into power, it will grant you a constitution for South Africa.'[24] This was an unexpected lifeline. Smuts grasped it eagerly and, just as Kitchener intended, passed on its message of hope to his colleagues. By 21 May all Boer opposition to peace was at an end and the main proposals had been drawn up, the principal terms being: that the Boers would acknowledge the King as their lawful ruler; that self-government would follow 'as soon as circumstances permit'; that there would be no question of enfranchising the black and coloured population before self-government; and that the financial assistance available to the Boers would be £3 million – a figure proposed by Kitchener, to Milner's obvious disapproval, during the course of the negotiations. The following day the British Cabinet approved the conditions and the Boers were instructed to return to Vereeniging to seek the agreement of the delegates. Milner had been out-manoeuvred, his position of unconditional surrender had been breached and the Boers had been left in no doubt that the peace terms they were considering constituted 'Kitchener's Peace'. On 31 May the terms were accepted and the peace treaty was signed in Kitchener's residence in Pretoria at eleven o'clock at night.

To the tired and dispirited Boer leaders Kitchener offered his hand, breaking the embarrassed silence with a sincere, 'Well, we are good friends now.' The war that was supposed only to have lasted three months had taken four months short of three years to be brought to a conclusion. The British had lost 22,000 casualties, many of them on account of inadequate medical provision, and the total cost to the British exchequer was £200 million. A total of 7,000 Boers died in the field and more than three times that number in the concentration camps. Much of the farming land in the former republics had been razed and ugly blockhouses and barbed wire covered the rest. Hundreds of Boer farmers were homeless.

Britain gained little materially from the Boer War. The secure, British-dominated South Africa of Milner's dreams never materialised and, by 1907, both the Transvaal and the Orange Free State were self-governing. Three years later the Union of South Africa was proclaimed and its first president was Louis Botha. For Britain, a military nation supposed to be capable of controlling and guarding its world Empire, great defects had been exposed in its army, both in terms of its equipment and management and in its size and mobility: it was for those reasons that Brodrick asked Kitchener to be the new broom at the War Office. But however much Britain's stock had fallen in the eyes of the world, Kitchener's peace was not without its advantages. During the two world wars of the twentieth century South African troops fought on Britain's side, thereby justifying Kitchener's hopes, expressed at the victory banquet in Johannesburg on 17 June, that the Boers would be 'an asset of considerable importance to the British Empire'. His handling of the Boers at Vereeniging, and his ability to acknowledge their sense of pride and patriotism, undoubtedly helped to bring about a lasting peace. If he failed to see that the treaty signed away the political rights of the native and the coloured populations then he was no more or less blinkered than any other British politician or civil servant involved in the negotiations. It was not until the end of the century that those issues were addressed when the Republic of South Africa held its first universal elections in 1994.

Kitchener returned to Britain on 20 June 1902, travelling from Cape Town on the SS *Orotava*. On the day of his departure all the ships in the great harbour were dressed in bunting from bow to stern, cheering crowds lined the quays and a military band played Auld Lang Syne. The enthusiastic scenes were repeated at Southampton on 11 July when the *Orotava* docked at 8.50 a.m. Twenty-five minutes later Kitchener, still wearing his South African service dress, came down the gangplank with French and Hamilton to be met by a military delegation and the Major of Southampton, who later presented him with the freedom of his town. In thanking him Kitchener was careful to request that the town's welcome to the returning soldiers would take a 'non-alcoholic direction'. Then, having accepted the Mayor's words of welcome, he pushed his way through the crowds to inspect this guard of honour, a unit of Yeomanry and a detachment of the Cameron Highlanders, his headquarters' guard in South Africa and his favourite regiment in Sudan. It was an emotional moment: he had pulled every string to have the Camerons accompany him on the *Orotava*, but to no avail. They had been detailed to travel at a later date on the SS *Walmer Castle*. While pushing through the western approaches, however, the faster Union Castle vessel had overtaken the *Orotava* and Kitchener had immediately ordered the captain to signal the passing liner that he expected the presence of the Camerons on the quay at Southampton. Much to Kitchener's chagrin there was no response to the signal but the Camerons had seen it. Kitchener was mightily pleased to see them and their presence put him in a good humour. For the first time in public he dropped his martial mask and beamed at everyone around him – it was on this occasion that the famous 'laughing cavalier' snapshot was taken, the only known photograph that shows him smiling in public.

After receiving the freedom of Southampton, and shortly before eleven o'clock, he joined the special train that was waiting to take him to London and further ceremonies. The carriages were covered in bunting and the engine carried in front a huge 'K' surrounded by laurel leaves. At Basingstoke it stopped briefly to allow that borough also to make Kitchener a freeman and at 12.50 p.m. it pulled into Paddington Station, where Kitchener was met by the Prince of Wales, the Dukes of Cambridge and Connaught and Lord Roberts. After a few brief words of welcome the party left in open carriages on a triumphal procession to St James's Palace, where Kitchener was entertained to lunch. The King's Coronation, which was supposed to have taken place a fortnight earlier, had been postponed due to Edward VII's illness and the grandstands erected along the processional route had been pressed into service for Kitchener's homecoming. It was a sensible move: thousands of Londoners had been waiting since dawn to catch a glimpse of Kitchener – the last time for many years that the capital city would be able to turn out in such numbers to welcome home a conquering hero.

In the afternoon the King presented Kitchener with the Grand Cross of St Michael and St George and made him a member of the newly founded Order of Merit. To those honours were added promotion to full general and he was also created a viscount, taking the title Kitchener of Khartoum and of Vaal in the Colony of Transvaal and of Aspall in the County of Suffolk. Parliament thanked him and awarded him £50,000, which he was rumoured to have invested in the Rand goldfields. While it was true that, like other investors interested in post-war South Africa, Kitchener did put some money into Rand Gold, he was too senisble to give his enemies any opportunity of casting doubts on his probity. On 26 January 1902 he had refused to take out shares in the South Africa Cold Storage Company as it had been awarded an army contract and his honourable dealings in personal money matters continued until shortly before his death, when he sold shares in a Canadian munitions firm after Lloyd George had contracted it to supply military weapons to the British Army. Not that Kitchener was indifferent to his own finances. Since the 1890s his financial adviser had been Sir Arthur Renshaw, who remained a shrewd consultant and friend: in 1902 Kitchener became a godfather to Renshaw's son, jocularly telling his friend that he had done 'his duty nobly on that score'. Renshaw performed other equally noble duties. Under his astute guidance Kitchener's bounty was placed in such growth areas as railway construction in Costa Rica, Mexico and the United States and in addition he looked after Kitchener's various family trust funds. While serving abroad in India and Egypt Kitchener had to meet fairly stiff expenses over and above his official allowance and that entailed considerable juggling of investments between Kitchener's bank accounts in Cairo, Calcutta and London.

The country, too, was anxious to pay its respects to Kitchener and the summer of 1902 saw him accepting the freedoms of several towns and cities as well as being much in demand as a speaker at public occasions. Kitchener hated making public speeches and vary rarely departed from the texts that were prepared for him by his ADCs. When confronted by the need to make an impromptu official utterance his usual means of defence was to excuse himself by saying that his audience probably knew more about the subject than he did. Only once did a public speech of his give a revelation of the inner man. That was in South Africa when he replied to Milner's eulogy at the victory banquet in the Wanderers' Hall in Johannesburg. Choking with emotion he touched briefly on the life of the soldier in the veldt, on the early morning rides, the tang of woodsmoke and the sense of shared comradeship. 'Though you may have to toil as before,' he told his audience, largely made up of soldiers, 'you can never quite be the same again. You have tasted the salt of life and its savour will never leave you.' Even Milner was forced to admit that it had been a good speech and that Kitchener had spoken well, if perhaps over-briefly; but that sense of soldierly reserve only served to add to the aura of martial glamour that surrounded Kitchener. Wherever he went in the months after his homecoming large crowds turned up to listen to him and to cheer him to the echo. And just as he had done in the wake of the Omdurman celebrations, he let it be known that instead of swords of honour he would prefer to be presented with gifts of gold plate or furniture. Those requests were eagerly granted and by the time Kitchener arrived in India he possessed several sumptuous dinner sets, which gave him great pleasure to show off when he entertained.

In the midst of the public adulation there were again those who refused to be charmed by Kitchener's victory in South Africa and who argued that his strategy had been brutal and uncaring. They pointed to the bludgeon of the blockhouse system and the associated sweeps and drives, to the wholesale burning of farms and above all to the introduction of the concentration camps. Today the phrase 'concentration camp' is inextricably bound up with the policies of the Nazi regime in Germany and so emotive is their use that the association of Kitchener's name with their introduction in South Africa would be enough to damn him were it not for the facts. There is no connection between the purpose of the British internment camps in South Africa and the purpose of the Nazi death camps in Germany and eastern Europe; the former were introduced for the protection of the population, the latter for extermination. That said, the British camps in South Africa were far from being places of recreation and should properly be termed internment camps.[25]

As the conflict in South Africa turned gradually into a guerrilla war at the beginning of 1901 both sides realised that Boer women and children were bound to be caught up in the front line of the fighting. Farms were used by the Boers as bases and Kitchener's tactics of farm burning meant that a large proportion of the population would be made homeless, hence the introduction of the protected laagers, or concentration camps, along the main railway routes. At the Middelburg peace talks Kitchener had told Botha that as long as the Boers continued to put pressure on their fellow countrymen to provide help for the commandos, he would be 'forced to take the very unpleasant and repugnant step of bringing in the women and children'.[26] Between then and the war's end 120,000 Boers were herded into fifty camps; of that number 26,000, mainly women and children, died of disease.

The presence of the camps and the high death rate were difficult to keep from the public gaze, even though Kitchener did his utmost to divert attention by constantly offering bland answers to Brodrick's questions. That they did become a matter for public debate was due in no small measure to the resourcefulness and energy of a remarkable woman, Emily Hobhouse, the daughter of a Cornish rector. Kitchener called her a 'bloody woman' and on her second visit to South Africa in October 1901 he had her arrested as a security risk before she could leave her ship in Cape Town harbour. By then, though, she had fulfilled the main points of a task that had begun that January – visiting the camps on behalf of the South African Women and Children's Defence Fund and making public her report. Those findings were not pleasing to the British conscience. 'If only the English people would try to exercise a little imagination [and] picture the whole miserable scene,' she reported back to her committee.[27] Families had been herded into the tented camps and forced to live on a meagre diet, medical facilities were primitive, water was frequently polluted, domestic arrangements squalid and no account had been made of the differing social and cultural backgrounds of the inmates. Many of the Boer families came from the remote areas of the Transvaal, where they lived in basic conditions of isolation: their ideas of domestic hygiene tended to be very different from those held by Boers who lived nearer the towns. In those chaotic conditions disease was endemic – at the time of Hobhouse's visit to the camps 30 per cent of all the children were dead or dying of enteric fever, dysentery, typhoid or malaria, in addition to the illnesses commonly associated with childhood, such as measles, whooping cough and diphtheria. The spectre of so many children being put at risk smacked too much of the Black Death and Emily Hobhouse's findings caused an outcry of righteous anger in the liberal press.

Henry Campbell-Bannerman, the Liberal leader, was moved to call Kitchener's camps the 'methods of barbarism' and, much to the discomfort of the Conservative administration, angry questions began to be asked in the House of Commons. For his part Kitchener preferred not to visit the camps and brushed off Brodrick's questions by telling him that he was told the inhabitants were 'happy enough'. On the question of hygiene he also said that he was considering prosecuting those mothers found neglecting their children. Kitchener looked on the camps as a means to an end and he found the details of administration boring. When political pressure began to build up he was equally happy to release those families who wanted to return to the Boer commandos. In December he wrote to De Wet informing him that 'all women and children at present in our camps who are willing to leave will be sent to your care, and I shall be happy to be informed where you desire that they should be handed over to you'.[28] To Kitchener's satisfaction several families took advantage of the offer for he knew that they would be a burden on De Wet's commandos.

Today in South Africa Kitchener is remembered not as the victor of Paardeberg, nor even as the engineer of the peace of Vereeniging. It is for the concentration camps that his name lives on. Visitors to the museums devoted to the Boer War – which South Africans know as *Tweede Vryheidsoorlog* (Second War of Independence) – are shown the powdered glass that Kitchener is supposed to have ordered to be sprinkled in the sugar given to the inmates of the camps, and there are stories of other outrages – such as poisoned food and fish hooks deliberately inserted in the bully beef. There is no more evidence for believing that Kitchener would have been the agent of such atrocities than there is for believing the other canard of the Boer War, that he shipped out prostitutes from London to Pretoria in order to compromise his senior officers and to discover which of them should be sacked for military inefficiency.[29] In both cases the facts are somewhat different. When the camps were first opened Kitchener ordered that there should be a basic ration scale made up of imported foodstuffs. Much of it was inferior in quality and caused violent stomach upsets that spread rapidly, leaving the Boer women to believe that they had been poisoned. There was also a blue substance in the sugar used as a whitening agent and its presence gave rise to the stories of powdered glass. As for the prostitutes, Kitchener had no need of them: when he purged his staff after taking command he simply marched into the leading hotels in Pretoria and sacked those officers whom he considered to be bar-room loafers.

8

INDIA: COMMANDER-IN-CHIEF

The Boer War had forced Britain to reappraise her imperial position, and with the death of Queen Victoria in 1901 something of the splendour of the Empire seemed to die with her. Gladstone had died in 1898 and, in July 1902, Salisbury retired from office leaving his Conservative administration in the hands of his nephew, A.J. Balfour. Others continued as before – Curzon in India, Cromer in Egypt and, until 1905, Milner in South Africa – but the heady days of Victorian imperial grandeur were ebbing away to be replaced by a more sober and reflective view of Britain's place in the world.[1] For the first time since the conclusion of the Napoleonic wars in 1815 there was an awareness that Britain could no longer stand alone, that other countries had caught up with her and were challenging her late nineteenth-century predominance in world affairs. Germany had begun building a battle fleet to rival the Royal Navy and throughout the conflict in South Africa her sentiments had tended towards the side of the Boers; Italy was now a nation state with interests in the Mediterranean and Near East; Japan had emerged as a world power, as had the United States of America, while Russia continued to threaten India's North-West Frontier. To end her 'splendid isolation' – as the policy had come to be known – Britain concluded ententes with Japan in 1902 and two years later with France, the country with whom she had almost gone to war over Fashoda. It was all a far cry from *The Times*' confident assertion on the day of the Diamond Jubilee celebrations in 1897 that the British

Empire was 'the mightiest and most beneficial empire ever known in the annals of mankind'.[2]

The politicians placed much of the blame for Britain's predicament on the army. Quite apart from the horrors of 'Black Week' in 1899 there was much else to deplore. Having effectively defeated the Boers in the field by May 1900 the army and its generals had then taken another two years to grind their enemy into submission. Reforms were now imperative and it was for that reason that Brodrick had told Kitchener that he would not be able to avoid the War Office for ever. For his part Kitchener had already admitted to Lady Cranborne that he would rather sweep a crossing than work with politicians at the War Office. At this stage in his career he was not prepared to risk his reputation for the grind of office work in London. Another consideration may have prompted him to refuse to be part of the reorganisation of the army: by then it was more than a quarter of a century since he had lived in Britain and in that period he had lost touch with day-to-day political life. It was not surprising that Kitchener wanted to spend the post-war years away from Whitehall in the relative calm of India.

Before leaving Britain in the autumn of 1902 Kitchener had made it clear to Curzon and to the India Office that he intended to enjoy his full leave before taking up his new appointment in India and he used that time well. At Hatfield he renewed and strengthened his friendship with Lady Cranborne, whose political influence was to be crucial in the months to come. In the following year she became the 4th Marchioness of Salisbury on her husband's accession to the title. Other aristocratic families also sought him as a guest: the Cowpers entertained him at Panshanger; the new Prime Minister, Balfour, at Whittingehame, his residence in East Lothian; and Kitchener also surfaced again in Lord Londonderry's circle, visiting him at his seats at Mount Stewart in Northern Ireland and Wynford Park near Stockton-on-Tees. Like Lady Cranborne, Lord Londonderry's wife Theresa was a brilliant hostess and inveterate string-puller who had taken Kitchener under her wing during his summer absences from Egypt and who had pressed his claims consistently in political circles. Kitchener owed much to the Londonderrys and it had even crossed his mind to enter into a matrimonial alliance with that great family. It had been put to him on many an occasion that if he wanted a career at home his ambitions would be assisted by the possession of a London residence and a wealthy wife and for some time he had toyed with the idea of proposing to Londonderry's daughter, Helen Mary Theresa.[3] Whether or not he actually proposed to her is unknown, but in 1902 she married the Earl of Ilchester. Pandeli Ralli put forward the name of a wealthy Greek heiress, a suggestion that did not appeal to Kitchener, who then put a stop to all further talk of arranged marriages. He was, as he had admitted to Millie all those years ago, her 'affectionate brother, unmarried and unlikely to be'.

Kitchener left for India on 17 October and travelled through Paris and Rome to Egypt, where he stayed with Cromer in order to visit the Aswan Dam and the newly built Gordon Memorial College in Khartoum. At the end of November he arrived in Bombay to take up the post of Commander-in-Chief of the army in India, second only in imperial significance to the Viceroy. Kitchener must have felt that the appointment was a watershed in his life, that his achievements marked him as a man whose destiny had been achieved for, as the liner carrying him to India made its way across the Red Sea, he took the opportunity to throw his collected correspondence overboard. From a historical point of view it was an unfortunate decision but from Kitchener's standpoint it may have seemed that he owed posterity nothing and that he had created a legend in his own lifetime.

The man who greeted him on his arrival in India probably felt the same way about himself. Kitchener had met George Curzon on several occasions at Hatfield and Panshanger and warmed to him, liking the man for his orderly mind and patrician temperament. More significantly, he liked his attractive American wife, Mary, whom he had first met at a ball in Egypt in 1892 and who had made an immediate impression on him. The daughter of a Chicago businessman, Levy Z. Leiter, Mary was beautiful, poised and wealthy, and she became another politically powerful lady to whom Kitchener was attracted. Like her husband she was determined that Kitchener's presence in India should add to the lustre of Curzon's reign as Viceroy and ever since they had met at

Hatfield in December 1898 there had been a tacit understanding that all three would meet up again in the near future. Curzon, who was then on the point of leaving for India, was greatly touched to receive a letter from Kitchener in which was enclosed 'a photo for Lady Curzon, to remind her of the man who means to take her down to dinner some day in India'.[4]

Since his triumph at Omdurman Kitchener had been determined to achieve the India command and in Curzon he had found a ready ally for his ambitions. As early as March 1900 it had been agreed that Curzon could have Kitchener once hostilities ceased in South Africa, even though Brodrick, one of Curzon's oldest friends, had warned him that India would never be able to hold the two men at the same time. Another friend, Sir Clinton Dawkins, a partner in the banking firm of J.P. Morgan who had known Kitchener while serving in Egypt as under-secretary for finance, offered even more candid advice: '(K) is spoken of as a great organiser, and with justice, is a great organiser in the sense that he can hold 100 threads in his hands and 1,000 details in his head, but that he is a great centraliser, and has very little appreciation of the proper organisation of a great administration.'[5] Curzon, though, did not accept the insights of either of his two old friends. Kitchener, he said, could be controlled; the soldier's lack of intellectual poise and his clumsy political interventions would be no match for the precision and agility of Curzon's own mind. Only Lady Curzon perhaps sensed danger and understood the true nature of the problem of two self-willed men working in tandem when she wrote to Kitchener shortly before he left London, entreating him to be gentle. 'I suppose you know that the prayer of the soldier [Indian Army] has been that the two giants will fall out – and it will be a grief for them to see you work in harmony, and to know the intense satisfaction it is to George that you are here at last.'[6]

Curzon was the eldest son of Lord Scarsdale, whose family seat was the elegant Adam mansion of Kedlestone Hall in Derbyshire. At Eton and later at Balliol he distinguished himself by his intellectual precocity and early conceived the ambition of becoming Viceroy of India before proceeding to take over the office of Prime Minister. He expected nothing less of himself and when, before he was forty, he had achieved his first goal there seemed little reason why he should not go on to become one of the greatest men of his generation. Curzon had achieved his successes by dint of hard work, intellectual ability and a refusal to allow himself to be overcome by the physical discomfort caused by a curvature to his spine. The problem had emerged while he was an undergraduate at Oxford and the pain caused by his partially crippled spine was to be a lifelong problem that he bore with great fortitude. Haughty in his behaviour to his subordinates, cunning in his dealings with politicians, an intellectual snob possessed of a high sense of purpose, Curzon was as uncompromising a person as Kitchener. But he had a blind spot in his evaluation of his coevals, and in Kitchener's case that was to prove disastrous. Within a half year of Kitchener's arrival in India, Curzon wrote to the Secretary of State for India, Lord George Hamilton, in the deprecating terms he used to employ when he wanted others to know that he was humiliating a colleague:

> Kitchener is an extraordinarily lonely man: being unmarried, he has nobody in his house except young officers greatly his inferiors in age and standing; he takes no advice from anybody; he spends the whole day in thinking over his own subjects and formulating great and daring schemes; he will not go and talk them over with the Military Department because he looks upon the latter as his sworn foe; he will not make friends with other Members of the Government, some of whom he cordially despises and openly criticises; he stands aloof and alone, a molten mass of devouring energy and burning ambition, without anybody to control or guide it in the right direction.[7]

Never was the description of a friend and close colleague so out of touch with reality. Kitchener was indeed consumed by 'burning ambition' and driven by 'devouring energy' but he was certainly neither 'lonely' nor 'alone'. At Treasury Gate, his official residence in Calcutta and later at Snowdon, his villa in Simla, Kitchener had thrown himself quickly into the social whirl and his dinner parties soon became a byword for culinary and social excellence. No detail, however small, was allowed to escape Kitchener's notice; before each party the dinner table would be inspected and woe betide the servant who made a mistake in the settings. Curzon's remarks about the members of his household was a cheap jibe. 'The Brat' was still with him as his ADC and he had appointed two other aides, both socially and politically well connected, R.J. Marker and Victor Brooke, the elder brother of the future Lord Alanbrooke. The experienced Hubert Hamilton joined him as his military secretary until 1905, when he was succeeded by William Birdwood, to complete a formidable household staff. With his aides he could relax and gossip about the social scene in India and recreations that he enjoyed, but when the time came for them to show their loyalty they displayed a fanatical belief in Kitchener that was matched only by their denigration of Curzon. More importantly from Kitchener's point of view, they did not keep their opinions to themselves. 'Conk' Marker had links to *The Times*, and his leaking of sensitive documents was to be a vital factor in the quarrel that was about to break out with Curzon. With his own lines of communication to the press and to Balfour's Cabinet secure, Kitchener had little need to befriend the members of the government of India or to give his approval to the officials of its Military Department.

To understand why two men, friends of long standing and united in their ideals of service to Empire, should have crossed swords, one has to turn to the labyrinthine ways in which the British rulers controlled their army in India. In essence, the Viceroy represented the British monarch and ruled on behalf of Parliament; the army was, therefore, subordinate to him. The Commander-in-Chief held the supreme executive control of the army and was responsible for its overall direction, including collection of intelligence, deployment of troops, discipline, promotion and training. However, the administration of the army – the control of its finances, the ordering of ordnance and the management of transport and supplies – was vested in the Military Member of the Viceroy's Council. The system of dual control had been worked out in Roberts's day to allow the Viceroy to have a military adviser while the Commander-in-Chief was absent on the many manoeuvres and inspections that took him away from the centre of government in Calcutta or Simla. It also maintained the constitutional point that the head of the army should not also be a politician. In theory, and given goodwill, it should have worked, but two related weaknesses had been built into the system. Firstly, the Military Member was a soldier, an officer lower in rank to the Commander-in-Chief; and secondly, the Commander-in-Chief was obliged to pass all policy proposals to the Military Member for sanctioning by the Viceroy. In the days of Kitchener's predecessor, General Sir Arthur Power Palmer, Curzon had made the machine run effectively enough, but the arrival of the new Commander-in-Chief soon revealed its flaws.

From William Birdwood, who had begun his career in the Indian Army and who had served in South Africa, Kitchener had learned something of the nature of dual control, but the lesson had not impressed him. While passing through Egypt, Kitchener had admitted to Cromer that his first initiative in India would be to abolish dual control and unite the positions of Commander-in-Chief and the Military Member, a proposal that his former political chief advised him to treat cautiously. Kitchener, though, was not the man to exercise prudence in such matters and within weeks of his arrival was pestering Curzon vigorously with ideas for reforming the terms of his command.

Curzon, who was still charmed to have Kitchener at his right hand, parried the demands skilfully and advised his new Commander-in-Chief to bide his time and to see how the system worked before he tampered with it. Such advice was, of course, anathema to Kitchener, who threw himself into finding other means of achieving his aims. 'Kitchener is mad keen about everything here,' Curzon enthused to Sir Schomberg MacDonnell, Balfour's private secretary. 'I never met so concentrated a man. He uses an argument. You answer him. He repeats it. You give him a second reply, even more cogent than the first. He repeats it again. You demolish him. He repeats it without alteration a third time. But he is agreeable as he is obstinate, and everyone here likes him.'[8] Once again Curzon was deceiving himself. Far from being demolished, Kitchener was grumbling secretly to Roberts that he found the military administration in India a gimcrack affair and that he was determined to change it: 'The only thing that excites officials out here is to get some of their relations or friends into some billet or other, or to arrange that some particular lady is stationed where they are.'[9]

What Curzon seemed not to have realised was that Kitchener could not operate unless he was fully in charge, that he was secretive by nature and disliked delegating responsibility. In Sudan and South Africa Kitchener had exercised supreme command; no less was going to suit him in India. It had also escaped Curzon's attention that Kitchener despised the standing Military Member, Major-General Sir Edmund Elles, a gunner who had previously served as Adjutant-General in India but had little operational experience.

There was one other weakness in Curzon's attempt to make Kitchener bow to his will: the opinion of the army in India. When it had been announced that Kitchener was to be the new Commander-in-Chief the army had treated the news as a bad joke. Palmer had spread around Lyttelton's nickname – 'K of Chaos' – maliciously and the notion that an officer devoid of Indian experience should be their new commander was met with incredulity.

Between then and the end of 1902 there had been a sea change in those opinions with the Viceroy taking Kitchener's place as the butt of the army's hostility. 'During my first two years in the country I found that Lord Curzon was very much disliked by the rank and file of the Army who all agreed that he was giving the natives too much rope.'[10] That is the disinterested voice of Frank Richards, at the time a private in the Royal Welch Fusiliers. From his reminiscences and the evidence of others it is clear that off-hand cruelty to Indian servants was the norm and that British soldiers in India expected to be allowed to maltreat 'bloody natives who claimed to be his brothers and equals'.[11] Curzon, to his credit, was determined that his Indian subjects should not be the victims of violence and neglect, 'I will not be party to any of the scandalous hushing up of bad cases of which there is too much in this country, or to the theory that a white man may kick or batter a black man to death with impunity because he is only "a damned nigger".'[12] He kept his word: after a Burmese woman was raped brutally by British soldiers in Rangoon in the summer of 1899 he had announced that any soldiers involved in similar incidents would be dealt with severely.

The move, far from winning him popularity for his sense of justice, only alienated him from some elements of British society in India and

INDIA: COMMANDER-IN-CHIEF

paved the way for further confrontation. In April 1902 the 9th Lancers arrived back in India after service in the Boer War and their homecoming was a signal for a drinking party that got out of control. Following a night's revels an Indian cook was beaten to death by two troopers of the 9th and the affair was covered up by the regiment. This was a great mistake, for when the victim's family complained Curzon lambasted the commanding officer of the 9th Lancers, accusing him of evasion and lack of candour. There was to be no 'scandalous hushing up'; instead the regiment was to receive a collective punishment with all leave being cancelled for nine months. The reprisals were not long in coming. The cavalry officers were well connected and they saw to it that Curzon was castigated for his rash decision. Such punishment, they argued, would only lower British prestige in India and make the white man a laughing stock at a time when the first stirrings of nationalist aspiration were being heard. Of course, Curzon's action survives as a monument to justice and decency but in the eyes of the 9th Lancers it betrayed him as an 'Indian-lover', someone who was willing to forfeit the strength of the British rule in order to gain a fleeting popularity. The regiment bore its disgrace in silence but at the Durbar in January 1903 – the celebration of the coronation of Edward VII as King-Emperor – the huge British crowd cheered the 9th Lancers as they rode by in the parade.

With the army sulking and with Kitchener demanding full control of his command, a showdown between the two men could not be avoided. There was hardly a Briton or an Indian who did not know of the enmity that had by now grown up between the two men, which in time came to be known as the battle between the Lord of the Realm (*Mulki Lat*) and the Lord of the Sword (*Jangi Lat*).[13]

To begin with, and in spite of their differences of opinion, relations between Kitchener and Curzon had been reasonably cordial. Kitchener told Lady Cranborne that Curzon was 'as kind as possible' and Curzon praised Kitchener's 'honesty and directness'. But by February an army order bearing Kitchener's signature was due to be issued by Elles, who had not taken the trouble to inform the Commander-in-Chief of its contents, a minor piece of discourtesy that Kitchener chose to turn into a slight. He demanded that Elles be sacked and threatened to resign unless his wishes were met. Curzon managed to smooth ruffled feathers but he was appalled by the reaction, not least because resignation was a threat he himself liked to use when thwarted in his plans. Then Kitchener set off on a tour of the frontier provinces, revelling in the freedom of riding over the long distances with his small staff, and basking in the acclaim that met him wherever he went: it was his prerogative to make a tour of inspection but it only served to remind Curzon that Kitchener's reputation stood higher than his.

Kitchener had promised sulkily that he would see the system in action before interfering with its workings, but all the while he schemed relentlessly to end dual control and to bring about Elles's downfall. Kitchener did not hesitate to use his big guns in demolishing his adversary. Roberts was kept in constant touch with his thinking, a discovery that led Curzon to rebuke Kitchener for passing signals behind his back relating to the control of the army in India. By way of revenge Curzon asked secretly for the army's cypher book so that he could intercept Kitchener's telegrams; what he did not know at that time was the extent of Kitchener's correspondence with Lady Cranborne, which was designed to be 'quite private' and which went through non-military channels. Slowly but surely Kitchener had been building up a case with her in the knowledge that the essential background information on dual control and his thoughts on the matter would be fed by her husband to Balfour, the final arbiter of the question.

Kitchener's dislike of Elles reached a new pitch at the end of May when the Military Member made a number of changes, largely of a grammatical nature, to an army order drafted by him and failed to give any notice of his emendations. Once again Kitchener threatened resignation; once again Curzon was forced to make peace. By then the Viceroy had grown used to the idea that neither the Cabinet nor the British public would stand for Kitchener standing down on a point of principle. On 4 June he told Hamilton gloomily that 'all sorts of fresh combats are ahead to which I look forward with an almost sickening apprehension'.[14]

Two further incidents, both of a private nature, helped to widen the rift between the two men. As with the earlier disagreements both were matters involving courtesy and pride but in that highly charged atmosphere both were blown up out of all proportion to their original significance. The Curzons liked to entertain sumptuously, Curzon believing that his reign as Viceroy should be remembered for the scale and drama of his public appearances: he also insisted on such occasions that protocol and precedence be observed. So, too, did Kitchener. During the hot season the Viceroy and his staff escaped each year to Simla to avoid the heat of the plains. There, in the shadow of the Himalayas, the British had erected an artificial English town and had brought into being a society that thrived on the minutiae of protocol, intrigue, gossip and an endless round of parties and balls. At one ball given that May in Viceregal Lodge, the Viceroy's rambling Gothic summer residence, the staff forgot to set a place for the Commander-in-Chief at the Viceroy's supper table. For a man who inspected personally his own table settings it was seen as a deliberate insult and in a fit of pique Kitchener ordered up his carriage. Without a word of explanation to anyone he drove off furiously into the night. Had he been less impetuous the matter could have been laughed off but Kitchener's reaction only made the incident seem worse than it really was and so the story grew, to be repeated and embellished by Simla's gossip-loving community.

'Now India is a place beyond all others where one must not take things too seriously', wrote Rudyard Kipling of hill station life. The problem was that Kitchener did and he brooded over the supper party incident. His temper was not improved when he discovered that Marker had offered his hand and had then been rejected by Daisy (Marguerite) Leiter, Mary Curzon's sister. To the Kitchener camp it seemed as if their man had been slighted and the 'insult' was magnified in their eyes when the distraught Marker asked to be allowed to resign his post as ADC in order to return home. From all accounts Lady Curzon's American sisters had behaved badly when they visited Simla, calling Curzon by his Christian name in public and gossiping with dancing partners about domestic life in Viceregal Lodge. Their high-spirited and naive behaviour had raised a few eyebrows but flirting and 'cool season engagements' were commonplace and no one would have given the Marker incident another thought had not Kitchener decided to side with his aide and to allow him to return home. (Back in London Marker was to become secretary to H.O. Arnold-Foster, the Secretary of State for War, and an important conduit of leaked information.)

Curzon was rightly alarmed by both incidents and by Kitchener's seemingly intransigent views on army reform. He told Brodrick, now Secretary for India, that he wished that Kitchener would show some tact, and to Mary he admitted that his Commander-in-Chief had become a menace to the well-being of British rule in India; but he understood, too, his impotence in the matter. It was he who had demanded Kitchener's presence in India and any disruption of that relationship would seem like ill will on his part. Fortunately for him, Kitchener's differences did not extend to Lady Curzon. To help heal the breach over the supper party incident she presented him with a pair of gold mustard pots to enhance his gold dinner plate. She also took to writing him discreet notes, asking him to forgive and forget for old times' sake and to be kind to her husband. 'Please do not answer,' she reminded him in a typical letter. 'Indeed there is no answer and I have only put in a human plea for a peaceful Finale to this miserable experience.'[15] Shortly before she went home on leave early in 1904, thinking her husband would not accept another term as Viceroy, she sent Kitchener three splendid candlesticks for his next birthday, 'when you will be taking a new Lady Viceroy down to dinner,' – her echo of Kitchener's hopeful words at Hatfield five years earlier being a sad reminder of happier days together.[16] After the upsets of Simla they spent several days at Naldera, the Viceroy's tented camp, where Kitchener was a constant visitor. 'A fine character with a perfect scorn of popularity,' was Lady Curzon's view of their military guest and she was also astute enough to see that Kitchener's determination was as tenacious as her husband's, thus making her intervention all the more vital to Curzon's cause.[17] Lady Curzon's charm seems to have worked for, by the middle of the year, Curzon was claiming that 'not a cloud flecks the sky' and that Kitchener had settled down to a bout of hard work in the best interests of the army. As far as the Viceroy was concerned, harmony had been restored; even Kitchener joined in the goodwill by telling Lady Cranborne on 1 July that Curzon was a 'first-rate' Viceroy and that all was well between them.

Lady Curzon's beauty and tranquillity – 'the romantic ideal' according to one witness – made her a delightful companion and her liking for Kitchener seems to have been genuine enough – 'there is a sort of bracing north wind of resolution and strenuousness about him, and a gentle spot about a woman which a woman is always quick to find.'[18] Fine words, but Kitchener was well aware that Curzon's term of office was coming to an end and he clung to the hope that a new Viceroy would be appointed who would be more amenable to his wishes. When Curzon announced in August that he would accept a further term as Viceroy, Kitchener was furious and his suspicions about Curzon's motives for accepting the extension were compounded when the Viceroy made it known that he would be taking six months' leave of absence. In Kitchener's book that was Curzon's chance to make political capital in London; to counter any such gains Kitchener immediately doubled his efforts to get his own way at home. Lady Salisbury, as Lady Cranborne had now become, remained his staunchest ally and her heart went out to him when he pleaded, somewhat sanctimoniously in the circumstances, that he wished that he had been 'created so that [I] could look on senseless obstructions, useless delays and multiplication of work with perfect equanimity'.[19] Her response was immediate – she sent a note from her husband, marked 'very private' requesting that Kitchener should find a way of providing the Prime Minister with more complete and up to date information about the position in India. For the beleaguered Kitchener it was a heart-warming document:

> A.J.B[alfour] is very much concerned about the situation in India. He is much hampered because the information K. sends is secret, and he therefore can't use it. He is doing his best to act through Roberts in order that the Govt. of India may be approached, officially or semi-officially, and an opportunity afforded for that Govt. to give, officially or semi-officially, this information which K. has given secretly to you. A.J.B. earnestly hopes that K. will do his best to make the effort successful.[20]

Curzon was right to suspect that Kitchener was working behind his back; but he still thought he could outwit him and that he could improve his own position while on leave. Unfortunately for those hopes, his long-standing friendship with Brodrick was on the wane and even Balfour was now inclined to admit that the reappointment to India had been a mistake. Cabinet concern was expressing itself not only over the vexed question of dual control but also, more strongly, over the partition of Bengal and Curzon's dealings with Afghanistan and the problem of frontier defence. It was this latter point that reopened the breach between Kitchener and Curzon. As part of his brief Kitchener had undertaken a study of the defence of India in the north-west, with particular regard for the possibility of Russian aggression. By June 1904 he had prepared a carefully worded document that was placed before the Committee of Imperial Defence in London while Curzon was home on leave. The memorandum, like many of Kitchener's policy documents, was strongly worded and to Curzon's mortification it placed the entire blame for the deficiencies in India's defence on the policy of dual control. That was not all: he had written at the same time to Brodrick underlining his dismay as to what would befall India were Russia to launch an attack in the north-west:

> There is no doubt if we had a big war on the frontier there would be a fearful crash and 'show-up' here. A system under which Transport, Supply, Remounts, Ordnance are entirely divorced from the executive command of the Army, and placed under an independent authority, is one which must cause an entire reorganisation as soon as war is declared, rather late to begin some people think … I am working as hard as I can … but I cannot help feeling what will be the good of having well trained and organised troops if they have not got ammunition, guns, horses, transport, and have to put up with defective supplies.[21]

This was a scenario that had long haunted British politicians – an undefended India lying at the mercy of Russian hordes – but Kitchener's memorandum also placed the Cabinet in another kind of quandary. To side with Kitchener's point of view must mean the resignation of Curzon; yet if Kitchener were to resign – a course he threatened again in September – the government could well be brought down by public outrage. An added complication was that Roberts, the only real expert on the matter, tended to side with Curzon, as he doubted whether Kitchener could combine successfully the two senior military offices in India. As the quarrel proceeded to its climax, Roberts shifted his opinions to suit Kitchener and throughout maintained a secret correspondence with his Indian commander. 'Please remember that your letters are treated in absolute confidence so write as openly as you like,' he had told him as early as June 1903.[22] Eventually, Kitchener's paper was taken off the agenda and by way of compromise Balfour suggested to Curzon that he should review the situation on his return to India at the end of the year.

Kitchener's own position had undoubtedly been strengthened, however: Balfour was being briefed by Lady Salisbury; Brodrick had abandoned the Curzon camp; and to cap it all, in October, Russia, which had gone to war earlier that year with Japan, almost dragged Britain into conflict. The Imperial Russian Navy, on its way from the Baltic to the Pacific, opened fire on British fishing trawlers on the Dogger Bank in the North Sea in the mistaken belief that they were Japanese gunboats. War with Russia suddenly became a possibility: the Royal Navy's Home Fleet was mobilised and the popular press clamoured for revenge. If Britain went to war, India's security would be threatened and in those circumstances it was impossible for Kitchener, Britain's greatest soldier, to resign on a point of procedure. 'As to power,' Kitchener told Lady Salisbury at the beginning of 1903, 'I do not want any more power outside the army, but I do want power to do good in the army; if I am incapable, why appoint me; if I fail, get rid of me, but why keep on a dead level of efficiency or drift backwards because you won't trust the person you appointed to do good?'[23]

Backed by the knowledge that the Cabinet had swung in his direction, Kitchener determined to bring the matter of dual control to a head with Curzon. He wanted, too, to destroy Elles, whom he found too 'narrow-minded and bigoted to a degree to be trusted' and he chose as his instrument a memorandum that he issued on New Year's Day 1905 calling for Elles's removal and for a complete reorganisation of the army in India.[24] The 'faulty, inefficient and incapable' machine that ran the army had to be rebuilt with the following three criteria in mind:

1. Dual control in the Army and the duplication of work in the Military Offices must cease.
2. The chief Military adviser must have direct access to the Viceroy and Government of India, without the intervention of an independent Military channel which only causes misinterpretation and distortion of the views put forward.
3. That under the supreme control of the Viceroy and Government of India the power of control over the Army must be conferred where responsibility is held to be.[25]

The memorandum was accompanied to Curzon's office with a note from Kitchener saying that he would resign unless dual control were ended, and further copies were despatched secretly to Marker in London.

Before the papers were discussed in Council, Elles was given the opportunity of replying to Kitchener's memorandum and of defending his own position. Patiently, he rehearsed the familiar arguments, that the Commander-in-Chief was responsible for running the army, the Military Member for organising it; no one man, he claimed, could perform both functions. Curzon went one better. In a brilliant summary of both positions he praised Kitchener as Britain's greatest military strategist and then went on to demolish his argument, listing his main points forcefully: that the Viceroy needed a Military Member to give advice to him during the Commander-in-Chief's absences; that under the constitution the Military Member was the legal representative of the government of India; and, finally, that any attempt to alter the status quo would result in the gradual evolution of a military dictatorship. All three papers were printed, and submitted to the Viceroy's Council on 10 March. Elles spoke first and defended his position eloquently before giving the floor to Kitchener. To everyone's astonishment Kitchener only made a brief comment stating that his case was contained in his paper and that he had nothing further to add. Kitchener never shone in debate but on this occasion it is possible that he realised that the vote would go against him and that silence was the best answer.

If so, Kitchener was correct in his evaluation. Curzon won the day and triumphantly sent a despatch to London outlining Kitchener's proposals and his Council's unanimous rejection of them. To this document

Kitchener was permitted to add a codicil recording his dissent from the Council's decision. In a moment of ill-conceived bravado Curzon described his adversary as 'a caged lion, dashing his bruised and lacerated head against the bars': but once again he was deluding himself. Kitchener might have lost the battle but he still had not lost the war. He had prepared his ground too well to allow the outcome of a single battle to deflect his purpose. The tenor of his correspondence with Lady Salisbury was now not only anti-dual control but also anti-Curzon; through Marker he had leaked enough confidential information to *The Times* to bring it on to his side, and he knew that the Cabinet was in his pocket. Just as he expected, Balfour attempted a disingenuous compromise that gave him more or less everything that he wanted. The Cabinet, on the recommendation of a sub-committee, decided that the Commander-in-Chief would be granted direct access to the Viceroy without having to go through the Military Member, who would now be counted as a civilian and would be known as the Military Supply Member; that the Commander-in-Chief would take over all administrative duties with the exception of supply and transport; and that the Military Supply Member would only advise the Viceroy on matters concerning finance. Curzon was further informed on 31 May that he would have to bow to the Cabinet's authority and that he would also have to accept the resignation of Sir Edmund Elles.

For Kitchener it was a sweeping victory. Against the wishes of the entire Viceroy's Council the Cabinet had given its assent to one man's wishes, for although dual control had not been rescinded, Kitchener had acquired most of the powers that he wanted. The ignominy of Balfour's position over dual control is revealed when it is compared to his government's thinking over the military position in Britain. In the previous year the Conservative government accepted one of the main proposals contained in the Esher Report on the reorganisation of the British Army, namely the abolition of the post of Commander-in-Chief and the division of War Office responsibilities under an Army Council. In other words, while Balfour and Brodrick were amongst those who accepted that no single person should control every aspect of army organisation in Britain, they were prepared to believe that such a system could be made to work in India.

Even at this late stage all might have been well had Curzon decided to live with the new arrangements: but in an evil hour he interviewed Kitchener on 25 June and stated baldly that he would resign unless Brodrick was told that the Military Supply Member should revert to the old title and be permitted to wear uniform. Curzon's resignation was something that Kitchener desired greatly and from Marker he had been led to believe that the Cabinet was prepared to let the Viceroy follow such a course should he ever propose it. However, common sense also suggested that both men should compromise but both were in such a highly charged and emotional state that coherent argument became impossible and it was Curzon who reached flashpoint first. According to Kitchener's evidence, Curzon, usually so aloof, broke down, burst into tears and demanded that his Commander-in-Chief support him. Kitchener, who had been 'prancing up and down his room talking to him very straight on the subject' was so completely taken aback by this turnabout that to his mild astonishment he submitted to Curzon's wishes. Later Kitchener admitted to Lady Salisbury that 'when he [Curzon] collapsed I rather lost my head' and that he thoroughly regretted his moment of kindness.[26] After he had pulled himself together Curzon put the episode at the back of his mind and set about trying to recover his position. On 18 July he rose in the Council and attacked the Cabinet for imposing a new form of military administration contrary to the wishes of his legislation. He ended up by claiming that thanks to his intervention the post of Military Supply Member had been converted to one of greater efficiency, a remark that was untrue and shocked Kitchener.

The end was not long in coming. In August Curzon thought to test his authority by insisting that his candidate, Major-General Sir Edmund Barrow, Elles's deputy, be appointed the Military Supply Member but the move was blocked by Brodrick, who ordered that Kitchener's wishes should be taken into account. (Brodrick had been told that Kitchener would never accept Barrow.) Forced into a corner, Curzon resigned on 12 August on the constitutional point that it was not up to the Commander-in-Chief to appoint his own Military Supply Member. The resignation was accepted and just over a fortnight later Lord Minto was appointed Viceroy in his stead. With their relationship now plumbing the depths, Kitchener and Curzon clashed again a few days later when the Viceroy accused Kitchener of not reading a document concerning the number of ordnance officers who would come under his control. Kitchener denied ever having seen the file but Curzon continued to press the point. Eventually, when the file was found in Kitchener's office, Curzon's demeanour suggested to Kitchener that he had been called a liar. 'In old days I suppose I should have called him out and shot him like a dog for his grossly insulting letter,' he told Lady Salisbury.[27]

Curzon stayed on in India until the autumn in order to welcome the Prince of Wales on his state visit to the country, a piece of hubris that cost him many friends. When he left on 23 October Kitchener had been persuaded by the intervention of Mary Curzon to take part in their final farewell to Simla but it turned out to be a less than edifying occasion. Surrounded by his loyal staff and in full dress uniform, Kitchener wordlessly shook the hand of the retiring Viceroy before turning to Lady Curzon and offering a simple 'goodbye'. Lady Curzon described the moment as being one of the most painful she had ever endured. A year later she was dead and her husband, first abandoned by the Conservatives, then ignored by the Liberals who came to power in 1906, was destined to spend many years in the political wilderness.

Before Curzon left India he determined to make public the documents relating to the row that would show the extent of Kitchener's secret correspondences. In this he was prevented from acting by the King, but he was given permission to publish the telegram of resignation containing his side of the argument. Kitchener insisted correctly that he should be offered the right of reply and the papers, together with a rejoinder by Curzon, were published in the London press on 25 August 1905. Three days later *The Times* called their publication a 'startling and unedifying spectacle' but although both men were blamed, the greater opprobrium was heaped upon Curzon, whose rejoinder was described as 'an offence against the public interest'. Marker had prepared the ground well. Only the *Spectator*, long antagonistic to Kitchener, spoke up for the Viceroy, declaring in an editorial of 2 September that the Commander-in-Chief had been given too much rope and that the thought of the army interfering in politics was an anathema to most right-thinking Englishmen. Not only was the exhibition of two distinguished men locked in public combat distasteful, the writer continued, but Kitchener had acted in a way injurious to the good of Empire:

> Lord Kitchener had just won his great controversy, to the injury of the future of India we think, but doubtless to his own contentment, and he should have rested on his laurels, and not have tried to jump on his opponent.[28]

The editorial added that the quarrel would give comfort to Indian nationalists, a theme taken up by other newspapers, but the *Spectator* remained a lone voice in censuring Kitchener. Most commentators were unanimous in their relief that the struggle was over and that Kitchener had come out on top, a victory described in some quarters as his greatest since Omdurman. It certainly did not harm his reputation. Within a year Brodrick, then out of power but still implacably hostile to Curzon, was congratulating Kitchener on 'how well the new organisation is going' and after the Prince of Wales had visited him during the winter of 1905–06 his letter of thanks recorded his delight 'that everything connected with the new system is working so smoothly and that you, the Viceroy, and the Secretary of State are so much in accord. It must be a sad disappointment to those who prophesied every evil result'.[29]

So massive in scale had this conflict been and so pre-eminent its protagonists that it tended to overshadow Kitchener's other achievements in India. These were not inconsiderable. He founded a staff college at Quetta based upon the British model at Camberley, having revised his belief that an army did not need officers well versed in strategy and administration. The war in South Africa had displayed to him the necessity of a twentieth-century army having a general staff and the Japanese victory over Russia in 1905 had brought home the need for a firm control of operations. Ian Hamilton, the official British observer at that war, had been a constant correspondent and his letters had dwelt on the high standard of the Japanese General Staff.

In India, a scheme for renumbering the Indian regiments and strengthening the more warlike Punjabi units was well received by all but the old guard, and, encouraged by the response, Kitchener proceeded to make a radical reorganisation of the army's divisions. Five were allotted to the North Command and four to the Southern Command, each of the nine divisional commanders being made responsible for the training of their men in readiness for war which, it was assumed, would be fought on the North-West Frontier. The deployment of the divisions allowed each to back up its neighbour, and, in order to improve transportation in time of war, Kitchener toyed with the idea of establishing a new railway network.

These were radical reforms as, following the Indian Mutiny of 1857, previous commanders were obsessed with the threat of insurrection and had maintained the army primarily as an instrument of internal control, if an imperfect one. Never far away from any Indian army cantonment was a British garrison, Indian units were not allowed artillery and the sepoys were armed with rifles of an earlier issue than those provided for their British counterparts. Kitchener changed all that. Sepoys were equipped with Lee-Metfords and, 'without any flourish of trumpets', steps were taken for the gradual process of commissioning Indian officers. The Mutiny, Kitchener said, should be forgotten and Indian and British soldiers should work in harmony. To that end he also reorganised the brigade structure so that each division should contain one British brigade to two Indian.

Much good work was done to improve the conditions of employment enjoyed by British officers in Indian regiments, many of whom had plumped for Indian service because expenses were lower than they might have been in a comparable British regiment. Levels of pay were increased for the sepoys and Kitchener also saw to it that more grants were made available for the purchase of kit, which in many regiments could be costly. Neither did he neglect his men's moral welfare. In October 1905 he issued a proclamation urging the British soldiers in India to forego the pleasures of the brothel and warning them of the terrors of venereal disease. Time might hang heavy on their hands, he admitted, but sport and regular exercise should ward off the temptations of physical lust. To those who succumbed – and many regiments maintained official brothels with prostitutes examined regularly by army doctors – Kitchener had nothing but contempt. 'What would your mothers, your sisters and your friends at home think of you if they saw you in hospital, degraded by this cause?' As a counter-attraction 'to those imprudent and reckless impulses that so often lead men astray' Kitchener instituted various sporting competitions and proficiency tests that he hoped would keep his men on the path of virtue.[30]

India gave its return in other ways. From the beginning of his appointment Kitchener determined that his dinner parties and dances should be second to none in their grandeur and he took great pains to lavish the best of hospitality on his guests. 'It was so sad saying goodbye yesterday and to think all our charming days are over,' wrote Lady Portland, who stayed with Kitchener in Calcutta. 'It seems like some sort of lovely dream now – and how one longs to have some means of fixing it in reality!'[31] The dream that Kitchener had created, though, was no illusion. His residence at Treasury Gate was refurbished and the gardens relaid with myriad flowers and shrubs supplied by the nearby Botanical Gardens. He also built an orchid house, but the changes he made in Calcutta were only a prelude to the splendour that was to be visited upon Simla.

For years, Snowdon, the Commander-in-Chief's bungalow, had been a drab hideaway offering little in the way of amenities for comfort or relaxation. As it was only a temporary residence the army supply department had never thought to beautify it, thinking that the supreme commander was above such trifles. That was before Kitchener entered their lives – by June 1907 he was able to boast to Lady Roberts that, 'I shall set up as a House Decorator when I leave here.'[32] Employing his usual energy Kitchener turned the house topsy-turvy, first of all enlarging the hall by removing a room and creating an 'L'-shaped space adorned with walnut panelling. Then he turned his attention to the dining room, for which he manufactured special lights to be placed behind the cornices. No detail was too small to escape his attention and he spared no one in his efforts to make Snowdon a place of beauty. William Birdwood, now on Kitchener's staff as military secretary, remembered that the aides had to accustom themselves to making vast amounts of papier mâché out of discarded files to create the decorative cornices for the ceiling, which was copied from Hatfield. A ballroom was added and the drawing room was designed and furnished by Sardar Ram Singh, the artist who succeeded Lockwood Kipling, Rudyard's father, as head of the School of Arts in Lahore. 'People are, I think, often inclined to say that room is too florid,' remarked Birdwood primly, 'and that was perhaps Lord Kitchener's taste; but I think all agree that it is a really fine room.' Naturally, the alterations were expensive even though most of them were undertaken by men of the Royal Engineers, but so anxious was Kitchener to have a sumptuous residence that he was fully prepared to meet 60 per cent of the total cost of 10,000 rupees (worth then about £850) from his own pocket.[33]

To exercise himself physically – for he had put on weight in South Africa and now had become quite portly and heavily jowelled – he took up shooting even though he was never a reliable shot. On one occasion in the Junga Hills near Simla he was refused a bumper of port after lunch by the solicitous Maxwell and bad temperedly took his revenge by immediately shooting a small deer and a cock pheasant with successive shots. 'Did you see those two shots?' he roared in triumph. 'Rather,' answered the aide. 'Splendid shots both of them.' 'Why the something something didn't you let me drink my port?' Kitchener shouted angrily before stomping off the hill in disgust.[34] Riding, his only recreation in South Africa, continued to occupy much of his energy, and he fostered, too, his interest in gardening. At Wildflower Hall, his well-named weekend cottage in Simla, he laid out an attractive garden, filling it with plants and shrubs he had found in the locality and which he looked on as his by right. 'He never hesitated to annex – I use a kind term – flowers and shrubs from my little garden to place in his own.' bemoaned one of his neighbours. Shortly after that unheralded visit Kitchener complained that the flowers would not grow quickly enough and lost interest in the project.[35] For indoor recreation he played bridge and took up billiards. At Snowdon the billiards room was inscribed by Kitchener with the motto, 'Strike and Fear Not', a challenge that he sometimes took over-literally; John Morley, the new Secretary for India, was fond of telling friends that Kitchener altered the score regularly to his own advantage when he thought no one was looking.

It had been while he was staying at Wildflower Hall that Kitchener was involved in an accident that left him partially incapacitated for the rest of his life. On 15 November 1903 he was riding alone into Simla along the military road that had been built in the time of Lord Dalhousie, Governor-General between 1847 and 1856, whose achievements included improvements to the country's roads and the rail system; at one point it was obliged to follow a tunnel through some high ground and it was there that the mishap occurred. As Kitchener rode through it, a startled Indian jumped out from one of the alcoves constructed for the protection of pedestrians, and caused the horse to shy. Normally Kitchener would have been able to bring it under control but in that dark and narrow space he had little room in which to manoeuvre and, as he struggled to calm the frightened beast, his left foot jammed in one of the wooden uprights protecting the alcove. At the same time he accidentally spurred the horse, which shot forward, twisting Kitchener's leg and breaking both the tibia and the fibula. Luckily both fractures were clean and the leg was to some extent protected by Kitchener's riding boot but he still suffered dreadful pain. The Indian who had startled him had run off in terror and when help did arrive the servants at first refused to enter the dark tunnel where the awesome *Jangi Lat* lay roaring in agony. Eventually Birdwood came on the scene with blankets and brandy and persuaded them to get Kitchener into a rickshaw, which hurried him back to Snowdon.[36]

Several hours after the accident the boot was cut off – a painful business for which Kitchener was given an anaesthetic – and the broken leg was set by army surgeons. But lacking even a primitive X-ray machine the doctors botched the job: when the plaster was removed it was found that the bones had knitted together crookedly and for the rest of his life Kitchener walked with a slight limp. As he began to recuperate Kitchener progressed from crutches to walking sticks and in his spare time he played bridge with his staff or read, but he was not a good patient. Maxwell did his best to humour him but Kitchener, to his dismay, found himself sinking into a mental torpor that only lifted once he was back in his office and grappling again with Curzon and the problem of dual control.

The broken leg was to have a curious sequel. Eight years later, when Kitchener was British Agent in Cairo, his ankle caused him so much pain that he was obliged to search around for a possible cure. Re-breaking and resetting the bones suggested itself as a possible solution but at that time British medical opinion had set its face against that operation, especially when the patient was a relatively elderly man. (Kitchener by then was over sixty.) It was a bloody operation involving surgery and temporary immobility but Kitchener was determined to go through with it and in the summer of 1911 he reported to Millie that he had found a Dr Kaileys in Dessau in Germany who was prepared to operate on the offending ankle. 'I hope to be in England in July', he told her, 'but do not expect to remain there long as I shall probably go to Germany and have me leg broken again and reset. They say they can make a good job of it. It will be rather a bore to lose my leave but it will be a blessing.' Before making the final arrangements he had checked the doctor's reputation with his old friend Slatin Pasha, who in addition to his accomplishments in the Arab world was well connected in Berlin and Vienna. He wrote to confirm that even though the operation might not be 100 per cent successful Kaileys had 'a good reputation'.[37]

In the end Kitchener's arrangements would not permit a visit to Dessau that year, but undeterred, he tried again in 1912 and would have gone through with the operation but for a bizarre warning. While staying at Marlborough House a message reached him through the office of the financier Alfred Rothschild that there was a German plot to disable him during the course of the operation. It seems that he had picked up the story from salon gossip in Berlin but King George V was impressed enough by the warning to order Kitchener to break off his arrangements, believing that his field marshal was too important an imperial asset to be jeopardised in Germany. Kitchener's operation never took place and the ankle remained a source of pain and discomfort, especially during the war years when he had to climb stairs every day in his London residence and at the War Office.

In April 1907 the Liberal administration offered Kitchener a two-year extension of his command in India, an invitation he was pleased to accept. He had by then made it perfectly clear that he had no intention of returning to London to involve himself in the reform of the War Office or the administration of the army. 'No more attempts at Army reform for me – either here or in England,' he told Lord Roberts, and he was as good as his word.[38] Ideally, he would have liked the appointment of British Ambassador to Turkey and he used to remind friends that he still held the rank of lieutenant-general in the Turkish Army and maintained several close friendships in the Sultan's inner circle in Constantinople. In that post he felt he could encourage the Turks to accept British influence and thus increase British prestige in the Muslim world. At other times he cast covetous eyes on the succession to Cromer in Egypt and hinted to Lady Salisbury that it would be a good stepping stone to the Viceroyalty of India, the post with which he hoped to crown his last years in public life. But the Liberals were not inclined to see Kitchener in any of these exalted positions, thinking him too closely associated with the interests of the Conservatives. Morley, who neither trusted nor liked Kitchener, thought it would be safer to keep him on in India for the time being.

In accepting the offer Kitchener knew that he was only marking time and he felt it would be a fine thing to spend it as agreeably as possible. Pleading ill health – he had been laid low by an irritating bout of fever – he requested a spell of leave that he would spend in the Far East recuperating and inspecting Indian Army garrisons. However, Morley, in an extremely clever letter turning down Kitchener's application, told him that the new coach of army administration in India could hardly hope to travel in a forward direction if its lynchpin were absent and it was unsafe to leave the army to its own devices at such a time. Kitchener had to drop the matter and with time running out on his appointment immersed himself in his hobbies. Orchids became a passion and he acquired a poodle on which he lavished much care and affection.

The social whirl continued to occupy him and he still presented the world with a picture of the hospitable and genial host; but underneath that surface gaiety he was becoming deeply introspective and unsure of his place in the world. His staff, his happy band of boys, had broken up, thus compounding his sense of isolation. Marker had remained in

England; Brooke had been appointed Minto's military secretary and 'The Brat' had become engaged to be married in 1906 while attending a staff course at Camberley. In his place was appointed Captain Oswald FitzGerald, like Maxwell an officer in the 18th Bengal Lancers, who was destined to spend the remainder of his life as Kitchener's constant companion who put his chief's interests above all others. Many resented the aura of quarantine 'Fitz' brought to Kitchener's entourage. Asquith dismissed him as Kitchener's 'familiar'; without any evidence others hinted at a homosexual relationship, but the truth was that Kitchener, however omnipotent he appeared in public, was becoming increasingly lonely in private. FitzGerald, a quiet orderly man twenty-five years his junior, provided him with agreeable company: he shared Kitchener's interests in the fine arts, enjoyed collecting and later became a partner in an east African estates and property enterprise. *Fidus Achates*, he remained with Kitchener to the end.

9

EGYPT AGAIN: PROCONSUL

The Liberals were to remain in power for the rest of the decade and beyond and while they held office the course of Kitchener's career after India was not to run so smoothly as before. With the new Viceroy, Lord Minto, he enjoyed a bluff, no-nonsense relationship based on the respect that the two men felt for each other and nurtured by dislike for Curzon. Kitchener's row with Curzon was public property but Minto's hostility, by its very nature, was of a more private origin. To satisfy Curzon's craving to stay on in India in order to meet the Prince of Wales, Minto had been forced to forgo the traditional ceremonial welcome and instead had been hurried in a closed carriage to Government House, where Curzon had greeted him wearing a smoking jacket and slippers. Minto never forgave the insult to his office but the dent to his pride was healed partially by Kitchener's warm words of welcome. Thereafter, he had nothing but good to say about his Commander-in-Chief and he was not slow in sharing his opinions with the India Office, calling Kitchener 'one of the few broad-minded soldiers I have ever met, very pleasant in conversation with a taste for gardening and art'.[1] John Morley, however, was less impressed by Kitchener's ambitions and refused to be charmed by Minto's increasingly breathless signals about the virtues of India's supreme military commander.

On taking over the India Office, Morley believed that it would be a good thing if the Indian Army had its powers restricted and early on in his office he told Kitchener that he would be 'most reluctant to sanction any increase in military expenditure'.[2] A committee was subsequently established to implement the changes, with the result that the following year – 1907 – it was recommended that Kitchener's army reorganisation should be spread over ten years instead of five and that other reforms such as the construction of new barracks be postponed. To block any expenditure on those schemes Morley further insisted that all new projects had to be referred to London for sanctioning by the India Office.

None of this new thinking appealed to Kitchener. Economy in military affairs had been a lodestar of his career but he was irritated that such cheese-paring should be proposed to him by a politician; throughout his life he preferred initiating ideas to submitting to them. He also felt that the cutbacks would wreck military efficiency but, as he realised that he could not afford another public quarrel with a senior political figure, he decided to maintain an air of accord with Morley. In private, though, both men had hard words to say about the other. To Morley, Kitchener was 'a fox', while Kitchener described Morley bluntly as 'pig-headed and dangerous'. Kitchener extended his distrust to the whole Liberal Party and stood aghast at the social reforms they were instituting in Britain at that time: they ought to be kicked out as quickly as possible, he told Lady Salisbury privately.

Ironically, Kitchener never worked again for a Conservative administration and as his time in India drew to a close in the spring of 1909 he began to worry about his future employment. In the old days it seemed that the Cecils just had to say the word for Kitchener to get his way, but the new administration refused to be cowed by Kitchener's veiled hints that he would leave Britain for good if suitable employment were not found for him. When Kitchener heard that Cromer had been succeeded in Egypt by Sir Eldon Gorst he came to believe that nothing but the post of Viceroy of India would suit him. In his pretensions he was supported by Minto, who was due to retire in 1910, and, more influentially, King Edward VII had put considerable pressure on the government to appoint his old friend to represent him in India. Morley, though, had long since decided that he did not want Kitchener with his 'arrogant bluster' to remain in India and he made it known that he would resign rather than ratify his appointment. The question of the succession to Minto dragged on through 1909 into 1910 as the Liberals agonised what to do with the country's most eminent soldier.

A solution was offered by their Secretary for War, R.B. Haldane, in July 1909. Haldane, a Scottish intellectual with degrees in philosophy and law, had been grappling with the problems of War Office reorganisation thrown up by the Esher Report of 1906 and it had been due to him that the Territorial Force had come into being, albeit against much powerful opposition. Under his guidance many other wise changes had been made: an Imperial General Staff was established, common field service manuals were issued to all arms and for the first time in its history the British Army was provided with an efficient staff organisation. Haldane also sanctioned the unofficial discussions between the British and the French staffs about mutual co-operation in time of war, a move that Kitchener thoroughly deprecated when he heard about it from Rawlinson. 'I do not like this,' he told him. 'We have no plan of our own and it will mean inevitably that we shall be tacked on to a French plan which might not suit us.'[3] The talks had been initiated at the time of the first Morocco crisis in 1906, when war between Germany and France seemed imminent and when Britain looked as if she might be dragged in on France's side.

Haldane also realised that the balance of world power had shifted dramatically since 1898 and that Britain needed a revised strategy. The country was no longer self-sufficient and the long-standing pattern of free trade meant that in time of war the country was at the mercy of seaborne supplies being cut off by an enemy. To meet that threat and to guard the British sea routes the Royal Navy was of paramount importance and the so-called 'blue water' policy was at the heart of British defence thinking. But the ships of the Royal Navy could only operate efficiently if the harbours and coaling stations along the imperial sea lanes were in British hands. The one vital gap in Britain's network seemed to be in the Mediterranean and the gateway to the passage to India through the Suez Canal: any break in the chain that linked the British bases in Gibraltar, Malta, Cyprus, Crete and Egypt could blight Britain's well-being in time of war. The solution, according to Haldane, was the creation of a Mediterranean Command, which was established in 1907 with the Duke of Connaught, the King's brother, as its first commander. When the Duke resigned in 1909 Haldane attempted to persuade Kitchener to take his place on the grounds that he would invest the role with a prestige it had not gained in its relatively short existence. On 7 July 1909 he put this proposition to Kitchener, adding as further inducements that he would be promoted to the rank of field marshal, that his salary would be enhanced by an additional £5,000 a year, that he would be given a palatial residence in Malta and that he would also occupy a position on the Committee of Imperial Defence. These were substantial rewards, but Kitchener was not tempted. He was out of sympathy with the reforms that Haldane had instituted at the War Office and was gradually losing touch with the innovations that were being made in the British Army. Haldane, however, had made a generous offer that had to be considered. Kitchener did not wish to return to London and a spell in a Maltese palace – with 'a beautiful garden', Haldane had added – would offer a pleasurable environment in which to live. He would have under his command the Egyptian Army, which knew and respected him and, as the post was new, he would be able to place upon it the imprimatur of his personality and ideas. Had he been a younger man it would have been a useful stepping stone but at the age of fifty-nine, with retirement beckoning, Kitchener realised that it would represent a mere sidestep. A few days later he replied that he could not accept the Mediterranean Command as he required a reasonable period of unemployment after so many years of continuous service to his country.

But Haldane and Morley were not to be diverted so easily and when the King intervened on their behalf by telling Kitchener that he attached 'great importance to his acceptance', Kitchener had little option but to obey his monarch's wishes. He was well rewarded for his loyalty. On 1 August a relieved Edward VII telegraphed personally to say that Kitchener's acceptance of the Command 'would in no way prejudice your being considered for any other higher appointment hereafter becoming vacant, which may be more agreeable to you'.[4] That clinched it. In Kitchener's mind – if not in Morley's or Haldane's – he would take the Mediterranean Command for a short time only, as an interlude to succeeding Minto in India.

To help sweeten the pill and to fall in with Kitchener's hints about his exhaustion and his need for a complete break, Morley sanctioned his plans for a visit to the Far East and Australia and New Zealand that would keep him gainfully employed and away from the rigours of the British winter. As his acceptance of the Mediterranean Command had still not been made public Kitchener may well have hoped that his ambitions for India were not yet extinguished and no doubt he also took heart from the constitutional crisis that had suddenly arisen in 1909 when the Liberals' budget was rejected in the House of Lords and a general election seemed imminent. His hopes were dashed, however: when the Liberals went to the country in January 1910 they were returned, though with a decreased majority.

In August Kitchener began a long series of farewells to India, beginning with an official banquet at the United Services Club in Simla on 20 August at which Minto paid generous tribute to his reforms, claiming that Kitchener had bequeathed India 'better trained, equipped and paid troops than she had ever had before'. Kitchener's successor in India was one of his divisional commanders, General Sir O'Moore Creagh VC, who came to bid him farewell at Poona before taking up the command himself. At the railway station, once the formalities were over, Creagh was astonished to discover that 'without saying "by your leave" he [Kitchener] had bagged the Commander-in-Chief's special railway carriage for his journey, to which he had no right.' To the consternation of everyone on the platform Kitchener set off on the first stage of his Far East tour in the princely style he had come to expect in India. 'I shortly left in a more modest one for Simla,' grumbled the vexed Creagh, who also admitted that it was to be several months before he could rid himself of the great man's presence, so formidable was the impression Kitchener had left behind him.[5]

Ostensibly Kitchener was going to the Far East at the invitation of the Japanese government, who were anxious to have him observe their annual manoeuvres; he had also carried with him invitations from the governments of Australia and New Zealand, who both wanted him to report on their defence capabilities. In addition to these official duties, and to make his six-month tour as agreeable as possible, time had been set aside for relaxation in China and the Dutch East Indies. Kitchener, for his part, decided to throw himself with gusto into the tour and to enjoy a long period of leave after some forty years' continuous service.

At the beginning of October he arrived in Shanghai, the centre of British influence in China, where he stayed at the China Association, 'a sort of Hurlingham without polo'. There he ate his way through several Chinese banquets, charmed local businessmen and haggled with dealers over the price of porcelain. A few days later he arrived in Peking, where the pattern was repeated on a grander scale, although not everyone was entranced by his presence. George Morrison, the China correspondent of *The Times*, was horrified to see Kitchener pocket several pieces of porcelain that had been laid out for his inspection at an official reception; and then hurriedly ordered his aides to follow suit.[6] So delighted were his hosts by his interest that no one had the nerve to question his actions or to ask him for something in return.

His first contact with Japan was made in Manchuria where, before travelling to Tokyo, he visited the battlefields of the Russo-Japanese war. The Japanese people had been flattered by his acceptance of their country's invitation and his reception was as tumultuous as any he had ever received in London. A palace was set aside for his use and he spent much of his spare time there and at the British embassy, where he met again the British diplomat Horace Rumbold, a friend from his days in Egypt, who had accompanied Kitchener on a visit to Suakin in 1894. Rumbold, a career diplomat, thought that Kitchener 'doesn't look a day older that when I saw him last, 7 years ago [in Cairo] on his way out to India'.[7] He enjoyed meeting him again but a week later saw him grumbling to his diary that Kitchener's visit had demanded his attendance at five dinners and two lunches in the soldier's honour. More enjoyably he accompanied Kitchener and his staff to a farewell banquet at which eighty beautiful geisha girls had been provided for the men's entertainment. 'I soon had a geisha on one knee, my arm around a second whilst a third cuddled up against me', he confided. The others followed his lead but not Kitchener. Each time a geisha tried to sit on his knee he blushingly pushed her away and the event ended with everyone — Kitchener excepted — playing 'a sort of game corresponding to "here we go round the mulberry bush", while one of the geisha squatted on the floor and thumped the drum.'[8] An explanation for Kitchener's repugnance of such frolics lies in Sir George Arthur's memory that such was the strength of Kitchener's chivalric feeling towards women that any indelicate story told in his company would meet with an immediate rebuke.

There was more to Kitchener's visit than the opportunity of dallying with dancing girls. The Japanese government was anxious to reinforce the 1902 alliance with Britain and hoped that a good report from Kitchener would allow them a freer hand in far eastern affairs. The Admiralty also wanted a strong Japan to counter German naval ambitions in the area and so free British warships on the China Station for service with the Home Fleet, and Kitchener agreed with that thinking. Although he was critical of some aspects of the Japanese army's manoeuvres he gave unstinted praise to its infantry and in reverential tones told Lady Salisbury that he admired greatly the nation's military spirit and the attention paid by the government to the needs of its army.

November was spent in Java and Christmas abroad the cruiser HMS *Encounter*, which took Kitchener on a brief Pacific tour before he began his Australian visit to Melbourne on New Year's Day 1910. For six weeks he visited military camps and watched manoeuvres; then on 18 February he published his findings in a report that called for the establishment of a military academy, the creation of a general staff and the provision of a home defence force. He also suggested that there should be improved lines of internal communication, including the construction of strategic railways, and that the country should be divided into ten military districts. His views were welcomed by the Australian Prime Minister, Alfred Deakin, and he received universal approbation for his statement that discipline in the army should take into account Australian needs and methods. During the South African war British officers had tended to be over-hard on Australian troops for their unwillingness to bow to British standards and style of military discipline and Kitchener's understanding attitude was seen as a step forward.

Indeed, during the Gallipoli campaign of 1915, when Australian troops were again fighting in an Imperial force, the war correspondent Charles Bean reported that most of the Anzac force exempted Kitchener from their general dislike of British commanders.[9]

From Melbourne Kitchener sailed for New Zealand, arriving at The Bluff on the South Island on 17 February. He immediately set the seal on what was to be a happy tour by proclaiming that he was no stranger to New Zealand as his father had owned property at Otago and that his sister still lived there. A special train took him to Dunedin, where he found awaiting him a large crowd whose enthusiasm outweighed its sense of decorum. The newspapers reported later that it resembled nothing less than a huge rugby scrum that had somehow allowed itself to get out of control. In the melee that followed, the Prime Minister of New Zealand, Sir Joseph Ward, was elbowed out of his official carriage and was forced to follow the procession in a hastily borrowed private motor car. This 'unfortunate blunder' occupied as much space as the description of Kitchener's welcome in the New Zealand daily press but, throughout the ordeal, Kitchener seemed to be amused greatly by the antics and surprised his staff by mingling with the crowd, talking to veterans with Boer War medals.

Something of that calm deserted him when he reached his hotel and picked up the local newspaper. An enterprising journalist had interviewed Millie about her famous brother and during the course of their discussion she had indiscreetly admitted that Kitchener was bored by women and that marriage was out of the question as he would soon tire of seeing the same face at breakfast each day. 'It is the funniest thing', she continued, 'to see him paying attention one day to a pretty girl and the next day to hear him wondering what her name is and when he met her. She imagines that she has the lion of London in her silken fetters while he has forgotten her existence.'[10] Kitchener was not at all amused by the article, still less by its implication that he was boorish.

Fortunately the tour of New Zealand offered no other contretemps and thereafter the press kept a respectful distance, only the *Wellington Dominion* remarking that underneath Kitchener's boyish smile lurked a 'cold, pitiless, unflinching, basilisk stare'. In Canterbury he praised the army cadet system which, as in Australia, he thought would provide New Zealand with a nucleus for its future military needs. At the tour's end he reported those views to Sir Joseph Ward, adding that the New Zealand army system should be similar in every respect to the Australian model so that in time of war the two countries could act as one.[11]

A sidelight of Kitchener's Australasian tour was the public interest he took in Freemasonry. He had been introduced by the Duke of Connaught and in his time had been Grand Master of Egypt and Sudan, and of the Punjab in India. At the time of his tour he was a Grand Junior Warden of England, a post that he took seriously, reminding Australian masons that masonry was 'based on strength and it is the object of my visit to Australia to do what I can to assist in carrying out that masonic objective'.[12] Kitchener remained an active mason until the end of his life and was particularly active in the organisation in Egypt, spending much of his time with the French *Grande Loge de la France* and the *Nil Loge*, both of which were affiliated to the Osiris and Star of the East Lodges. Masonry was an important binding to his already well-established network of social and political connections in Britain.

From New Zealand Kitchener crossed the Pacific, changing ships in Tahiti, and landed at San Francisco on 7 April after a rough crossing. For the rest of his short tour he played the tourist, visiting the Yosemite Valley in California before setting out across the country by way of Chicago for New York, where he gave two interviews, one of which he ended by declaring that he was 'perfectly safe in saying that New York, should be proud of her beautiful women'.[13] On the east coast part of his four-day visit was spent visiting West Point, the American military academy, which he announced should be the model for other countries to follow; he also found time to inspect the Altman fine art collection in the Metropolitan Museum of Art and was entertained to dinner by the Pilgrims Club. He spent only twelve days in the United States because, the moment his ship docked in San Francisco, news reached him from friends in London that suggested the nomination of the next Viceroy to India was now imminent and that he should be in London to press his claims. On 20 April he left New York on board the SS *Oceanic* and six days later he was in residence in Belgrave Square.

EGYPT AGAIN: PROCONSUL

Hurriedly he arranged interviews with Morley and with the King, who promised unreserved support. However, as Asquith was out of the country, no decision could be reached until the early summer. Having already accepted the Mediterranean Command, Kitchener now said he would rather be unemployed than go to such a billet and told Haldane that he was opposed to the posting. Morley replied that Haldane had his acceptance in writing, and that he himself would resign if he were put under pressure to accept Kitchener as the next Viceroy. Morley was keen on appointing another man, Sir Charles Hardinge, a permanent under-secretary at the Foreign Office. Privately, Morley told friends that there would be political unrest in India if Kitchener were appointed and that his presence might undo much of the trust created by the India Councils Act of 1909, the Liberals' first step towards parliamentary democracy in India that introduced elections to the country's legislative councils. In his desire to win allies Kitchener dropped his mask of taciturnity, not always to good effect: Esher noted in his journals that Kitchener was becoming too voluble in his dealings and he warned him 'not to threaten John Morley, as he is a strong, proud and obstinate man'.[14] His advice was to no avail. At a private dinner with Morley, which Esher attended, Kitchener showed himself at his worst with inevitable results: 'That night, supposed to be guarded and silent, he was lush of talk, with a copiousness of indiscreet opinion, praise and blame that made Lord Morley say afterwards, "Never, never shall he go to India."'[15]

Morley outmanoeuvred Kitchener, but his final victory was due in no small measure to the death of King Edward VII on 6 May. The loss of that vital prop of support was fatal to Kitchener's interests and a month later Morley undertook the 'disagreeable task' of finally crushing any hope Kitchener had of attaining the Viceregal post. Hardinge, he told him, had been selected instead. The news was a bitter blow to Kitchener and made the more unpalatable by the knowledge that, had Edward lived, he might well have been able to persuade Asquith to overrule the Secretary for India. So sure had Kitchener been of the post that he had even selected his staff. His chagrin was completed by the lack of interest the Liberal Cabinet showed in his welfare. On 13 June, to no comment, Haldane announced that Kitchener would not now be taking up the Mediterranean Command.

For the first time in his life Kitchener was unemployed, a state of affairs which, to his surprise, he found quite congenial, deciding to use the free time to his own advantage. Later that summer he went to Ireland, visiting his childhood homes in the company of FitzGerald, and then he embarked on his customary social round of Britain's stately homes. With winter approaching his dread of spending it in England encouraged him to travel to east Africa, making up a shooting party that included his nephew Toby and FitzGerald.

It was at this time in his life, too, that Kitchener began to think again about putting down roots. Having enjoyed hospitality in the great houses of England, it had long been his ambition to own a country house himself in which he could entertain in style and which would reflect both his artistic interests and the honours his career had brought him. In the autumn of 1910 he found such a place near Canterbury called Broome Park. Once the home of the Oxenden family, it had been built between 1635 and 1638 and it was (and is) considered to be one of the finest extant examples of Caroline architecture in England. The purchase – it cost Kitchener £14,000 – was completed on his return to England in April 1911 and for the remaining five years of his life Kitchener lavished great care and attention on beautifying the building and laying out the gardens to his precise specifications. From his designs, which are deposited in the Chapter House of Canterbury Cathedral, it is easy to see that nothing was too small to earn Kitchener's attention. He maintained a voluminous correspondence with his estate manager, Walter Western, and each letter emphasised in minute detail his plans for the restructuring, refurbishing and relaying of the grounds, and gave precise instructions for the design of such highly personal interior details as the monogrammed 'K.K.' walls in the entrance hall or the sitting-room at the north end of the house with its stone chimney piece embracing Kitchener's family motto, 'Thorough'.

In his enthusiasm for the new estate he found an unlikely ally in his neighbour at nearby Knole, Lady Victoria Sackville, another of those Victorian grandes dames who first swam into his ken while he was

Sirdar of the Egyptian Army in the 1890s.[16] She had thought him at first a 'rough diamond' but she warmed quickly to his interests in house decoration and was able to help him with the designs for the Jacobean ornamentation of the drawing room, which Kitchener wanted to base on the model at Knole. Her marriage to her cousin Lionel Sackville-West was in difficulties at that time and she had recently been through a messy court case involving the ownership of Knole. She took solace in Kitchener's company, enjoying greatly the sense of passion he brought to improving his estate. Lady Sackville also advised on the furnishings for Broome Park and scoured London's shops for him while Kitchener was out of the country. Kitchener repaid some of those favours by entertaining her daughter Vita while he was British Agent in Egypt – and at a dinner party he astonished her by remarking in answer to a question about his interest in Egyptian art that he could not really think much of a people who had painted the same cat for 4,000 years![17]

As well as Knole, Kitchener copied details from other great houses he had known in the past, the staircase with its heraldic finials and decorated balustrade being a replica of the staircase at Hatfield, the model for many of the changes he had wrought in his lodge at Simla. In the interior Kitchener's engineering instincts came into play. He wanted a larger, wider and taller entrance hall and to obtain it he ordered drastic structural alterations – the floor was raised to the base of the windows and the roof was stripped off to be replaced by metal girders, the old wood being used for the hall panelling and staircase. Not everyone, though, was happy with the results. The country house correspondent of *Country Life* remarked later that, 'The entrance hall as remodelled is undeniably fine work of its kind, but the effect of the elaborate Jacobean woodwork, the pendant ceiling and the two great marble fireplaces is rather overwhelming.'[18]

The purchase of Broome Park was not completed until April 1911 but that winter, as Kitchener and his party made their stately way across east Africa past the great lakes of Albert Nyanza and Victoria Nyanza, he was already about to become a man of property. So entranced had Kitchener been by the landscape he found in Kenya and so intrigued by the possibilities that existed for its exploitation as farming land that he was determined to purchase a property under a scheme then being run by the British East Africa Corporation. His choice fell on Muhoroni, an estate near the Uganda railway 38 miles from the Victoria Nyanza.

Kitchener had bought the east African estate with the firm intention of wintering in Kenya and spending his summers in England at Broome, but he was destined never to return to Muhoroni. On arriving at Mombasa in March 1911 he received word from King George V that he wished Kitchener to return to take charge of the troops at his Coronation on 22 June. Kitchener travelled home immediately, appropriately enough on the German liner *Feldmarschall,* and broke his journey at Ligorno, where he was introduced to Kaiser Wilhelm II. Kitchener was determined that his deployment of the troops at the Coronation should be as well planned as possible and he threw himself into the arrangements with all his customary energy. His reward was to be appointed a Knight of the Order of St Patrick, then Ireland's highest chivalric honour. In the weeks after the Coronation Kitchener spent much of his time with the Desborough family at the invitation of Lady Desborough, who had been sitting behind him at the Coronation where she 'was sorely tempted to chop my prayer-book on your head to make you look up! What would you have said?'[19] As the tone of her letter suggests, the Desboroughs remained good friends and Kitchener lavished much attention on their sons, Billy and Julian. In such company Kitchener could relax and admit that he cared not what the future might bring, even retirement.

Lack of money, though, prevented such a course of action. Broome Park, he reckoned, would eat up his capital and he began to sound out friends about being appointed to remunerative public positions that would offer him a salary without too much work having to be done in return. The response was his appointment to the board of the London, Chatham and Dover Railway, which paid a salary, and to the Presidency of the North London Association of Boy Scouts, which did not. To the press it seemed inexplicable that the great Lord Kitchener should have been reduced to worrying about suburban railway timetables and awarding proficiency badges to earnest teenage boys, although, in his thorough way, Kitchener used both posts to good advantage: he persuaded the railway company to improve its services to Canterbury and his Scouts were given leave to camp at Broome provided they helped in the gardens.

Questions were also asked in the House of Commons about the lack of confidence being shown in Kitchener by the Liberal government and on 15 June J.E.B. Seely, the Under-Secretary for War, had to defend his government's position against a determined Conservative attack by brushing aside the persistent questions with a smooth politician's declaration that, 'It is considered undesirable in the interests of our state to express any opinion as to the qualifications and claims of particular officers for particular posts in the service.' He added that Kitchener had been offered a seat on the Committee of Imperial Defence but failed to admit that the Liberal Foreign Secretary, Sir Edward Grey, had already entered into talks with Kitchener.

Early in 1911 Sir Eldon Gorst, the British Agent in Egypt, was dying of cancer and it was clear that a replacement would have to be found to succeed him. In normal circumstances Kitchener would have been the obvious choice but his quarrel with Curzon had convinced many Liberals that his military training and outlook would cloud his judgement in a post that was primarily civilian and diplomatic. To ascertain that Kitchener understood that the appointment was in no sense military in character, Grey met him on 19 June in the week following the Conservative questions in the House of Commons. Grey had made his move in the knowledge that he had the support of Lord Cromer who, having first opposed Kitchener's claims, now believed that he was the only man capable of ruling Egypt at a time when nationalist agitation was on the increase. The King, too, had made it known that he would like to see Kitchener in Cairo: the question was, could Kitchener adapt himself to a civilian gubernatorial appointment? It was known that he still lusted after the Indian post and those with long memories remembered his diffident approach to the governance of Sudan. Kitchener, though, was convinced. He genuinely liked Egypt and the Egyptians, recalling that it was there he had made his reputation: there was no question but that he would accept the invitation and the stipulations attached to it by Sir Edward Grey.

At the end of June he travelled to Dublin to be invested as a Knight of St Patrick and he returned to London on 12 July for further talks at the Foreign Office. Gorst had died two days earlier and on 16 July Grey announced Kitchener's appointment in the House of Commons. To the left wing of the Liberal Party this was seen as a sell-out and Grey was forced to parry several leading questions about Kitchener's suitability for the diplomatic post, although most sections of the Commons were pleased with his appointment. *The Times* summed up the general feeling in its editorial the next day: 'The duties he has now to perform are novel to him and his countrymen will look forward with much interest, but with confidence, to see how he will discharge them. He has proved himself a great soldier, and a great military administrator. They expect him to prove himself a great civilian.'[20]

Kitchener was delighted. He had served – with varying degrees of success – three great Victorian imperial pro-consuls, Cromer, Milner and Curzon. Now it was his chance to join their number and he told friends that he was determined that his rule should be as renowned and as dazzling as any that had gone before. Triumph in Egypt, he reasoned, would surely open the gateway to India, for he still had not lost sight of becoming Viceroy.

Accordingly, the rest of that summer was spent making the arrangements for his departure. FitzGerald would accompany him as his military secretary and two French chefs were added to his staff. He made plans for his gold plate and dinner services to be shipped out to Egypt while the rest of his treasures were left at Broome Park in the custody of his estate manager. After making a round of farewells to his closest friends – the Desboroughs, the Salisburys and Pandeli Ralli – he left for Egypt from Liverpool Street Station on 16 September, unannounced, except for the presence of a troop of Boy Scouts who had camped at Broome and who had come to see him off.

If Kitchener rejoiced in his appointment to Egypt, then with very few exceptions the Egyptians were overjoyed to see him at the helm of their country. In Sudan, South Africa and India, Kitchener had been largely indifferent to the native population and had cared little about their language, culture or political aspirations. Egypt, though, was different.

He spoke Arabic, appreciated their culture and understood their admiration for a personality as their ruler; but in his own unbending way Kitchener also admired the Egyptian people for their simplicity of outlook. He had lived in the country for fourteen years, the time of his rise to power, and he looked on it as his spiritual home. One of his civil servants remembered that during a difficult interview on financial matters, Kitchener's attitude was one of ill-concealed boredom until the official forecast that the changes would benefit the ordinary Egyptians. 'When I mentioned the fellahin,' he continued, 'his face lighted up wondrously.'[21]

Enough was known about those susceptibilities to suggest that Kitchener's period in Cairo would be a happy one. 'If a man like Lord Kitchener existed in every country,' wrote the leader writer of *Al-Bassir* shortly after his arrival, 'the dead would return to life, the poor would be rich, science and freedom would spread, and everybody would be happy.' Even allowing for the hyperbole the comment was typical of the warmth of the welcome awaiting Kitchener when his ship docked at Alexandria on 28 September. Cheering crowds lined the route that took him in the Khedive's carriage to the palace, where he presented his credentials to the same Abbas Hilmi whom he had humbled all those years ago while Sirdar of the Egyptian Army. His relationship with the Khedive was to be of obvious importance and the two men greeted each other with an icy formality that disguised their inner feelings. Abbas Hilmi had never forgiven Kitchener for the sleight to his young self in 1894 and he had smarted at the appointment of a man he detested. Within a few months, the enmity between the two men was to break out again but on that warm, late summer's evening the new British Agent's words had a soothing ring:

> I am particularly pleased with the prospect of being called upon to maintain the deep sympathy which animated my predecessor in his relations with your Highness, and I hope that this sympathy, added to a friendship to Egypt of long date, will facilitate for me the task I have at heart, namely, watching over to the best of my power, and with the approval of your Highness, the prosperity of Egypt.[22]

The following evening Kitchener arrived by special train in Cairo, where he was driven to Kasr-al-Dubara, the British Residency, and as his carriage and escort swung into his new and dignified home set among carefully tended lawns on the banks of the Nile, the last cheers died down: *Al-Lurd Kuchner* had returned to the country that he knew best of all.

The Egypt that awaited Kitchener was held fast in the mould that Cromer had fashioned for it. The pretence that Britain acted only in an advisory role was maintained by the presence of an Egyptian General Assembly and Legislative Council, by the use of the Egyptian national flag and by the facade of the Khedive's allegiance to the Sultan of Turkey; but Egypt was still very much an imperial outpost in British possession. Abbas Hilmi was merely a puppet and for many years Cromer had been the country's autocratic ruler. Under his regime formidable engineering and irrigation works had been put in hand and institutions of a peculiarly British style — from the police forces to the railway system — had come into being, but political reform had been slow in coming.

After Cromer's departure in 1907 Gorst had been given his post by a Liberal government who had backed him in his determination to introduce an element of democracy. Local government was strengthened, more Egyptians were employed in the civil service and Gorst took a more tolerant approach to nationalists arrested in public disturbances, but those belated concessions had failed to soothe nationalist passions. In February 1910 the Prime Minister, Boutros Ghali Pasha, a Copt, was assassinated in a Cairo street and in the year that followed Egypt became a hotbed of nationalist groups of different political opinions united only by their call of 'Egypt for the Egyptians!' Gorst's illness had led to so much indecision in Cairo that the Liberals had been forced to back-pedal on their policy of gradual reform in Egypt: Grey assured the Commons that, 'Lord Kitchener goes to continue our work in Egypt and to promote progress as far and as fast as it is reasonable to do it,' but privately he told Kitchener that what Egypt needed was a strong man.[23]

Within a day of his arrival Kitchener demonstrated that potency. War had broken out between Italy and Turkey over the occupation of Tripoli in neighbouring Libya. As the Sultan's nominal subject Egypt could have been obliged to lend assistance to Turkey but Britain declared neutrality in the dispute and Egypt had to follow suit. This announcement shocked Islamic nationalists, whose hearts were with their co-religionists, but by a mixture of firm-handedness and patience Kitchener kept Egypt out of the conflict. When a group of Muslim army officers asked to be allowed to volunteer for the Turkish Army, Kitchener immediately gave permission, on the understanding that other officers would be promoted to take their places and that they would be placed on the reserve list on their return. The requests were promptly withdrawn. Egypt's neutrality assured, Kitchener turned to the weightier matter of domestic reforms in which he proved himself to be an ideal, if autocratic, governor. Using the methods that had won him his military successes he cut through the civil administrative machinery to achieve his desired goal: those methods infuriated the British civil servants but to the Egyptians, who did not always admire imported political institutions, he appeared as their saviour. As P.G. Elgood, an administrator in the Department of Finance, recalled, Kitchener was utterly ruthless in weeding out his officials: 'Mentally he was accustomed to divide officials into two classes: those who were useful to his plans, and those who were not.' [24]

He set his seal on his working methods shortly after his arrival. When Ronald Storrs, his gifted Oriental Secretary, told him that several senior British officials intended to resign or take early retirement rather than work with the new administration, Kitchener pointed to a drawer in his desk and rapped out an order, 'You'd better go down to the Club and let it be known that I've always kept printed acceptance forms for resignations, only requiring the name to be added to become effective.' [25] There was no more talk of resignations but, later, Storrs discovered that the drawer contained only a supply of cigars to which Kitchener had become increasingly addicted. Something of a chain-smoker, Kitchener's favourite method of working was to stride around the room, pulling at a cigar, while he threw out orders and ideas for his staff to pick up. As he had done so often in the past many of his solutions to problems bordered on the absurd, but would be proposed to get a reaction. At other times he would listen silently to a discussion before introducing his own answer and then brooking no opposition.

Under these circumstances his staff, which in addition to FitzGerald and Storrs, included Lord Colum Crichton-Stuart, son of the Marquess of Bute, had to keep on their toes, but sometimes Kitchener's methods could backfire. When he foresaw problems at the Department of Finance he sacked the adviser, Sir Paul Harvey, and appointed as his successor his old ADC, Lord Edward Cecil, whom he knew would be more amenable. He then turned his mind to irrigation and, priding himself on his engineering abilities, designed a chain of pumping stations capable of taking water to outlying areas, a scheme irrigation experts criticised because of its cost. The most formidable opponent was Sir William Willcocks, the Egyptian government's drainage expert, who kept up a running battle with Kitchener over his schemes and other plans to raise further the height of the Aswan dam, which he had designed. Willcocks was too important a figure to brush aside and their disagreement rumbled on until early in 1914, when Kitchener told his staff to let his opponent 'have the field for himself'.

In addition to improving the country's irrigation schemes, which he saw as the key to agricultural improvement, Kitchener was determined to do away with medieval systems of land tenure and to improve the lot of the fellahin, the ordinary Egyptian small farmer. In 1912 he passed the Homestead Exemption Law – known as the 5 Feddan Law, because it referred to farms of five feddans or under. (A feddan is equal, roughly, to an acre.) Based on the successful Punjab Land Alienation Act of 1900 that did much to free Punjabi farmers from the yoke of their landlords, the act gave security of tenure, limited to 9 per cent interest on money borrowed for improvements, and paved the way for the establishment of village savings banks and communal warehouses. It checked borrowing and encouraged thrift, and its introduction was appreciated by the Egyptian peasantry. Whenever Kitchener made one of his many tours of inspection in country areas he would be greeted by banners proclaiming 'Welcome to Lord Kitchener. The Friend of the Fellah'.

Landowners and senior officials were sceptical about the innovations and Kitchener's reasons for introducing them: in their eyes he was a 'socialist' who had usurped the traditional flow of capital and credit. The stories of their opposition merely amused Kitchener, who affronted his critics further by mingling freely with the fellahin and making sure that, in true sultanic fashion, the doors of his residence were open at all times to anyone who cared to call. On one occasion a deputation from a village in the Galiouba province sent a letter asking for Kitchener's intervention to provide them with more water. Kitchener replied immediately that he would meet their deputation but that on no account were they to incur any expense by purchasing new clothes for the occasion. Wherever he went he refused to stand on ceremony and his easy ability to remember names and the intricacies of family relationships, important elements of Muslim etiquette, won him many friends. His staff, who accompanied him everywhere, soon found that he was at his happiest when he was out on tour, inspecting the many improvements he had set in train: the new pumping stations, the warehouses, the metalled stretch of road between Cairo and Alexandria, or the hospitals and clinics built by the Public Health department. Under his guidance a Ministry of Agriculture also came into being, although he was unsuccessful in his efforts to finance it through a system of death duties imposed on the wealthy landowners.

Gorst had begun a gradual programme of liberalisation by introducing Egyptians into public offices and by following a policy of non-interference in affairs that did not directly concern the British. These innovations, coming hard on the heels of Cromer's autocracy, did nothing to appease the more extreme nationalists but only served to fuel their claims. Many nationalists were middle-class intellectuals who came to regard Kitchener's concern for the fellahin as a paternalistic sop. Political assassination was rife: several plots directed against Kitchener were uncovered by the police, including an attempt on his life in April 1913. Kitchener had been told by Grey to show a firm hand but he was also obliged by his Liberal masters to continue Gorst's reforms.

The solution Kitchener adopted was to give with one hand and to take away with the other. To combat the tide of nationalistic agitation he summarily closed five radical newspapers, including the influential *Al-Akhbar*, and ordered the arrest of all agitators. He then set about imposing a form of government he thought would be more suitable and serviceable than any that had existed previously and would be acceptable to most Egyptians. In his first annual report Kitchener had doubted the wisdom of introducing democratic institutions in an oriental country, believing that 'party spirit is to them [the Egyptians] like strong drink to uncivilised African natives', but, whether he liked it or not, Egypt possessed two political assemblies, the Legislative Council and the General Assembly, both of an advisory nature. It was no part of Kitchener's intention to devolve greater responsibility on either body – he told Grey that it would be 'insane' to give the Egyptians 'a larger measure of power and control' – but his military instincts told him that the present system was unwieldy and wasteful of effort.

The result was his implementation of the Organic Law in 1913, which abolished both institutions and created a single council, the Legislative Assembly, which had a higher proportion of elected members, sixty-six, to nominated members, seventeen. The new body was granted extended powers to delay legislation and to prevent taxation being introduced without discussion, but it remained like its predecessors essentially a consultative and deliberative body. Having worked hard on its details Kitchener took no further interest in the new assembly and, indeed, he was absent from Egypt when the reforms were announced. Ideally, Kitchener would have liked to have seen the charade of the British Agency disappearing, the Khedive deposed, and the creation in their place of a British Viceroyalty as grand as its Indian cousin. Kitchener, of course, wanted to be the first holder of such an omnipotent title and dreamed, too, of adding territories discarded by the Ottoman Empire. In his mind's eye he could envisage the creation of a mighty British sphere of influence in the eastern Mediterranean extending across Mesopotamia (modern Iraq) and down the Euphrates to the Persian Gulf.

Having stamped an authority on Egypt that seemed to some observers to be as potent as any exercised by the pharaohs, Kitchener resolved that his domestic affairs should be equally sublime. Whenever he went on tours of inspection he was accompanied by servants wearing a gold and red uniform of his own design and he always travelled in the best railway carriages that Wagons-Lit could provide, equipped with the finest furnishings and provided with lavish menus. At Kasr-al-Dubara he built a new ballroom and refurbished the reception rooms so he could entertain in the style he felt his position demanded. The life obviously suited him because to his visitors and to British residents in Cairo he seemed more relaxed in his manner. A visiting journalist called at the Residency and, after sending in his card to FitzGerald, was ushered into the drawing room. While he was admiring the view across the lawns to the Nile and the pyramids beyond, his reverie was interrupted by Kitchener, smoking a cigar and eager to discuss his latest irrigation project. In the old days he would have dealt with the journalist through one of his aides. His new-found ease seemed to know no bounds. Whereas Cromer – and even the liberal Gorst – had only extended official invitations to a token Egyptian or two, Kitchener's garden parties were well attended by Egyptian army officers and officials, to whom he always made a point of showing a warm welcome.

His regal style of entertaining extended, naturally enough, to royalty. He threw a party for the German Crown Prince when he visited Cairo, he invited his aristocratic friends from England to join him on shooting trips down the Nile and one of his first duties in 1911 had been to receive King George V and Queen Mary in Port Said. Two years later he arranged for the same Royal couple to land at Port Sudan on their way home from a tour of India. It was a magnificent occasion, attended by the leading sheikhs, who set up a great tented village, anxious to pay homage to Kitchener's King with displays of their own wealth and temporal power. Those who witnessed it looked on the event as a meeting between equals, with Kitchener, resplendent in full-dress uniform, towering over King George as each sheikh was brought up in turn to be introduced to the monarch. The hospitality was returned during Kitchener's summer leave: in 1912 and 1913 he spent part of the summer at Balmoral and the rest at Broome Park, where he lived in his agent's house until the alterations were completed.

Although Kitchener enjoyed his annual leaves in England, he found he was increasingly out of kilter with the times and had been particularly distressed when his niece Frances Parker joined the suffragette movement. In 1912 she was arrested during a demonstration in London and sentenced to four months imprisonment. Having paid for her education at Cambridge, Kitchener felt she owed her family a greater sense of loyalty and he bluntly wrote to Millie to tell her so:

> Please do not send any suffragette ladies to me as you know my feelings on the subject. I am quite disgusted to think what Frances may have attempted. Whatever her feelings on the subject may be I cannot help thinking she might have some consideration for her family. I can do absolutely nothing in the matter. One of her associates wrote to me about it.

Failing to get any family support, Frances went on hunger strike but was freed under the terms of the 'Cat and Mouse' Act, which was introduced to enable imprisoned suffragettes in poor health to be released. Two years later she was re-arrested in Scotland under the alias 'Janet Arthur' after taking part in an attempt to blow up the cottage in Alloway in Ayrshire that was the birthplace of the poet Robert Burns.[26] During the First World War she served in the Women's Army Auxiliary Corps and was appointed OBE. Her brother, 'Wallier' Parker, had served on his uncle's staff in Khartoum in 1899 and after working with Military Intelligence in Cairo had accepted the command of the Cairo Police School. Remembering his uncle's injunction that family connections did not carry with them any promise of preferment and that every man should rise or fall through his own efforts, 'Wallier' Parker did not seek Kitchener's company at the Residency, but his intelligence work, including the training of spies at the police college, did fall within the British Agent's sphere of political interest.[27]

The British presence in the Middle East centred on the protection of the Suez Canal, the main imperial artery, and on the presence of a strong buffer between India and Europe to protect the overland route east. Southern Persia, which gave Britain its major oil supplies, was also a vital sphere of influence and control of the Persian Gulf was in British hands. Parker's work among the Sinai tribes had helped to keep most of them pro-British although its interests in the whole area had been threatened by a change of direction in Ottoman rule following the Young Turks' revolt of 1907. There had been, too, the added complication of the Balkan revolts of 1911 and the upsurge of Slav

EGYPT AGAIN: PROCONSUL

nationalism and breakdown of Ottoman authority in Europe, which had led to friction between the newly independent state of Serbia and Austria–Hungary. Traditionally Britain had tended to support the Sultan of Turkey but her influence had been undermined increasingly by the presence there of Germany and by the swing of Turkish opinion to Kaiser Wilhelm II, who had declared that he was the true defender of Islam. Like their British counterparts, German agents infiltrated the lands of the Middle East, often in the guise of archaeologists, and set about influencing the desert tribes against the British. To meet that threat British agents worked long and hard to maintain Britain's hold over tribes friendly to her, a task that bore fruit in the Arab revolt of 1916 and the decisive defeat of the Turks in Palestine in 1918.

Kitchener was deeply interested in the moves and counter-moves reported to him by the Sirdar, his old friend Sir Reginald Wingate, and important sheikhs representing a variety of nationalist opinions were constant visitors to the Residency. While the nationalist movement had manifested itself in Egypt in a pro-Egyptian, anti-British agitation and in plots against his life, in the Sinai and further east there were tribes anxious to accept British support in the conspiracies against the Turks. In Kitchener they found a ready audience. His friendly discussions with Abdullah Ibn Husain, the son of the Sharif of Mecca, paved the way for that powerful ruler to support Britain during the First World War and to refuse the Ottoman command that all tribes should proclaim holy war against the British infidels.

On 17 June 1914, shortly before Kitchener was due to take his annual leave, it was announced from Buckingham Palace that he had been created an Earl, an honour that gave him a great deal of pleasure; and two days later he set off on the first part of his journey home from Alexandria to Marseilles. He would never see Egypt again.

Of all the countries in which he had served, Egypt had given Kitchener the most satisfaction. From his early friendships with discerning Egyptians and Levantines he had refined his love of fine art and antiques until collecting had become first a hobby and then an obsession. His knowledge of Arabic and his acquaintance with Muslim etiquette had opened doors in his understanding of diplomatic behaviour, and in his early manhood the long rides over the desert wastes with his Arab scouts had given him a taste for companionship in extremity whose savour had never entirely disappeared. Egypt, he often admitted to friends, was his spiritual home and its inhabitants the best of friends. And the Egyptians did not forget him. Serving in Egypt in the Arab Bureau during the summer of 1916 at the time of Kitchener's death, Ronald Storrs heard a grief-stricken Egyptian cry out: '*Al-Lurd, al-Lurd mat. Allah yir hamel!*' (The Lord is dead. May God be merciful to him.)[28]

10

WAR LORD: RAISING THE NEW ARMIES

After arriving at Dover on 23 June Kitchener travelled to Broome Park to inspect progress and then set off on a series of country house visits, beginning at Taplow Court. It was while he was there that news of the assassination of Archduke Franz Ferdinand, heir to the throne of Austria–Hungary, was announced in the morning papers of Monday 29 June. To most British people, waiting for the summer holiday season to begin, events in Bosnia's capital, Sarajevo, seemed remote and unimportant but, with his knowledge of the ramifications of Balkan politics and Germany's interest there, Kitchener was less sanguine. Turning to his hosts at breakfast he remarked laconically, 'This will mean war.' Few others believed him and most people were inclined to regard the assassination as being little more than a minor irritation concerning only the Balkan countries.

What followed next was the well-documented progression towards a global confrontation with demands being issued, threats being made and positions becoming entrenched as Europe marched inexorably towards confrontation. The first flashpoint came on 23 July when Austria–Hungary issued an ultimatum to Serbia making ten demands for the suppression of Serb nationalist groups, the punishment of the assassins and participation in the judicial process. Serbia was given forty-eight hours to comply but stopped short of allowing Austria–Hungary to take part in the trial of the assassins – Gabriel Princip and his associates – arguing that it should be referred to the International Court at The Hague. The response seemed sufficient to avert a wider crisis but already diplomacy was proving powerless to stop Europe's drift towards war. Both countries mobilised their armed forces as Germany, Austria–Hungary's main ally, encouraged Vienna to take decisive action against the Serbs before any other country intervened in the crisis. On 28 July, confident of German support, Austria–Hungary declared war on Serbia and the European house of cards began to collapse. The following day, Russia, Serbia's traditional friend and protector, began to mobilise its forces along the border with Austria and within twenty-four hours this was followed by the order for full mobilisation.

This bellicose move, designed to warn Vienna not to trifle with Serbia, brought an ultimatum from Germany, demanding that Russia cease her preparations for war. A second ultimatum was sent to Russia's ally, France. When no suitable responses were forthcoming from either St Petersburg or Paris, Germany declared war on Russia on 1 August and on France two days later. Even at that late hour Britain had no obligation to become involved and Grey kept up a flurry of diplomatic messages to the different capitals of Europe; but the die was cast when the German General Staff agreed to keep to the letter of their war plans. These, the result of years of careful planning, centred on a swift knock-out blow to France – estimated to require no longer than forty days – thus allowing the German Army then to concentrate on defeating the Russians in the east. The only drawback was that the punch had to be delivered through Belgium and Belgium's neutrality was guaranteed by Britain in a treaty of 1839. It was a calculated risk whether or not Britain honoured its terms. On 4 August units of the German Army crossed the Belgian frontier, an irreversible decision that led to Grey demanding from Berlin an assurance by midnight that the country's neutrality would be respected. When this was not forthcoming Britain declared herself to be at war with Germany.

During the uneasy days before that climax, Kitchener had increased the number of his official appointments, although like others in London he had not abandoned the social round. On 21 July he lunched with the German Ambassador, Prince Lichnowsky, who agreed that the crisis in the Balkans, and Austria–Hungary's aggressive attitude, must lead to war. Eight days later Kitchener lunched with Asquith and Winston Churchill, now First Lord of the Admiralty, and argued that Britain could never again claim the right to be a world power if she did not stand firm with the French against any invasion by Germany or Austria–Hungary. The meeting drew Kitchener into the Cabinet's thinking on the international situation and his own reasoning made a deep impression on Asquith. While addressing the House of Commons on 3 August Grey echoed Kitchener's words on the absolute necessity of supporting France: 'If we stood aside, our moral position would be such as to have lost us all respect.'[1] But in spite of the confidence placed in him by the Cabinet and the value he knew they placed on his experience, Kitchener did not want to remain in London if war was declared. His proper place, he told the King, was in Egypt.

With the situation in Europe deteriorating, the government ordered all heads of overseas missions on leave in Britain to return to their posts on 31 July. In the absence of further orders Kitchener prepared to return to Cairo on the overland route through France to Marseilles, where a cruiser would take him to Egypt. He spent the weekend at Broome and told Storrs, who was staying at Rochester, to meet him at Dover on Monday 3 August to catch the one o'clock steamer to Calais. Storrs met him shortly before midday and was mildly surprised to find Kitchener pacing the deck in a state of nervous anxiety. The captain had been ordered to start immediately but the demands of the railway timetable on a bank holiday weekend, and the late arrival of the boat train, had persuaded him to delay departure. While FitzGerald and Cecil were urging that their chief's orders had to be obeyed they were interrupted by a telephone message from the Prime Minister ordering him to return to London.[2] Storrs never forgot the look of dread on Kitchener's face or the feeling of resignation that accompanied the party as they made their way back to the capital, where a further message awaited him from Asquith: 'with matters in their present critical condition I was anxious that you should not get beyond the reach of personal consultation and advice.'[3] Kitchener was not trying to run away from his responsibilities – he was, after all returning to his posting in Egypt – but he had never lost his fear of being placed in the War Office in a position where he would be subservient to a Cabinet minister.

He had reason to be worried because Britain was entering the war without settled leadership at the War Office. Following the earlier resignation of J.E.B. Seely in the wake of the Curragh Mutiny,[4] Asquith had taken over responsibility for the position of Secretary of State for War and his first thought had been to hand it over to Haldane, at that time Lord Chancellor. Kitchener's presence in England changed everything. That same day *The Times* carried a leader arguing Kitchener's claims for appointment to the War Office and the cry was taken up by other newspapers, including the normally cautious Liberal *Westminster Gazette* whose editor, J.A. Spender, argued that if Kitchener were allowed to return to Egypt 'there would tomorrow be such an uproar against the Government as had not been known in our time'.[5] Appointing Kitchener was an obvious solution but first Asquith had to persuade colleagues who might baulk at a soldier being appointed to a Cabinet post normally held by a civilian. He had also to persuade Grey that Kitchener would serve his country more efficiently in London and that Egypt could be left in other hands. At the same time, Haldane was keen to keep Kitchener out of the Cabinet, but his claims had been undermined by a newspaper campaign, headed by Lord Northcliffe, that maintained Haldane's alleged German sympathies (he had once stated that he looked on Germany as his spiritual home) would make him unacceptable to the French.

The flurry of press comment helped Asquith to make up his mind that Kitchener was the only realistic appointment or, as his colleague Walter Runciman, President of the Board of Trade, remarked, there was a great advantage for Asquith of 'having the unattackable K at the War Office and at his board'.[6] After returning to London, Kitchener met Asquith on 4 August and, having been persuaded that it was his duty to accept the post of Secretary of State for War, he insisted that it should not entail parliamentary duties and that he would be allowed to return to Egypt once the war was over. Although there is no record of the proceedings, Asquith agreed to those conditions and the appointment was announced on the evening of the following day.[7] Kitchener thus became the first serving soldier to sit in the Cabinet since General Monck in 1660 and for his pains he drew three salaries: in addition to his field marshal's pay he received £5,000 as Secretary of State and a special allowance of £1,140.

In his diary Asquith admitted that Kitchener's appointment was 'a hazardous experiment', but he vindicated his decision by adding that the emergency needed a strong man capable of carrying the country into war.[8] Whatever his qualms, though, they were not shared by the rest of the country as The Times reported the following day:

> We need hardly say with what profound satisfaction and relief we hear of Lord Kitchener's appointment as Secretary of State for War. Since the suggestion has been put forward by The Times during the past two days there has been abundant testimony to the confidence which his name inspires in the public at this tremendous crisis. It was unthinkable, indeed, that so great a military asset should be wasted at such a time, and we heartily congratulate the Government on the promptitude with which they have confirmed the popular choice. In the huge task of equipping and dispatching our land forces, as well as perfecting the measures for protecting these shores, Lord Kitchener's services will be invaluable. Let us repeat that the appointment will be equally welcome to our friends on the Continent.[9]

The Times' leader was typical of the enthusiasm shown once the news became public. To the man in the street all was well now that Britain had secured the services of its greatest soldier in its hour of need, and much of the anxiety that had gripped the nation on 4 August evaporated when the headlines announced Britain's new warlord. In their eyes Kitchener could do no wrong. His imperial progress had seen him defeat all who had dared to stand before him and his very presence – his huge frame, the luxuriant moustache, the fixity of his gaze – had become a symbol of British pluck and resolve. In short, he was nothing less than a national institution whose existence would strike terror into the hearts of Britain's enemies. In that respect Asquith had shown great discernment in engineering Kitchener's services at such a critical time. As he admitted to his confidante, Venetia Stanley, on the evening he made the announcement, no other public figure in the country could possibly have achieved the same effect.[10]

Kitchener took up his appointment with characteristic energy, standing for no opposition to his immediate plans. He arranged for FitzGerald to remain with him as his military secretary and to his staff came two additional secretaries, Herbert Creedy and Sir George Arthur. Before his first day was out, he had also commandeered the services of an official motor car and had made arrangements to move into rented accommodation at 2 Carlton Gardens, which he acquired from Lady Wantage (in March 1915 the King gave him an official residence at York House, St James's Palace, where he lived as he had done in India and Egypt, in the company of his closest members of staff). That sense of drive and expediency also appealed to the public: to their mind, once Kitchener had taken on a task, he would not rest until he had seen it through to its completion. Within a day or two, most people were talking about the war being over by Christmas.

They had other reasons for being so confident, since they had been assured that the war would be won at sea by the ships of the Royal Navy. Meanwhile, in France, the small but highly professional British Expeditionary Force (BEF) would help the French Army to repulse the Germans, holding them up long enough to be crushed by the Russian steamroller from the east. That was also the strategic scenario favoured by most professional soldiers, who forgot that the American Civil War had dragged on four years, the Russo-Japanese War for two, let alone the stalemate of the Boer War. Very few people envisaged that it would be a war of entrenchment. Indeed it was an indication of British optimism that volunteers were invited originally to sign on for six months, or for the duration of the war, whichever was the longer. The smooth mobilisation of the BEF, the best equipped and most professional army to have left Britain's shores, was a further example of the no-nonsense approach that would surely give a short, sharp riposte to German pretensions.

WAR LORD: RAISING THE NEW ARMIES

That sense of enthusiastic conviction gave the early weeks of the war an unreal quality, creating a feeling that war was a glorious adventure and that man had been transformed and liberated from the doldrums of a hum-drum existence. That sentiment finds its truest expression in Rupert Brooke's poem 'Peace' and in Herbert Asquith's equally emotionally charged sonnet 'The Volunteer', but it struck a chord, too, in the actions of ordinary people, who felt ennobled by the exhilaration of war. 'This was too much for me to resist,' admitted sixteen-year-old George Coppard, 'and as if drawn by a magnet, I knew I had to enlist straightaway.'[11]

On 6 August the government authorised an increase to the army of 500,000 men and the first recruiting posters appeared in the streets the following day, announcing: 'An addition of 100,000 men to His Majesty's Regular Army is immediately necessary in the present grave National Emergency. Lord Kitchener is confident that this appeal will be at once responded to by all those who have the safety of our Empire at heart.' By 12 September 478,893 men had volunteered and of a total of 5.7 million who eventually served their country by the end of the war 2.46 million had enlisted by the end of 1915.[12]

One of the first to recognise that need for manpower had been Kitchener. When he entered the House of Lords on 25 August to make his maiden speech, he caused some amusement by mistakenly sitting on the episcopal benches, but his words produced very few smiles:

> The Empires with whom we are at war have called to the Colours almost their entire male population. The principle which we on our part shall observe is this – that while their maximum force undergoes a steady diminution, the reinforcements we prepare shall steadily and increasingly flow out until we have an Army in the field which, in numbers not less than in quality, will not be unworthy of the power and responsibilities of the British Empire. I cannot at this stage say what will be the limits of the forces required, or what measures may eventually become necessary to supply and maintain them. The scale of the Field Army which we are now calling into being is large and may rise in the course of the next six or seven months to a total of thirty divisions continually maintained in the field. But if the war should be protracted, and if its fortunes should be varied or adverse, exertions and sacrifices beyond any which have

been demanded will be required from the whole nation and Empire, and where they are required we may be sure that they will not be denied to the extreme needs of the State by Parliament or the people.[13]

Of all the members of Asquith's Cabinet, Kitchener was the first to understand that not only would the war be a long one, but that it would need a greatly enlarged British Army to win it. A few days earlier he had told the Cabinet that the war would last at least three years and that Britain would require one million men under arms. His remarks astonished his colleagues, who held to the view that the war would be won at sea, with Germany being defeated in Europe by the combined military might of France and Russia.

With the help of hindsight those same colleagues praised Kitchener after the war for his wonderful intuition, implying that he had come to those conclusions through military instinct rather than through reasoning. Such a reading, though, does not take into account Kitchener's own grasp of the military situation or of his past experience. A glance at Kitchener's military career shows that, not only was he used to fighting wars of long duration, but that he had won his greatest victories by dint of superior numbers: in Sudan, at the Atbara and Omdurman he had used his forces to crush the Mahdists; in South Africa, at Paardeberg, he had been the only field commander to attempt to grind the Boers into the ground at Cronje's laager; and later in the war his army, 250,000 strong, held down the enemy with their drives and sweeps. No other British commander in modern times had ever used his men in such great numbers to achieve his objective. Faced by war in France against a numerically superior enemy, Kitchener was employing the tactics that had served him in the past.

Like other commanders of his age, Kitchener had also studied the American Civil War, which had dragged on for four years and which had seen a nation in arms. To his friends Kitchener would point out that Lee had surrendered to Grant at Appomattox because he no longer had enough men to fight on his side, a fate that could have been avoided had the southern states possessed a military machine capable of realising its full quota of trained soldiers. Other lessons from the past flooded back into his mind: he was fond of reminding the French technical adviser to the British government, the Marquis de Chasseloup Laubat, that Napoleon had eventually been beaten because he could not replace the huge number of fighting men he had lost in Spain and during the invasion of Russia. To prevent that fate befalling Britain, a large volunteer army would have to be found. Spring 1915 was the earliest date for the arrival in France of battalions of the 'New Army' or, as it also came to be called, the 'Kitchener Army'. Until that happened, argued Kitchener, the Russians would have to put pressure on the Germans in the east, thus relieving the French who, with the BEF, were grappling with the German offensive in Flanders. This was unconventional thinking to most members of the Cabinet but such was their belief in Kitchener's authority that his strategy was adopted.

The problem facing Kitchener was how to create out of nothing the New Armies, the aim being to raise seventy divisions plus a supply of reserves. For generations the British people had refused to tolerate conscription and by tradition the army had always been small and professional. During the Boer War volunteers had flocked into the army, giving some junior generals such as Hunter and Macdonald cause to believe that compulsory service should be introduced, but theirs were minority voices. Most senior soldiers did not want to see the professional army becoming a civilian mob. The Liberal government had, from the beginning, also turned its face against conscription, although it had toyed with the idea of introducing it in 1906 as part and parcel of Haldane's reforms and the creation of the Territorial Force. For one thing, most Liberal ministers felt that any measure of compulsion would infringe individual liberties, and for another, they were chary of offending the trades unions. Chancellor of the Exchequer David Lloyd George spoke for many of his Liberal colleagues when he claimed in 1910, 'No party dare touch it [conscription] because of the violent prejudices which would be excited even if it were suspected that a Government contemplated the possibility of establishing anything of the kind.'[14]

Nevertheless, the idea of Britain's young manhood serving a term in the colours refused to go away: in 1905 Lord Roberts took up the cause of the National Service League, which advocated a period of service in the armed services for all young men. It rested its case primarily on the need for a strong army for home defence, arguing that Germany was preparing for a war of invasion and that the Royal Navy would be unable to prevent it happening. As late as 1912 Roberts was claiming that, once Germany had achieved naval and military superiority, she would make a lethal strike across the North Sea that Britain would be powerless to resist. The claim caused uproar. A motion was raised in the House of Commons for the field marshal's pension to be reduced and the Liberal press roundly condemned him for scaremongering. While Roberts was correct in his assessment that Germany was re-arming with war in mind, he was stretching a point in suggesting that Britain's home defences were so weak that any invasion could not be repelled: the Territorial Force had been created for just such a purpose. The other weakness in the League's argument was that its proposed national servicemen would only have been employed in home defence, whereas any war in the future would be fought overseas. What killed off any hope of the League succeeding in its aims, however, was the overwhelming dislike most people felt for compulsory military service. In peacetime, conscription was never a serious political argument.

However, despite that widespread opposition, it may be asked: why did Kitchener not choose to introduce conscription in August 1914, at the outbreak of the war? Had he given the word the country would surely have rallied to the call, so high was the regard in which he was held. With the backing of those Conservative and Liberal MPs who had advocated conscription Kitchener could have made a stand on the issue but, as he told colleagues, he was out of touch with the arguments that had raged before the war. Out of loyalty to Asquith he fell in with the Cabinet's wishes that for the time being conscription should not become a political issue, but there was a more compelling argument to Kitchener's decision. Kitchener was not convinced that national service was a valid alternative to securing men who were keen and enthusiastic to join the Regular Army. If New Armies had to be raised then he held to the belief that the men should be volunteers, not civilian conscripts, and that the New Army battalions would be linked to the regimental structure of the Regular Army. No new regiments would be raised but the existing regiments would be allowed to expand their battalion strength: and by the war's end a not untypical regiment such as The Highland Light Infantry had up to twenty-six battalions on its strength instead of the normal, peacetime, two Regular battalions and several Territorial Force battalions. In that way, Kitchener argued, the volunteers could be assimilated quickly into the New Armies and no new machinery would have to be assembled to deal with conscripts.

To confirm the logic of his thinking he pointed out that it had taken France and Germany some thirty years to perfect the administration of their conscript armies; how could Britain equal that feat within a few months? Besides, he was not unaware of the magic of his personal magnetism in gaining new recruits. 'I have held up my finger and the men are flocking to me in thousands,' he was often heard to remark in the War Office whenever the idea of compulsory service was bruited by his colleagues.[15] He might have added, too, that voluntary service seemed to be both fair and virtuous to those who joined up or to those who allowed their employees to enlist. 'The employer allowed a percentage of his men to go,' noted Brigadier-General C.R. Ballard. 'Instead of grumbling about compulsion, he felt a glow of virtue over doing his bit. The rich merchant, whose chauffeur had enlisted, sweated virtue as he walked to the office. Everybody felt the uplift that comes from voluntary service.'[16]

The army that Kitchener inherited in August 1914 was the force that had been brought into being by Haldane's army reforms and on the outbreak of war its establishment consisted of the following numbers:

Regular Army, 247,432
Army Reserve, 145,347
Special Reserve, 63,933
Channel Islands Militia, 5,613
Territorial Force, 268,777
Territorial Reserve, 2,082
Bermuda and Isle of Man Volunteers, 330[17]

Of the Regular Army, 120,000 men were serving abroad while the remainder made up the six divisions of the BEF, which was expected to form Britain's contribution to a land war in Europe, fighting on the left flank of the French Army. In the event the BEF on August 1914 consisted of four infantry divisions and one cavalry division: it was a fine, well-disciplined force possessing efficient ancillary services, up to date equipment and modern armaments. The official historian of the war called it 'incomparably the best trained, best organised and best equipped British Army which ever went forth to war' although ominously, he added the rider 'except in the matter of numbers'.[18] Pitted against it and the French Army were seventy-eight German divisions. By the years' end there were eight British infantry divisions of the Regular Army in France together with the Guards brigade and four Territorial divisions; by then Kitchener's forecast that a million men would be needed and that the war would last until 1917 had been shown to be correct. The race was now on to train the new Kitchener divisions for deployment in France by the late spring of the following year.

One solution presented itself to Kitchener as a possible alternative to hurrying the volunteer New Armies into being – the men of the Territorial Force. Although they had been earmarked for home defence under the Haldane reforms, at least 20,000 men of their number had volunteered to serve overseas and the first of them arrived in France on 1 September. Formed in 1907 by the Territorial and Reserve Forces Bill and mustered the following year, the Territorial Force was intended to provide the country with a second line of defence of part-time soldiers to replace the old Yeomanry and Volunteers, whose primary task was the defence of Britain in time of war. In that way, the Regular Army would be freed to concentrate on its overseas garrisons and on fighting a war in Europe. Haldane also hoped that the Territorial Force would act as a bridge between the public and the military: 'No longer,' he claimed at a public meeting in Manchester in 1907, 'would there be that gap between the army on the one hand and the public on the other.'[19]

It was a pious hope for, from its inception, controversy dogged the Territorial Force. Apart from a short period in 1909 when an invasion scare swept through Britain and recruitment rose to 270,000, annual recruiting figures were disappointing and when war broke out it was 47,317 men short of its establishment figure and the annual wastage rate was 12.5 per cent. One of the problems was that the Regular Army had failed to take the Territorials seriously, although Major-General Douglas Haig, as Director of Military Training, had given Haldane sterling service at the War Office in helping to create the force. As Territorial soldiers only trained once a week and attended a fortnight's camp once a year, senior Regular officers looked upon them as little more than an ill-trained civilian rabble that used up valuable resources. A further problem was that the Territorial Force was only partially under War Office control, the local units being organised and run by civilian County Associations under the presidency of the local lord-lieutenant. There were, of course, excellent Territorial units and a total of 692 Territorial battalions were mustered, with 318 seeing operational service abroad, but as a means of raising the New Armies, the Territorial Force was a non-starter.

Kitchener had been out of the country when the Territorial Force had been formed and, uninterested in the arguments that had raged about army reform between 1906 and 1912, he knew little about the system. Initially, though, he was inclined to include it marginally in his plans, telling the House of Lords in his second speech on 17 September that:

> The Territorial Force is making great strides in efficiency, and will before many months be ready to take a share in the campaign … the soldier-like qualities evinced by the Force are an assurance to the Government that they may count to the full upon its readiness to play its part wherever the exigencies of the military situation may demand.[20]

But the more he explored its labyrinthine connection to the War Office, the more convinced Kitchener became that the Territorials would have to play a subsidiary role. Partly, he thought it was wrong to disrupt the predetermined plan that the Territorials should be committed to home defence – Kitchener looked on a German invasion as an outside possibility – and partly he dismissed the force as a 'town clerk's army' that would disrupt army discipline. More importantly, though, Kitchener was anxious to stamp his own authority on the New Armies. In Egypt, as Sirdar, he had created an army after his own design, and in India he had defeated Curzon in his battle to impose his ideas of military administration; he now wanted to build an army that he alone could control through the existing organisation at the War Office.

Inevitably, his attitudes caused a good deal of offence to those Liberals who admired the Territorials. Asquith admitted privately that, 'Lord Kitchener has rather demoralised the War Office with his bull in a china shop manners and methods, and particularly his ignorance of & indifference to the Territorials';[21] and after the war Haldane condemned Kitchener for not using the Territorial organisation, complaining that, 'I was unable to prevail on him to adopt, or even to make much use of the Territorial organisation I had provided.'[22] While Haldane had a point that the County Associations could have offered a means of channelling the new recruits, Kitchener was right to keep the Territorials in a secondary role in the early part of 1914. Its members had volunteered for four years' part-time service, mainly at home; therefore it was wrong, Kitchener argued, to change in mid-stream their conditions of service. Besides, the first recruiting figures convinced him that a volunteer army based on the existing army structure and responsible only to him could be brought quickly into being, trained and soon be sent to France; and his decision was justified by the results: by October there were enough men for twelve new divisions and by June 1916 thirty Kitchener divisions had been raised, seeing service in France, Palestine, Mesopotamia, Salonika and at Gallipoli.

To bring his New Armies into being Kitchener made use of three propaganda channels for the recruitment of volunteers – an official government agency, the press and voluntary, ad hoc, local and national recruiting committees. The first of these was the all-party Parliamentary Recruiting Committee (PRC), whose purpose was to solve the problem of 'how the grave issues of the war should be fully comprehended by the people and thereby give a powerful impetus to recruiting'. Financed by the War Office and reliant on the administrative structures of the main parliamentary parties, the committee opened its campaign early in September with a direct appeal that was posted to eight million voters. This was followed by a hastily arranged nationwide timetable of public speeches given by politicians and public figures to encourage men to enlist. Some of those rallies organised by the PRC were highly emotional affairs accompanied by the singing of patriotic songs, much flag waving and the appearance of a finely turned out recruiting sergeant. Popular artists including Harry Lauder offered their services free of charge and the movement spawned Phyllis Dane's famous call-to-arms embodied in her song 'We don't want to lose you, but we think you ought to go'. Soon it became *de rigueur* at all meetings to feature prominently Kitchener's portrait.

From the outset the PRC had realised the importance of Kitchener to its campaign and Kitchener had been equally ready to lend whatever help he could. The appearance in *London Opinion* of 15 September 1914 of Alfred Leete's famous portrayal of Kitchener with an outstretched finger proclaiming that he 'wants YOU – JOIN YOUR COUNTRY'S ARMY!' was taken up by the committee. With its added appeal, 'God Save the King', it appeared in several variations and became the most instantly recognisable symbol of Kitchener's desire to raise a huge volunteer army, although there is little evidence that its use as a poster was widespread. Even so, the use of Kitchener's features was a masterstroke: everyone knew the extravagant moustache and the firm, confident eyes. By the beginning of January 1915 *The Times* was able to report that Britain was a nation in arms and that the success of the recruiting campaign was due to Kitchener and his portrait:

> Posters appealing to recruits are to be seen on every hoarding, in most shop windows, in omnibuses, tramcars and commercial vans. The great base of Nelson's Pillar is covered with them. Their number and variety are remarkable. Everywhere Lord Kitchener sternly points a monstrously big finger, exclaiming 'I Want You'. Another bill says: 'Lord Kitchener wants another 100,000 men'. ('My word,' remarked a lonely spinster according to a current joke, 'one would do me!')[23]

The PRC also had at its command the services of the Caxton Advertising Agency, whose contract with the War Office to advertise for recruits was worth £6,000. Its owner, Sir Hedley Le Bas, began his career in the army as a trooper in the 15th Hussars and founded his agency in 1899. Taking Kitchener into his confidence, he secured a promise that as far as was practicable Kitchener's name would be linked personally with the appeals. Thus posters appeared asking, 'What is your answer to Lord Kitchener's call?' or declaring that, 'Lord Kitchener is much gratified with the response already made to the Appeal for additional men for His Majesty's Army'. By the end of the war the PRC had produced 54 million posters, leaflets and other advertisements, 12,000 public rallies had been held and 20,000 speeches made.

The press, too, played its part. Kitchener's appeal for the first 100,000 recruits appeared in the pages of *The Times* and the *Daily Mail* and in the early months of the war his name was associated closely with the call, 'Your King and Country need You'. Aware that the newspapers could prove a double-edged sword, Kitchener was not loath to praise their editors when they toed his line; when they attacked him or his policies he was in favour of censoring them or even of closing them down. 'The idea of Lord Kitchener was that all information should be held back from the public,' said Sir Arthur Markham to the House of Commons on 1 September the day after the notorious 'Amiens Dispatch' appeared in a special Sunday issue of *The Times*. Written by Arthur Moore, it was headlined 'Broken British Regiments Battling against Odds' and it painted a dire picture of the heavy losses sustained by II Corps during the Mons retreat. Kitchener immediately issued a strongly worded rebuttal through the Press Bureau. Questions were asked in Parliament about the right of newspapers to publish their own versions of what was happening in France and for a time the freedom of the press hung in the balance. Ironically, one of the factors that shielded *The Times* was that the publication of the despatch actually encouraged recruiting, F.E. Smith, who was the censor, even admitting that he added a sentence or two pointing up the need for more volunteers. 'I have been asked by Lord Kitchener as far as possible to assist his object which was, of course, to obtain recruits,' was Smith's explanation during the debate in the House of Commons.[24] Thereafter, Kitchener kept the press at a distance and the first official war correspondents were not allowed to go to France until May 1915. Until then Kitchener put his relationship with the press on a military footing, with eyewitness briefings being provided by Colonel Ernest Swinton, an engineering officer who had served with him in South Africa.[25]

By 12 September the first 100,000 men had been recruited and been formed into six divisions, numbered 9 to 14, following the Regular Army divisions. (In the British Army of the First World War, four battalions made up a brigade, three brigades a division.) These were men of a different stamp from the recruits of earlier years. Most were better educated, better fed and fitter, and they came from all walks of life. Above all, they were keen. 'They became soldiers in spirit overnight,' recalled one of the officers who helped to train them, 'willing to learn and to learn quickly, so as to get it all over as soon as possible.'[26] In the first flush of enthusiasm the War Office's problem was not to raise sufficient numbers of recruits so much as what to do with them once they had enlisted. So great was the pressure on the existing army structure that recruits frequently went short of uniforms, weapons with which to train and even accommodation. Vast tented encampments soon mushroomed in civic parks, farmers' fields and in country estates as would-be soldiers drilled with broomsticks while still wearing their best suits. To meet the shortages production of khaki uniforms and boots had to be stepped up, supplies were purchased from the USA and the Post Office helped out with blue uniforms surplus to requirements. Every hardship was met with good humour by the recruits, who quickly soaked up the essential *esprit de corps* of the regimental battalions to which they belonged. To train them, NCOs who had last seen service in South Africa were called up out of retirement and elderly majors, who had failed to win promotion in peacetime, returned to lead battalions as colonels. On the whole these 'dug-outs', as they were called mischievously, served their men well and by the time the first Kitchener divisions embarked for France they had a good conceit of themselves and their abilities.

To encourage the flow of the recruits Kitchener agreed to lower the upper age limit to thirty-five and the physical standards to a minimum of 5ft 6in (this was reduced again before the year was out to 5ft 3in).

He also agreed to a system of deferred enlistment whereby men could enlist and be held in reserve until they were needed. Another innovation was his approval of the formation of 'Pals' battalions, so called because they kept together in one unit volunteers from cities and towns or from working, sporting or recreational backgrounds. The first Pals battalion was formed on 28 August in Liverpool and within a week there were three more. In all, 304 Pals battalions were formed from such diverse backgrounds as cricket clubs, public schools, shipyards and coal-mines. It seemed a fortuitous idea, one that Kitchener was happy to encourage. 'The atmosphere was wonderful,' said a soldier of the 18th West Yorkshire Regiment (2nd Bradford Pals), 'a gang of lads all together and more or less of the same age, with the same ideas – they all wanted to travel and to see life and adventure, you know, just something different.'[27] It proved a popular concept but it reaped a bitter harvest. At the Battle of the Somme in July 1916 the 16th Highland Light Infantry (Boys Brigade) lost 554 killed or wounded, all from the same part of Glasgow and all associated with the Boys Brigade.

Contrary to a belief that grew up after the war, that the soldiers risked everything while the generals were uncaring about casualties – the 'lions led by donkeys' theory – Kitchener never accustomed himself to the size of the casualty lists. 'This isn't war!' he exclaimed to Sir Edward Grey on more than one occasion. Confronted by the growing lists of casualties that appeared each day in the newspapers, he would blame front-line commanders for wasting men's lives in useless attacks on heavily defended German trenches. 'I never mind ordering a soldier to face danger,' he would say, 'but I will not have soldiers murdered.' Hysterical stories about German atrocities left him unmoved and unconvinced. After being told a highly coloured story, Kitchener cut the speaker short by saying, 'What is the good of discussing that incident? All war is an outrage!'[28] It was a far cry from Paardeberg and the uproar that had greeted the 1,200 casualties sustained in one day's fighting.

However much he worried about the casualty lists and however depressed he became about the static nature of the war in France, Kitchener never failed to inspect the battalions of the New Armies before they embarked for war service. Having brought them into being,

Kitchener regarded it as his duty to see them off and perhaps to offer them hope and encouragement, too. Often the inspections were hastily arranged affairs lacking any military pomp, but whatever the conditions or the weather, Kitchener was present, a gleam of pride and satisfaction in his eyes as he watched the passing ranks. The memory would live on in the minds of those who experienced them, as it did with George Coppard:

> We were beginning to shape like real soldiers and I began to wonder when we would go overseas. At the end of February came another move, this time as part of our training. The battalion assembled and commenced the first stage of marching to Aldershot, roughly a hundred miles, in full kit, less ammunition. The march was done in easy stages and took nine days. At East Grinstead we marched past Sir Archibald Hunter, GOC Aldershot Command. On the next day Lord Kitchener became the highlight of our journey. There was a good deal of wind-up before this event, and we were ordered to make a model salute and get the colour of Kitchener's eyes. On the command 'Eyes right', I swung my head smartly and stared searchingly into the grey eyes. I was disappointed for they were so heavily hooded. In his greatcoat Kitchener looked very big, but so baggy and grey – nothing like the dark handsome posters of him which were displayed all over the country.[29]

Unfortunately, not all soldiers of the Regular Army shared Coppard's optimism. From the beginning of the war, the BEF's commander, Field Marshal Sir John French, had privately expressed his disapproval of Kitchener's thinking. At the first meeting of the War Council, held in the afternoon of 5 August, he had clashed with Kitchener over the possible duration of the war: like most senior officers he felt that it would be relatively short and had demanded that five divisions be sent to France as part of the expeditionary force instead of the four proposed by Kitchener. The following day the Cabinet accepted Kitchener's recommendation, a decision that deeply disturbed French. Always prone to be suspicious of his colleagues, he came to believe that Kitchener deliberately wanted to starve him of troops. As time went on he came to be haunted, too, by the spectre of Kitchener assuming command of the New Armies once they were in the field, thereby claiming the ultimate victory. The decision to withdraw selected officers and NCOs from the BEF to train the New Armies only served to harden that sense of mistrust.

French's concerns were fuelled by Brigadier-General Henry Wilson, his deputy chief of staff, who was openly contemptuous of 'K's "shadow armies" for shadow campaigns at unknown and distant dates'.[30] Wilson, an articulate, though vain and impetuous man, had told friends that he refused to be 'bullied [by Kitchener] especially when he talks such nonsense'.[31] Another concern was that, in the recruitment of the New Armies and their establishment by division, too much emphasis was being placed on local association. Many doubted the wisdom of raising Pals battalions, believing that men from the same background might band together to resist military authority or refuse to fight if the going got tough, for fear of high casualties. Far better, they reasoned, to disperse the men in battalions throughout the Regular Army. That uneasiness reached its peak in the question of what to do with recruits from Ireland and Wales, areas of Britain which, unlike Scotland, were not noted for providing the British Army with large numbers of reliable recruits.

Traditionally, Welsh people tended to disregard the armed forces as a means of making a living. Nonconformist preachers had taught their congregations to condemn militarism, and in the South Wales mining communities there was active prejudice against the army following its intervention in the Cambrian miners' strike and the Tonypandy riots of 1910. Recruiting was always going to be a problem in Wales and the question of separate and distinguishable Welsh units might not have become an issue had it not been for the intervention of Lloyd George. In the Queen's Hall in London on 19 September 1914, he made a strong case for the creation of a 'Welsh Army in the field' in the shape a recognised Welsh Army Corps. His proposal, together with a demand for the provision of Nonconformist chaplains for the Welsh troops, caused a row when the Cabinet met on 28 October. Kitchener angrily told his colleagues that he would resign rather than comply with Lloyd George's demands and could not see any reason why Welshmen should be treated separately.

Asquith managed to curb Kitchener's temper and to placate Lloyd George, but it was only a temporary truce. Two days later the row erupted again when it was revealed that Welsh soldiers had been forbidden to speak Welsh, even in private. Once again Kitchener refused to recognise the powerful emotions involved: he told Asquith that the Welsh as a nation tended to be wild, insubordinate and were not to be trusted. At the Cabinet meeting, though, he decided to back down in the face of Lloyd George's arguments, a tactical retreat that temporarily patched up the quarrel between the two men. Three days later he promoted a Welsh protégé, Colonel Owen Thomas, to be the general commanding in North Wales, thus moving Lloyd George to admit to Asquith that 'he [Kitchener] is a big man, & what is more does things in a big way'.[32] Later in the war, in February 1915, Kitchener also sanctioned the formation of the Welsh Guards, although in private he used to joke that the women of Wales had only pressed their men into service to claim the 12s 6d a week separation allowance.

Kitchener had been forced to back down over the Welsh recruiting issue largely because he faced a powerful and persuasive opponent in Lloyd George. Unfortunately he was unable to take the same attitude to Irish recruiting.

When war broke out Asquith and John Redmond, the parliamentary leader of the Irish Nationalists, agreed that the Irish Home Rule Act should be put on the statute book and that it should be suspended for twelve months or the duration of the war, whichever should prove the longer. At the same time the Ulster Unionists agreed not to press their Amending Bill for the permanent exclusion of the six northern counties. Thus war in Europe temporarily stilled in Ireland the passions that had been threatening to spill over into civil war. In the Ulster counties the unionist leader Sir Edward Carson had 50,000 men in arms, thanks to the organisation of the Ulster Volunteers and to the importation of 24,000 modern rifles and ammunition through the ports of Larne and Bangor. As a counter-balance there was the Irish Volunteer force in the south, made up of a mixture of homerulers and extreme nationalists armed with rifles provided by Irish nationalist sympathisers.

As the call for recruits began to gather momentum, Carson and Redmond jockeyed for political position by offering their Volunteers in the service of the Crown. In so doing, both men were united in their arguments that, by joining up, the men would have earned the right to make political demands once the war was over. There the similarities ended. Lieutenant-General Sir George Richardson, the commander of the Ulster Volunteers, told his men that while they remained in arms they would prove their loyalty to the King and be a permanent reminder to Westminster of Ulster's undying opposition to Home Rule. Redmond, on the other hand, looked on the war as being a struggle for the rights of small nations in which Ireland had to play a historic part. By dedicating themselves to his cause, he told his men, Ireland would earn the right to Home Rule. He also added that by serving Ireland they would provide her with a permanent Irish defence force. In contrast to the crude rhetoric of Richardson and Carson, this was an attractive argument that many members of the Volunteers were prepared to accept (a group of extremists disagreed, remaining the Irish Volunteers while the Redmondite rump became the National Volunteers). When Redmond addressed the press on 19 September, the day after the Home Rule Act was added to the statute book, he reminded them that nothing less than an identifiable 'Irish Brigade' would satisfy the ambitions of his countrymen, who wanted to 'gain national credit for their deeds, and feel like other communities of the Empire, that she too has contributed an army bearing her name in this historic struggle.' His appeal revived the memory of the Wild Geese, the Irish mercenaries who had fought in continental armies under the historical title of the Irish Brigade. Unhappily for future British-Irish relations, Kitchener did not see it in that romantic light, being too prejudiced against Home Rule and more concerned with the realpolitik of recent events in the country of his birth.

Among the first battalions to cross over to France with the BEF were units from the Irish home garrison and their place had been taken by battalions of the Territorial Force. A logical solution to the question of home defence for Ireland would have been the formation of a national reserve force, the provision of which had been a subject for debate in the War Office during the immediate pre-war years (Haldane's measures did not extend to Ireland). Some senior officers in Irish command had argued the case for a volunteer reserve force that would be similar in character and formation to the Territorials, but their pleas had been met with hostility from War Office officials, many of whom were sympathetic to the Ulster cause. The argument dragged on to no avail for four years. Each time senior Irish officers put forward compromise plans, such as confining the force to ex-soldiers, these were stonewalled by officials and politicians who feared that disaffected Irishmen would join up only to turn their guns against the British. At the outset of hostilities Redmond offered the services of the National Volunteers, producing a plan whereby his men would be quartered in military barracks to provide a police and home defence capability. This offer was rejected by Kitchener, who regarded the National Volunteers as rebels in sheep's clothing. The same fear was at the back of his mind when he considered Redmond's requests for a distinctive Irish division, with its own badge and colours, based on Irish volunteers and Irishmen living in Britain who wanted their national identity to be recognised in a tangible way.

On 6 August Redmond met Kitchener at the War Office, where he faced an icy reception. 'Get me 5,000 men and I will say thank you,' Kitchener told him. 'Get me 10,000 and I will take off my hat to you.'[33] Redmond put his demands to Asquith a day later, drawing from the Prime Minister, with whom he had enjoyed a fruitful relationship, the promise in the House of Commons that, 'Lord Kitchener will do everything in his power by consultation with gentlemen in Ireland to arrange for the full equipment and organisation of the Irish Volunteers.' A month later, while visiting Dublin, Asquith changed his tune by promising Redmond that an Irish Army Corps would be established and in a speech at the Mansion House he went out of his way to reassure Irishmen that their national aspirations would be satisfied if they joined the British Army:

> Don't let them be afraid that by joining the colours they will lose their identity and become absorbed in some invertebrate mass, or, what is perhaps equally

repugnant, be artificially distributed into units which have no national cohesion or character.[34]

The idea of using the National Volunteers being a non-starter, Asquith and Redmond turned their energies to persuading Kitchener that an Irish infantry division should be formed.

Eventually it was announced in October that the 16th Division being raised at Mallow would be known as the 16th (Irish) Division and that it would be commanded by Lieutenant-General Sir Lawrence Parsons, an Irishman but no supporter of home rule. He gave offence by appointing Ulster Protestants to senior posts and blocking the way of Catholics, including Redmond's son William, who was refused a commission. (Later he won a DSO for gallantry serving as a subaltern in the Irish Guards.) In despair Redmond sent Parsons a list of suitable Catholic officers who were qualified to command at brigade and battalion level but this disappeared into the War Office filing system with the tart acknowledgement that, 'Lord Kitchener is glad to have this by him for consideration when vacancies occur.'[35] Of equal importance to Redmond and to the men of the 16th Division was that it should have its own cap badge, preferably incorporating the national emblem, the harp. Parsons, though, disagreed, preferring that the men should keep their regimental badges. In this he was supported by Kitchener, who suggested the compromise of a shamrock shoulder strap.

Kitchener's obduracy and the War Office's tardiness in meeting Redmond's requests affected Irish recruiting, so that when Kitchener complained in public that Ireland was not doing her bit, it was with little justification. 'Only 1,200 men are needed,' he said of the 49th Brigade, which was made up largely of Irish recruits, 'and if Ireland finds itself unable to fill up the vacancies, which seems incredible in view of the large number of men of recruitable age in Ireland, steps will be taken to bring the depleted battalions to strength.'[36] Kitchener would counter any opposition by saying that if he had his way the Irish recruits would be dispersed throughout the British Army so that they would not appear in its ranks as a cohesive unit. It should be said by way of redress that the British Army was held in considerable contempt by a large section of the Irish population, many of whom regarded it as an army of occupation.

After an increasingly acrimonious correspondence with Redmond in July and August 1915, Kitchener agreed to compromise by providing the Irish recruits with a semblance of national identity in the army. His reasons for so doing were encouraged both by a growing admiration for Redmond's doggedness and by the genuine concern he felt about the lack of recognition given to the bravery of the Royal Dublin Fusiliers and the Royal Munster Fusiliers at Gallipoli. At a meeting on 29 September 1915 held in the War Office and attended by Augustine Birrell, H.J. Tennant and Redmond, Kitchener announced that, 'Ireland, in his opinion, did magnificently in the matter of recruiting.' Other points to which he agreed, were:

1. The appointment, if possible, of Lord Cavan, Irish Guards, to succeed Parsons.
2. The appointment of Catholic officers to high command.
3. The 16th to be given official recognition as the 'Irish' Division.
4. The creation of Special Irish Reserve Battalions.
5. The establishment of an Irish recruiting department.[37]

On the question of the employment of National Volunteers as reserves, Kitchener refused to be drawn, repeating his view that if they were trained, armed and kept together in military units there would be civil war in the country once the war was over. But those same arguments were not applied to the men from the Six Counties who, mainly as Ulster Volunteers, made up the 36th (Ulster) Division with their own distinctive uniforms and badges. Of those men a contemporary observer said, 'No military force since Cromwell's Ironsides had such determined political unity – or religious fervour.'[38] In the eyes of the world the 36th was an 'Ulster' division in a way which the 16th could never be a wholly 'Irish' division.

Kitchener's reasoning was based partly on his childhood experiences in the south-west of Ireland, where he had been encouraged to look on the Irish as a subject race, and partly on his political prejudices. As a

Conservative he was against giving Home Rule to Ireland and tended to support the aims of Carson's unionists: as a soldier, too, he looked on the National Volunteers as rebels, remembering that Irish nationalist volunteers had fought in South Africa on the Boer side under the leadership of Major John MacBride, the ill-starred husband of Maud Gonne, the Irish patriot. His experience, albeit second-hand, of recent British-Irish relations also convinced him that an armed Ireland would present a threat to Britain; giving the National Volunteers arms and recognition would have entailed the kind of risks that Kitchener was not prepared to take. Nevertheless, as the minutes of his meeting with Redmond demonstrate, he was prepared to compromise and the 16th Division fought throughout the war as the 'Irish' division. That little publicity was given to these changes was due largely to the prevailing political situation; any hint of a pro-Irish stance was met with distrust by the British press, whereas anything to do with Ulster tended to be reported positively. Kitchener had little to gain by announcing the results of his meeting, Redmond, for his part, having adopted a pro-British stance, failed to deliver the goods and his subsequent humiliation helped to fulfil Kitchener's prophecy that sooner or later Ireland would be plunged into a war of rebellion. By then it was already too late as recruitment in Ireland in 1915 had slumped to 23,015, half as many as had volunteered in the previous year.

The drop in Irish recruiting was matched by an equally disastrous fall-off in Britain and by the spring of 1915 the figures were low enough to alarm the Cabinet. For example, the average daily return of recruits in Manchester was ninety-four in February compared to 541 five months earlier.[39] The heady days of a rush to the colours being a thing of the past, the government introduced the compromise measure of the National Registration Bill (July 1915) whereby a register would be compiled of all men aged between fifteen and sixty-five. Out of it came the Derby Scheme, administered by Lord Derby, Under-Secretary for War and a popular political orator, especially in the north of England. The basis of the scheme was that men from the register aged between eighteen and forty-one would sign up, or 'attest', but would be called up as and when they were needed, depending on such factors as the importance of their jobs to the war effort or whether or not they were married, the object being to enlist first of all young bachelors in unskilled jobs. Attesting the recruits was left in the hands of local tribunals, who were not always the best judges of a recruit's suitability, and the scheme frequently fell foul of corrupt practices. Nevertheless, the principle of voluntary recruiting, so dear to most Liberals, remained intact until the beginning of 1916 when the Military Service Bill was passed, automatically transferring all attested single men on the register to the Army Reserve. Even that measure failed to bring in the desired numbers and conscription became law in May 1916 with the passing of the National Military Service Act. Thus, at one stroke, compulsory service, so long resisted in Britain, became the law of the land at a time when the country was facing its hour of greatest need.

The battle for and against conscription had been long and bitter, much of it being fought against the background of the strained political loyalties of the day: in May 1915 Asquith was forced to form a coalition government with a new Cabinet. For although the idea of conscription was generally abhorred by the Liberals and promoted by the Conservatives, it was not always discussed on party political lines: Lloyd George approved of its introduction while Conservatives such as Lord Lansdowne stood against it. Kitchener, too, was against compulsion, holding long to the belief that voluntary service was the only realistic answer to the military manpower problem; thus he lent his support to the Derby Scheme in the hope that it would raise the necessary numbers and stave off the introduction of conscription. His reasoning was partly an old-fashioned belief in the integrity of the voluntary principle; partly, too, he regarded conscription as a last ditch to be employed after 1917 if the war was still continuing; also he had been appalled by the huge losses of 1915 and doubted if the country would be able to afford a huge standing army even in wartime.

All Kitchener's training and experience had pointed to the volunteer solution: it was practical, economical, and would quickly provide the required numbers of men. The proof of the pudding was in the eating. The New Armies acquitted themselves well in France in 1915, often fighting against better trained and better armed German divisions;

oblivious of hardships and the unacceptable casualty rate, they fought with tenacity and courage at the battles of Ypres, Neuve Chapelle, Aubers Ridge and Loos. That they did so was due in no small measure to the loyalty they felt to the man who had called them into being. No other British war leader of the day could have created them and then have demanded such standards of service and such sacrifices from them. After Kitchener's death, *Punch* paid homage to him as 'The Maker of Armies' and *The Times* was no less homiletic, saying that, 'The great armies that he called into being are his living monument, and no nobler monument, has been raised to man.'[140] Without Kitchener's vision and drive the outcome of the First World War, once it had reached stalemate in France, would have been very different.

As well as raising the New Armies Kitchener had to feed and arm them – as Secretary for War he was also responsible for munitions, supply and strategy. Under Haldane's reforms the structure at the War Office provided the Secretary for War with four principal lieutenants: the Adjutant-General (Lieutenant-General Sir Henry Sclater) dealt with army personnel, the Quarter-Master General (Major-General Sir James Cowans) with supplies, the Master-General of the Ordnance (Major-General Sir Stanley von Donop) with munitions and the Chief of the Imperial General Staff (Lieutenant-General Sir James Wolfe-Murray) with strategy. There was an Army Council to advise on policy and the Secretary for War had a seat in the Cabinet: during his tenure Kitchener used to sit at Asquith's right hand. In theory the structure was similar to the reorganisation that Kitchener had attempted to foist on Curzon in India but in practice it allowed Kitchener to act as a one-man band, a situation ideally suited to his temperament. Most of the best staff officers were in France with the BEF, thus denuding the War Office. Those who remained quailed when on Kitchener's first day in office he discovered that the pen provided for him would not work. 'Dear me,' he muttered to Arthur. 'What a War Office! Not a scrap of Army and not a pen that will write!'[141] That lack of effective organisation and Asquith's refusal to put his Cabinet on a proper war footing allowed Kitchener great freedom in the first twelve months of the war. Given to being secretive and to evolving his strategy and plans without recourse to discussion, Kitchener appeared to be over-dictatorial to some Cabinet colleagues, including Lloyd George, and simply terrifying to those who stood in awe of him.

Asquith, who to some extent had tied his fortunes to Kitchener, supported his Secretary for War by shielding him inside and outside the Cabinet but even he could not protect him from himself. Faced by questions on policy from his colleagues, Kitchener would display that same mixture of taciturnity and loquacity that had earlier cost him the Viceroyalty of India. A question on French's tactics would be met by a return to the earlier discussion on the disestablishment of the Welsh church; an enquiry about 18-pounder field gun ammunition would see Kitchener talking disjointedly about Carson's Amending Bill. Much of his behaviour was due to political naivety, but Kitchener was also possessed of a good deal of bureaucratic cunning. Often his garrulity was a smokescreen, for he never lost his conviction that the free availability of military information was bad for security.

He had good reason to complain on that score. Asquith used to tell his innermost secrets to Venetia Stanley and on one occasion he distractedly threw a Cabinet paper out of the window of his car as it passed through Roehampton. Grey had to remonstrate with his colleagues to keep secure their papers after sensitive files had been found by the police in St James's Park. The worst feature, though, of security in wartime London was society gossip.

Walter Page, the American ambassador, admitted that through his contacts in Mayfair and Belgravia he possessed the best intelligence gathering unit of any of the neutral countries. Lloyd George shared the secrets of Cabinet meetings regularly with newspaper magnates including Northcliffe. Secret military movements were discussed openly at dinner parties so that senior officers often found it easier to talk about their futures with well-placed hostesses than to go to the relevant military quarter. Faced by such an intolerable situation – which did improve, admittedly, as the war progressed – Kitchener became increasingly secretive and unwilling either to explain his actions to his colleagues or to share his opinions with them. All his fears about married men discussing secrets with their wives returned to the surface and at times he showed a degree of deviousness and obscurantism that infuriated Cabinet ministers. Politicians such as Esher complained that Kitchener's 'form of speech was Cromwellian in its obscurity and incohesion'. Kitchener's retort was that he would tell his colleagues all they wanted to know if they would only divorce their wives.[42] Kitchener never quite accustomed himself to the fact that he was a soldier occupying a position normally held by a civilian; that stance offended those who had to work with him, politicians unused to the mechanics of operating a smooth military machine.

Privately Kitchener admitted that he would have preferred to have adopted Cromwell's title of Captain-General so he would have overall command of the army and of the running of the war. It was in that mood that he faced up to the two other great problems thrown up by the war — munitions and strategy.

At the peak of his career, 1914: Field Marshal Earl Kitchener, Secretary of State for War.

2 On his mother's knee, with his eldest brother, Henry Elliott Chevallier, and his sister, Frances Emily (Millie) Jane.

His birthplace, Gunsborough House near Listowel.

His early home, Crotta House, Kilflynn.

5, 6, 7 Youth and early manhood
(*above*) Sporting side-curls, with two of his brothers and his sister; (*below*) the main street of Ballylongford, the village nearest to the Crotta estate, as it was in 1916.

As a cadet at the Royal Military Academy at Woolwich.

9 As a lieutenant in the Royal Engineers.

10, 11 On survey work
(*above*) In Palestine, 1875; (*below*) in Cyprus, 1878.

12 'The Champion of Civilisation' in a khaki patrol jacket, with Khartoum in the background.

13 As Sirdar of the Egyptian Army.

14, 15, 16 The Sudan campaign, 1883–85
(*above*) Pictured in heroic pose at the head of troops advancing on Dongola; (*opposite top*) the Gordon relief expedition: Kitchener with his guides at Korti, just before the start across the desert; (*opposite bottom*) a collage from the *Illustrated London News* Kitchener memorial number, in honour of the victory at Omdurman.

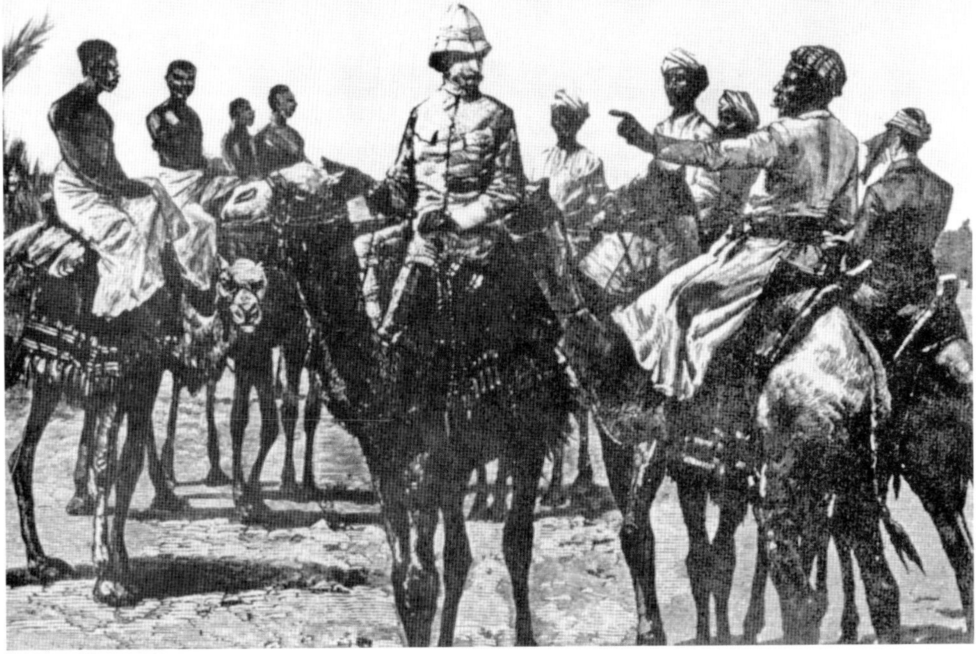

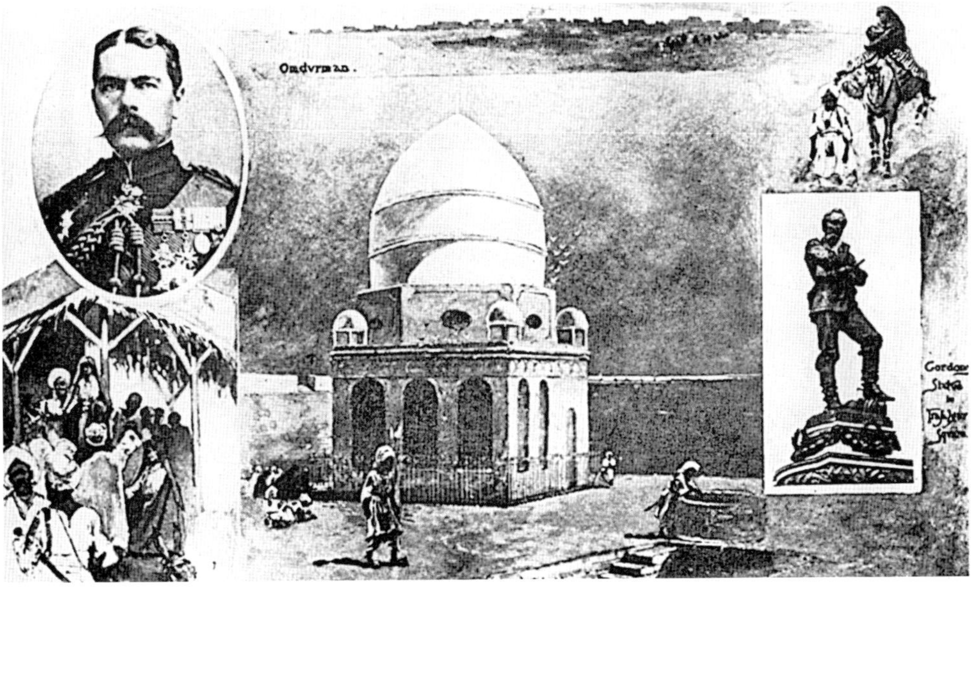
Omdurman.
Gordon

WELCOME!

BRITANNIA. "SIRDAR! I THANK YOU! I AM PROUD OF YOU!"

"It was not merely a great victory for Egypt and Great Britain, but it was a great victory for civilisation."
(*Lord Rosebery at Perth, October* 24. "*Times*" *report*.)

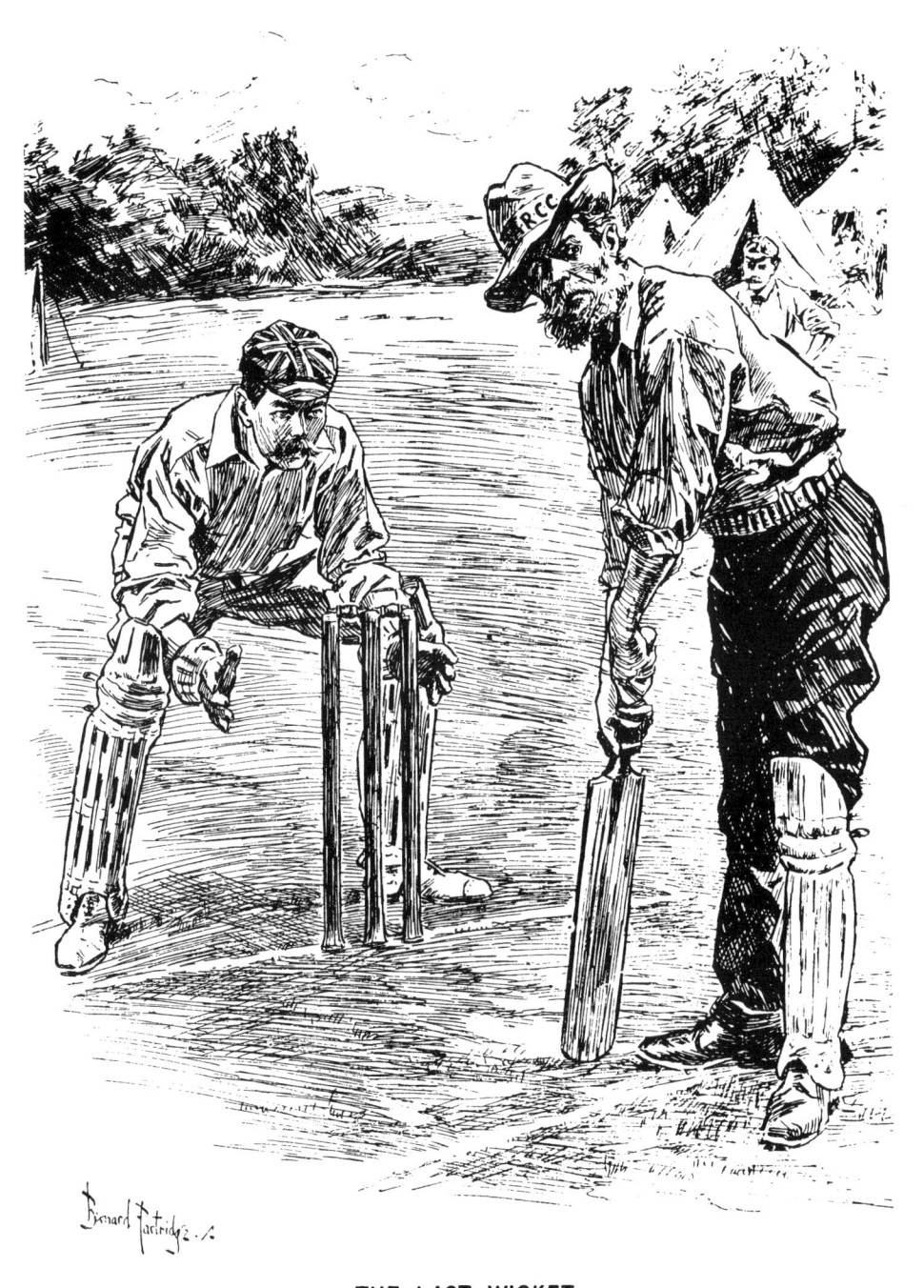

THE LAST WICKET.

Kitchener (Captain and Wicket-keeper). "HE HAS KEPT US IN THE FIELD A DEUCE OF A TIME; BUT WE'LL GET HIM NOW WE'VE CLOSED IN FOR CATCHES!"

19, 20, 21 The Boer War
(*above left*) In South African campaign uniform with his ADC Frank Maxwell, 'The Brat'; (*above right*) pictured exchanging compliments with Boer leaders in 1902; (*below*) the peace conference that ended the war.

22, 23, 24 (*above left and below*) A hero's welcome for the victor of the Boer War; (*above right*) in full regalia – Kitchener began the campaign as a major-general and finished as a general.

25 Replying to the toast to his health proposed by the Prince of Wales at the St James's Palace banquet held in his honour on 12 July 1902.

26 (*opposite*) A caricature of Kitchener in evening dress published by *Vanity Fair*, 23 February 1899.

Spy

EASTWARD HO!

Britannia (to India). "WE CAN ILL SPARE HIM; BUT YOU SEE WE GIVE YOU OF OUR BEST!"

28, 29, 30 India, 1902–09
(*above left*) With King George V; (*above right*) leaving Simla in September 1909; (*below*) visiting wounded Indians at Brighton during the Great War: Kitchener retained a close interest in the army, which, as commander-in-chief, he reorganised.

31 In full dress uniform as field marshal.

32 Entering the Khedive's state coach at Alexandria on his arrival there as British agent in Egypt, 27 September 1911.

33, 34 Secretary of State for War
(*above*) A portrayal of Lord Roberts's visit to his former Chief of Staff, now installed in the War Office; (*below*) watching troops march past as Basingstoke.

35, 36 Kitchener's Army
(*above*) Reviewing men of the New Armies at Woking, September 1914; (*below*) inspecting the guard of honour before the recruiting meeting at Guildhall on 9 July 1915.

37 The famous recruiting poster.

38 Going to face his critics: Kitchener leaving the War Office for his meeting with MPs on 2 June 1916.

39, 40 Anzac, 13 November 1915
(*above*) On the beach with General Birdwood, addressing the Australians; (*below*) returning with the general through the trenches to the beach from Russell's Top and Bully Beef Sap.

41 With Sir Edward Grey in Paris.

42 Bidding Admiral Jellicoe farewell on board HMS *Iron Duke*.

43 The Wartime Economy Meeting at Guildhall, March 1916. In the front row, ranging from left of the speaker, are Kitchener, Mrs Bonham-Carter, Mr Balfour and Cardinal Bourne, with Mr McKenna, Chancellor of the Exchequer, disappearing off the edge of the photograph.

44 At Broome Park, with inmates of the Manor Court Army Nursing Home, Folkestone, whom Kitchener invited to visit his beautiful Kentish seat.

45 30 May 1916, addressing the House of Lords for the last time.

46 Members of the party aboard the *Hampshire* who went down with Kitchener (taken from the *Illustrated London News* memorial number).

47 'The Sinking of HMS *Hampshire*' by Charles Pears.

48 The last post for a great soldier-statesman: a drawing of the supreme moment of the Kitchener memorial service.

THE LOST CHIEF.
IN MEMORY OF FIELD-MARSHAL EARL KITCHENER, MAKER OF ARMIES.

11

THE NEED FOR SHELLS

On 17 September 1914, after bringing the House of Lords up to date on the military situation in France and giving reassurances about the steady influx of recruits to the New Armies, Kitchener admitted that, 'Our chief difficulty is one of matériel rather than personnel.' He went on to say that:

> Strenuous endeavours are being made to cope with the unprecedented situation, and that thanks to the public spirit of all grades in the various industries affected, to whom we have appealed to co-operate with us and who are devoting all their energy to the task, our requirements will, I feel sure, be met with all possible speed.[1]

From the beginning of the war Kitchener understood that not only was the BEF too small to make any great impact on the European theatre of war in the short term, but also that it was hopelessly short of artillery pieces, shells, small arms and ammunition to fight a lengthy campaign. At the outbreak of war the army possessed 800,000 rifles, half of which were the standard Short Magazine Lee-Enfield (SMLE), but the annual rate of production was a modest 50,000. In the front line each infantryman was issued with 150 rounds of ammunition carried in pouches, but they also took with them a bandolier of 100 rounds that was all too frequently misplaced or left behind on leaving the trenches. Machine guns were also a problem, with the ageing Maxim being replaced by the Vickers on the basis of two guns for each battalion. Again, production was slow and the problem was exacerbated by a decision taken in November 1914 to increase the allocation to four per battalion. The smaller air-cooled Lewis gun was also coming into service but at the beginning of 1915 its numbers were also limited to four guns per battalion. As for artillery support, of the 500 field guns in France only twenty-four were 5in 60-pounders, the rest were 18 and 13-pounders and 4.5in howitzers. No one in the War Office or on the General Staff had been able to forecast that a modern war would need additional heavy weapons and large amounts of ammunition of all kinds.

Later, it became received opinion to claim that Kitchener's early understanding of the shortage of weapons and shells was as much a sudden gleam of insight as was his decision to raise the New Armies. This is only partially true. Kitchener made mistakes in his handling of munitions and on many occasions he was guilty of under-estimating the quantities that would be required by the armies in France, but his earliest communiqués to Field Marshal Sir John French, Commander-in-Chief of the BEF, expressed his opinion that shortage of shells and ammunition could cause overwhelming difficulties:

> The supply of ammunition gives me great anxiety … Do not think that we are keeping any munitions back. All we can gather is being sent, but at the present rate of expenditure we are certain before long to run short, and then to produce a small daily allowance per gun will be impossible. I hope to increase the ammunition being sent today.[2]

'Did they remember,' he asked his staff at the War Office, 'when they went headlong into a war like this that they were without an army, and without any preparation to equip one?'[3] The BEF might have been the best equipped army to have left Britain's shores, but it was designed to fight a limited war of short duration; the casualties and losses of equipment during the retreat from Mons had revealed to everyone how untenable would be its position if it could not be adequately re-supplied. Kitchener, who had based his military reputation on carefully

THE NEED FOR SHELLS

building up stocks before delivering a decisive blow, was appalled by the situation that revealed itself to him.

In the wake of the recriminations following the Boer War, various reforms had been instituted in the army command structure and in its administration. These included the establishment of an Ordnance Board of ammunition experts headed by the Master-General of Ordnance (MGO) to meet the army's requirements for weapons and munition supplies. It worked on the principle of supply and demand. Once the commanding officer of a unit decided his requirements a request was sent to the War Office; the Secretary of State, having authorised it, would pass it to the Master-General of Ordnance. If the matériel was held in stock by any of the state-owned works the order would be completed; if not, there was an alternative method involving a search by the Director of Army Contracts for quotations for their supply from private firms. It was a cumbrous method, surrounded by red tape, which drove many senior commanders to distraction: orders could take up to six months to be fulfilled.

While delays in peacetime were little more than irritants, in wartime they could be disastrous. On the outbreak of war, Asquith had authorised the Chancellor of the Exchequer, Lloyd George, to allow the Director of Army Contracts to place orders without first asking for quotations, thus freeing the Ordnance Board from Treasury control. This helped speed up orders but it could not undo the legacy of pre-war recommendations that the Board's reserve supplies and ammunition should be sufficient to maintain seven divisions in a limited campaign such as all colonial campaigns had been. In an attempt to undo that damage Lloyd George then placed £20 million for extending the country's armaments capacity at the disposal of the MGO, Major-General Sir Stanley von Donop. However, Donop chose to hoard the funds rather that spend them quickly and effectively and by September the BEF was experiencing a severe shortage of artillery shells. French was forced to limit the rate of fire of his 18-pounders to fourteen rounds a day while receiving only half that number on a daily basis. According to Major-General William Robertson, quartermaster-general of the BEF, 'The insufficiency of guns and ammunition was even more serious than the shortage of personnel, and there was less excuse for it.'[14]

Robertson was writing after the war and with the benefit of hindsight. On the other hand, as his speech to the House of Lords revealed, Kitchener was concerned about the problem from the outset, and in private he was outspoken about the munitions supply system. Equipping the BEF, he said, was rather like shopping for a straw hat at Harrods.[5] In place of that piecemeal approach he advocated the creation of a large-scale armaments industry and the centralisation of military supplies to the armed forces.

Kitchener's comment about shopkeeping was not misplaced. Under the Ordnance Board there were two sources of munitions supply for the army and navy. One was a group of state-owned factories including the Royal Arsenal at Woolwich (heavy armaments), Birmingham and Enfield (small arms), Waltham Abbey (explosives), and the more recently created Royal Aircraft Factory at Farnborough. The second was a group of private manufacturers that produced armaments to War Office specifications and which provided about 20 per cent of the total needs of the British Army. This group included Vickers, Armstrong Whitworth, Cammell Laird, Beardmore and the Coventry Ordnance Works, all of which produced armaments and munitions as and when needed by the War Office. Thus, the government's ordnance factories tailored their output to an agreed formula drawn up before the war, while the private sector only came into play at War Office instigation. Both systems were unwieldy in wartime and in Kitchener's view neither would stand the pressure placed upon them. When he first met the heads of the private manufacturing companies he told them bluntly that they had to think of supplying armaments and ammunition for terms of years, not months.

The real difficulty facing Kitchener was how to bring into being a munitions industry capable of meeting the demands of an ever-expanding army when so many factors combined to conspire against him. Very few soldiers or politicians had begun to understand the nature of the trench warfare and artillery bombardments on the Western Front, and even fewer had grasped how Britain's military power was linked to the nation's industrial and economic capacity. According to Sir George Riddell, the newspaper owner who acted as liaison officer between the government and the press, the MGO's staff was so surprised by the sudden availability of funds and the removal of restrictions that it became catatonic when faced by the need to develop quickly a new system of munitions supply. 'Von Donop and the others who are at the head of Ordnance know all about guns,' he noted in his diary, 'but have no wide view of the situation.'[6]

If one problem was the head-in-the-sand attitude adopted by the War Office, then another was the inability of the ordnance factories, public and private, to adapt to the needs of modern warfare. None had re-tooled their machinery to manufacture weapons or shells in any capacity – the Royal Arsenal at Woolwich still put explosives in the shells by hand, the result of a lack of machine development. Neither had the manufacturers taken any steps to safeguard their supplies. In peacetime Britain had depended on the German chemical industry to provide the nitrate for high explosives: the loss of that market meant that another source had to be found elsewhere. Gauges used to determine the correct size of fuses were also in short supply and had to be imported from the United States. An added complication was the lack of agreement over what kind of weapons and shells would be most effective. The general pre-war opinion was that shrapnel was superior to high explosives in the bombardment of enemy positions: it quickly became clear that the German trenches and barbed wire emplacements could only be destroyed by high-explosive shells but these were only being manufactured at the meagre rate of 45,000 a month. Machine guns, the new 'Queen of the Battlefield', were also in short supply; many had been lost in the first months of the war and by December 1914 only 226 Vickers guns had been produced.[7]

Perhaps the scale of the problem is best illustrated by the supply figures of weapons to the army between 1902 and August 1914. During that period only 657 18-pounder guns, the army's staple artillery weapon, had been manufactured and the total number of guns and howitzers ordered and supplied amounted to 957, or an average of eighty per year.[8] This was principally due to the economies that had been forced on the army, but the lack of foresight shown by the General Staff was also a contributory factor.

Before Kitchener could step up the production of guns and ammunition he had to secure the support of the labour force. In the first wave of patriotic enthusiasm large numbers of skilled workers had enlisted, thereby denuding essential industries of as much as 25 per cent of their workforce. On 8 September Kitchener appealed to fully trained tradesmen and skilled workers to remain in their jobs, and later the War Office sent out a directive to recruiting officers instructing them not to sign up men from reserved occupations. Kitchener also gave his blessing to the introduction of a system of war service badges to be worn by munition workers to show that they were engaged in essential war work.[9] Ideally, Kitchener would have preferred a total ban on all skilled men joining up, but such a move would have offended those politicians anxious to prevent government interference in labour agreements. Only the Board of Trade, with its network of Labour Exchanges, had direct dealings with the relationship between employers and the workforce. This suggested to Kitchener that it should come under the control of the War Office with the Board of Trade's President, Walter Runciman, sharing with him the title of Joint Secretary of State for War. The proposal, with its hint of government control of industry, met with a sharp rebuttal from Asquith but it offers a clue to the direction of Kitchener's thinking – that the war could only be won once the army's entire needs, men, weapons, supply and strategy, were centrally controlled with the minimum of political interference.

By the end of 1914 the government's munitions workforce was still 6,000 men short and the situation was even worse in the private sector. In a bid to attract more workers the Board of Trade instructed its Labour Exchanges to concentrate on finding men from the ranks of the unemployed, from skilled refugees and from engineers involved in non-governmental work. Steps were also taken to relax trade union restriction on the use of semi-skilled workers. This move, along with an agreement that trade unions involved in war work would not strike, was designed to remain in effect for the duration of the war but it was often honoured only in the breach. Under the terms of the Defence of the Realm legislation and the Munitions of War Act strikes were officially forbidden during the war but that did not prevent confrontations between management and the workforce and the subsequent withdrawal of labour. A strike by 200,000 South Wales miners went ahead in March 1915 in spite of the new laws and the Miners' Federation's full demands were met by the employers. A month earlier, engineers in Glasgow had gone on strike in pursuit of a claim for an additional two pence an hour and, although it was settled a fortnight later, Clydeside found itself saddled with a reputation for militancy that remained with it throughout the war and beyond.[10]

The situation required tact and diplomacy as many trade union leaders were sensitive about surrendering hard-won rights but Kitchener, in return for their support, promised that he would hold off for as long as possible the introduction of conscription. Arthur Henderson, the leader of the Labour Party, later admitted that Kitchener 'recognised that no section of the nation contributed more in human wealth than did the working class. I found him free from all prejudice and frankly and sincerely sympathetic in his attitude towards Labour.'[11]

Kitchener believed that the problems of increased production and the regular supply of workers to industry could only be solved under the aegis of the War Office. All his instincts suggested that he should assume total control of the problem, yet such a policy was bound to lead him into conflict with his colleagues. As early as 30 October 1914 Lloyd George clashed with Kitchener, telling him at a Cabinet meeting that 'he [K] was only one among 19, and must stand criticism in the same way as any other member of the Cabinet'.[12] At the time Lloyd George was slowly forming the opinion that he was the only politician capable of leading the country to victory. His forceful personality and his messianic zeal made him a formidable opponent and, as his private papers have revealed, he threw himself into the war with all the ardour of an armchair general. On 14 September he proposed to the Cabinet that a committee should be established to investigate the whole question of armaments and munitions supplies, a suggestion that met with hostility from Kitchener, who had always been suspicious of committees. 'I am sorry to say,' Kitchener warned Asquith, 'that if these outside committees are thrown upon me, it makes more work than I can do.'[13] Kitchener's stature within the Cabinet won the day for his point of view but a month later French's pleas for the provision of more shells could no longer be ignored.

On 12 October a Shells Committee was formed by Asquith with Kitchener as chairman, thus keeping it under War Office control, and with its membership drawn from the ranks of the Cabinet – Lloyd George, Churchill, Haldane, Runciman, Reginald McKenna (Home Secretary) and Lord Lucas (President of the Board of Agriculture). Although it came to be seen as a broken reed – Kitchener eventually refused to attend its meetings, pleading pressure of work – the Shells Committee did succeed in two vital areas. It was able to persuade von Donop to increase the number of 18-pounder guns on order from 900 to 2,100, while at the same time speeding up their delivery dates. To increase production further the committee also made finance available for the industrial expansion of four of the main private armaments manufacturers, a step that tested to the full the Liberals traditional antipathy to government intervention in the private sector. The Shells Committee only met six times and had its teeth drawn by Kitchener's intransigent attitude to outside interference, but it introduced Cabinet members to the munitions problem and the difficulties facing Kitchener in keeping French's army fully supplied.

In addition to being severely hampered by shortage of shells the BEF had also to accustom itself to the new conditions of warfare on the Western Front. Trench warfare meant that accurate rifle fire became less important than the ability to batter down enemy defences. Trench mortars, heavy grenades and periscopes were in great demand but, as von Donop was informed by Major-General Frederick Wing, commanding the artillery in 3rd Division, not only were existing stocks in short supply but many of the weapons were simply not up to the task:

> As it seems probable that a considerable amount of trench warfare will have to be carried out before the Germans are beaten, I beg to point out that our troops are at present at a considerable disadvantage in the above aspects owing to having no trench mortars and also owing to the fact that the lyddite shell of our 4.5" howitzers hardly ever detonate.[14]

As Kitchener had already pointed out, the problem of a lack of matériel was proving to be the deciding factor in the battles on the Western Front. However, equally clearly, the system had also failed to solve the problem or to bring new and enhanced weapons into the field. By the end of the first quarter of 1915 Kitchener estimated that 481,000 high-explosive shells should have been produced: due to the difficulties he had inherited the actual figure was only 52,000. The knowledge that the goods had not been delivered only served to heighten the conflict between Kitchener and Lloyd George, who returned to the attack in February 1915. The outcome was a meeting, chaired at 10 Downing Street by Asquith on 5 March, which recommended the establishment of a Munitions Committee with full executive powers.

This was agreed and the following fortnight was spent ironing out the final details of its composition and duties; on 23 March it was announced that a War Supplies Committee had been established to mobilise the sources of supply to meet the demands of the armed forces. This time, the committee would report directly to the Cabinet, thus challenging the paramountcy of War Office control. Kitchener, who had not been invited to attend the final meeting, was enraged by the proposal and reminded Asquith angrily that it took time to introduce new means of production. In the House of Lords on 15 March he had also placed some of the blame on the inadequate size of the workforce and on the 'slack work' of a minority. The following day he took steps to remedy that by creating an Armaments Output Committee that would deal with manpower problems through the offices of a successful industrialist, George Booth, a cousin of Millie's husband, Harry Parker.

Booth had been an adviser of Kitchener's since the beginning of the war and, as was the case with others who worked for him, he had developed a fierce loyalty to his chief. All his industrial and business expertise told him that the problem went beyond labour shortages, that only by spreading orders for munitions among all private engineering firms would the full supply of armaments and munitions be achieved. That course, however, would only intensify the growing quarrel between Kitchener and Lloyd George, who now claimed to A.J. Balfour, that the War Supplies Committee had been set up 'for the purpose not merely of supervising existing work but for organising our engineering reserves for the purpose of increasing the output'. He also added that Kitchener refused to hand over control and warned Balfour that he meant to dominate the committee through a tame chairman.[15] What Kitchener had done was to refuse the committee any information from War Office sources and to ban it from interfering in existing War Office areas of supply. The stage was set for a battle that, in the long term, was as bitterly contested as the earlier power struggle between Kitchener and Curzon.

Matters came to a head on 26 March when Kitchener threatened Asquith that he would resign if further civilian committees were foisted on the War Office; at the same time Lloyd George retorted that he would wash his hands of the whole business but not before he had passed on his feelings to the press. In Kitchener's mind he was fighting not just for War Office independence, but also attempting to preserve the right of soldiers to fight the war in their own way. In his view the duty of politicians was not to interfere in practical matters such as the provision of 18-pounder shells, but to provide a framework in which military men could work. Division of effort would only lower the odds for a successful outcome. This was an argument similar to the one he had brought to bear in India when he fought tooth and nail to bring the Supply Department under the aegis of the Commander-in-Chief.

Lloyd George saw matters rather differently. Although he shared Kitchener's aim of creating a centrally controlled means of supplying the army, he viewed the shortages on the Western Front and the inefficiency of existing weapons as evidence of gross blunders made by the War Office. In particular he singled out von Donop for blame, accusing him not only of holding up supplies but also of being constitutionally incapable of envisaging war on a grand scale, a view shared by Sir George Riddell. Von Donop was a slow thinker who achieved his best results by dint of careful estimation: to the dismay of his colleagues he would ponderously produce a slide rule and volumes of paper when confronted with the simplest request for figures. In place of what he called a 'quartermaster mentality' Lloyd George advocated the creation of a separate department, or ministry, for munitions that would be capable of harnessing the nation's industrial and manpower resources. This new organisation would be run by civil servants responsible to the Cabinet and owe formal allegiance to the military through the War Office. To those who had witnessed the Kitchener–Curzon struggle, the arguments had a familiar ring. Lloyd George regarded Kitchener as a plodding soldier with an unreceptive mind, Kitchener looked on Lloyd George as a political slyboots who would stop at nothing to get his way.

Faced by a private row that threatened to become public knowledge, Asquith was forced to compromise. On the one hand he could not antagonise Kitchener, whose Armaments Output Committee had been announced on 7 April; neither was he prepared to force Lloyd George into resignation. *The Times* had already begun to criticise the War Office's management of munitions and had also questioned Booth's appointment, asking how 'this solitary shipowner' would fit into 'a reluctant world of soldiers'. Having taken evidence from both sides, therefore, Asquith announced on 8 April that a new Munitions Committee would be established under the chairmanship of Lloyd George 'to ensure the promptest and most efficient application of all the available resources of the country to the manufacture and supply of munitions of war for the army and navy'.[16] The War Office's Armaments Output Committee was, in theory, subordinate to this new committee and to bridge any gap between the two it was agreed that Booth should attend meetings of both.

Like most compromises the new arrangement did not suit either protagonist. Lloyd George's satisfaction at seeing the creation of a separate committee for munitions soon evaporated when he discovered that it had to look to the War Office for all its technical information and he soon found Kitchener at his stonewalling worst. At a Cabinet meeting on 19 April Kitchener turned on Lloyd George for disclosing to the Munitions Committee the number of men that had been sent to France that month. Lloyd George countered that such information was essential if his committee was to supply the new divisions with the correct amounts of guns and ammunition. In the resulting row Kitchener threatened to resign but not before telling his colleagues that their security failings prevented him from sharing confidential War Office information.

Unused to the cut and thrust of political debate and frequently hurt by the aggressive rhetoric used in Cabinet meetings, Kitchener would retreat into taciturnity or blame his colleagues petulantly, and then threaten resignation. A few days later, he was persuaded by Lloyd George to announce in Parliament the numbers of men despatched to France – the very information he had been trying to withhold – so that he could appease opposition demands for action on recruiting and munitions. Critics hostile to Kitchener claimed at the time that the mixture of brooding silence and sudden rages betrayed his political naivety, but frequently they were a subterfuge allowing Kitchener a tactical retreat to rethink his position. Another tactic he used at this time was to claim he could not fathom the British political system. 'The people here do not understand, me,' he would tell friends, 'and I do not understand them.'[17]

In a last-ditch attempt to strengthen his position Kitchener appointed Sir Percy Girouard, by then the Managing Director of Armstrong Whitworth, to join him at the War Office to advise on the output of munitions. Although Girouard had been a soldier, like Booth he was now a businessman, unused to War Office fetters. It was obvious that the War Office would not be able to control either man and when Girouard put forward a scheme for the establishment of National Shells Factories, Kitchener announced on 28 April that in future Girouard and Booth would be 'authorised to act without further reference to the Secretary of State'.[18] The writing was on the wall: Kitchener was admitting that his department was unable to control the complete supply and manufacture of armaments and munitions. Faced by recruiting difficulties as well as by the crisis in Gallipoli and the failure of the spring offensive in France, Kitchener could no longer find the time – or, perhaps, the energy – to concentrate on meeting the army's needs for additional supplies. As he had forecast a year earlier, this could only be achieved once the threat of Cabinet interference had receded and munitions were controlled from a central source. A Ministry of Munitions with Lloyd George at its head was created on 26 May 1915, but its establishment owed as much to the progress of the war as it did to political intrigue and to newspaper interference in the collision between Kitchener and Lloyd George.

THE NEED FOR SHELLS

To answer French complaints that Britain had not been fully committed to the war on the Western Front, 1915 had seen a number of attacks on the seemingly impregnable German lines. The results were not encouraging. There had been a breakthrough at Neuve Chapelle on 10 March but the battle quickly became a slogging match with predictably high casualties. Undeterred, the French continued to insist on frontal attacks, throwing vast numbers of men at the enemy in Artois and Champagne in a fresh attempt to rid their homeland of the enemy. On 9 May they attacked along a 4-mile sector of the front between Lens and Arras while simultaneously, Sir John French's British forces launched an attack on the German positions at Aubers Ridge that was preceded by an artillery barrage of such intensity that it seemed to all who witnessed it to herald the complete destruction of the enemy's lines. Unfortunately the heavily guarded German trenches, bristling with machine gun emplacements, had scarcely been breached by the British bombardment and when the main attack went in, line upon line of British infantrymen fell before the concentrated German fire. The artillery had not only failed to breach the German defences, it had given the enemy ample notice of an infantry attack, allowing the Germans to regroup and counter-attack. But shortage of shells was not the only cause of the defeat at Aubers Ridge. As at Neuve Chapelle, the British General Staff had failed to come to terms with the new lessons of trench warfare, mainly the need to co-ordinate the original attack and to use reserves to exploit the initial breakthrough.

French claimed that Aubers Ridge would be one of the greatest battles the world had ever seen. By the day's end it had become another killing ground, the result of ill-prepared British infantry being hurled against an enemy protected by invulnerable defences. The attack was continued in the Festubert sector a week later but the whole sorry episode was not called off until the middle of June. For French it was a disaster and undermined his position as commander of the British forces in France. He would not have been human had he not tried either to exonerate his leadership or to find a convenient scapegoat. During the early part of 1915 he had asked for munitions and still more munitions. By 12 May his Military Secretary, Captain Arthur FitzGerald, and his ADC, Captain Frederick Guest, were back in London priming critics including Lloyd George, Balfour and Bonar Law about the shortage of shells that had lost the battle. A memorandum, carefully presented by French, showed the number of shells requested against those actually supplied. At the same time, French joined Lloyd George and the newspaper magnate Lord Northcliffe in an attempt to have Kitchener removed from the War Office. None of the three men harboured any love for Kitchener in 1915. Northcliffe blamed him personally for the recent death in action of a favourite nephew and had already clashed with him over the use of war correspondents in France. Lloyd George, in spite of the cordiality that suffused his correspondence, intrigued on a grand scale to undermine Kitchener's authority: the publication after the war of letters and diaries written by him and his associates is ample proof of the dislike and disdain he felt for Kitchener.[19] For his part, French had come to despise his former colleague. 'I devoutly wish we could get rid of Kitchener at the War Office,' he told his mistress, Winifred Bennett. 'I'm sure nothing will go right whilst he is there. It is so hard to have enemies *in front* and *behind*.'[20] The passing of confidential information to the opposition leaders and to Kitchener's enemy Lloyd George, only served to provide them with political ammunition; it was not enough in itself to cause a public outcry. To ensure the widest possible coverage of his claims, therefore, French had to involve the press and that is where his friendship with Northcliffe came in. On 1 May the newspaper baron had written to French offering him advice on how to gain the maximum publicity for his case:

> A short and very vigorous statement from you to a private correspondent (the usual way of making things public in England) would, I believe, render the Government's position impossible, and enable you to secure the publication of that which would tell the people here the truth and thus bring public pressure upon the Government to stop men and munitions pouring away to the Dardanelles as they are at present.[21]

French, who was no stranger to the value of the press, had as his guest at GHQ Colonel Repington, the war correspondent of *The Times*, a man who raised wildly contrasting emotions in those who knew him. Some, like Haig, loathed him – earlier that week he had dismissed him from First Army headquarters. Others who found him charming and debonair were quick to forget that he had been obliged to leave the army after an indiscreet affair with the wife of Sir William Edward Garstin, a senior official in the Egyptian government.

During the course of the Battle of Aubers Ridge Repington had been disturbed and upset by the casualties sustained by his old regiment, The Rifle Brigade. Already hostile to his old chief, Kitchener, on account of his attitude to the press, he grasped eagerly French's offer to show him the confidential figures for the number of shells used in the battle.

A fortnight after Northcliffe's letter to French, under lurid headlines in The Times – 'Need for Shells', 'British Attacks Checked', 'Limited Supply the Case' and 'A Lesson from France' – Repington laid the blame for French's losses on the lack of shells: 'The attacks were well planned and valiantly conducted. The infantry did splendidly, but the conditions were too hard. The want of an unlimited supply of high explosive was a fatal bar to our success.' In an editorial Geoffrey Dawson was more forthright. He hinted strongly that the blame should be laid fairly and squarely on the government's shoulders. If the French Army was so well supplied, he asked, why was not the BEF?

> This is a war of artillery, and more and more it is coming to depend upon the supplies of ammunition. From every source we are told that the new German infantry formations are in good cases inferior to our own, but that their artillery is good and lavishly supplied. If we equal the enemy in this respect our cause is won. British soldiers died in vain on Aubers Ridge on Sunday because more shells are needed. The Government, who have so seriously failed to organise adequately our national resources must bear their share of the grave responsibility.[22]

This was a serious accusation. On 20 April Asquith had assured munitions workers in Newcastle that no British Army in the nation's history had 'been maintained in a campaign with better or more adequate equipment', a damaging statement to have made when it was widely known that munitions were in short supply. Questions were asked in the House of Commons on that very point on 17 May only to be brushed aside with the promise that the government would investigate the position. Later, Asquith blamed Kitchener for assuring him that all was well, but in all his statements to the Cabinet and in the House of Lords Kitchener had consistently exercised caution on the subject of the supply of munitions – witness his paper on 'The State of the War', a document that, incidentally, gives the lie to the criticism that Kitchener was lacking in candour:

> It must be remembered that the manufacture of armaments and munitions of war is a highly specialised industry, and the resources of the nation devoted to such supplies were very circumscribed; any attempt, therefore, to expand suddenly must be fraught with unexpected difficulties and disappointments. [23]

In addition, Kitchener had in his possession a letter from French dated 2 May stating that 'the ammunition will be all right'. When he wrote that, French had been anxious to win Kitchener's permission to assault the Aubers Ridge; in the heat of his conversation with Repington the contradiction was no doubt forgotten. Kitchener, for his part, kept quiet about the letter, telling friends that he was fighting the Germans, not Sir John French.

This attack on the government, and the disclosures made by French, were not enough to bring it down. All indeed would have been well for it had not Admiral Fisher, the First Sea Lord, taken it into his head to resign over a disagreement with Churchill over the level of naval support for the Gallipoli campaign. This gave the Conservatives the opportunity to end their wartime truce with the Liberals and to demand the formation of a coalition government. On 17 May, the day on which parliamentary questions were being asked about the disclosures in *The Times*, Asquith demanded his Cabinet's resignation and a separate battle began to appoint a Coalition Cabinet that was announced a week later, on 25 May. Other factors had also combined to bring down the Liberal administration: the munitions crisis, the recent sinking of the liner RMS *Lusitania* by a German U-boat, the first

THE NEED FOR SHELLS

Zeppelin raids on London, the failure of the campaign in Gallipoli to achieve a breakthrough and the high casualty lists in France.

Aware that Asquith was forming a new government and that the reshuffle offered an opportunity to bring down Kitchener, Northcliffe stepped up his criticism. In a hotly worded editorial, published in *The Times*, he openly laid the entire blame for the mismanagement of the war on Kitchener:

> Men died in heaps upon the Aubers Ridge ten days ago because the field guns were short, and gravely short, of high explosive shells. Our sole purpose is to ensure that such a lamentable defect shall be made good as soon as possible. Lord Kitchener must bear his share of the responsibility, because against much wise advice he insisted upon keeping in his own hands the control of questions with which the War Office was far too preoccupied to deal. He could not raise immense new Armies, and direct industrial organisation as well; yet that is what he tried to do, and the result was confusion.[24]

In the same edition the French and the German supply systems were subjected to extravagant praise, the inference being that Britain's was second-rate, if not worse. A few days later John Buchan, in France as *The Times*'s special correspondent, added his voice to the controversy with a description of the Battle of Aubers Ridge that ended with an oblique attack on Kitchener's part in it:

> All the strategy and tactics of the war depend today upon one burning fact. The enemy has got an amazingly powerful machine and unless we can provide ourselves with a machine of equal vigour he will nullify the superior fighting quality of our men. That machine consists in a great number of heavy guns and machine-guns, and an apparently unlimited supply of high explosives.[25]

If the articles in *The Times* at least had the virtue of a decent literary style, those that appeared in Northcliffe's other newspaper, the *Daily Mail*, depended on sensationalism for their effect. On 21 May its headlines announced 'The Shells Scandal' and 'Lord Kitchener's Tragic Blunder', and the ensuing article suggested it was time for Kitchener to go. Its publication turned the tide. Shocked by Northcliffe's presumption the British public came down firmly on Kitchener's side. Copies of both newspapers were burned by members of the Stock Exchange, who also placed a placard outside the *Daily Mail*'s editorial offices with the legend 'The Allies of the Hun'. For a while the circulations of both newspapers plummeted and Lloyd George was forced to tell Northcliffe that, such was the strength of Kitchener's public standing, attacks upon him only redounded to the discredit of the accusers.

Throughout the crisis Kitchener behaved with dignity and self-restraint even though he had been sorely provoked. His friends rallied to support him and letters condemning French's behaviour flocked into the War Office. From France, Rawlinson lamented the absence of the 'oneness of purpose which activated everybody' during the Sudan campaign, the Duke of Connaught expressed his 'disgust at the disgraceful campaign', as did Lord Esher, who went on to warn Kitchener that it was part of a plot hatched by Northcliffe and Lloyd George to get the latter into 10 Downing Street.[26] The normally reticent and cautious Haig was more forthright in his condemnation when writing to FitzGerald, Kitchener's military secretary:

> I feel I must send you a line to tell you how thoroughly disgusted we all are here at the attacks which the Harmsworth reptile press have made on Lord K. It is most unfair and most unpatriotic at the present time. That 'Times' has published several articles for which the editor would have been shot in any other country but England. We in the First Army have a grudge against Repington who in an article on the 18th inst. gave away the position of our heavy batteries at Le Cateau with the result that they were suddenly shelled and many casualties caused. I think it was quite wrong to allow such a deceitful fellow to come to the front at all.[27]

From Buckingham Palace King George V made his statement on the affair by creating Kitchener a Knight of the Garter and by making discreet representations to Asquith proposing the appointment of Kitchener as supreme commander of Britain's forces. Kitchener's only comment on the matter was to ask French calmly why he had allowed

THE NEED FOR SHELLS

Repington access to GHQ. 'Unless war correspondents are allowed by the Cabinet,' he warned, 'I do not think it is right for you to allow Repington to be out with the army.' This mild rap over the knuckles met with a testy reply. 'Repington is an old friend of mine and has constantly stayed with me for the last 10 or 12 years. He was here for a day or two in an entirely personal capacity. I really have no time to attend to such matters.'[28]

Kitchener, anxious not to prolong the quarrel with his senior commander in the field, or to draw too much attention to the War Office, kept his temper. Perhaps, too, he recalled that it was the discreet leaking of confidential papers that helped him get his way during the dispute with Curzon. He could hardly chide French for having taken the same path himself. By 23 May Esher was able to tell FitzGerald that French was 'both certainly ashamed of and annoyed with his gang of mischievous friends'.[29] Things returned to normal at GHQ and in the Cabinet reshuffle Kitchener was confirmed as Secretary of State for War with Lloyd George going to the newly created Ministry of Munitions. Apart from Bonar Law, who received a relatively minor appointment at the Colonial Office, the only casualties were Churchill and Haldane, both of whom lost their ministries.

Thus ended the struggle that came to be known as the 'Battle of the Shells'. Kitchener lost control of munitions supply and production to Lloyd George, whose earlier warnings appeared to have been vindicated. French stayed on in France, although he was never again to enjoy the same degree of trust at the War Office. Northcliffe turned his attention to other things and took up the cause of demanding conscription. On the face of it, Kitchener was the loser and Lloyd George the winner. Certainly, after the war, Lloyd George claimed that Britain had been pulled back from the brink of disaster by the creation of the Ministry of Munitions and by his galvanisation of the war effort. According to his view, Kitchener's chaotic and inefficient methods were swept away and replaced by Lloyd George's dynamism and his businesslike approach. It is a claim that bears little relationship to the facts.

At that time Asquith felt that Lloyd George's behaviour towards Kitchener left 'a disagreeable taste in one's mouth'. A century later there is still a hint of such an aftertaste in the papers relating to the struggle and the parts played by the main protagonists. Throughout the first half of 1915 Lloyd George kept up a barrage of subterfuge, scheming secretly with politicians in both parties, while claiming openly to have solidarity with Kitchener and his work at the War Office. Kitchener could be equally devious, and there is little doubt that on occasions his secretiveness enraged Lloyd George, but he believed genuinely that in time of war personal animosities should be put to one side. When pressed by colleagues to put a stop to Northcliffe's venomous attacks, Kitchener merely replied that, 'Our job is to get on with the War – it will be quite enough time to answer these when we have won it.' The day after Lloyd George's appointment he sent him a magnanimous letter of congratulation, proposing warmly that they should work in harmony in the future. The gesture was characteristic of Kitchener at that time. Also, Churchill later recorded that Kitchener was the only member of the Cabinet to say farewell to him and Haldane when they resigned from office.[30] Several attempts had been made to push Kitchener into a siding but Asquith refused to be moved, realising that however much the soldier's political star might have fallen, he still enjoyed great popularity.

The crisis saw a new stoicism emerge in Kitchener's personality. Northcliffe's allegations and the strife in the Cabinet were enough to shake any man who was not strong and resolute, and throughout the episode Kitchener behaved with great dignity and purpose. Margot Asquith, however, thought this behaviour betrayed 'deplorable weakness', telling him once the crisis was over, 'You have been weak over Northcliffe as I told you before. Very weak.'[31] It was not weakness, though, that drove Kitchener to silence. Rather, what encouraged him to hold his peace was his belief that he should be above such matters, and a dread that to open his mouth would be to expose too many of the War Office's methods of working. Also to be considered was the nature of his opponents. He believed that French was a military lightweight, having already told Asquith that he was 'not a really scientific soldier' and that he was incapable of leading large armies in the field. Northcliffe he regarded with supreme contempt. Only Lloyd George with his bare-faced ambition and his belief in the power of sheer personality – a belief shared by Kitchener – posed any threat and he was now safely ensconced at the Ministry of Munitions.

Before the war Lloyd George preached a policy of pacifism and arms control to such good effect that it could be claimed fairly that the wartime shortages were also of his making. At the outbreak of hostilities his conversion to the needs of military supply and demand was therefore all the more remarkable and his claims should be seen against that background. When he moved to Munitions – he stayed until July 1916 when he achieved his dream of succeeding Kitchener at the War Office – Lloyd George made a number of important changes to improve the supply and production of shells and other munitions: a statistics branch was established to monitor the army's needs; scientists and engineers were called upon to experiment with new weapons to meet the changing needs of war, especially new types of trench grenades and mortars; and most importantly of all he managed to overcome Liberal scruples about state control of industry. By the war's end it was generally admitted that Lloyd George's introduction of 'war socialism' had given the Ministry of Munitions a previously unheard of advantage in harnessing the nation's industrial resources. For all those reasons, and for the later successes in tank and aircraft production, Lloyd George felt that he could claim full credit for changing the face of wartime munitions supply. His assertions were supported by several of his Cabinet colleagues, including Churchill who later wrote that the success of the Ministry was due 'in the first instance to Mr Lloyd George, who gathered together the great majority of these able men, and whose foresight in creating the national factories laid the foundations for subsequent production'.[32]

When Lloyd George, Churchill and others made those claims Kitchener was no longer alive to answer them; but the facts speak for the part he played in laying the foundations of Britain's munitions industry. The shells used at the Battle of the Somme in July 1916 came principally from the supplies Kitchener had created during his stewardship at the War Office. In the short time during which he had control of munitions, Kitchener increased the number of contracts for the manufacture of high-explosive shells, he had started to draw the private firms into the network of national munitions supply and, at his instigation, sensible agreements were entered into with the trade unions over restrictive practices and 'dilution', the policy by which semi-skilled workers could be introduced to more demanding work normally executed by skilled workers.

That Kitchener had been able to keep up with the army's requests, in addition to all his other worries, was an extraordinary achievement. During the first nine months of the war he increased the army's stock of lorries from 80 to 8,100, motorcycles from 15 to 3,000; 1,000 motor ambulances were supplied and he also had to arrange for the daily provision of 35,000 gallons of petrol to meet the needs of his newly mechanised army. Nor were supplies to the troops forgotten. By May 1915 Kitchener had arranged for the provision of 7,962,000 pairs of boots, 8,812,268 jackets, 9,465,052 pairs of trousers, 3,609,374 greatcoats and 4,902,720 caps. The size of the increase can be best gauged when it is considered that the holdings of those items in the pre-war army did not exceed a quarter of a million of each.[33] Kitchener was also able to tell his colleagues that such was the increase in overall production that the munitions factories could now produce in three days the amount of ammunition normally manufactured in one year in peacetime. For a man whose previous military campaigns had been marked by a tendency to treat economy as a military necessity, this was largesse on a grand scale. By the spring of 1915, though, it was obvious to everyone that the task was too great, that the needs of war demanded a new organisation to meet them.

Not that Kitchener was without his blind spots. He was slow to understand French's demands for large quantities of high-explosive shells, and he was guilty of blaming the BEF for wasting ammunition without regard to supplies. There was, too, his well-known comment about the machine gun, which has become one of the great myths of the First World War. Like other senior officers whose wartime experience only extended to colonial campaigns, Kitchener regarded the weapon as an irrelevance and had found it to be of limited used in South Africa. Little thought had been given to its deployment, infantry

THE NEED FOR SHELLS

commanders preferring the steady and rapid fire of their riflemen to transporting unwieldy Maxim guns around the battlefield. At the outbreak of war the BEF possessed two Vickers machine guns per battalion but it soon became obvious that more would be needed. Kitchener's attitude to the question of those supplies has often been repeated: it finds its most risible form in the story told by Sir Eric Geddes, former Managing Director of the North Eastern Railway, who worked for Lloyd George at the Ministry of Munitions.

Towards the end of 1915 Geddes went to the War Office to request the proportions of rifles to machine guns that would be required nine months hence, only to receive the unhelpful reply from Kitchener, 'Do you think that I am God Almighty that I can tell you what is wanted nine months ahead?'

'No Sir,' said Geddes, 'and I do not think that I am either, but we have to work it out between us and try to get it right.'

Kitchener thought for a second before retorting, 'I want as much of both as you can produce.'

When pressed by Geddes to be more precise, Kitchener said that two machine guns per battalion was the minimum and four the maximum. Anything above four was a luxury. Geddes wrote down Kitchener's requirements, asked him to sign the document and returned to the Ministry of Munitions. When it was shown to Lloyd George, he turned to Geddes and said, 'Multiply that by four, double that for luck, and double that again for contingencies. The sum of four, multiplied by four, multiplies by two, equals sixty-four, and provide that per battalion.'[34]

Later, Geddes framed Kitchener's order and kept it in his office as a reminder of what he took to be the Secretary of State for War's lack of foresight. Had that incident been the whole story, Kitchener would indeed have been blameworthy and Lloyd George the army's saviour, but as the level of military supplies in 1915 demonstrates, it should be seen in context. Up until December 1914 only 266 Vickers guns had been produced out of 1,792 ordered. By July 1915 the army had received just over 1,000 of these weapons and no infantry battalion was ever to be equipped with the number of machine guns promised by Lloyd George, although by the war's end most battalions had been equipped with one Lewis gun for every two platoons. The only formation ever to receive sixty-four Vickers guns was the Machine Gun Corps, a specialist gunnery regiment founded in October 1915 that eventually had 288 machine gun companies, consisting of four sections with each one equipped with four guns.

What is often forgotten is that Kitchener had to plan the increased production and supply of weapons and ammunition from meagre beginnings. Pre-war economies allied to a lack of vision meant that his earliest efforts had to be circumscribed and that it would take many months for his labours to bear fruit.

The best comment on his munitions work was left to George Booth who, throughout his period at the War Office, had been amused by Kitchener's gentlemanly reserve in refusing to mention their distant family connection. After the Memorial Service held for Kitchener in St Paul's Cathedral the week after his death, Booth accepted a lift from Lloyd George, who made his customary observation that he saw Kitchener as a lighthouse, a sudden blinding flash of light followed by utter darkness. Booth disagreed. 'Kitchener was a great man,' he said. 'He was inexplicable at times, but he really knew the big things.'[35]

That month, June 1916, saw the final delivery of the 13,995,360 rounds of artillery and howitzer ammunition that had been produced at Kitchener's instigation since the beginning of the year. Between then and December 1916 the figure rose to 35,407,193 rounds. It was a far cry from the 1,363,700 rounds Kitchener had been able to eke out of the impoverished munitions industry during the first five months of the war.[36]

12

STRATEGY ON THREE FRONTS

On 2 January 1915 Kitchener wrote to Sir John French summarising the position facing the Allied armies in France and asking for his comments:

> I suppose that we must now recognise that the French Army cannot make a sufficient break through the German lines of defence to cause a complete change of the situation and bring about the retreat of the German forces for northern Belgium – if that is so, then the German lines in France may be looked upon as a fortress that cannot be carried by assault and also cannot be invested with the result that the lines can only be held by an investing force while operations proceed elsewhere.[1]

It was a useful flash of military insight, illuminating perfectly the stalemate of the Western Front and provoking the central strategic argument of the war. With the armies of France, Britain and Germany locked in a long defensive line that stretched from the coastal plain of Belgium to the mountains of Switzerland there was no room for them to manoeuvre or for the generals to make dashing feinting attacks on their enemies' flanks. In place of move and counter-move, trenches and heavily defended emplacements had been constructed to defy assault:

by the end of 1914 it was obvious to Kitchener that Britain and France still did not possess sufficient munitions and men to make full-frontal attacks a paying proposition in terms of tactical advantage. Something more dexterous was required and so began the debate between the 'westerners', men including French who argued that Germany could only be beaten convincingly in Europe, and the 'easterners' who put their faith in Britain's traditional 'blue water' policy, the use of the navy to gain military advantages elsewhere. The latter school, of which Churchill was a leading exponent, believed that the war could be won more effectively, and certainly more cheaply, by employing the ships of the Royal Navy to help win decisive battles away from the European theatre of operations.

Caught in the middle of French's demands for increases in men and ammunition to mount more effective attacks on the German lines and Churchill's insistent suggestions for an attack on the Dardanelles to relieve Turkish pressure on Russia – he had raised the idea in September and again at a meeting of the War Council on 25 November 1914 – Kitchener decided to play a waiting game, realising that the size and resources of the BEF prevented Britain from making any decisive military moves either in France or elsewhere. Until the New Armies had been raised and equipped, with sufficient reserves to fight a lengthy campaign, Kitchener based his strategy on an understanding of the following three fronts: defence of the British homeland, the Western fronts and their interaction with Russia and the need to relieve the pressure on Russia with limited demonstrations either in the Balkans or the Dardanelles.

Each of these fronts and the events that shaped them had a bearing on what was happening elsewhere. They form the central thrust of Kitchener's strategic thinking, demonstrating that he had a thorough understanding of the two-fronted nature of the war and of its global application. But, of course, he had to work within the limits of the organisation and administrative machine of the war that he found when he became Secretary of State in August 1914.

As the most influential adviser to the Prime Minister, Kitchener sat at Asquith's right hand during Cabinet meetings and during the early months of the war his fellow ministers tended not to question any of his edicts. Like his predecessors, Asquith did not employ a secretary to take notes or write minutes and tried invariably to reach a consensus among his colleagues before coming to any decision. A clever parliamentarian, with an instinctive flair for being right, or for appearing to be so, Asquith had enjoyed six years of power alongside an equally secure and discerning Cabinet. Into their midst Kitchener made his way with some difficulty. His earlier relationships with politicians had either been one-to-one, as in India where he dealt directly with the Secretary of State for India, or behind the scenes at convivial places such as Hatfield and Panshanger. Now he had been thrown into a system where all decisions had to be seen to be taken by the Cabinet; small wonder that in such company and unused to its debating conventions, Kitchener appeared tongue-tied and prone to adopting 'eastern' methods of plenipotentiary rule.

However, even to a committed believer in parliamentary democracy such as Asquith, the Cabinet system was too unwieldy an instrument with which to wage a war. A specially convened Council of War numbering Cabinet ministers and officers of the General Staff had met on 5 August to discuss the deployment of the BEF but since then direction of the war had reverted to the Cabinet. Business requiring instant decisions was resolved on an ad hoc basis. For instance, when Kitchener was ordered to go to France to assess the military position on 1 September 1914, his instructions came from Asquith acting in concert with McKenna and Jack Pease, the President of the Board of Education, who both happened to be dining that night at 10 Downing Street.

Advising the Cabinet was the Committee of Imperial Defence with its own secretariat but it too was large and unwieldy with a preponderance of members used only to working in peacetime conditions. In an attempt to weld things together, at the end of November, Asquith formed the War Council, composed of the following members under his chairmanship: Kitchener, Churchill, Lloyd George, Grey, Balfour representing the opposition, Fisher the First Sea Lord and Wolfe-Murray, the new Chief of the Imperial General Staff (CIGS) in succession to General Sir Charles Douglas, who died in October. Later this was expanded to include thirteen members but as an administrative body it proved only to be an adjunct of the Cabinet, incapable of dynamic and individual action. As Edwin Montagu, then Chancellor of the Duchy of Lancaster and later Minister of Munitions, remembered, it was a spineless creation. 'You do not get discussions in the War Council differing materially from those in Cabinet,' he told its secretary, Maurice Hankey. 'You have the same protagonists in both; and all you do is substitute a different set of spectators.'[2]

Thus, with a Cabinet unsure of the correct attitude to take in the prosecution of the war, yet mindful of its democratic traditions, Kitchener was placed in something of a cleft stick. Asquith offered little guidance in the first instance, with the result that Kitchener's natural instincts to assume autocratic control were given full rein. Nor were the leading lights of the General Staff in a position to guide him as by the end of August they were all in France with the BEF, where Haig commanded I Corps and Smith-Dorrien II Corps. Other generals whom Kitchener trusted and who could have proved useful to him, old friends such as Rawlinson and Birdwood, were also in the field, leaving only antiquated staff officers who were terrified of Kitchener. Sir Charles Harris, the Director of Finance, described Kitchener's handling of the first meeting of War Office heads of department as 'hell with the lid off', with Kitchener showing complete contempt for his CIGS, Sir James Wolfe-Murray (soon to be replaced by the equally ineffective Sir Archibald Murray).[3]

Each day Kitchener would appear at the War Office wearing the blue undress uniform of a field marshal of the British Army. When speaking in the House of Lords he would wear a formal frock coat with a silk top hat for the short walk from the War Office to Westminster. For troop inspections he wore khaki uniform. Invariably smart, he was something of a dandy, reminding friends that his figure was still good enough not to require a corset, a claim not always borne out by his photographs, which show him gradually putting on weight as the war progressed.

In the decade before the outbreak of war the invasion of Britain by a hostile country – usually depicted as France or Germany – had been a topic for discussion in military circles and a lurid subject for popular fiction. Even reputable papers such as *The Times* published warnings that Britain was being infiltrated by a secret German army posing in the guise of bandsmen, waiters, jewellers and such like. So universal was this fear that in 1908 when Guy Du Maurier, a major of the Royal Fusiliers, presented his 'invasion scare' play *An Englishman's Home* in London's West End, the War Office arranged for a recruiting booth to be placed in the foyer. It was against that background that Haldane's Territorial Force had come into being and the threat of invasion was taken very seriously by the authorities at the War Office. In the autumn of 1908 the Committee of Imperial Defence (CID) considered the subject and concluded that, although a 'bolt from the blue' was unlikely, the possibility remained of a limited invasion by a force numbering some 70,000 men. To meet that eventuality they recommended that two divisions of regular troops should always be kept in Britain to support the Territorial forces. Contingency plans were also drawn up to transport troops to the scene of any attack and every Territorial unit was allocated a specific stretch of coastline to defend.[4]

Although it is unlikely that Kitchener paid much heed to the invasion scare stories he was not inclined to ignore the CID's findings and home defence was constantly in his mind for much of 1914. Nor was he alone. Towards the end of October Grey wrote to him about the possibility of a German attack on the Armstrong Whitworth munitions works at Elswick in Northumberland, where 'there are plenty of open bays … where transports could be beached and a force rapidly landed. It would be well worthwhile for the Germans deliberately to sacrifice 30 or 40 thousand or more if they could disable Elswick before their men were stopped or taken.'[5]

Kitchener was able to calm the Foreign Secretary – who had a home in Northumberland – by reminding him of the presence of strong fortifications around the factory and of seven infantry battalions based at Newcastle. But the scare refused to disappear. On 21 October, Churchill admitted in Cabinet that the Royal Navy might not be able to prevent a German invasion as the primary task of his capital ships was attack not defence. In that case the limited numbers of submarines and torpedo boats might be insufficient to stop a German invasion fleet.

For a few weeks invasion fever gripped the War Office and the Admiralty. Ian Hamilton was put in charge of a central defence force, mines were laid at strategic coastal points and patrols were stepped up.

Those fears amused Asquith, who told Venetia Stanley that 'the possibility of German invasion ... pre-occupies and alarms the mind of Kitchener', but it was not any 'bolt from the blue' that gave Kitchener restless nights.[6] Rather it was a fear that if the Germans defeated the allies in France they would then be ideally placed to launch a cross-Channel invasion. Kitchener thought little of the French Army, fearing that the Germans would walk through them 'like partridges', and to Hankey he confided his fear of a French collapse on the Western Front. For those reasons he thought it vital that Russia should continue to engage the Germans in the east until the New Armies were created and ready for service. Should the Russians fail, the Germans would be free to concentrate on the Western Front, overrun France and attack Britain from the Channel ports. It was with that scenario in mind that Kitchener persuaded the Cabinet on 6 August that only four divisions of the BEF should be sent to France, two remaining in Britain until further mobilisation of the Regular and Territorial forces had taken place.

For his concern over home defence Kitchener drew the scorn of Asquith and Churchill. Even friends such as Rawlinson counselled him that the Germans were unlikely to attack Britain 'without accepting battle with the High Seas fleet in the North Sea which is what our Navy professes to have been longing for since the war began'.[7] But the trouble that Kitchener took over the threat of invasion and its implications for the direction of the war in Europe lies at the root of his overall strategy and his understanding of the relationships between the various fronts: keep Britain secure against invasion and lend support to Russia until such time as the New Armies were ready to deliver decisive blows on the Western Front.

The British strategy for the war in Europe had been first discussed with the French in 1906 and finalised in 1911: basically it called for the deployment of the BEF on the left of the French Army, which, in turn, would make its offensive against the Germans in Alsace. When the Council of War met on 5 August various other possibilities were aired but none of them emerged as a serious contender to the pre-arranged plan. A landing in Belgium to aid the Belgian Army and to attack the German advance from the flank was ruled out on account of the dangers inherent in the longer sea crossing, and a muted proposal to keep the BEF at home until home defences had been organised was dismissed as being liable to upset the French preparations. Major-General Henry Wilson, to whom had fallen the responsibility of liaising with the French, skilfully steered the discussion towards the absolute necessity of offering maximum support on the French left, a conclusion that was ratified by the Cabinet on the following day. Privately, Wilson thought little of the British high command, telling his diary that French and Haig had discussed strategy like idiots, and showed nothing but contempt for Kitchener, whom he detested.

Having forecast a lengthy war Kitchener was not only anxious about the security of home defence, but he also preached caution in employing too great a proportion of Britain's professional army on the battlefront. Should it fall to a German advance Britain would then be denied the core around which its volunteer armies would be built. For that reason he disagreed with the pre-arranged concentration at Maubeuge, which lay midway along the Franco-Belgian border on the French side. Such a deployment, Kitchener argued, would place the BEF in great peril as he believed the Germans would make a wide sweep through Belgium north of the Sambre-Meuse line. Having drawn Britain into the war by invading Belgium there was every reason to believe that they would exploit their new tactical advantage. To offset that danger Kitchener proposed the concentration of the BEF north of Paris, at Amiens, where it could prepare for engagement with the enemy beyond the danger of a surprise attack.

French and Wilson disagreed, feeling that any change in the plans would alienate the French and make them suspicious of British motives. Believing the war would be a short one, French was also anxious to get into the field as quickly as possible to cover the north of the French line while Joffre, the French commander, pushed his armies through Lorraine into Germany. Once that happened, the Germans would be forced to pull out of Belgium to meet the French attack. This strategy, known as Plan XVII, had been drawn up by the French general staff to counter the threat of the Schlieffen Plan by which the German invasion of France would come north of Metz through Belgium to the west of Paris in a rapid encircling movement. Wilson placed great faith in the offensive nature of Plan XVII and promoted consistently a bullish forward deployment at Maubeuge. Kitchener, on the other hand, held out for the safer option of Amiens. To him it seemed inconceivable that the Germans would attack in any strength through southern Belgium and the Ardennes while the relatively undefended northern plain was theirs for the taking. Neither did he believe that the French offensive in Lorraine would be successful, in which assessment he proved to be right: by the end of August all French forward movement had foundered on the heavily defended German border positions.

The argument over whether to deploy at Maubeuge or Amiens lasted for three hours, with Kitchener eventually giving way. This decision was finally taken by Asquith, who was chary of disagreeing with his senior field commander. Mobilisation, which had been ordered at four o'clock in the afternoon on 4 August, was under way five days later and by 20 August the BEF was standing to on its concentration arc between Maubeuge and Le Cateau.

Kitchener's formal instructions to French were of necessity vague but they produced a sensible enough summary of the situation. The BEF was to co-operate with the French Army but to avoid unnecessary casualties. At the same time 'while every effort must be made to coincide most sympathetically with the plans and wishes of our Ally', Sir John French was told that he would not be placed under French command. That contradiction was to be the cause of much misunderstanding, intensified by the fact that Joffre was not made privy to Kitchener's instructions.[8] To make matters worse, French himself had a low opinion of his allies' social standing, reminding Kitchener that 'one always has to remember the class these French generals usually come from'.[9] Unfortunately those feelings were reciprocated by General Lanzerac, whose 5th Army lay to the right of the BEF. When French arrived at Lanzerac's headquarters at Rethel he was met with a haughty greeting that suggested the BEF was merely a last-minute gatecrasher. Having successfully enraged French, Lanzerac proceeded to deepen his suspicions by refusing to understand the British field marshal's attempts to discuss strategy in French. The meeting broke up with French convinced that Lanzerac was planning an offensive, whereas attack was the last thing on his mind. The following day the BEF moved up to its positions along the Mons-Givry line and it was there that it engaged General von Kluck's First German Army on 23 August.

There were further difficulties with communication. French had failed to understand the nature of the intelligence reports given to him by cavalry scouts and reconnaissance aircraft, so he had underestimated the size of the German army opposing him. Instead of the one corps and two cavalry divisions forecast by Wilson, the German Army was more than twice that size – two-and-a-half army corps plus cavalry and artillery. There was the added disadvantage that a considerable gap had opened up between the BEF and Lanzerac's 5th Army, which by then was in the first stages of retreat. French agreed to stand at Mons and cover him but the fall of the fortress of Namur that same day convinced him that withdrawal was the only sensible option if the BEF were to be saved. As Kitchener had forecast, French's force was in danger of being wiped out before it had made any impact on the war. As early as 19 August Kitchener had warned French that the Germans were developing a movement on their right flank to the north of the Meuse and he added that the force consisted of five army corps.[10]

Churchill never forgot the 'apparition of Kitchener Agonistes' when the latter arrived at the Admiralty to give him the news of the fighting at Mons and the dangers it presented to Britain. One false move by French and Britain's professional army would be given a knock-out punch by the advancing German forces now pushing forward in a ponderous right hook. After the confidence expressed by French in his earlier communications the news that he would have to retreat came as a severe shock to Kitchener. Pulling himself together he sent a generous telegram to French congratulating him on the composure of the British troops and asking for more information.

That Kitchener's worst fears were confounded was largely due to German ineptness and British professionalism. Unaccountably General von Moltke, the German Chief of Staff, moved four divisions to East

Prussia to counter the Russian advance and used seven other divisions in time-consuming sieges at Maubeuge and Giret. At the same time he ordered his centre and left flank to attack in a pincer movement around Verdun while the right flank wheeled sharply to the east of Paris. Had this alteration to the Schlieffen Plan succeeded, von Moltke would have split the Allied forces as his predecessors had done at Sedan. Instead, the movement over-extended his lines of communication and allowed Joffre to regroup his forces for the ensuing Battle of the Marne. A third factor, not to be overlooked, was the experience and tenacity of the BEF. Its fighting qualities were more than a match for the pursuing German troops, as it showed at Le Cateau where Smith-Dorrien's II Corps fought a determined and successful rearguard action.

Had French kept his nerve during the week that followed the Battle of Mons all might have been well, but his optimism of early August had given way to despair. Always prone to live off his nerves, and volatile in his interpretation of events, French became convinced that he had been deserted by his allies to the right and that he was standing alone. Into his mind floated Kitchener's admonition not to expose British forces to unnecessary attack and by the end of August he was certain the BEF's future safety lay in pulling it out of the line west of the Seine towards the Channel port of Le Havre. To Kitchener, such a move, announced in a telegram of 31 August, not only smacked of cowardice but also threatened the already fragile British-French relationship. After wiring for further information Kitchener gained Cabinet approval to order French to stay in line with Joffre's forces:

> The government are exceedingly anxious lest your force, at this stage of the campaign in particular, should, owing to your proposed retirement so far from the line, not be able to co-operate closely with our allies and render them continual support. They expect that you will, as far as possible, conform to the plans of General Joffre for the conduct of the campaign.[11]

This unequivocal command drew from French the disclaimer that such a policy would be a disaster, that his troops were shattered and that he had lost all confidence in the French generals. In the face of his commander's refusal to obey an order Kitchener felt that further telegrams would serve no purpose and that he should cross over to France himself to steady British nerves.

On 1 September he gained hurried approval for his visit from Asquith, who noted with some satisfaction that Kitchener was going to France to put the fear of God into French and his staff. Such a point of view was hardly constructive but the Prime Minister was sufficiently mystified by French's panic to take the unusual step of allowing a politician to visit the front. All previous usages of war pointed to the fact that the direction of the army should be left to the commander in the field; but here was a senior Cabinet minister making his appearance on territory reserved for soldiers. To French, his mind already poisoned by Wilson, this was an outright insult and he showed little grace at the meeting, which was held in Paris at the British Embassy in the presence of various diplomats and politicians: Sir Francis Bertie, the British Ambassador, Alexandre Millerand, the French Minister of War, René Viviani, his Prime Minister, and General Huguet, the influential French liaison officer. French himself was in a markedly irritable mood, complaining to everyone that the meeting would have to be short as he was needed at the front. He was further piqued when he saw that Kitchener was wearing the uniform of a field marshal and had announced to Bertie his intention of inspecting the men at the front. This was not only an insult, but a veiled threat. Not only was he jealous of Kitchener's superior political authority, he also knew that Kitchener's military knowledge would tell him that the BEF was still capable of holding its place on the French left. French's alarm was almost tangible, Huguet noting that compared to Kitchener's calm and reflective bearing he looked sour and impetuous. Eventually Kitchener took French aside to discuss the problem in private. Although no official record was kept at the time, from the tenor of Kitchener's message to the Cabinet iron had obviously been put into the commander's soul:

> French's troops are now engaged in the fighting line where he will remain conforming to the movements of the French army though at the same time acting with caution to avoid being in any way unsupported on his flanks.[12]

To underline the agreement Kitchener copied the message to French, adding that he was to regard its conclusions as an 'instruction'; French was left in no doubt that retreat was out of the question.

The Paris meeting left in French a lasting feeling of resentment towards Kitchener. Already suspicious about Kitchener's motives in keeping two divisions in Britain, French now believed that the War Office was taking too great an interest in his handling of the army in France. The incident became public knowledge and Churchill, who was liked by both men, was asked by Asquith to intervene. However, the relationship, forged in South Africa, was irreparable. The mercurial French would try to establish a sense of camaraderie in his correspondence, telling Kitchener that 'the same mutual understanding exists between us now as always', but when he added in the same letter, 'don't think that I forget South Africa so easily!'[13] Kitchener ignored the proffered hand. The war he was now waging was far removed from the early morning dash to Kimberley or the romantic charge of French's cavalry at Klip Drift. This was Paardeberg writ large.

By 3 September French was working again in full concert with Joffre and his force played a useful role in the Battle of the Marne. Ten days later the Germans had retreated, Paris had been saved and there had been no significant breakthrough. All along the new front on the River Aisne, on both sides, trenches began to be dug. The war of movement on the Western Front was slowly grinding to a halt.

Only one area was still open to further movement: Flanders and the coastal plain with its strategically valuable Channel ports. To French it offered the possibility of outflanking the Germans while the Belgians covered him from the north: even at this late stage he dreamed of a breakthrough and of invading Germany by Christmas. Joffre agreed to the new deployment of the BEF towards Ypres, conceding French's point that the area would provide better opportunities for the more mobile BEF to attack the German flank. But on 28 September, as the British Army corps pushed their way along the Ypres Salient, news arrived that the Belgian Army was besieged in Antwerp, the Germans having also realised that the area provided the last chance for a decisive advance. Kitchener, ever fearful of German assault through northern

STRATEGY ON THREE FRONTS

Belgium and the fall of the Channel ports, intervened quickly. Three days later he ordered the 7th Division, sent to reinforce the BEF, to move to the defence of Antwerp, his decision being spurred on by evidence that the Belgian government was intent on abandoning the city. Frantic efforts were made to encourage Joffre to send reinforcements and French was asked to detach part of his army for the defence force, which would be commanded by Rawlinson.

In all, Kitchener managed to rustle up 53,000 men for the defence of Antwerp in an exercise that showed him at his best. With Asquith absent in Dublin, Kitchener and Grey had to take charge. (At one point it looked as if Churchill, a Cabinet Minister, would have to remain in Antwerp as garrison commander, having been despatched by Kitchener to the city to try to prevent the Belgian government from retiring.) In spite of all the frantic Allied efforts, though, Antwerp fell on 10 October and the BEF, with Rawlinson's force regrouped at Ypres where it met an advancing German army also intent on a flanking movement. The resulting battle, the First Battle of Ypres, lasted from 12 October to 11 November, during which time the original British Expeditionary Force was given a terrible mauling.

At the height of the battle Kitchener crossed over to Dunkirk to discuss the military situation with Millerand and Generals Joffre and Foch, the commander of the French armies in the north. Their object was to persuade Kitchener to send more British troops to France to reinforce the Allied line against the increasing intensity of German attacks and to still French fears that the BEF was on the point of withdrawing. Kitchener was unmoved by their pleas, telling Joffre that the New Armies would not be ready until the following year and that he was unwilling to commit them piecemeal to the Western Front. This refusal alarmed the French, who now believed that not only were the British averse to fighting the Germans in Europe, but any help they gave would be less than wholehearted. Taking this to signify French dissatisfaction with Britain's high command, Kitchener offered immediately to replace French and suggested Ian Hamilton, an offer Joffre declined. Unfortunately for all concerned, Foch repeated the story four days later to Wilson, who lost no time in telling French. The news renewed

French's hatred for Kitchener and in a state of fury he despatched his ADC to London to complain personally to Asquith. Faced by another major row between his top two military men the Prime Minister wrote soothingly to French and Churchill intervened again, assuring him that 'you are our man and we are going to stand by you'.[14] Once again French was mollified, on this occasion being prepared to accept the explanation that Kitchener's offer had been made in the face of French complaints and suspicions. A month later Kitchener and French met for the last time on terms of intimacy when they joined Asquith at Walmer Castle to discuss strategy for 1915. On the way back to London Kitchener drove with French to Broome, a visit that French later remembered as being 'the last of all the many days of happy personal intercourse which I spent with my old South African chief'.[15]

The meeting, held on 20 December, also introduced French and Asquith to Kitchener's thinking on the two-fronted nature of the war and the significance of Russia as an ally. In Kitchener's view, if the Russian armies were driven further back beyond the River Vistula by Ludendorff's counter-attack of 15 December, then the Germans would be able to release more troops for service on the Western Front. In that case the British and French armies would be put under severe pressure at a time when they had been weakened by the fighting at Ypres and the Aisne. However, French disagreed with this prognosis and remained confident that the allies could easily contain the German menace should it materialise. During the Battle of Ypres the Germans had used large numbers of inexperienced reservists, giving rise to a belief that the German front-line troops were no match for the British soldier. The two men parted, albeit amicably, but with different views of the strategic situation. French continued to look for victory through offensives in the west; Kitchener believed that any moves in Flanders or France were dictated by what was happening in Russia. The only change agreed upon at the meeting was the replacement of Sir Archibald Murray as CIGS by Sir William Robertson.

At this stage in the war Kitchener found it difficult to persuade his colleagues of the continuing importance of Russia as an ally. To them the Russians were merely the 'steamroller' that would crush Germany on the Eastern Front. Although the Russian Army had failed to make its expected breakthrough Kitchener still felt that it was central to Allied strategy. On 18 December he had therefore been alarmed to receive evidence that the Russian Army had run short of munitions during the German offensive on the Bzura-Ravka line, a message that convinced him a major German victory was in the offing. On that evening he doubted whether the British-French line would be able to hold in the face of the German reinforcements that would be hurled at it. For that reason Kitchener was lukewarm about the further offensives bruited by Joffre and French. The casualties inflicted during the autumn campaign in Flanders, the inability of the allies to make a breakthrough, the absence of a major British force in France and the neutralisation of the Royal Navy seemed to Kitchener to demonstrate a need to rethink British policy. From December 1914 this was to be determined by an understanding of the difficulties facing Russia and the need to relieve pressure on her by bolstering the Western Front until the arrival of the New Armies and by investigating limited offensives elsewhere. Kitchener had seen the link between the two fronts as early as 4 October when he had given tentative expression to his thinking in a letter to the British Ambassador in Russia, George Buchanan:

> It is important that we should be kept accurately and continuously informed as to real progress of the fighting in the Eastern frontier of Germany in the next few weeks. Upon this will depend critical decisions that we shall have to take as regards sending troops abroad or keeping them at home.[16]

As the threat of invasion began to recede and the position stabilised on the Western Front Kitchener realised that events in France and Flanders were dependent on what was happening in Eastern Europe. He asked his staff to keep him fully briefed on the fighting on the Russian front and in this he was fortunate to have the assistance of four able officers attached in different capacities to the Russian Army: Colonel A.F.W. Knox, Military Attaché, Captain James Blair, his assistant, Captain J.F. Neilson with the Russian Army in the field and Major-General John Hanbury-Williams, the Head of the Military

Mission. This latter officer, an experienced military administrator, had been detached from the General Staff on the outbreak of hostilities to serve in St Petersburg as Head of the British Military Mission and his signals were a vital means of supplying Kitchener with news of the current state of affairs in the east. When he wrote on 20 December that 'Russia will have to remain on defensive until their wants can be supplied', Kitchener was alarmed enough by the news to demand further efforts of Russian Supply Committed, which he had set up at the War Office Under the Chairmanship of U.F. Wintour of the Board of Trade.[17] Ensuring that Russia received sufficient weapons, munitions and finance to purchase them from the United States became a vital cog in Kitchener's war effort. To him the successful conclusion of the war depended on a Russian army remaining in the field until Britain's New Armies were ready to play a decisive role on the Western Front, thus forcing Germany to fight hard on two fronts. Until that time he advised a policy for the British armies of active-defence in Flanders. It was with that strategy in mind that Kitchener listened to proposals for opening other fronts.

Kitchener's letter of 2 January 1915 to Sir John French had articulated the problem facing him and his fellow strategists in the War Council: with the fighting on the Western Front facing stalemate, should attempts be made to discover military advantages elsewhere? French thought not, replying that the Western Front was the only one on which the Germans could be beaten decisively once additional men and munitions had been made available. If a second front had to be opened, he continued, Serbia should be encouraged to attack Austria–Hungary or, alternatively, a combined operations assault made on the Belgian coast.

Kitchener was opposed to any immediate offensives in Flanders but he realised too that the policy of active-defence could draw heavy German attacks on the Allied line. Under other circumstances he might not have been averse to sending French more men and supplies but he did not want to commit these until the Russians had stabilised their position on the Eastern Front. But on the same day he wrote to French, a telegram was received at the Foreign Office from the Grand

Duke Nicholas requesting that the Allies make a 'demonstration' against Turkey in order to relieve pressure on her troops in the Caucasus. This plea renewed fears in Whitehall that any further Russian setbacks might lead her to sue for peace with Germany, thus allowing Turkey, Germany's ally, to strike at Egypt and freeing Austro-Hungarian forces for the Western Front. To prevent this, and to give Russia the support that Kitchener knew she needed, the War Council turned its attention in the opening weeks of 1915 to the rival claims of the 'westerners' and the 'easterners'.

Kitchener insisted that any War Council decision had to allow for the fact that Britain's reserves were limited and that a substantial number had to be earmarked for future use in Flanders. On 7 and 8 January the War Council rehearsed the possibilities that presented themselves. Lloyd George favoured the transference of British military strength to the Balkans, where Austria–Hungary and Turkey might be beaten by a 'Balkan League' consisting of Serbia, Romania and Greece.[18] Such a move would require a landing at Salonika or the principal Adriatic ports, but until Italy's support was assured Kitchener considered this to be a non-starter. The one promising area was an invasion through the Dardanelles, to capture the Gallipoli Peninsula and to allow the navy's capital ships to strike at Constantinople, thus ending Russia's isolation from the Mediterranean. Accordingly, Kitchener was asked to investigate this possibility further. At the same time plans for further offensives in Flanders were postponed, although French's disappointment was softened by the reassuring promise that 'for the present, the main theatre of operations for British forces should be alongside the French Army, and that this should continue as long as France was liable to successful invasion and required armed support'.[19]

French, though, was not to be so easily appeased. To gain maximum political advantage, his reply to Kitchener was copied to the Prime Minister with the result that his confident prediction of a British breakthrough to the Dutch border was shown to the War Council. The incident did little to help the relationship between the two soldiers, bringing a sharp rebuke from Kitchener, who knew that French was also drumming up support through Wilson's presence in London, but it did work to French's advantage. When the War Council met again on 13 January French was at his eloquent best, even managing to persuade Kitchener to agree to plans for a spring offensive in Flanders, with an attack on Zeebrugge to coincide with Joffre's attack at Arras and Rheims. It was finally agreed to pass French's scheme, although no decision about timing was to be taken until February when Kitchener hoped to be in a position to commit the 29th Division, the last Regular Army force at his disposal. The deployment of this division satisfied French as he believed that the War Council would be unable to reach a consensus on which front to open, that to wage war against Turkey would be 'to play the German game, and to bring about the end which Germany had in mind when she induced Turkey to join in the war – namely, to draw off troops from the decisive spot, which is Germany herself'.[20]

However, the War Council, having opened up the possibility of war on other fronts, kept the idea firmly on the agenda. It had been agreed it was imperative both to relieve pressure on Russia and to take the fight to the enemy; the question was, in which arena? Kitchener forecast that a military assault on the Dardanelles would require 150,000 men and that any other front would require equally large numbers of troops. As French had thought, no backers could be found for any of the options on the table, a stalemate that cast a long shadow over the Council's deliberations. As the winter's day drew to a close the members of the War Council were seized by collective despair. It was at that crucial point, when morale was low and men tired, that Churchill lifted the gloom with a carefully prepared proposal for a purely naval assault on the Dardanelles. His timing could not have been better: just as the War Council was beginning to accept the need for a long fight to the end in Europe, here was a plan that offered the prospect of a cheap victory on another front. Troops would be unnecessary, for the Royal Navy's battleships would force the Narrows, break into the Sea of Marmara and bombard Constantinople, thus crushing Turkey with one fell blow. The knock-on effect would bring the Balkan states into the war on the Allied side and free Russia to concentrate on defeating Germany; the Austro-Hungarian Empire would falter and the Germans would find their rear threatened by the British and French. Not only did

Churchill promise that the Turks would flee before the might of a naval bombardment, but the battleships employed would be of obsolete design (though heavily gunned) so that any losses would not affect the efficiency of the Grand Fleet. As a clincher he also offered the services of the brand-new dreadnought, HMS *Queen Elizabeth*, whose mighty 15in guns could be tested against the Turkish forts.

To Kitchener, whose first choice had been a landing at Alexandretta on the Syrian coast to cut Turkish lines of communication, Churchill's intervention was a godsend. In the first place it would satisfy a call for action to relieve pressure on Russia, secondly it would not require a major force of troops, and thirdly it removed the necessity of committing any of Britain's reserves until the Russians started their spring offensive and the New Armies were ready for service in Flanders. It also allowed him breathing space to consider the deployment of British troops elsewhere and to discuss further Lloyd George's Balkan plans with the French.

In the opening days of the war Britain had made great diplomatic efforts not to damage the susceptibilities of Turkey, a country that had previously been considered a friendly power. Unknown to Britain, though, the Turks had secretly signed a treaty with Germany on 3 August and any hopes of retrieving the situation were dashed when two new Turkish warships – paid for by public subscription in Turkey – were prevented from leaving their British yards. This was a sensible precaution but it enraged the Turks and allowed the Germans to appear as Turkey's friend by offering them two new warships, the *Goeben* and the *Breslau*, complete with crews. By the end of September the Dardanelles had been closed and, when the Turkish fleet bombarded the Russian Black Sea ports, hostilities became inevitable – although Britain held off until 5 November before declaring war.

The advent of Turkey into the war upset the strategic balance in two ways. It cut off Russia from the west through her vital supply route to the Mediterranean and it weakened Russia's war effort by drawing away her troops to fight in the Caucasus; it also threatened Egypt and the Suez Canal. Thus the defeat of Turkey was essential to protect British interests in the Near East and to free Russia from having to fight on an additional front. Steps were taken to prevent that eventuality. By declaring Egypt to be a protectorate and deposing Abbas Hilmi, Britain secured control of the country that was also garrisoned by eight battalions of Indian infantry, the 42nd Territorial Division (East Lancashire) and by the Anzacs, troops from Australia and New Zealand. Command of the force was given to General Sir John Maxwell, another Kitchener protégé. Kitchener's earlier work with Arab nationalist leaders such as Abdullah Ibn Husain had done much to neutralise the Sultan of Turkey's call for Muslims to wage holy war against Britain, and in the event the Suez Canal was never seriously threatened. The war against Turkey was destined to be fought on three main fronts: the long-drawn-out campaign in Mesopotamia to protect British oil interests, the Desert War culminating in the triumphant Syrian campaign of 1918, and the Dardanelles (Gallipoli).

Despite his belief that Britain should be cautious, Kitchener was fully alive to the dangers created by Turkey's entry into the war. As early as 31 August he was studying a Greek plan to land troops on the Gallipoli Peninsula to capture the Turkish forts with British and French naval support. Due to Britain's conciliatory attitude towards Turkey the plan was shelved: had the attack gone ahead it would undoubtedly have succeeded as the Turks had only two divisions on the peninsula, encamped in ill-equipped forts. A naval attack on 3 November, led by a squadron of warships under Rear-Admiral Sackville Carden, achieved some success by destroying the outer fortifications and terrifying the Turkish garrison but, in the long term, it proved disadvantageous to Britain. The ease with which its ships had carried out the bombardment convinced the Admiralty, against all previous naval practice, that battleships could take on the forts; it also warned the German advisers in Turkey to reinforce the positions and to bring in more efficient guns. Churchill, who had been bewitched by the idea of an attack through the Dardanelles ever since the Greek invasion had been broached, first raised the idea of a combined operation at the War Council on 25 November but he could then find no takers largely because Kitchener had become obsessive about conserving Britain's military reserves.

STRATEGY ON THREE FRONTS

The re-thinking of British strategy in January 1915 brought the Dardanelles proposals into greater focus. Before then, Churchill had kept it warm, winning Fisher over to his side and securing confirmation from Carden that British warships could take on the Turkish forts. With a War Council ready to accept anything that might produce cheap victories away from the deadlock in Europe, Churchill offered the Royal Navy as the instrument with which to defeat Turkey. Today his proposals smack more of optimism than tactical reality, but such was the mood of the War Council on 13 January that a purely naval attack through the Dardanelles was approved. No one asked how the ships, once in the Sea of Marmara, were to capture Constantinople. Two weeks later at another War Council, Fisher attempted to resign over a split with Churchill but was prevented from doing so by Kitchener, who pulled him aside and told him that he had 'to stick to the thing'. If there were any other misgivings, no other member of the Council or its advisers cared to voice them.

The preliminary bombardments began on 19 February, the main attack going in a month later on 18 March when, for the last time in British naval history, a line of battleships went into action as they had done in the days of gunboat diplomacy, to silence the Turkish guns and force their way through the Narrows. At the end of a day of sound and fury three capital ships had been destroyed and three more badly damaged. Only four Turkish gun platforms had been hit. Four days later, Rear-Admiral de Robeck, successor to the ailing Carden, signalled London that troops would now be necessary to clear the peninsula. The Gallipoli campaign, which lasted from April 1915 until January 1916 and which was to cost the Allies a quarter of a million casualties in return for no strategic advantage, was about to begin. Its failure, made the more poignant by Churchill's heady advocacy, cast a long shadow over his career and almost broke Kitchener's reputation.

Between 13 and 28 January, when final approval was given to the naval attack on the Dardanelles, Kitchener met his senior advisers to discuss the possibility of deploying troops in theatres other than the Western Front.[21] The key point in their discussion was how to influence events in the Balkans, where Serbia had suddenly come under the threat of Austrian attack and Bulgaria seemed to be on the point of throwing in her lot with Germany. Any British demonstration there, allied to a naval success in the Dardanelles, could bring Greece and Romania into the war on the Allied side, where their large armies could be employed against Turkey. Apart from those diplomatic considerations, the sub-committee had to consider the best ways of aiding Russia. Kitchener was largely of the opinion that any lull on the Western Front caused by the removal of British troops would allow the Germans to remove units from Flanders to the Eastern Front with disastrous results for the Russians. For that reason he was interested only in a limited use of British troops in the Mediterranean. He may not have had any faith in the French ability to break through the German lines in the west, but he realised that their presence did tie down large numbers of Germans who would otherwise be used against the Russians. However, each member of the committee was agreed that the threat of enemy success in the Balkans warranted the despatch of a British expeditionary force to Greece. This recommendation was ratified by the War Council on 9 February.

At the beginning of February Lloyd George travelled to Paris to persuade the French to commit an infantry division to the Mediterranean front. Its use was opposed by both Kitchener and Joffre, but political expediency dictated that the presence of a French contingent would allow a French voice to be heard in any ensuing peace treaty: the French still harboured nineteenth-century fears of British political domination in the eastern Mediterranean. In turn, Kitchener agreed to commit the 29th Division to the Balkans, where it would be quartered on the island of Lemnos as a mobile reserve. This division was made up of regular soldiers who were serving abroad before the war and it was regarded by French and Joffre as the trump card in Kitchener's hand. Were it to be transferred to France it would add its weight to French's spring offensive; but should it be used in the Mediterranean Joffre would regard the deployment as evidence of Britain's lack of commitment to the Western Front. During the weeks that followed the decision to send it to the Balkans became a pawn as Kitchener attempted to find the correct balance between opening up a new front in the Mediterranean and shoring up the Western Front (at this point the Dardanelles campaign was still considered to be the responsibility of the Admiralty).

The decision to send the 29th Division to the Mediterranean had been taken mainly on the strength of attracting Greece and Romania into the war on the Allied side and of preventing Bulgaria falling under German domination. It was also felt that its presence there could be of limited use in the Dardanelles should the navy require any military support. However, the offer of two British and French divisions was considered to be too meagre to tempt Greece, which was also alarmed enough by Russian reverses in Poland to object to an Allied military presence in the country. These defeats also set alarm bells ringing in Kitchener's mind. Fearing that the German gains in the east would result in the loss of the Warsaw–Petrograd railway, thus allowing the rapid transport of German troops to the west, Kitchener ordered the 29th to remain in Britain until the situation became clearer. It was only when Russia achieved a series of victories in the Carpathians towards the end of February that he felt he could afford to order the 29th to take up its original Mediterranean deployment. By that time, though, senior naval opinion in London was swinging inexorably to the position that a decisive victory in the Dardanelles could only be achieved by the use of troops.[22]

The slow drift towards the opening of a front against Turkey had been caused by a number of factors: the inability to forge a coherent campaign for the Balkans, the need to maintain Britain's diplomatic position in the face of any imminent Turkish collapse, Churchill's insistence on a purely naval attack, and Kitchener's fears of a Russian collapse on the Eastern Front. There was, too, Kitchener's knowledge of the area. 'If the Fleet cannot get through the Straits unaided, the Army will have to see the business through,' he told the War Council on 24 February. 'The effect of a defeat in the Orient would be very serious. There can be no going back. The publicity of the announcement has committed us.'[23]

Throughout this period Kitchener had shown great prudence. To have committed the 29th Division while the Russian front was unstable would have been folly, but his statement to the War Council that troops would be needed in the Dardanelles should not be regarded as contradictory. Kitchener still held to his belief that the Western Front was the only strategic area where victory could be won but that no large offensives should be launched until the following year. He also saw the political value of a 'demonstration' in the eastern Mediterranean. Where he erred was to commit a major force, including the 29th Division, in response to naval requests without giving thought to the consequences. By launching it against the Turks on the Gallipoli peninsula, Kitchener had committed Britain to a long-drawn-out campaign that would eventually require troops and munitions on a scale second only to the Western Front. Once landed, it would have to be supplied, re-equipped and reinforced, yet when the final decision was taken on 10 March little thought seems to have been given to those requirements, partly because, until the last minute, Kitchener hoped that the troops would not be required in any great numbers.

Acting without a General Staff – which in normal circumstances would have advised on the logistics of a landing and consequent occupation of the peninsula – Kitchener relied on his military intuition. To his way of thinking the Dardanelles could be captured by the Royal Navy, with a later landing on the Gallipoli peninsula to hold what had been won by the battleships' guns. At no time before 10 March had any great consideration been given to the tactics to be employed. As he had done in the past, Kitchener took the attitude that this was territory that belonged properly to the commander on the spot, in this case to General Sir Ian Hamilton, his Chief of Staff in the latter stages of the Boer War. He had been appointed on 12 March and his description of the fateful meeting with Kitchener gives a good idea of the air of improvisation which surrounded the Gallipoli expedition:

> Opening the door I bade him good morning and walked up to his desk, where he went on writing like a graven image. After a moment he looked up and said in a matter-of-fact tone, 'We are sending a military force to support the fleet now at the Dardanelles and you are to have command.' At that moment K wished me to bow, leave the room and make a start as I did some thirteen years ago.[24]

STRATEGY ON THREE FRONTS

Hamilton was now given five weeks in which to organise an invasion against a heavily defenced enemy. Even had he been allowed more time it is doubtful whether the War Office was in a position to provide him with the information, advice and requirements necessary to land a large military force on hostile territory. The dismal story of the planning failures, lack of foresight and bungling by the British commanders has been told many times.[25] Little attempt was made to reconnoitre the proposed landing beaches or to ascertain the military opposition that would face the Allied units, and the notion that it would be a 'combined operation' with the navy remained nothing more than a pious hope. Instead of sweeping in after the guns had engaged the forts, the troops would be required to go in cold under the shadow of the fleet.

At dawn on 25 April the military attack on the Gallipoli peninsula began, with the main landings being made on the beaches at the southern tip and the Anzac force landing at Y beach further to the north, near Ari Burnu. After almost a fortnight of heavy fighting Hamilton had to admit to Kitchener on 8 May that:

> The result of the operation has been failure, as my object remains unachieved. The fortifications and their machine guns were too scientific [they were not] and too strongly held to be rushed, although I had every available man on duty. Our troops have done all that flesh and blood can do against semi-permanent works [they were not] and they are not to be able to carry them. More and more munitions will be able to do so.[26]

Confronted by heavy casualties and a shortage of ammunition of all kinds, Hamilton appealed to Kitchener for reinforcements, his message arriving on his desk just as the shells crisis was about to break in the aftermath of Aubers Ridge. Initially, Kitchener was inclined to help Hamilton and, much to French's disgust, ordered the despatch to Gallipoli of 20,000 rounds of 18-pounder shells from the BEF's reserves (these were replaced a day later). On the subject of replacement troops, though, Kitchener was not sanguine, knowing that the recent losses at Neuve Chapelle and Aubers Ridge would have to be made good sooner rather than later both to appease the French and to draw pressure off the Russians.

A new factor had also been introduced on the Eastern Front. A force composed of the German Eleventh Army and the Austro-Hungarian Fourth Army, under the command of Field Marshal August von Mackensen, had broken through the Russian line at Gorlice-Tarnow. The prospect of a Russian Army in retreat and the creation of a new line further east put immediate pressure on the French and the British forces in France to draw German attention on the Western Front, a prospect that certainly did not appeal to Kitchener in view of the failure of the spring offensive. Nevertheless, he could neither ignore Russia's plight nor avoid the possibility that the Germans might then be in a position to throw their victorious divisions against the French and British lines. A flurry of telegrams passed between him and Hanbury-Williams, the head of the Military Mission to the Russian Army, during May as Kitchener attempted to gauge the relative strength of the Russian Army and to ascertain what was happening on the Eastern Front:

> The reports we have received concerning the Russian retirement in the Carpathians and in Galicia are very disquieting. Can you tell me privately how serious their defeat has been in this theatre and whether it is possible for them to take effective steps to arrest the German and Austrian advance, or whether we are to expect further retirements? The Russians, according to our information, now hold the line Dvernik-Sanok-Ropchitse-Shchutzin and have been driven back on the Lower Nida. Is this correct? What do their recent losses amount to approximately?[27]

Kitchener wanted to help Russia by supplying it with sufficient weapons to replace those lost at Gorlice-Tarnow but events at home made large-scale provision impossible. The Grand Duke Nicholas wanted greater efforts to be made at Gallipoli, even going so far as to promise Hamilton 4,000 Russian troops, an offer that was subsequently withdrawn. To Kitchener this was unrealistic because so small a force would make little impact on the Turkish lines, now heavily reinforced during the lull in the fighting. 'The situation there [Gallipoli] is one of great difficulty,' he told Hanbury-Williams to inform the Russians, 'owing to the drain on our ammunition supplies, caused by protracted operations against trenches which additional troops would not shorten'.[28] One way out of the problem, he added, would be for Russia to put pressure on Bulgaria to join the Allied side, but this proposal fell on deaf ears (after a careful balancing act Bulgaria threw in her lot with the Germans in September, thus precipitating the later operations in the Balkans).

With the Dardanelles campaign in stalemate, Kitchener outlined his thinking to the Grand Duke through a secret message to Hanbury-Williams on 21 June:

> I do not anticipate the enemy withdrawing further troops from the Western Front at an early date, in view of the strong and successful offensive being maintained by the French and ourselves. I quite realise the Russian difficulties consequent on lack of rifles and gun ammunition. You should, however, urge the Grand Duke not to abandon the line of the Vistula between Ivangorod and Novo Giorgevsk and the line of defences between Novo Giorgevsk and Grodno if it can possibly be avoided. These lines were held in the early stages of the War at a time when the Russian mobilisation was far from complete. Should the enemy gain possession of them, our Ally would be faced with a very difficult problem when – some months hence, or early next year – the munitions question has been overcome, and it becomes possible to assume the offensive.[29]

If the Russians could hold out until 1916 the combined might of Britain and France would then be able to break through in the west, thus drawing the German Army away from Russia. In the meantime, Britain would do her best to rearm Russia, to hold the Western Front and to keep up the pressure on Turkey in the Dardanelles. This was considered by many Russians to be too small an effort, the belief growing in Petrograd that Britain would fight to the last drop of Russian blood; but given the circumstances there was little else that Kitchener could promise. Britain was still not in a position to throw large armies into the field, nor did she yet possess the technological means to wage war on a grand scale.

When the War Council met to discuss the conflicting calls for replacements, Kitchener stalled by suggesting that the only answer was 'to maintain the defensive role hitherto imposed upon us'.[30] The point of view was accepted by his colleagues. That same day, 14 May, Repington's 'Need for Shells' article appeared in *The Times* and eleven days later the coalition Cabinet came to power. Under the new administration a Dardanelles Committee was formed, with Asquith as chairman, to deal with eastern strategy and it was to that body that Kitchener and Churchill spoke on 7 June. In a memorandum prepared on 28 May Kitchener rehearsed the alternatives that presented themselves: to evacuate Gallipoli and lose not only prestige but also political advantages in the Near East, or to continue the status quo; at the same time he introduced the news that he could now afford to give Hamilton three additional divisions in addition to the 42nd Territorial Division that had already been sent. Churchill backed this latter proposal, arguing for a new offensive and this view was accepted by the Cabinet two days later. A fifth division was added to the force on 28 June.

Encouraged by this good news, which he took to be a sign of total support, Hamilton planned a new attack from the southern tip of Gallipoli, with a subsidiary attack going in further north on the Aegean coast at Suvla Bay aimed at dissecting the peninsula and opening the way for an attack on the forts at the Narrows. But just as Hamilton's army had been reinforced, so too had the Turks'. Their tenacious fighting and a lack of vision and enterprise on the part of the Allied commanders marked the failure of the second military phase during the third week of August, with Hamilton's forces still having no more than a toehold on the peninsula. By the end of the month the idea was gaining ground in the Cabinet that the Dardanelles operation should be shut down in favour of increased action on the Western Front or an expedition to the Balkans. The crunch came on 17 August, when Hamilton sent a request to the War Office for 95,000 reinforcements plus equipment. On receiving the message Kitchener wrote to Asquith explaining why he would be unable to accede to Hamilton's wishes:

> To send such reinforcements as those asked for would be a very serious step to take at the present moment when an offensive in France is necessary to relieve pressure in Russia and keep the French Army and people steady – Sir John French is strongly against doing so and I personally feel that it is not certain that even if they were sent the result would be decisive and relieve us of the Dardanelles incubus.[31]

Three days later the Dardanelles Committee agreed that it would be impossible to support Hamilton while replacements were needed urgently in France both to maintain the active-defence policy on the Western Front and to relieve the hard-pressed Russians. Kitchener argued that continued inaction by the British would harm their relationship with France, where talk of negotiating a separate peace was growing. When Churchill protested that this went against all received opinion, that the New Armies would not be ready to mount fresh offensives until 1916, Kitchener rounded on him with the grim remark that 'we had to make war as we must, not as we would like to.'[32] Although the final decision about what to do with the force in the Dardanelles was not taken until November, and Kitchener refused to lose sight of the possibilities there, the meeting on 20 August marked the beginning of the end. Initially, the Dardanelles had offered a means of drawing Turkish troops away from Russia, at the same time demonstrating to the Russian people Britain's sense of purpose, and had it been successful it would have won important diplomatic gains. However loath he was to abandon it completely Kitchener realised by August that the Dardanelles could only continue to be a drain on British resources. To understand his conclusions we have to go back to the first week of July when British and French leaders met in Calais to discuss the future conduct of the war and Britain's part in it.

On 24 June, prior to the conference, French and Joffre had met to prepare a united front for the conference, based on the argument that Britain had to commit its forces more fully to the Western Front to make up for the French losses of the spring and to allay French fears that she was attempting to aggrandise her position in the Near East. Joffre remained confident that he could wear down the Germans and achieve a breakthrough at the German salient near Noyon but this would require a British offensive in Flanders. Later that day, during the joint staff talks, Sir John French promised that he would 'assist as far as he could in any attack of the French Army; it is a duty we owe to the Russians to co-operate'.[33]

This compromise worked on two levels: it gave Britain a breathing space to determine the situation in Gallipoli and it gave the French much-needed assurance of British commitment to the Western Front. A month later, though, Joffre renewed his bid for an outright offensive in Flanders. On 16 August Kitchener crossed over to France to discuss those plans with Joffre and during the course of the meeting, to avoid a split with the French, he changed his mind and gave his approval for a British attack at Loos in September. His decision contradicted previous tactical thinking but it was governed by a desire to keep the French happy and by news elsewhere of Allied disaster. On 4 August Warsaw had fallen to the Germans, who were harrying the Russians deep into their own country. Buchanan, the British ambassador in Russia, had warned Kitchener that the defeats found people in Petrograd greatly depressed and nervous, with talk of revolution in the air. Unless the British took up the offensive in France at the expense of the Dardanelles the Russians might well seek a separate peace with Germany. On this reading Kitchener's decision to commit to an autumn offensive was due mainly to his interpretation of events on the Eastern Front and the Russian reaction to them. Two days after returning to London Kitchener sent a telegram to Hanbury-Williams urging him to tell the Grand Duke that Britain would do her best to help Russia by pressing home the offensive with the 'utmost vigour'.

The events of the summer of 1915 proved to be the high-water mark of Kitchener's strategic thinking. Throughout this period Kitchener preached the primacy of the Western Front as the only sure means of defeating Germany, provided always that the Russians did not falter in the east. From the urgency of his telegrams to Hanbury-Williams and Buchanan, and from the depth of information they provided, it is apparent that Kitchener had a good understanding not only of the Russian front but how events there affected British strategy.

STRATEGY ON THREE FRONTS

Had Kitchener been able to articulate his policies to his colleagues all might have been well, but when he did speak on vital matters of planning or strategy his utterances tended to appear oracular or puzzlingly contradictory. Nevertheless, until September 1915 the reins of that strategy were firmly in his hands; thereafter, three events conspired to weaken his authority at the War Office: a failure to take steps to counter the Austro-Hungarian invasion of Serbia, French's setback at the Battle of Loos and his own wavering attitude towards British withdrawal from the Dardanelles. For a year that had begun with such high hopes, 1915 was doomed to end in bitter disappointment.

13

EROSION OF POWER

Once Britain had committed to joining Joffre's autumn offensive in September 1915, it became necessary to deny Hamilton the reinforcements and heavy mortars he had requested for use at Suvla Bay. This placed Kitchener in a quandary but help came from an unexpected quarter. While he agitated about the potential disaster facing the Allies at Gallipoli, France offered six divisions to assist Hamilton on the Asiatic side of the Dardanelles but this offer, born of internecine politicking in Paris, came to nothing. Joffre, recognising the challenge to his authority, successfully blocked the provision of troops for the expedition because he needed them for the Western Front. At the same time, too, France began switching her attention from the Dardanelles to the Balkans.

From the outset of the war Bulgaria had been courted by both sides and eventually signed a military agreement with the Central Powers on 6 September. Two weeks later she began to mobilise her large but antiquated armed forces, complete with artillery drawn by oxen. The decision was not just triggered by German blandishments – Russian setbacks that summer and the British failure at Suvla Bay also served to convince the Bulgarians that they should join what appeared to be the winning side. However, the move alarmed the French and the government was subjected to intense public pressure to go to the aid of Serbia, an ally and a long-standing enemy of Bulgaria. The matter was settled on 22 September when previously neutral Greece offered the Allies landing facilities at the port of Salonika to deploy forces in support of Serbia. The French government made ready to send the necessary forces but the British Cabinet was more cautious. France continued to keep up moral pressure for assistance to be given to Serbia through Salonika, arguing that a combined Allied operation would encourage the creation of a proposed Balkan League led by Serbia to threaten Austria–Hungary and open the back door into Germany. On 24 September, the government acceded to French requests and agreed to commit two divisions to an Allied landing at Salonika. These would be drawn from Hamilton's force at Gallipoli.

Kitchener viewed the Balkans as a battlefront with considerable suspicion. His reading of the situation told him that the region's traditional instability and the antagonisms and jealousies fomented in the aftermath of the Balkans War of 1913 meant that any Balkan League would be a non-starter unless Russia, the traditional friend of the Slavs, achieved a substantial victory over the Austro-Hungarians. As that seemed unlikely in 1915, Kitchener hoped that Serbia would take refuge behind its mountainous frontiers and postpone any action against Bulgaria until such time as the Allied armies had arrived:

> Serbia would be playing into German hands by precipitating hostilities with Bulgaria and at the present juncture any such action would be most unwise while we are arranging to send troops to Salonika in order to enable the Greeks to support Serbia. The Serbians should ensure their country from attack from the north and not allow their feeling with regard to Bulgaria to precipitate matters.[1]

Repeated telegrams from Kitchener to Colonel George Fraser Phillips, the Military Attaché with the Serbians, reveal that he feared being lured into another Gallipoli with the Allied armies being bottled up on the coast, devoid of tactical advantage. Much depended, therefore, on the attitude of the Greeks, whose offer of support had been made by their Prime Minister, Eleftherios Venizelos, and it was on that obstacle that the Allied effort was to stumble. A series of contradictory private telegrams from Venizelos arrived in London during the last week of September confusing the Dardanelles Committee and inducing in Kitchener a feeling of profound helplessness. On 30 September Kitchener told Hankey that 'so much time was wasted in talking to these people that he simply couldn't get time to do his work at the War Office'. Ominously, Hankey thought that Kitchener's 'queer state' and 'hysterical condition' might lead to a nervous breakdown.[2]

Kitchener's anxieties had been caused mainly by his workload and by the incessant demands of the pro-Balkans faction in the Cabinet, headed by Lloyd George and Edward Carson, the Attorney-General and a leading Irish unionist. But the Greek dithering did not help: Venizelos's indecision had come about because King Constantine, a brother-in-law of Kaiser Wilhelm II, was worried enough by the Allied failure in Gallipoli to hesitate committing his country to war. On 5 October the Dardanelles Committee agreed to provide 64,000 men to a British-French force only to discover that evening that Venizelos had been sacked by the king. The following day von Mackensen's forces swept over the Danube towards Serbia and on 9 October Belgrade was forced to surrender: as had happened at the Dardanelles, any Allied intervention was doomed before it had even begun.

The intricacies of the Balkan situation, and the need to evolve a military strategy to meet them, came at the worst possible time for Kitchener. Not only was he feeling the strain of overwork – largely self-inflicted, it must be said – but he was aware of the dangers of opening another front at a time when British prestige was already at risk in the area due to the stalemate at Gallipoli. 'I pace my room at night,' he admitted to Asquith, 'and see the boats fired at and capsizing, and the drowning men.'[3] A terrible feeling of despair swept over him. Kitchener liked Hamilton, yet the constraints of British policy prevented him from offering him any immediate assistance.

Into the midst of this muddle and uncertainty came news of the failure of the Battle of Loos, which had begun on 25 September. This was the offensive to which Kitchener had given his approval in August and its mismanagement by Field Marshal French was a terrible blow. Although Haig's First Army had made an early breakthrough, French's failure to deploy his reserves halted the momentum and led eventually to a German counter-attack. When the fighting died down at the beginning of October French's army had suffered 50,380 casualties (killed, wounded and missing) for little strategic or territorial advantage. French's muddled leadership led to a breach with Haig and to calls for his dismissal by Cabinet members. As Kitchener had committed them to that course of action he was not beyond criticism and from the beginning of October that year his position at the War Office was suddenly tenuous.

The first move was taken by Asquith, who insisted that Kitchener's administration of the War Office should now be bolstered by the reconstitution of a General Staff. Kitchener accepted the change to please Asquith, but in Cabinet his occasionally secretive and devious behaviour was now being put repeatedly to the test. With confusion dominating the Dardanelles Committee, and with an increasingly hostile Cabinet, Kitchener began to lose touch with his war aims, which he could not manage single-handedly. At the same time, too, he had to face insistent demands for the introduction of conscription from ministers, including Lloyd George and Carson.

Both were experienced politicians who found little difficulty in outflanking Kitchener and bewildering him during Cabinet meetings. Carson, a shrewd barrister, tended to treat Kitchener as a hostile witness while Lloyd George employed his superior political rhetoric to ridicule Kitchener's awkward attempts to explain his strategic thinking.[4] The shakiness of Kitchener's position is illustrated by a Cabinet meeting of 9 October during which the rival claims of the Balkans and Gallipoli were discussed. Acting on impulse, Lloyd George asked Kitchener if any news had been received of von Mackensen's threatened advance into Serbia. Taken by surprise, Kitchener responded that up until the meeting he was unaware that any intelligence reports had come his way, a forgivable admission during a time of crisis. Pressed by Lloyd George, Asquith arranged for the War Office to be telephoned and back came the reply that the news of the German attack had been received the day before. On this occasion Kitchener might have been let down by his staff, but the incident convinced Lloyd George and others that he had lost control of the direction of the war.[5] As Hankey remarked frequently, Kitchener ran the War Office by bludgeoning everyone into agreeing with him and brooking no opposition to his thinking. His staff knew of his dislike of the Balkans, so the vital telegram had presumably been filed away to avoid a row, but it was a damaging omission.

During the meeting Lloyd George and Carson had been further inflamed by a joint-staff paper, prepared under Kitchener's direction, advocating the reinforcement of the Dardanelles by eight divisions but stressing the strategic primacy of the Western Front. It also poured scorn on proposals for reinforcing the British-French force at Salonika by arguing that it was now too late to save Serbia.[6] Two days later the British Balkanists found an unlikely ally in Joffre. Thoroughly shaken by the failure of the Allied offensive in Flanders and Champagne, and disgusted by attempts to remove him from office, Joffre came up with a plan to send more men to the Balkans to protect the Serbian right. The expedition, he continued, could win important strategic advances by holding the railway line from Salonika north to Uskub, thereby helping to block the Central Powers' attempt to dominate the Balkans through Bulgaria. Joffre's argument also took into account the fact that the six French divisions earmarked for Salonika would be commanded by his enemy, General Maurice Sarrail, thus keeping him out of the country, far from the intrigues of Paris. In the interests of the entente the Cabinet agreed to a compromise: four divisions earmarked for deployment in Egypt would be diverted to Salonika thereby bringing the British contribution to five divisions in all.[7]

Kitchener pointed out that Joffre's plans for Salonika would stretch the Allied line to breaking point and he refused to give them any credence, thereby instigating another clash with Lloyd George. He responded to the latter's surmise that the presence of a large British-French force at Salonika would encourage the Balkan states to combine by stating that Britain simply could not afford the troops, which were needed for the Western Front and Gallipoli. However, Kitchener did concede that the entry of Bulgaria into the war had tipped the strategic balance by presenting Germany with the opportunity of sending supplies directly to Turkey by the overland route. Should the Turks be able to pour more guns and well-armed men into the Gallipoli peninsula Hamilton's already weakened forces would not be able to offer much resistance. Any such disaster would put further pressure on the

Russians and destroy British credibility in the Muslim world: in that case Kitchener knew that he would have to find some way of reinforcing the British forces in the Near East.

To ascertain the position Kitchener asked Hamilton on 11 October to let him know the probable losses his army would sustain if the order were given to withdraw. In a reply that finished him as a commander, but which impressed Kitchener as an accurate estimate, Hamilton assessed that half his force might be lost if the positions were abandoned under the fire of Turkish guns. This pessimism brought renewed demands for Hamilton's replacement but also strengthened Kitchener's resolve against evacuation. Three days later the War Committee ordered that Hamilton should be replaced by General Sir Charles Monro, the forthright commander of the British Third Army in France.

The sacking of Hamilton had been in the air for some time. Lieutenant-General Sir Frederick Stopford, the corps commander at Suvla Bay, sacked by Hamilton, led the criticism and he was supported by others including Captain Guy Dawnay, an officer on Hamilton's staff who presented an unexpurgated version of the operation to the Cabinet. Asquith then allowed the War Committee to have sight of a vitriolic attack on Hamilton written by Keith Murdoch, an Australian war correspondent who blamed everyone else for the failure bar the Anzac corps under Birdwood's command. It was at this time, too, that demands grew for French's replacement, moves led by Haig, who enjoyed great influence at court through his wife's appointment as maid of honour to Queen Alexandra. Although Kitchener had little love for French and had been bitterly disappointed by Hamilton's failure, he was disgusted by the political intrigues, which he knew were directed at him as well. When he met Birdwood in Gallipoli a month later his first words to him echoed his sentiments, 'I can't tell you how glad I am to have you with me again, Birdie, and to be away from all those bloody politicians!'[8]

That Kitchener's standing had fallen to this new low in mid-October was mainly due to the Balkans-Dardanelles imbroglio but it was not helped by events on other political fronts. In the midst of the crisis and the growing pressure to find some way of changing the direction of the war, Curzon, now back in parliamentary life as Lord Privy Seal, held a private dinner for ministerial colleagues anxious to see conscription introduced as quickly as possible. In their eyes this could only be achieved if Kitchener gave his support to the scheme, so high was his standing both with the general public and with the Tory rank and file at Westminster. Kitchener, though, refused to be drawn and when Asquith learned about the plot on 17 October he wrote an anguished letter begging Kitchener to stand firm:

> We are (as you realise) in a most critical situation. You and I have since the war began worked in daily intimacy and unbroken confidence. And you know well that, in every exigent crisis, I have given you – as you have given me – loyal and unstinting support.
>
> I should like you to know that what is now going on is being engineered by men (Curzon, Lloyd George and some others) whose real object is to oust you. They know well that I give no countenance to their projects, and consequently they have conceived the idea of using you against me. God knows that we should both of us be glad to be set free. But we cannot and ought not. So long as you and I stand together, we carry the whole country with us. Otherwise the Deluge! …
>
> … I do not appeal to personal considerations, but I am certain, in the interests of the Country, and of the effective prosecution of the war, that it is essential that you and I should stand together, and that the intrigue, which has for its main object both to divide and to discredit us both, should be frustrated.[9]

Margot Asquith had also written to him earlier, begging, 'Don't let Curzon score,' but it was her husband's letter that pulled at Kitchener's heartstrings.[10] The following day he met Asquith at 10 Downing Street and reaffirmed his support for the voluntary system of raising the New Armies. By nailing his colours to Asquith's mast Kitchener enraged many Conservatives at a time when he could ill afford to lose any public support, yet the incident shows Kitchener at his loyal best. It was Asquith who had brought him into the Cabinet at the beginning of the war and it was therefore to him that Kitchener felt he owed his allegiance.

Matters came to a head on 31 October when Lloyd George wrote a long letter to Asquith cataloguing his criticisms of Kitchener's management of the war and ending with the threat that he would make its contents public unless it were discussed in Cabinet. In comparison to Kitchener's understated loyalty to Asquith, Lloyd George's attack was not just unfair; it was also less than truthful. In essence it boiled down to two major complaints, namely that Kitchener's inability to organise the mass manufacture of munitions had led to the military disasters on the Western Front; and, that Kitchener had failed to take cognisance of events in the Balkans early in the war and thereafter failed to present a coherent British response. The letter was skilfully argued but as a letter designed to make political capital it does not do justice to Kitchener.

Munitions were no longer the problem they had been at the beginning of the war and, by the end of 1915, had reached a reasonable level of output. French's botched offensive at Loos could hardly be ascribed to a shortage of ammunition; rather, as at Neuve Chapelle and Aubers Ridge, the British collapse had been caused by the failure of GHQ to produce a workable plan. That was not the responsibility of Kitchener but of the officers on the spot. It was also unfair to blame Kitchener for the shilly-shallying attitude to the Balkans. Lloyd George had indeed warned the Cabinet of the danger to Serbia if Bulgaria declared war but, as far as Kitchener was concerned, the British response was the responsibility of the Foreign Office. All too often Grey and his officials either failed to tell the War Office of their moves or took no account of the military situation before entering into political commitments.

Faced by a Cabinet revolt more serious than the earlier shells crisis, Asquith hedged his bets. He owed Kitchener a debt of loyalty yet he knew that his colleagues were tired of War Office tardiness and its Secretary's obstructive and seemingly contradictory behaviour. He had already toyed with the idea of resurrecting the post of Commander-in-Chief and filling it with Kitchener, a proposal that Kitchener himself, egged on by Esher, had considered earlier that year. He also suggested an appointment as generalissimo of the British armies in the Near East and India but Kitchener refused both offers, preferring to stick to the War Office. To have decided otherwise, Kitchener parried, would have been to give up in mid-stream and destroy national unity.

To avoid a public row and to prevent a split in the Cabinet, Asquith changed tack and suggested that Kitchener should go to the Dardanelles to inspect the situation himself. In his absence Asquith would take temporary responsibility for the War Office as he had done in the wake of the Curragh incident. This was agreed on 3 November, much to the satisfaction of Kitchener's enemies who hoped that he would not come back. Those impious thoughts were reasonably well founded for not only was Kitchener going to a war zone through the submarine-infested Mediterranean but, if the Gallipoli situation were as complicated as it sounded, then Kitchener might be persuaded to stay on to command the Allied force there. Either way, when the time came for his departure Kitchener acted with such dignity that Lloyd George was not a little ashamed of the events he had put in train. Just before the end of the Cabinet meeting on the morning of 4 November Kitchener left to make his final preparations. With little fuss he got up from the table, nodded discreetly at Asquith and left the room: his bearing left a vivid enough impression on Lloyd George for him to relate what happened to Frances Stevenson, his wartime secretary and mistress, who wrote it up in her diary:

> Not a word spoken! He might have been going out to lunch. He knew as well as anyone that it was for good he was leaving, but not a sign of his countenance or demeanour gave evidence of this. D [Lloyd George] says that he felt a lump in his throat, and he thinks many other members of the Cabinet were touched also. Crewe passed a rather significant note across to D. Personally I think it is rather a cowardly thing the P.M. had done.[11]

Asquith had had little choice. Kitchener's departure cleared the air and removed him from the Cabinet at a time when his very presence caused offence. 'We avoid by this method of procedure the immediate supersession of K as War Minister,' Asquith told Lloyd George, 'while attaining the same result.'[12]

Kitchener's absence allowed changes to be made in the political and military hierarchy. A new War Committee was formed, consisting of Asquith, Balfour, Lloyd George, McKenna, Bonar Law and then later Grey and Kitchener. At the War Office further props of Kitchener's authority were removed when the Ordnance Board's responsibilities, mainly research and development, were transferred to the Ministry of Munitions. To more lasting effect, Asquith began negotiations with Robertson to take over as CIGS in a revised role that would give him control of strategy with direct access to the War Committee, and steps were also taken to replace French with Haig – the one move of which Kitchener did approve. When he returned, Kitchener found he had lost control completely of munitions and strategy and that his powers had been eroded considerably. But neither Asquith nor Lloyd George had been prepared to grasp the nettle and remove him completely from office. That they were not prepared to do so was due entirely to the standing and prestige Kitchener still enjoyed with the British public. That was such an important consideration that when the *Globe* reported on 6 November that Kitchener was on the point of resignation and when it repeated the story the next day, the Press Bureau ordered its suppression. Although other attempts were made later in the year to curtail Kitchener's authority, no minister ever dared risk public disapproval by proposing that he should be sacked.

By the time Kitchener left for the east no final decision had been taken about which front to support, although the voices of the 'evacuationists' and of the pro-Balkanists were becoming more insistent, fired by a report from Monro that recommended total evacuation. He had based his findings on the exhausted state of the troops and on the hopelessness of their position; he had also asked his three corps commanders at Gallipoli to give him an independent assessment – Julian Byng and Francis Davies replied that they supported his conclusions, but Birdwood disagreed and argued for the retention of the front. This simply confused Kitchener, who travelled to the Dardanelles through Marseilles where the cruiser HMS *Dartmouth* carried him to Mudros. Ignoring pleas from his staff that his safety was imperilled, Kitchener proceeded on a thorough inspection that took him frequently into the firing line. At the Anzac beaches his presence – unannounced on security grounds – was greeted with an immediate display of enthusiasm from the battle-hardened Australian and New Zealand soldiers. As Birdwood remembered:

> It was quite a spontaneous demonstration and pleased Lord Kitchener more, I dare say, than he would have cared to show. Wherever he went, the ovation which broke out from the men was such as to make one anxious lest the Turks should notice it and guess the cause. At some points, where the enemy were only a few yards away, it was with difficulty that they were prevented from cheering. The men were dressed in their ordinary working garb, and Lord Kitchener seemed unusually at home amongst this crowd of toilers. The strong, interested face of the one gazing on the intent weather-tanned countenance of the others, as he questioned them and told them the King's message, made a picture not readily forgotten.[13]

Whatever their loyalty inspired in Kitchener, the difficulties of the terrain and the hardships they had suffered certainly had a profound effect on him. That night he confessed to Birdwood that what he had seen had thoroughly depressed him. 'Thank God, Birdie, I came to see this for myself. I had no idea of the difficulties you were up against. I think you have all done wonders.'[14]

Following a series of conferences with the British naval and military commanders, his first report to Asquith suggested he would recommend withdrawal at Suvla and Anzac while retaining a presence at Cape Helles to save face. This merely echoed Monro's advice but Kitchener had more to say about Britain's strategic responsibilities in the area. Given the extent of the British evacuation, he argued, Turkey would be free to attack Egypt and threaten the Suez Canal. To prevent that happening he proposed to use a portion of the Gallipoli force for a landing at Ayah Bay in the Gulf of Iskanderun, thus reopening the Alexandretta project. This startled Asquith enough to pass it on to the General Staff, who advised against the scheme on the grounds that it would require a larger force of troops than Kitchener had predicted. This idea was finally put into cold storage on 17 November when the French objected to a British military presence near Syria, traditionally regarded as their sphere of influence in the eastern Mediterranean.

Kitchener travelled onwards to Greece on 16 November to explain Allied war intentions and to prevent any possibility of the neutral Greek Army clashing with Allied forces at Salonika. In his meetings with King Constantine and later with his political leaders,

Kitchener proved again his flair for diplomacy that had served him so well in Egypt and Sudan. As the Kaiser's brother-in-law, Constantine found himself in a difficult position as, although he wanted to remain neutral, he realised that his country was dependent on British influence in the eastern Mediterranean. Showing a polite regard for the king's domestic problems, Kitchener pointed out that Britain would eventually triumph over Germany because at the end of the day she would be able to put into the field vastly superior numbers of men.

By 21 November Kitchener was back in Mudros, where he penned his final report recommending partial withdrawal and the implementation of a plan to prevent any Turkish attack on Egypt. During his tour of inspection Kitchener's messages to Asquith had begun to betray contradiction and indecision. On the one hand he had placed his job on the line before leaving London by refusing to order total evacuation, yet a telegram to Asquith of 15 November spoke of the difficulties involved in staying on:

> The country is much more difficult than I imagined and the Turkish positions are natural fortresses which, if not taken by surprise at first, could be held against very serious attack by larger forces than have been engaged.[15]

The uneven tenor of Kitchener's telegrams probably influenced Asquith, more than any other factor, to accept the majority view of the War Committee that the Gallipoli front should be closed down and the troops completely withdrawn. What now swayed the War Committee was Kitchener's continuing insistence that Egypt was in danger and could only be protected by cutting off the country to the north of Syria – the War Office view was that the garrisoning of Egypt's frontiers provided the best means of defence – so it was by his own petard that Kitchener was almost hoisted.

When Kitchener began to insist to the War Committee that the fall of Egypt could herald Britain's defeat and the end of the war, Asquith saw his chance. If that were so, he retorted, if matters were so serious there, would it not be preferable for Kitchener to remain in the Near East and to assume control of Egypt? Kitchener refused to be tempted:

> I think it is essential that I should return to England to give you full information of the situation out here, and to make the necessary arrangements to carry out the policy decided on. I personally can do no good in Egypt.[16]

But the lust for Kitchener's blood was coursing strongly in the War Committee. If he would not accept the Egyptian command, then he should remain in Gallipoli to oversee the evacuation. As this would involve problems of military precedence with Kitchener, a field marshal, taking the place of Monro, a lieutenant-general, the suggestion was shelved, only to be replaced by a counter-proposal that Kitchener return to his old job in Cairo where his presence would still civilian fears of a Turkish invasion. By then (23 November) Kitchener was well aware of his colleagues' machinations and he replied firmly that under the circumstances he was returning home immediately. To Asquith's query about the safety of Egypt he reported that he had briefed Sir Henry McMahon, the High Commissioner, on the prevailing political situation in Cairo and was confident that he could deal with any difficulties that might arise.

A week later, Kitchener had returned to London. On his way home he stopped in Rome where he was presented to King Victor Emmanuel and decorated with the Order of the Grand Cordon of St Maurice and St Lazarus. While in Rome he admitted to Sir Rennell Rodd, the British ambassador, that he was thoroughly disgusted by the confusions sown by his fellow members of the War Committee and that their duplicity made it impossible for him to continue working with them. Shortly after arriving home he went to 10 Downing Street to carry out the threat of resignation he had made to Rodd in Rome. Not for the first time, though, Kitchener was deflected from such a drastic course of action by an appeal to national unity.

Kitchener had now been placed in the unsatisfactory position of seeing his duties at War Minister reduced to recruiting and administration and of knowing that his colleagues, having plotted against him once, would no doubt continue to do so. Storm clouds remained around his head and they broke again a week later over the Cabinet's Salonika policy and over the difficulties he was facing in reaching agreement on a working relationship with Robertson, his new CIGS. This time Asquith thought that the time had come to sideline Kitchener by appointing him a roving Commander-in-Chief, telling Hankey that, while he wanted to 'use his [Kitchener's] great name and authority as a popular idol', he wanted him to be removed from the corridors of power.[17] Rumours of Kitchener's resignation reached Petrograd, where an anxious Hanbury-Williams owned to being 'much disturbed by rumours that you are about to hand over the seals of office to someone else'.[18] Such a gesture, he continued, would be bound to damage the fragile British-Russian alliance and he urged Kitchener to think again. More significantly, the threat reached the ears of King George V through Robertson, who said that Kitchener's removal would be a national disaster, a point of view with which the King agreed. In the face of such powerful promptings Kitchener agreed to remain in office, although the final decision was made more palatable by Robertson's readiness to compromise with his new colleague.

That his threats of resignation were not motivated by caprice can be judged by examining the prevailing conditions in the upper reaches of government during the last months of 1915. Far from having decided finally to evacuate Gallipoli, a minority within the Cabinet led by Curzon still clung on to the possibility of keeping the British troops on the peninsula in the interests of British standing in the Muslim world. This group found solace in the vacillating attitudes of the naval and military leaders and in the fear that evacuation would involve unacceptably high casualties. But their best hope of support came in a paper from Hankey that, having reviewed the military position, recommended the retention of British forces.[19] The main thrust of Hankey's argument was that any evacuation would not only damage Britain's standing but also her treaty obligations with Russia. He also suggested that withdrawal was out of the question because 'we are already long past the time when the continuance of fine weather can be counted on', a telling argument as the onset of wintry weather was already adding to the miseries of the troops on the peninsula. In his opinion the situation could be retrieved if four divisions were withdrawn from Salonika on the understanding that the front would be closed down.

Hankey's paper was not without its merits and Kitchener grasped eagerly at this straw, hardly surprisingly given his stated view. Knowing that the Mesopotamian campaign had foundered with a British and Indian force besieged in Kut, Kitchener favoured a policy of resolution against the Turks. Like Hankey, he was concerned too that no evacuation should be attempted at that late date in the year. The following two days were spent in Calais attempting to persuade France that the time had come to withdraw from the Balkans. Although Asquith showed surprising firmness in arguing the British case, he was eventually thwarted by the well-worn argument that British hesitancy in the Balkans would damage the entente. British resolve, weakened by this argument, crumbled when Tsar Nicholas II sent a personal plea to King George V asking for the retention of the British forces in Salonika. Even if the Calais conference had succeeded, the Dardanelles campaign was already doomed. Monro had telegraphed Kitchener in his absence that any new initiative would fail and that even if four divisions were sent from Salonika all element of surprise would have been lost. On 7 December the Cabinet approved the evacuation of the Anzac and Suvla beachheads and two weeks later, on Robertson's recommendation, Cape Helles was also ordered to be shut down. After the disasters of 1915 the only good news was that the evacuations were completed quickly and efficiently and without the heavy loss of life that Hamilton had feared.

The failure of the Allied campaign at Gallipoli has provided history with one of its great unanswered conundrums. If only the tactics, the leadership, the reinforcements and the munitions had been better, runs the argument, then a sordid defeat could have been a glittering triumph. In theory, the original reasons for the campaign had much to recommend them, but at the end of the day a complete absence of Allied strategic aims and the half-hearted conduct of the campaign must account for its failure and for the waste of so many lives and so much equipment. As for Salonika, the British troops, as promised to the French, stayed on in the Balkans until the end of the war, accomplishing little and causing the Central Powers no trouble. Ludendorff called Salonika the 'greatest internment camp of the war' and it seems a fair assessment.

EROSION OF POWER

As the Gallipoli campaign was entering its death throes Kitchener's attention was being diverted by the French concern for the Balkans and by events on the home front, where unexpected hitches had arisen in his relationship with his new CIGS. Not that Kitchener disliked Sir William Robertson, a bluff, level-headed general who had risen from the ranks. Rather, it was the constitutional nature of their relationship that troubled him. At their first meeting Kitchener had assured Robertson that 'he would be only too glad to rid himself of some of the work he had hitherto been compelled to do, if he could but find someone to relieve him of it.'[20] He went on to tell Robertson that he should pay no heed either to Cabinet gossip or to the prevailing hostility of men such as Lloyd George. Although Robertson was sympathetic to those pleas, before agreeing to anything he asked for permission to prepare a memorandum of agreement that would lay down the ground rules of their professional relationship. This, Robertson was perfectly entitled to do and, as he had been assured by Asquith that he was both to advise and to direct the Cabinet on strategy, he felt able to call the tune. The main points of his paper to Kitchener, dated 5 December, were encapsulated in the following demands: that a War Council should direct policy through information provided by CIGS; that the CIGS should sign all operational orders and that he should be the fulcrum for communication with the battlefronts; that the Secretary for War should deal only with administration and recruiting – his peacetime function – and that his voice should not be in the ascendancy at the War Office.[21] To Kitchener these latter points presented a wounding neutralisation of his authority and he offered his resignation to Asquith immediately with the hint that some other politician might be found to accept Robertson's recommendations.

At that juncture the situation was retrieved by Robertson's good sense and by the intervention of the King and of the feline Esher. While he was in France discussing the Balkans position on 9 December Kitchener was persuaded by Esher to meet Robertson in Paris, where the two men, much to their surprise, managed to reach a sensible agreement. As Robertson's suggestion that he should sign orders breached the constitutional responsibility of the Secretary of State for War for the conduct of the war, the new CIGS readily fell in with Kitchener's proposal that orders should be signed 'under the authority of the Secretary for War'. It was further agreed to remove the reference to the neutralisation of Kitchener's voice at the War Office, and the so-called 'Kitchener–Robertson Compact' came into effect by Order in Council on 27 January 1916. Much to the surprise of Asquith, who had entertained thoughts of a rift between the two men, Kitchener and Robertson got on well together. Shortly before Christmas, Kitchener wrote to Haig emphasising the importance he placed on Robertson's appointment for the future conduct of the war:

> I am looking forward to getting Robertson who will I am sure greatly help me here. I have the utmost confidence in his loyal support on sometimes difficult occasions owing to political interference and I am sure we will get on well together.[22]

Robertson, for his part, found Kitchener an equally agreeable colleague, 'a fine character, lovable and straight', and it was left to Asquith to rue the formation of the new partnership.[23] Having hoped to muzzle Kitchener while keeping him in the public eye he found Robertson to be an equally thorny proposition. As the sole source of military advice to the Cabinet, Robertson, a committed 'westerner', was only prepared to think in terms of France and Flanders and his first action was to order the evacuation of Cape Helles on 23 December. Thereafter, Robertson's main concern was to prop up and reinforce the Western Front in preparation for the summer offensive on the Somme.

As Kitchener prepared to spend Christmas with his staff at York House he found time to count the gains and losses of the old year. Munitions, once such a burden to the War Office, was now a separate ministry and beginning to bear the fruits of the year's labours, and strategy, with which he had wrestled single-handedly from the beginning of the war, had rightly become a matter for the General Staff under Robertson. The Russian front appeared to be stable, as did the Western Front, in spite of the hideous loss of life that had been borne mainly by the Russians and the French. Gallipoli had been a failure, thus preventing the Ottoman Empire from being a decisive theatre of war but providing the politicians with the opportunity of dividing up the spoils with a series of secret treaties and understandings that would be brought into play once the war was over – Russia to receive Constantinople, France Syria, Britain to keep Egypt and to establish an independent state for the Arabs.

Kitchener played a significant role in reaching those secret – and later, much reviled – compacts, but by the end of 1915 he was coming to the view that the war should not be about conquest as far as Germany was concerned. To Haig he confided that only a decisive victory over the Germans followed by a fair peace treaty would prevent further war in Europe.[24] Any compromise with the Germans or the meting out of harsh conditions would only lead to a fresh outbreak of hostilities within five years when Britain might be unprepared and without allies. In that case all the hardships endured by all countries would be for naught. During the first months of 1916, therefore, he gave some thought to the problem and in so doing has left history with the tantalising notion that, had he lived to command a seat at the table dictating terms to the Germans, his voice would have been raised against the more punitive clauses of the Treaty of Versailles. Shortly before his death he told Derby that if the Allies presented Alsace and Lorraine to France, Germany would not rest until she had reclaimed them through a 'war of revenge'. By the same token, the confiscation of Germany's colonies would leave Germany with a similar desire 'to engage in war for new territory'.[25]

But by what means a decisive victory was to be gained was as much beyond the ken of Kitchener as it was beyond his colleagues. He had no theories how to break the stalemate of trench warfare and his frequently uttered remark 'this isn't war' sums up the sense of hopelessness and futility that had gripped the British high command by the end of 1915. Besides, the war had aged him. Sixteen months of controlling every aspect of Britain's war effort – recruiting, supply and strategy – had left its mark on him, mentally and physically. When Rennel Rodd, a friend of twenty years' standing, met him in Rome that November he had been shocked to find Kitchener in a state of exhaustion, and 'rather perplexed and conscious of his isolation'.[26]

At home in London, George Arthur and FitzGerald conspired to lift some of the burden of responsibility from his shoulders by persuading Kitchener to spend his spare time at Broome Park, where he found solace working in the garden. The estate was also used as a recuperation camp for wounded soldiers, in whose welfare Kitchener took a good deal of interest, providing them with comforts and taking time off in their company to talk to them about their experiences. Like French, now superseded and commanding the Home Forces, Kitchener had never accustomed himself to the British losses of 1915, which, although small in comparison to French or Russian casualties, had brought home to the public the harsher side of war. Hardly a family in Britain did not have a male relation in uniform and many volunteers had already added their names to the casualty lists that appeared each day with monotonous regularity in the British press.

Kitchener, too, had suffered losses, among them Julian Grenfell, the gifted son of the Desboroughs, and his brother Billy. 'My dear Lord K, my dear friend,' wrote Lady Desborough in reply to Kitchener's anguished letter of regret, 'you were always so good to Julian and Billy. I seem often to see them walking on each side of you at Wrest when they were very young ... I am writing to you to say that you must not grieve for us.'[27]

Death had also claimed other friends. Lord Roberts had died within earshot of the guns in France, visiting the Indian Army contingents in November 1914, while closer to Kitchener's heart there had been other and sadder losses. Of his staff in India, most were dead by the end of 1915. Major Victor Brooke had been killed in action in September 1914, one of the first British officers to fall in France. Major-General Hubert Hamilton was killed leading the 3rd Division on 14 October that same year, and Colonel R.J. Marker, who had lost his heart to Lady Curzon's sister, died of wounds in November.

Earlier in his career Kitchener had made stoicism in the face of public grief a virtue and those who knew only the myth of the stern taskmaster bereft of emotion were frequently surprised by his displays of emotion in private. The deaths of all his friends shattered him and made it more difficult for him to come to terms with the effect that war was having on British society. Whereas in South Africa he had refused to be moved by the losses at Paardeberg, by 1915 he could neither make light of the continuing British casualties nor could he come to terms with them. It was almost as if he were carrying alone upon his shoulders the entire responsibility for the Allied war effort. During the winter of 1914–15, after a long day spent discussing Joffre's requirements with the Marquis de Chasseloup Laubat, Kitchener came to a point where he had to tell him that the British response would fall short of what was expected. Turning to the French diplomat 'in a deep and half-strangled voice as if he were suffering agonies of pain', Kitchener admitted the sorry truth that he had done all that he could to help. 'Tell Joffre …' he said, 'tell my friend Joffre that I am sorry … so very sorry that I cannot do more.' The conference at an end, those present were embarrassed to find Kitchener in tears; then catching their looks, 'as if he was ashamed of himself and what he seems to consider a weakness, he quickly puts back his spectacles'.[28] It was not an isolated incident. To Lady Desborough he had also written that he wished he could find a way of doing more for the war effort, and it was at this same time that he made his anguished appeal to Lord Derby asking him to say what more he (Kitchener) could do to help the country. 'I am doing all that I can,' he said, 'yet I still feel that I am leaving much undone.'[29]

Despite all the problems of 1915, Kitchener never lost the support of the majority of the British people and in their eyes he remained the supreme war leader, the epitome of the nation's, and the Empire's, sense of purpose. 'The Constable of Britain', Churchill called him and in that guise he accomplished for Britain what Hindenburg did for Germany. 'Rightly or wrongly, probably wrongly,' he confided to Haig at the beginning of 1916, 'the people believe in me. It is not therefore me that the politicians are afraid of, but what the people would say to them if I were to go.'[30] Happily, his relationship with the new Commander-in-Chief continued in the same intimate vein. Whereas French had preferred to adopt a state of continuing hostility, employing discord instead of discretion, Haig never allowed himself to become confused by the apparent clash between Kitchener's senior military rank and his political employment. Whenever Kitchener visited the front, Haig always provided him with a guard of honour and full military courtesies, treating him both as an honoured guest and as a military and political superior.

By that time, though, the responsibility for overall strategy had passed to the General Staff acting in tandem with the commander in the field. This new state of affairs might have given Haig less freedom of action than had been accorded to Sir John French but it did provide a cushion between him and the War Office. Moreover, Haig was in complete agreement with Robertson that the principal aim of the Allies for the remainder of the war should be 'the application of maximum strength in the West, subject only to such reductions as might be rendered necessary by defensive considerations in the East'.[31] To that end Haig and Robertson began planning the best means not only of attacking the German lines in France and Flanders but of drawing German reserves into battle and then wearing them down.

The bullish offensive policies planned for the spring and summer of 1916 had their origin in a meeting of the Allied staffs held at Chantilly on 6 December 1915. At Joffre's insistence it had been agreed that an attack on the German lines in the west would be matched by a Russian offensive and followed by an Italian attack on the Austro-Hungarians (Italy had entered the war on the Allied side in the spring). Little attempt had been made to co-ordinate this Allied strategical decision but Joffre's confidence in its success had been boosted by the steady growth of British forces in France. As a result of Kitchener's work earlier in the war Haig had at his disposal in January 1916 thirty-eight divisions, with a further nineteen divisions promised for the summer. Added to the Belgian and French armies, this gave the Allies a superiority of 139 divisions to the German's 117. The difficulty had arisen in the generals' interpretation of how to use them to best advantage. Joffre wanted to continue a war of attrition – harrying attacks on the German lines designed to wear them down – whereas Haig favoured a policy of all-out offence preceded by a number of diversionary attacks to confuse the enemy. Robertson and Kitchener supported Haig's theory but they failed to convince the War Committee, who formulated a wary policy of non-committal on 13 January: undeterred, Haig continued to discuss with Joffre a summer offensive at a point where the Allied lines joined on the River Somme.

The War Committee's oscillation was largely of its own making. Having appointed Robertson to direct strategy they now found themselves tied to an offensive policy on the Western Front, although many members still harboured dreams of a grand, liberating campaign in the Balkans. All that had been achieved by the neutralisation of Kitchener was a swing towards the west and the subjugation of the War Committee to Robertson's opinions.

While the attrition-offensive debate continued it was made redundant by the Germans when they attacked the French fortress of Verdun on 21 February. This relatively unimportant French position was regarded by most French tacticians as being surplus to their defensive requirements, and caution suggested a French withdrawal to straighten their lines between St Mihiel and Rheims. But tactical sense knew nothing of French pride. Verdun became a symbol of French resistance and Pétain – who had been ordered to defend it to the last man – made his name with his famous phrase, 'They shall not pass.' By the time that the fighting died down at the end of June the French had sustained 315,000 casualties, the army had come close to mutiny and neither the Germans nor the French had gained any tactical advantage.

The fighting, though, did force Britain's hand. At the height of the crisis Haig answered Joffre's appeal for help by extending the British line and – against Kitchener's better judgement – by bringing forward the planned British offensive to 1 July. This merely confirmed Kitchener's belief that British war aims were tied too closely to French strategy to allow much freedom of action. Ideally he would have preferred to have waited until later in the year, or even until 1917 when the British Army would have numerical superiority over the French and when its command would hold the whip hand of tactical control. After a meeting with Joffre on 29 March, Kitchener advised Haig to 'husband the strength' of the British Army in France and to be cautious of French attempts to use British troops to fill their own positions in the line. Kitchener's suspicions had been reinforced by other items on the agenda, such as the French proposal for a fresh offensive in the Balkans. By this time Kitchener and Robertson both believed that not only was that battlefront a dead letter but that the time had also come to withdraw one British division from Salonika for re-deployment in France. As the Serbian Army had now regrouped, this suggestion made sense but the French refusal to accept the British proposal only made Kitchener believe more strongly than ever that the French were only interested in territorial gains in the Balkans and the Near East.

Once back in London, Robertson presented his proposals to the War Committee in a paper entitled 'Future Military Operations', which called for acceptance of the French status quo in Salonika and a summer offensive in France. Although Kitchener was concerned lest a British offensive should over-stretch the country's resources, he supported Robertson's plans, which were accepted by the Cabinet on 7 April. This was destined to be Kitchener's last hand in the direction of the war.

Although shorn of most of his responsibilities, Kitchener did not allow himself any hours of idleness at the War Office. He remained a member of the War Committee and his duties as Secretary for War drew him into the new technological advances being made in the weapons of war. Ernest Swinton, the officer of Engineers whom he had appointed to provide 'eye witness' accounts for the British press, had since moved on to become an enthusiastic supporter of the new 'landships', or tanks, which had begun development at the beginning of 1915. His notion that these ungainly craft would be able to smash holes in the German defences to be exploited by the infantry had met with initial scepticism at the War Office, but after seeing trials of the improved 'Big Willie' tank at Hatfield in February 1916 Kitchener was an enthusiastic convert to the cause of tank warfare. Under his orders forty tanks were ordered to be constructed and the first crews were trained as members of the Heavy Section, Machine Gun Corps.

Kitchener also took a keen interest in the development of aircraft for reconnaissance and bombing roles and in concert with Balfour he spent a good deal of time in March 1916 promoting the development of a suitable 'airship-destroyer', a seaplane strong enough to carry the 3in guns necessary to destroy the German Zeppelins then beginning to cause civilian alarm with their night-time bomb attacks on the south-eastern counties of England.

EROSION OF POWER

Events in Russia also continued to interest Kitchener. At his instigation a Russian staff officer, General Gilinski, attended British-French staff conferences and he also arranged for Russian officers to be attached to British regiments in France to gain some experience of the fighting there. In return, Major-General C.E. Callwell, former Director of Operations at the War Office, went to Russia in March to observe the military situation in Armenia and Persia. Much of Kitchener's concern was born of his desire to assist Russia and to keep himself up to date with events on the Eastern Front, but with the French appearing intransigent over Salonika, Kitchener was also anxious to bring the Russian staff round to the idea that the Western Front had to be the decisive theatre of operations. On 28 February Hanbury-Williams reported the partial success of Kitchener's initiatives, tempered by the Russians' continuing insistence that the Balkans could still offer the key to the back door to Germany:

> Have communicated parts of your two letters to the Emperor and the Chief of the General Staff. I think the latter now recognises that France is the main theatre, but he is still of the opinion that some sort of offensive should be undertaken at the same time from Salonika. His point is that an offensive even if only towards Sofia would prevent the Bulgarians from threatening Roumania, would enable the Serbian army to be utilised, and would produce a good effect on Greece, which, according to his latest information, is beginning to change her policy and might even join us. If she did so, the Anglo-French forces now at Salonika, joined by Serbians and Greeks, should amount to at least 450,000 men which he considers would be strong enough for decisive measures against Bulgaria without materially affecting operations in France.[32]

With the supply of rifles hampered by a hard winter at Archangel, Russia was still short of weapons for her summer offensive. The need to step up those supplies, and to discuss a future strategy that would underline British war aims, meant that sooner or later Britain, through her Secretary of War, would have to discuss these issues face to face with her Russian ally.

14

AN UNPITIED SACRIFICE

The idea that Britain should send a high level mission to Russia had been in many politicians' minds since the beginning of the war. Although her interests were well served by Buchanan and by Hanbury-Williams, Britain had never enjoyed the opportunity of discussing strategy, munitions and common war aims with Russian leaders, a failing that Kitchener had suggested should be remedied as early as 1914. Several senior Russian officers had come to Britain since then, mainly to discuss munitions, and there was a permanent military mission headed by Major-General E.K. Hermonius, an experienced military engineer with long experience of weapons procurement. However, there were no staff talks to compare with those held at regular intervals with the French, with the result that by the end of 1915 the feeling was growing in Russia that Britain's sole role was to supply the Russians with military supplies and money to finish off the war. 'They want us to put a big bag of money on their doorstep,' Knox reported, and 'then run away.'[1] Connected to that belief was the slightly contemptuous suggestion that Britain, not being a first-class military power, was unable to make a decisive military contribution to the Allied war effort.

In January the Cabinet had taken its first steps to present Britain's efforts in a more acceptable light by establishing a propaganda bureau in Petrograd. Their choice to head the initiative fell on the gifted diplomat and man of letters, Maurice Baring, but he refused the post, preferring to continue his staff work with the Royal Flying Corps in

France. While the search went on for a possible replacement, Buchanan argued that the Russians wanted not words but guns for their coming summer offensive. Acting in the spirit of the Chantilly conference of the previous December, Russia was planning a major strike against the Germans in Poland coupled to an advance in the south-west against the Austro-Hungarians. From their huge resources of manpower the Russian armies had been replaced and reinforced to a strength of 130 divisions, but in spite of improvements the troops were still woefully short of heavy field guns and rifles.

To help ease the situation, the War Office had persuaded the Italians to supply Russia with rifles in the previous autumn and the Russian Supply Committee, now headed by Booth, had managed to step up the supply of munitions through Murmansk. The problem had now arisen: how was Russia to pay? Knox had not been far wrong in his assessment of Russian sentiments. Many senior Russian Army officers and politicians did regard Britain as a bottomless pit of finance and by the spring of 1916 the British Exchequer was worried that the Russian balance of payments had become lopsided with an accumulation of credits to be debited once the war was over. When Buchanan and others began to voice their concern that popular unrest in Russia could lead to war weariness and the overthrow of the government, the Cabinet began to pay more attention to the Russian situation. If the summer offensive failed and political agitation continued, the Russians might even be forced to sue for a separate peace. To avoid that possibility it was agreed at the end of April to despatch a political mission to Russia both to discuss the supply of munitions and their payment and to stiffen Russian resolve.

Initially, Asquith toyed with the idea of sending a team consisting of Lloyd George, to discuss munitions, and McKenna, to disentangle the financial problem, but at the Cabinet meeting on 28 April Kitchener suddenly announced that he would like to head the mission. Within a fortnight of his suggestion Hanbury-Williams was able to report that it was a common knowledge in Petrograd that Kitchener would be visiting Russia. On 12 May he passed on this intelligence to the War Office:

> There are rumours of a visit here which I know would give much pleasure to H.M. who spoke to me about it last night. I hope it will materialise as I feel sure that there are many reasons which make such a visit useful, if it were feasible.[2]

By the time Hanbury-Williams's message was received in London the Russian ambassador in London, Count Benckendorff, had issued Tsar Nicholas II's official invitation to Kitchener on 13 May. Two days later Kitchener replied that 'nothing would give [me] greater pleasure than to visit Russia, but at present the arrangements for my so doing are not finally settled and I shall have to see the King and Prime Minister on the subject before I can let you know at what date I shall be able to avail myself of His Majesty's kind invitation'.[3]

With security in wartime London notoriously lax and with Petrograd known to be a hotbed of gossip and intrigue, the possibility that Kitchener might visit Russia was widely known in both capitals by the middle of May. Even had the politicians chosen to keep silent on the matter there were other channels of communication equally leaky and open to interception. From the time of his arrival in Petrograd in October 1914 Hanbury-Williams had complained about Russia's 'great contempt for ordinary military cyphers', a state of affairs that had seen him resorting to the use of King's Messengers for the passage of all but the most vital messages to Kitchener.[4]

Such had been his haste in leaving London that the War Office had failed to provide him with a personal cypher so that most wires and letters went through normal diplomatic channels. Knox had also complained on this score, reminding Kitchener and other colleagues on several occasions that their messages were liable to be intercepted. 'Remember no cable from you to me is confidential,' he was warned by Ellershaw, the munitions expert, on 26 May, 'no matter how much you may mark it so.'[5] Knox's and Hanbury-Williams's concern was not so much about the messages falling into Russian hands but about the damage done when their contents became public or semi-public knowledge. The German intelligence service in Petrograd was well developed and efficient and could rely on the support of large numbers of influential Russians who still thought that their country would be best served by an alliance between the Romanov and Hohenzollern imperial families. Later, both Knox and Hanbury-Williams admitted that Kitchener's impending visit was common knowledge in Petrograd by the third week of May.

On 16 May Kitchener confessed to Hanbury-Williams that although his invitation had been received, no firm arrangements had been made, largely because the Cabinet's attention had been diverted by the events of the Easter Rising in Dublin (an Irish republican citizens' army had held units of the British Army at bay for almost a week between 24 and 29 April before being forced to surrender). In its wake Britain had executed fifteen rebel leaders, thus creating a terrible feeling of bitterness in Ireland that Asquith hoped might be placated by sending Lloyd George to Dublin to deal with Irish affairs. The appointment also prevented Lloyd George from having any further role to play in the Russian mission and by 26 May it had been finally agreed that only Kitchener should go, with McKenna remaining in London. That Asquith and his colleagues on the War Committee should have decided that Kitchener should be Britain's sole political representative was hardly surprising. Kitchener had an unparalleled reputation amongst Russian leaders, his name was still all-powerful and his personality had been unsullied by the setbacks of the previous year. It was therefore widely assumed in both capitals that, under the shadow of his influence, British and Russian officials would be able to iron out the financial difficulties and strategical misunderstandings that were in danger of threatening the alliance:

On 26 May Kitchener told the Russian ambassador that the War Committee had authorised him to accept the Tsar's invitation and that he hoped to formalise his travel arrangements within a week. The next day the following message was sent to Hanbury-Williams confirming that the visit was now going ahead:

> Lord Kitchener intends to accept the gracious invitation of the Emperor. Please arrange for Neilson to meet Lord Kitchener at Archangel and to be attached to his staff during the visit. The party will consist of Earl Kitchener, Sir Frederick Donaldson, Brig-General Ellershaw, Lieut-Col. FitzGerald, Mr O'Beirne, F.O., Mr Robertson, Assistant to Sir F. Donaldson, 2/Lieut McPherson, one clerk, one detective-inspector and three servants. Should arrive Archangel 9th of June.[6]

It was a good mix. O'Beirne had served at the British embassy in Petrograd and had an unrivalled knowledge of Russian affairs, Ellershaw had been Britain's emissary in the Russian arms' negotiations since May 1915, and Donaldson was technical adviser to the Ministry of Munitions. At Kitchener's instigation, McPherson, an officer in his favourite regiment, the Cameron Highlanders, was ordered to accompany the party as interpreter. Arrangements for the trip were left in the hands of the Admiralty, who sent a signal on 26 May to Admiral Jellicoe at Scapa Flow, the base of the Home Fleet in the Orkney Islands. The date 5 June was suggested and Jellicoe was ordered to detach a cruiser from one of his squadrons to take the mission to Archangel with all proper regard to speed and safety. Jellicoe responded the following day proposing the use of the armoured cruiser HMS *Hampshire*, provided that sufficient coal supplies could be made available to her for the return journey. The Admiralty replied a few hours later agreeing to the *Hampshire* and ordering Jellicoe to despatch a collier to the anchorage at Yukanskie.

Although 5 June had been fixed upon as the best date for the departure of the mission with an arrival in Petrograd planned six days later, an unexpected hitch over the weekend of 3–4 June almost put the trip in jeopardy. Acting on information from Hanbury-Williams that he might not be able to accomplish much in so short a time – the return journey was expected to commence on 21 June – Kitchener suggested that he should call off the arrangements altogether. Having almost been superseded during his previous absence Kitchener was determined to spend a very short time away from London; it was only Hanbury-Williams's reply that the Tsar considered the trip to be of the utmost importance that calmed Kitchener's uneasiness. Not that he was against making the journey. Quite apart from the interest he had taken in Russia's war aims from the beginning of the war, he had always wanted to visit Russia and was looking forward to the interlude. Callwell, who had recently returned from Russia, met him at the War Office on 27 May to advise him about what kit to take with him and noted that 'the Field Marshal was in rare spirits, looking forward eagerly to his time in Russia, merry as a schoolboy starting for his holidays, only anxious to be off'.[7] Asquith, too, was pleased to see Kitchener in such a light frame of mind and noticed that he refused to be downcast by the King's refusal to allow him to take decorations to Russia to present to high-ranking officers.

Only one cloud blotted his horizon. On 21 May Sir Ivor Herbert, Liberal MP for South Monmouthshire and a supporter of conscription, rose in the House of Commons to move that the Secretary for War's salary be reduced by a token £100. This formality was a traditional means for Parliament to show lack of confidence in a minister and it brought to a head months of back-bench frustration with Kitchener's methods of running the war, but as Kitchener could not attend meetings of the House of Commons he had to be defended. With an eloquence that had the House ringing with cheers, Asquith spoke up for his colleague, grandiloquently emphasising the debt that the country and the Empire owed its greatest soldier. Since the beginning of 1916 Asquith's faith in Kitchener had been eroded badly and there had been times when he would have been glad to see Kitchener go, but on this occasion he shielded his colleague skilfully and reproved those who had attacked him. Herbert's motion was defeated easily but Kitchener, who had been forewarned of the attack, had already made a contingency plan to cover his line of retreat. To the surprise of the crowded House, H.J. Tennant, his Under-Secretary for War, announced that Kitchener would meet members for an informal briefing session on 2 June when he would discuss with them the direction of the war. So many Members of Parliament asked to attend the meeting that it was decided to move the venue from the War Office to a committee room at Westminster. Ironically, perhaps, this turned out to be Room 15, the room in which the Irish Party had met in December 1890 to depose Charles Parnell from their leadership.

Thoughts of going down the same path did not cross Kitchener's mind when he arrived at Westminster shortly before 11.30 a.m. on Friday 2 June. Wearing the undress uniform of the Royal Engineers, Kitchener strode into the committee room and addressed the packed assembly from a carefully prepared speech. 'I feel sure that Members must realise that my previous work in life has not been of a kind to make me into a ready debater,' he told them, 'nor to prepare me for the various twists and turns of argument.'[8] But what followed next was a revelation to all who had gathered to hear him. Speaking with a calm authority he rehearsed the problems that had faced him at the outbreak of war and continued to discuss the means by which most of them had been solved or nearly solved. Equipment, transport, ammunition, and conscription were but a few of the topics he covered in a wide-ranging deposition of the army's current status. His performance drew applause from the MPs present and, when questions were asked, he was again equal to the task, speaking with an assurance and geniality that charmed and surprised his inquisitors. Throughout the war Kitchener had refused to be drawn into public debate, partly because he lacked confidence in his oratory, partly because he was secretive by inclination and also because he thought that public utterances presented too much of a security risk. Only in France during staff talks had he been able to dominate proceedings and then only because he spoke fluent French.

Thoroughly satisfied by his success Kitchener spent the Saturday morning at the War Office before lunching with the King, who was moved enough by the story of the previous day's triumph to pass on the news to Haig in France:'Lord K's meeting with the House of Commons went off much better than was expected and might almost be called a success – it was thought that K with his weakness in argument would be badly heckled and get flustered. But he did not, and made a very good statement, carefully prepared beforehand.'[9] The King had always taken the keenest interest in Kitchener's affairs and considered that his handling of a potentially explosive political situation had been unexpected and quite masterly. Having briefed his sovereign on the importance of the Russian mission Kitchener motored down to Broome Park, where he spent the rest of the day putting final touches to a sunken rose garden he had embellished with an ornate fountain and a suite of four bronze statues depicting pairs of young boys in athletic poses. The following day, early in the morning, saw him back at the War Office to take care of a number of personal matters, including the sale of some shares in a Canadian munitions firm that had been awarded a government contract recently, and to put his signature to legal papers relating to his east African estate. By mid-afternoon he was ready to go, and his official car arrived to take him to King's Cross railway station where a through-carriage had been reserved on the overnight express to Edinburgh. From there he would continue on to Thurso and the short sea journey over the Pentland Firth to Scapa Flow.

Creedy and Arthur were already at the station to see the party off but there was a last-minute hitch when it was discovered that O'Beirne's cypher clerk had gone mistakenly to London Bridge station. Unwilling to be the cause of any disruption, Kitchener left orders for the offending clerk to be found and sent on north with O'Beirne by special train. At 4.40 p.m. the train drew out of the station carrying Kitchener and his party north on the first leg of his journey. Kitchener's last words to his friends on the platform were uttered from the carriage window – 'Look after things while I am away'. Arthur remembered afterwards that a sad look crossed Kitchener's face as he spoke and then, as if ashamed, he took his seat in the compartment and looked away out of the window until the train started.[10]

Once informed of the War Minister's departure, the Admiralty sent a signal to naval headquarters at Scapa informing them of the time of Kitchener's arrival in Thurso the following day and requesting that a torpedo boat destroyer, HMS *Oak*, wait in readiness to take the party from Scrabster (Thurso's harbour) across to Orkney. Earlier in the day it had been decided to overrule Kitchener's request to join the *Hampshire* at Scrabster, owing to the danger of submarine attack during the short sea crossing.

At the headquarters of the Grand Fleet that weekend, the atmosphere was dominated by a curious mixture of confusion and elation. Throughout Saturday the big ships of Jellicoe's battle fleet had been slipping back into the haven of Scapa after their indecisive encounter with the German High Seas Fleet off the coast of Jutland. Battle-weary and strained by two days of engagement with the enemy, during which they had lost three battlecruisers, three cruisers and eight destroyers, the survivors licked their wounds and began the lengthy task of recoaling and replenishing their supplies. Life at the shore station at Longhope was no less busy. All through the day a flurry of messages counting the cost of the battle had been flashed to the Admiralty, putting the signals' staff under considerable pressure, and by midday the harassed naval staff was snowed under with the paperwork involved in resupplying the fleet and counting the ships and their manifests as they came back in. Among those they noted as having sustained light damage was the *Hampshire*, which had reached home base just as the brief northern night was beginning to fall.

During the Battle of Jutland *Hampshire* had been part of Rear-Admiral Heath's 2nd Cruiser Squadron, acting as the connecting ship between it and the 4th Light Cruiser Squadron, and on 30 May had rammed and sunk one of the German U-boats despatched by Admiral Scheer to attack the naval bases at Rosyth, Invergordon and Scapa. It was a task to which her captain and crew had become thoroughly accustomed, having spent most of the previous year on anti-submarine patrols between the Moray Firth and the Minches, even surviving a submarine attack on 1 July 1915 when a torpedo fired by *U-25* failed to explode. At the outbreak of war *Hampshire* had been attached to the China Station and had taken part in the pursuit of the *Emden*, the notorious German surface raider that accounted for the loss of so many Allied merchantmen in 1914. Her final task that year had been to escort troopships taking Anzac troops to Egypt. On returning to Britain she had refitted at the Harland and Wolff yards in Belfast where her forward and aft 7.5in guns had been re-sited on the upper decks. On Wednesday 16 February 1916 *Hampshire* steamed out of Belfast Lough, passed south of Rathlin and Skerryvore, and rounded the Butt of Lewis to take up station at Scapa with Jellicoe's armoured cruiser squadrons. According to Stoker F.L. Sims, the last survivor of her crew – nineteen at the time of the disaster – life on board the cruiser was 'like one big happy family' and the captain, H.J. Savill, was considered to be a well-liked, capable and experienced officer.[11]

Although somewhat venerable – she had been laid down in 1902 at Elswick's on the Tyne and been first commissioned in August 1905 – *Hampshire* was far from being obsolescent. Her sister ship, HMS *Caernavon*, had played an important role in the Battle of the Falklands in December 1914 and the 'Devonshire' class, to which both ships belonged, was still considered to be capable of fulfilling a front-line role.

AN UNPITIED SACRIFICE

Of the ships available to Jellicoe at Scapa, *Hampshire* was therefore an ideal choice (she had previously transported Kitchener from Egypt to Malta in 1912). With a top speed of 22½ knots and lightly armoured with a modest 6,665 tons of Krupp plating she possessed a good turn of speed for a ship of her size; more to the point for Jellicoe's present requirements, her bunkering capacity allowed for 1,600 tons of coal, making her an ideal long-range vessel. With a displacement of 10,850 tons, an overall length of 450ft, beam of 68½ft and maximum draft of 25½ft, she was strong, powerful and well suited for the voyage to Archangel, which would take her around the North Cape of Norway.[12]

Although the decision to use the *Hampshire* had been taken on 27 May, Captain Savill was not given his sailing orders until the morning of Sunday 4 June and no one in the crew knew the precise purpose of their mission until they saw Kitchener come aboard the following day. Jellicoe's instructions ordered Savill to proceed out of Scapa eastabout along the east coast of South Ronaldshay and to steer with all due repair to Latitude 62° North of Stadlandet, where her destroyer screen would leave her. Thereafter she was to reduce speed and zigzag to avoid the possibility of submarine attack, the final part of the signal reinforcing the absolute necessity of maintaining a high level of vigilance in that area:

> Every precaution to be taken against enemy submarines. They have recently been reported to be off Stadlandet in latitude 62° N; no information has been received that they are operating further north.[13]

After recoaling, Savill moved *Hampshire* from her mooring to take up position near Jellicoe's flagship, the battleship HMS *Iron Duke*. For the rest of the day the crew continued the business of clearing the decks and making good the surface damage. Below deck the captain's cabin, used as a war station room at Jutland, was tidied up and made more acceptable for *Hampshire's* distinguished passenger.

The following morning, 5 June, Kitchener's train pulled into Thurso station, having completed the last part of its 700-mile journey over the single-line track from Inverness. Before joining the *Oak* at Scrabster his

THE KITCHENER ENIGMA

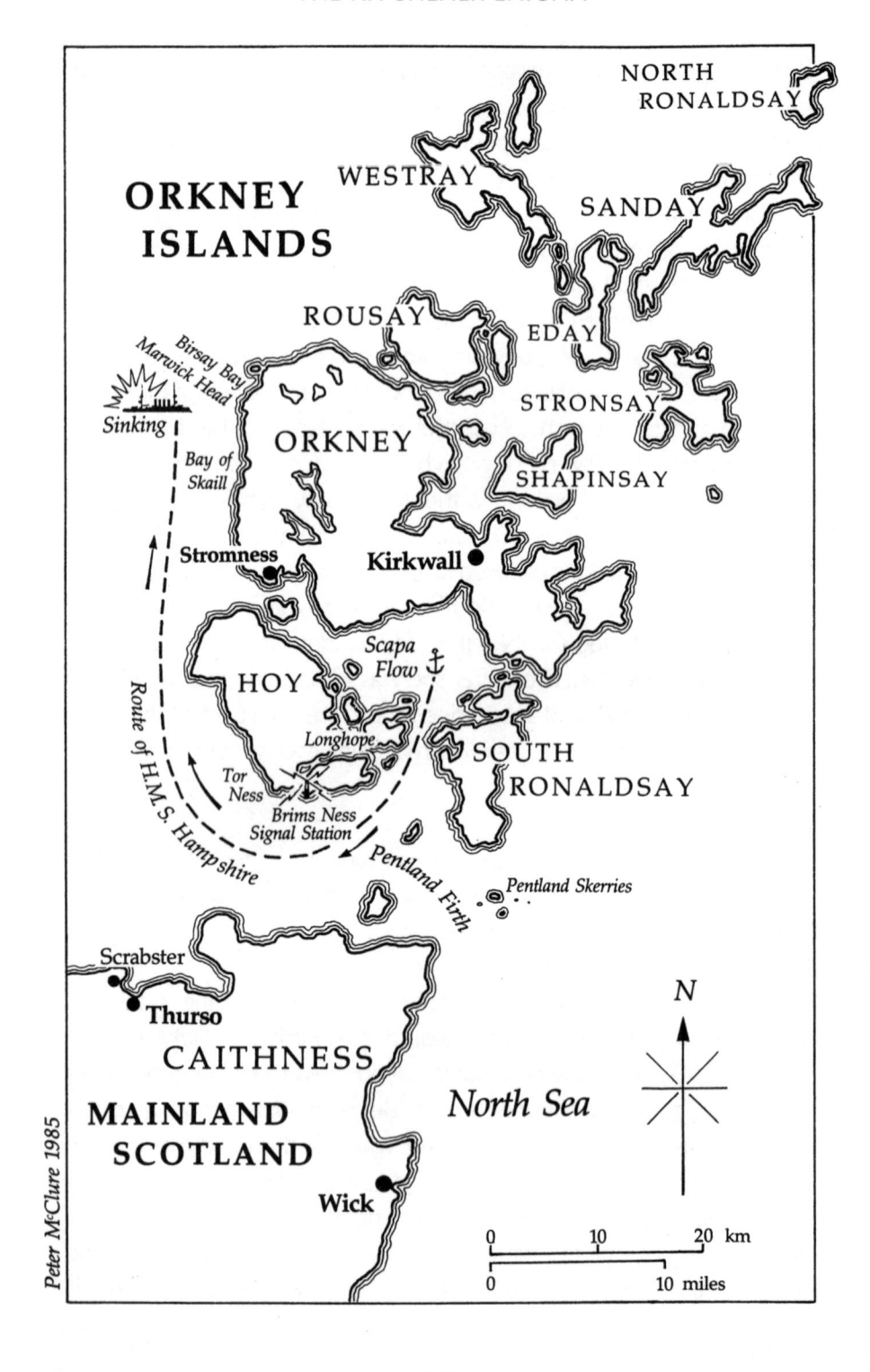

AN UNPITIED SACRIFICE

party stretched their legs and walked around the harbour, contemplating the short sea journey that lay ahead of them. To the north lay Orkney, around two hours away, but across the waters of the Pentland Firth, which had been whipped up by a strong gale from the north-east. Shortly before midday the *Oak* arrived at Scapa to tie up alongside the *Iron Duke*. It was still raining hard with a high wind blowing and it was with some difficulty that Kitchener and his party negotiated the narrow gangway between the two ships. Kitchener had requested this brief interlude in order to discuss with Jellicoe and his staff the events of the Battle of Jutland and its aftermath. Talk over lunch turned to whether or not it could be considered a British victory – while the German fleet had turned away, the British had lost more capital ships – and to the possible damage to British naval prestige on account of the strategic stalemate in the North Sea. Relaxing after his rough crossing, Kitchener was at his most affable, telling his hosts that he was looking forward to his brief break in Russia, almost as if his mission were a holiday.[14]

To the alarm of the flag officers present, though, he explained to Jellicoe that he expected the round trip to last three weeks and wanted to be back at Scapa on or around 21 June. The exigencies of such a timetable would entail a double return trip for the *Hampshire* and that Jellicoe was not prepared to risk. After lunch permission was requested from the Admiralty for the cruiser to stay at Archangel for the duration of Kitchener's visit. This was granted at 6.08 p.m. once the *Hampshire* was under way and it was relayed at 6.40 p.m. Savill replied almost an hour later, at 7.35 p.m. It was to be his last message.

The question of the *Hampshire*'s return was not the only problem with which the naval staff was wrestling that afternoon. All day long a gale had blown from the north-east and still showed no sign of abating. To those who knew the waters such conditions ruled out the eastabout route as being too rough for the cruiser and her destroyer screen. The alternatives were to sail westabouts as far as Cape Wrath before turning north into the main mercantile route to Murmansk and Archangel, or to sail westabouts through the Pentland Firth and then north along the west coast of Hoy, a route commonly taken by fleet auxiliaries and coast merchantmen. The first choice was turned down when it became known that Admiral Preston's fleet of minesweepers had been prevented by the rough seas from sweeping the western channel. This left the Hoy route as being the only acceptable passage: it was chosen both because it offered the ships a lee from the islands, thus allowing the destroyers to keep up with the *Hampshire*. More to the point, because no craft had ever been harmed in the area it was commonly assumed that no German minelayer had dared to operate so close to the enemy shore.

The decision to take that route was Jellicoe's first mistake; his second was to misinterpret the meteorological conditions prevailing in Orkney. From the Admiralty had come the forecast that the north-easterly winds would abate later in the day to be replaced by a more violent front from the north-west Atlantic:

> The decision proves that those present did not comprehend what type of air structure was prevailing at the time. For within an hour the storm centre passed and the wind backed sharply to the north-west. The conditions were exactly the reverse of those anticipated. Even fiercer than the north-east gale was the north-west blast that swept the swelling waters against a jagged coast. Analysis of the storm structure shows that a definite, well-known type of cyclone was passing from the Atlantic to the North Sea and was about to recurve, before heading north-east into Arctic regions. The forecaster would have warned against starting under such conditions; for haste could only mean danger and delay.[15]

That analysis, written seven years later, is a classic definition of the weather conditions prevailing in Orkney that afternoon, but it was also available to Jellicoe's Flag officers from the Admiralty's meteorological office. The forecast said that by late afternoon the wind would back to the north-west but at four o'clock it was still blowing hard from the north-east and showed no sign of abating. As Kitchener was clearly anxious to be on his way, the naval staff ignored the forecast: Savill was ordered to keep to the previously arranged westabout route when the weather conditions pointed to the wisdom of delaying departure for at least twenty-four hours.

AN UNPITIED SACRIFICE

Shortly after 4 p.m. Kitchener passed over to the *Hampshire* in the fleet drifter *Mayberry*. Through the rain he could just make out the distant shapes of his escort destroyers, *Unity* and *Victor*, passing out of their anchorages to make for the rendezvous off Tor Point. As Jellicoe and his staff watched the *Mayberry* work her way across the choppy waters they were not to know that they had committed a third and fatal mistake. They had failed to take into account the nature of the German submarine offensive prior to the Battle of Jutland and, more seriously, they had paid no attention to a vital message about submarine activity on *Hampshire*'s route that had arrived at Longhope that afternoon.

From the very beginning of the war the Admiralty had developed, in its famous Room 40, a highly sophisticated branch of its Naval Intelligence Department (NID). Its first coup had come in October 1914 after the German cruiser *Magdeburg* had been sunk by Russian naval vessels in the Gulf of Finland. While the German ship was under fire a signals' officer attempted to destroy the secret cypher book but was killed before he could do so. In a rare piece of co-operation the Russian Navy passed on the codebook and cyphers to the Admiralty; henceforth Captain W.R. Hall and his colleagues in Room 40 could decipher every German naval wireless transmission and plot every German ship movement. Other evidence came from the interrogation of German sailors, from Allied agents operating in occupied Belgium, neutral Spain and Norway, and from the investigation of sunken wrecks, but the Admiralty's trump card was to be able to intercept and decode German naval signals.

By the beginning of 1916, still unaware of the extent of British intelligence gathering, the German Navy had further perfected its wireless telegraphy techniques. Directional signals could be beamed from bases such as Sylt far out into the North Sea, giving German naval staff an accurate picture of the deployment of their ships and providing U-boat commanders with necessary information about Allied ship movements. With information thus gained from the Germans' own wireless intercepts and from their agents stationed in Britain, German naval staff had an accurate picture of ship movements from British ports. Typical of the kind of transmission made around the time of the Battle of Jutland was this serial message of 30 May, directed from Bruges to all U-boats on patrol in the northern approaches:

> Steamer TRUWOR, black, 3,600 tons, under Spanish flag with Spanish neutral markings on both sides, without name, without markings on funnel, is ready for sea at Blyth. Archangel given as destination. She is carrying contraband and probably proceeding on 31st May at high water.[16]

While transmissions of that kind provided the U-boat captains with useful information about their prey, they also gave the Admiralty precise bearings of the U-boats' own positions. Once the message from Bruges had been received, any U-boat in the immediate vicinity of the *Truwor*'s route would reply, giving details of her position and state of readiness for attack. Those vital messages were picked up by directional frequency stations on the British coast, forming a network that stretched from the Wash in the south to Shetland in the north. From these listening posts, and from coastal patrols, the men in Room 40 were able to build up a fairly precise picture of U-boat movements, the type of craft being used, its characteristics and, sometimes, even the name of the commander.

The evidence of the record book Submarine Reports: Home Waters shows just how accurate was that information in the fortnight before Jutland when Admiral Scheer had ordered a determined submarine assault on the Royal Navy's east coast anchorages.[17] The warnings were passed on to Operations Division for transmission to Scapa but like so many of the other intercepted messages gained by NID they were mistakenly filed away, or not acted upon. The main difficulty lay at the Admiralty, where the methods used by NID had not yet gained the confidence of the staff officers in Operations, who made their own interpretation of the intercepts passed to them. Consequently, many vital messages earmarked for transmission never got through or, if they did, were given a low priority.[18] Unfortunately, the same habit continued after the battle, and in the confusion at the Admiralty and Scapa high-priority messages about submarine movements and sightings were either forgotten or lost amidst the welter of paperwork at naval headquarters.

Before the great sea battle it had been Admiral Scheer's plan to use Admiral Hipper's battlecruisers as a decoy to lure the ships of the Grand Fleet out into the North Sea, where they would be set upon by the combined forces of his High Seas Fleet and his strategically placed submarine pack. To that end, 18 U-boats had been ordered to patrol the main British naval approaches at the end of May: two small minelayers, *U-43* and *U-44*, cruised north to Scapa, eight hunter-killers of recent build covered the Firth of Forth and a further two each watched the Humber and the Dutch coast off Terschelling. Finally, three ocean-going submarine minelayers of a new design were sent to mine the sea lanes off Orkney, the Moray Firth and the Firth of Forth. The first of this class to sail was *U-74*, which left Wilhelmshaven on 13 May under the command of Erwin Weisbach. Her sister boat, the *U-72*, sailed ten days later but was forced to return to base after failing to lay her mines off the Isle of May in the Firth of Forth. Lastly, the *U-75*, commanded by Kurt Beitzen, remained off Sylt until 24 May when she was ordered to proceed to Orkney to lay her mines off the west coast, to the north of Marwick Head, on the precise course that Jellicoe was to select for the *Hampshire*.

Five nights later Beitzen laid his mines in five groups of four across the seaway running 2 miles off the west coast of the Orkney mainland. Arranged in irregular lines running north-west to south-east, each mine was moored 30ft below high water, too deep to harm small ships such as minesweepers and fishing boats, but deadly to ships of larger draught. His work completed, Beitzen retired to the safer waters of the north-west triangle off Cape Wrath and did not return to his home base until 11 June.[19] The tragedy was that, although Beitzen's cruise, taking him between Orkney and Fair Isle, had been undetected by local naval patrols, its movements and those of its sister boats had been intercepted by Room 40. Not only that, but from the level of submarine activity in the North Sea, Operations had been forewarned of German intentions. Thus at the very time that Kitchener's journey was being planned, the Admiralty in London and Jellicoe at Scapa possessed sufficient information to warn them that the *Hampshire* would have to run the risk of submarine attack, by torpedo or mine, during her North Sea passage.

Apart from the wireless intercepts upon which Operations placed such little faith, the first tangible evidence had come on 27 May when Weisbach had been forced to surface his boat east of Peterhead. Three armed trawlers, *Searanger*, *Oku* and *Rodino*, happened to be in the vicinity and, seeing the U-boat on the surface with its sail flying, immediately opened fire. Weisbach attempted to dive before the trawlers found his range but in so doing he veered his craft into the path of another armed trawler, *Kimberley*, which opened fire at close range. Before the U-boat sank the trawler skippers had ample opportunity to log the details of the submarine's type and its armaments. Other evidence, equally telling, came three days later, on 30 May, when the destroyer *Trident* was attacked in the North Sea. That same afternoon the cruiser *Galatea* narrowly missed being torpedoed by the *U-32* off the Pentland Skerries and, ironically, *Hampshire* was herself involved in another submarine scare when she gave chase to probably the same U-boat on 1 June while returning to Scapa.

By that time the extent of Scheer's submarine offensive had been plotted accurately by British naval intelligence and information about each cruise and its purpose had been passed on to Operations.[20] Two intercepts, dated 31 May and 1 June, relate to *U-75* and showed her to be west of Orkney: knowing that she was of the new ocean-going minelaying class, the purpose of her mission must have been realised. From the evidence of another signal, warning of a U-boat off the Pentland Skerries logged at 4.15 p.m. on 3 June, it is certain that information about *U-75*'s movements had been transmitted to naval headquarters at Longhope. The news about the Pentland Skerries' sighting reached Jellicoe's hands, providing him with another reason to abandon the eastabout route for the *Hampshire*: had he and his staff paid equal attention to the signals regarding the *U-75* and to three vital messages logged on 5 June, they would have reached a similar conclusion about the use of the new route west of Orkney.

The first of these signals – all timed and dated from the Cape Wrath station – arrived at Longhope at 2.40 p.m., reporting a submarine northeast of Cape Wrath, travelling west. It was repeated at 5.15 p.m. with conclusive evidence of surface contact with the U-boat being sent two hours later:

AN UNPITIED SACRIFICE

> Following intercepted from Armed Yacht 024 to R.A. Stornoway. A Trawler 1798 reports information received from Grimsby trawler 8 a.m. Submarine sighted 2 a.m. 10' N.E. of Cape Wrath steering W.[21]

This was Beitzen's *U-75*. By the time that the second and third signals had been logged, *Hampshire* was already at sea but as she was still in wireless contact with Longhope there was still time to warn her of the danger. Having ignored the first signal earlier in the afternoon the naval staff allowed Savill to sail on into an area now known to be threatened by a U-boat of the minelaying class. The strain of overwork, the confusion sown in the aftermath of Jutland and the last-minute rush to prepare Kitchener's mission are all reasons why these vital messages were overlooked but they cannot mask the fact that Jellicoe and his staff had blundered. Not only did they misread the weather forecast but they ignored or misplaced vital messages warning of the presence of a U-boat in the vicinity of the passage chosen for the *Hampshire* and her hapless passengers.

At 4.45 p.m. *Hampshire* had slipped her mooring buoy and passed out of Scapa Flow through the Hoxa Gate, west into the stormy waters of the Pentland Firth. The first the crew knew of their important passenger was when the *Mayberry* came alongside. Stoker Sims, who was working on the steam pinnace, had a good view of him and his party as they negotiated the companionway up to the main deck. 'We didn't even know he was coming aboard until the last few minutes,' he recalled when interviewed in 1984. 'We didn't know what was happening until we saw him and his staff. It wasn't half a rough night.' Sims stayed on in the pinnace for the next two hours cleaning out her steam engine. At the time he thought it a thankless task – the pinnace had been sent out as a picket boat earlier that afternoon on a fruitless errand to pick up Kitchener and his party from *Iron Duke* – but it was one that was to save his own life.

In anticipation of the expected heavy seas everything on the *Hampshire*'s deck had been battened down with only the hatch to 14 Mess remaining open for Sims's use once his work on the pinnace had been finished. Making 19 knots against the conflicting tide races and huge seas of the Pentland Firth, *Hampshire* reached Tor Point, off the south-west tip of Hoy, on time at 5.45 p.m. to find *Unity* and *Victor* waiting in readiness. Built in 1913 as 'K' class destroyers, neither ship had the weight or the strength to cope with the prevailing weather conditions – they were only 257ft long and displaced a mere 928 tons – but they pushed themselves into line behind *Hampshire* as the little group turned north past the prominent landmark of the Old Man of Hoy, a spectacular 450ft high seastack by the island's precipitous cliffs.

It was when they entered the open seas to the west that Savill discovered he was now facing a completely different weather pattern. The wind had backed to the north-west and instead of the expected lee from the island he found that he was facing a head-on gale. Ordering the group to make 18 knots, Savill took his ship as far as possible into the shore to try to gain a measure of protection, but within an hour it had become obvious that the destroyer escorts could not keep up with the faster and more powerful cruiser. In spite of two reductions of speed down to 15 knots, *Victor*, then *Unity*, signalled to report that in such seas they could not hope to make more than 10 knots. As a further reduction in *Hampshire*'s speed would make her unmanageable while shipping a heavy sea, Savill ordered *Unity* to return to base at 6.20 p.m. and repeated the order to *Victor* ten minutes later, leaving his ship to plunge on alone through the force nine gale. Shortly before 7.30 p.m., just as the routine order 'stand by hammocks' was being piped, Sims finished his work on the pinnace and made his way to the 14 Mess hatch leading down to the ship's interior. He only had time to wash his hands in preparation for supper when the *Hampshire* was rocked by a violent explosion and began to yaw in the heavy seas.

'A terrific blast went through the ship shaking her from stem to stern,' remembered another survivor, Shipwright William Charles Phillips. 'Something out of the ordinary had happened, and the fumes which began to spread gave evidence that we had probably struck a mine.'[22] The worst had happened. Bucking her way through the storm, *Hampshire* had dropped on to one of Beitzen's mines moored 30ft below high water, tearing a huge hole between the bows and the bridge. It was nearly 7.45 p.m.; her position was roughly 1½ miles from the shore between the Brough of Birsay and Marwick Head, shaping a course of N.30°E.

The fumes and the caustic smoke from the mine's explosion caused a flash-fire in Sims's mess and many of his mates were burned horribly before they could reach the safety of the deck. Knowing that the magazine was next to their mess, below the bridge, there was a desperate rush to get up the companionway, away from the noxious fumes and the danger of imminent explosion. Sims was one of the lucky members of Mess 14. When *Hampshire* struck the mine he was standing by the ladder leading to the hatch and he lost no time in clambering up it to safety – 'the first thing you do is up that bleeding ladder!' On deck he found a scene he has never forgotten. The cruiser was settling quickly by the bows and frantic attempts were being made to launch the ship's boats before the angle became acute. But in such conditions escape was impossible: those boats that were lowered were smashed to matchwood on the *Hampshire*'s side by the waves below. Only the Carley rafts remained and these had been thrown overboard with scores of sailors jumping into the water after them. These large oval craft – simple rafts with an encircling band of thick cork – were to save young Sims's life:

> We dived up the ladder and over the side. Some of the seamen had already got them big Carley floats with the ropes round them. Of course we had dived over the side and I managed to get hold of one of them and they hauled us in. The seamen were saying, 'Come on, let's get clear or she'll draw us down with her.' And they paddled it and got away from her. I got one of the ropes around me and hung on to her.

Elsewhere, men were not so lucky. Many of the stokers had been badly injured by an exploding boiler in the engine room and, although there was no panic, it was taking them a long time to get up through the hatches on to the deck. The explosion had also knocked out the ship's electrical system, plunging their escape routes into darkness and making their progress all the more difficult. Equally, the loss of power now meant that Savill had been denied any possibility of making wireless contact with the shore.

Foremost in the captain's mind was the need to get Kitchener on deck so that he could try to get him away in the ship's galley. While standing on the half-deck by the hatch to the Gun Room Flat, Petty Officer Wilfred Wesson heard an officer call from the bridge, 'Make a gangway for Lord Kitchener.'[23] Seconds later, Kitchener and FitzGerald, dressed in greatcoats, passed up the forebridge, where it had become obvious to the naval officers that all hope had to be abandoned of getting a boat away from the sinking cruiser.

Kitchener was last seen alive by Leading Seaman Charles Rogerson, who observed him standing on deck with the faithful FitzGerald. 'He went down with the ship,' he recalled ten years later. 'Captain was calling to Lord K to go to a boat but Lord K apparently did not hear him or else took no notice. He had walked calmly from his cabin when the explosion occurred and waited equally calmly while preparations were made to abandon ship.'[24] In those circumstances there was little hope of escape. Kitchener hated cold weather and even had he got off the *Hampshire*, he would surely have perished very quickly in the bitterly cold waters. Faced by impending doom, the last view anyone had of Kitchener is of him standing impassively on the cruiser's deck as she began to settle in the heavy seas.

Fifteen minutes after she struck the mine, *Hampshire* went down by the bows, her stern rising high in the water before seeming to somersault forward as she plunged out of sight below the waves. All that remained on the storm-tossed sea was a litter of wreckage and three Carley rafts that were being drawn inexorably by the tide towards the rocky cliffs of Birsay and Sandwick. Those survivors in the rafts now faced a fate worse than the pounding seas: they knew that even if exposure did not claim them, they would have to take their chances on an inhospitable shore where the cliffs towered 300ft above the rocks and reefs below. In the following hour many men were to give up and die in the cold seas while others tried pathetically to paddle their huge raft towards the safety of the Bay of Skaill, the one inlet on the coast where safety beckoned.

Those who managed to scramble on to the rocky shore owed their lives to the people of the surrounding area, who had hurried to the clifftops in response to news of the disaster. Only one of the rafts reached the safety of the Bay of Skaill – the other two were swept into narrow inlets somewhat to the north where rescue was more difficult. Few of the sailors could remember what had happened to them. Fred Sims woke to find himself tucked up in the bed of a crofting family called Harvey, who plied him with tea and cigarettes and tended his burns. 'They'd pulled over a hundred of us up,' he recalls, 'but it was only the first few they got hold of come round all right.' Shortly after midnight a naval officer arrived at the Harveys' house and told Sims that transport would come the next day to take him back to Scapa where his burns would receive attention. He was also warned not to divulge any information about the sinking or about Kitchener's presence on the ship.

The disaster had been witnessed by a handful of the inhabitants of Marwick, including James Gaudie of Nether Skaill, who had been drawn to the shore by the violence of the *Hampshire*'s explosions. 'The ship was half under water', when he saw it. 'I reckoned it was at least one and a half miles off shore. Hazy, raining, and a lot of harsh sea, and just a raw fog, damp feeling. The sea was breaking it up just like it had been a reef or rock.'[25]

Another witness of the sinking was Joe Angus of Stromness, then stationed with the Territorial Force shore patrol in the nearby palace of Birsay, a twelfth-century ruin of great religious and historical importance to the islands:

> By this time there was quite a few of the local people about the palace there watching the scene, and some of the womenfolk were really in tears. In fact it was really a sad sight to behold but we could no nothing about it. Very stormy night, the sea was running high and the wind was blowing down the coast.[26]

Angus had come on duty at eight o'clock, just as the *Hampshire* was going down by the head with 'a volume of smoke and flames immediately behind the bridge'. His first instinct was to send a telegram to the Commander of the Western Patrol in Stromness but in his agitation two small errors were made, both of which confused the authorities: it was timed, wrongly, at 7.45 p.m. and its contents gave little clue to the emergency of the situation. The telegram was wired from Birsay Post Office, with a copy to the Commander of the Royal Garrison Artillery in Kirkwall, and it read 'Battle Cruiser seems in distress between Marwick Head and Brough of Birsay'. On receiving the news, Captain F.M. Walker, the Western Patrol's commanding officer, ordered two vessels to stand by in Stromness harbour – the armed yacht *Jason II* and the trawler *Cambodia* – until he received further information. Not knowing either the identity of the 'battlecruiser' or the movement of British ships that day, he was in some doubt about the message's authenticity. While his staff was asking Birsay for more detailed information, a further message was received from Angus's patrol. It arrived at 8.20 p.m. and read baldly 'Vessel down'. This time there could be no doubt and Walker acted promptly. His two rescue ships were ordered to make ready and he took steps to telephone the information to Vice-Admiral Brock at Longhope.

The rescue operation ran into difficulties before it had even begun. Confused, unnecessarily, by the mention of the term 'battlecruiser' – *Hampshire* was an armoured cruiser, a different class altogether – Brock dithered. Instead of ordering a flotilla of rescue ships into the area he felt obliged to confirm Birsay's telegrams before acting. The signal station at Brimsness, on the south-west tip of Hoy, was asked about ship's movements that evening and back came the reply that *Hampshire* had passed at 6.46 p.m. At the same time a third, agitated signal arrived at Stromness, timed at 8.35 p.m., reading 'Four funnel cruiser sunk 20 minutes ago. No assistance arrived yet. Send ships to pick up bodies'. Now was the time to act, and to his credit Brock did what he could to launch a creditable rescue attempt. *Jason II* and *Cambodia* put to sea from Stromness and by 9.10 p.m. four destroyers, including the recently returned *Unity* and *Victor*, left Scapa to begin their search off Marwick Head one and a half hours later.[27] They were joined by the ex-Cunard tender *Flying Kestrel* and two other trawlers, *Northward* and *Renzo*. Later in the night other vessels moved into the area and, throughout the small hours of the morning, beneath the destroyers' searchlights, they swept through the heavy seas. Their harvest was meagre – only a handful of corpses and

AN UNPITIED SACRIFICE

what wreckage had managed to break away from the sinking cruiser. Just after the first light the *Flying Kestrel* picked up the body of FitzGerald, but in spite of an extensive search that continued well into the following day Kitchener's body was never found. Of the ship's company of 655 only twelve survived, the lucky ones who were plucked out of their Carley rafts and resuscitated by the people of Orkney.

In spite of the thoroughness of the search and the efforts put into it by the sailors, it was a case of too little too late. Walker's delay at Stromness is understandable as the first message from Birsay was imprecise but Brock's failure to act seems inexcusable. He had been one of the guests at Jellicoe's lunch party on the *Iron Duke* and had been made privy to *Hampshire*'s course – Walker's telephone call and the subsequent message from Birsay should have alerted him but he continued to prefer caution to action before issuing any orders. For an officer of his experience to have been puzzled by the use of the word 'battlecruiser' was unforgivable. Given that he knew the importance of Kitchener's mission, and the route it would take, he must have known that the messages from Birsay could refer only to one ship, the *Hampshire*.

To compound the confusion, the shore patrols from Stromness and Kirkwall, which had been despatched by motor car, got lost on the way to Birsay. This was perhaps understandable as the roads in the district are confusing and roadsigns had been removed for the duration of the war but it did add to the delay. At the same time local susceptibilities were injured when the men of the RNLI lifeboat at Stromness were refused permission to assist the rescue as Brock, knowing that Kitchener was aboard the *Hampshire*, wanted to keep the operation a naval affair on security grounds (in fact the Stromness lifeboat did not put to sea at all during the First World War but the incident fuelled local stories that the rescue had been botched badly). However, in the light of the weather and sea conditions off Marwick Head that evening it seems unlikely that the earlier arrival of the rescue craft would have added to the number of survivors. Nevertheless, at the end of a day of naval blunders, the delays and confusions were perhaps symptomatic of a lack of care in the Royal Navy's safeguarding of the life of Britain's principal war leader.

At 8.10 a.m. on 6 June Jellicoe signalled to the Admiralty his deep regret that *Hampshire* had been lost to a torpedo or mine and that there was very little hope of survivors. By three o'clock in the afternoon his worst fears about Kitchener's fate were confirmed by the news of the discovery of FitzGerald's body and by the pitiful size of the list of survivors. It was his worst moment. To his friend Admiral Sir Henry Jackson, the First Sea Lord, he wrote that evening that the loss of the *Hampshire*, 'a national disaster of the first magnitude, has naturally caused me the deepest distress, as I feel in a measure responsible as I ordered her movements ... My luck is dead out for the present I am afraid.'[28]

For the naval high command, security was the first priority. Knowing that Kitchener was carrying secret documents that could have floated away from the wreckage, the Admiralty ordered Jellicoe to maintain a strict watch and to make the coastal strip on the west of the Orkney mainland out of bounds to the local people. A special metal-lined shell to be used as a coffin was put aside in case Kitchener's body was found and was to be used to convey it secretly back to London. Orders were also given to maintain a high degree of secrecy should the body or any trace of it be found. Acting in those interests Jellicoe suspended all communications between Orkney and mainland Scotland, largely because he did not want to divulge either the extent of the rescue operations or the position where the *Hampshire* went down. Those necessary measures created a number of local myths that still enjoy currency in the islands. There are few people who do not know someone who in turn knew another who recounted one of the following stories as 'gospel truth': that soldiers turned would-be rescuers away from the shores at gunpoint, that the Stromness lifeboat was forcibly prevented from taking part in the search for survivors, and that the *Hampshire* had been sent to her doom through the machinations of enemy spies.[29]

If Jellicoe had been thoroughly dismayed by the disaster, the news caused panic and confusion when it was announced in London at lunchtime on Tuesday 6 June. As the evening newspapers went on sale in the busy streets traffic came to a standstill and a large crowd began to form outside the War Office, where the blinds were drawn and the Union flag flew at half-mast. The shock of Kitchener's death was so profound that years later many people remembered in detail what they were doing when it was announced. To them it seemed that the centre had been torn out of their lives leaving them alone in a world that was suddenly unsure and unsafe. By evening a rumour was sweeping through London that Kitchener was still alive and travelling to Russia by other means, that the announcement had been a decoy to fool the Germans. Rumours of that kind became more exaggerated and nonsensical as the weeks progressed and the most common romance was that, King Arthur-like, Kitchener had cheated death and was waiting in hiding for the opportunity to return to lead his country to victory. Many of those rumours became myths, inspired by a common need to reject the fact of Kitchener's death, and it would take many years for the more potent of these to die down. Not a few were given additional credence by Millie Parker, Kitchener's sister, who foolishly encouraged any number of quacks, fakers and other con men to make money or publicity out of claims that Kitchener was either still alive in another guise or that secret agencies – Irish, German and even British – had murdered him by blowing up the *Hampshire*. Other stories suggested that the secret of his departure had been betrayed to the Germans who, forewarned, had despatched a U-boat to lie in wait off Orkney for the *Hampshire* to sail into her path. This rumour, in particular, was to resurface again in the 1920s when it was given added, if mistaken, support by Kitchener's official biographer, Sir George Arthur.

The news of Kitchener's death dominated the morning papers of 7 June. Little was given away about the *Hampshire*'s position, other than that she had been lost off Orkney en route to Russia and news editors were left to piece together their stories as best they could. Elsewhere, colleagues paid handsome tribute to Kitchener's powers of leadership and to the unique role he had played in bringing Britain to the state of readiness necessary to fight and win a major European war. As might have been expected, the emphasis was on his imperial triumphs, culminating in August 1914 when, 'cometh the hour, cometh the man', he stepped forward into the limelight of his countrymen's affections to lead them in their greatest hour of need. Little was said about recent setbacks and disagreements; rather, the mood was restrained and elegiac. Allied to that sense of loss was a feeling of bewilderment, almost as if Britain's ship of state had foundered.

Curiously, the tone in the German press was equally temperate when it was announced the following day. Most of the leading newspapers concentrated on Kitchener's service to the Empire, adding that his later years had been frustrated by political intrigue: in a society that did not separate so severely its military and civilian elements, it did not seem strange that Kitchener, a soldier, should have occupied a high political post. What did surprise most German commentators was the information that Kitchener had been sent to Russia in what seemed to be a ship of questionable vintage. Others suggested that the *Hampshire* might have been torpedoed by a German submarine but the naval authorities never made any statement about the sinking or the role played by *U-75*. At the time the news was breaking of the *Hampshire*'s loss German naval high command was unaware of Beitzen's exact position and it was not until he returned on 11 June that the picture could be put together and placed in the German records.

Beitzen's instructions had been clear enough and he had carried them out to the letter. In response to Scheer's orders he had laid his mines off the west coast of Orkney in readiness for the departure of the Grand Fleet, while *U-43* and *U-44* watched the eastern approaches to Scapa. As it happened Jellicoe's ships were not troubled by that trap but, through British complacency and mismanagement, the *U-75* did sink a British armoured cruiser carrying the important prize of Lord Kitchener. Thus, a minor aspect of tactical planning, added to a large measure of luck, allowed the Germans to claim one success from their submarine initiative at Jutland. For doing his duty Beitzen was awarded the Iron Cross, First Class, on 20 June, but in the interests of security the award was given little publicity in the German press. It was noted by British naval intelligence, however. When news of Beitzen's award was picked up from Holland, in the pages of the Enschede newspaper *Tubantia*, it was logged by NID and placed in the *U-75*'s growing file.[30]

One German newspaper, though, seemed to make capital out of the disaster. On 7 June – the day on which the news of Kitchener's death occupied the British press – the *Leipziger Neuste Nachrichten* put the news in a front-page story that suggested the secret of Kitchener's mission had been betrayed to Germany and that in some way the sinking of the *Hampshire* had been neatly planned by the German naval authorities:

> One is tempted to repeat, regarding England, the old adage: 'It never rains but it pours'. It is a hard blow for England, and one that will strike home all the harder since morale in England, in spite of all official glossing over and propaganda, is still deeply depressed by the massive losses suffered by the British fleet. To Great Britain, indeed to the whole of the British Empire, the loss of Kitchener counts more than that of an army. It is as if our Hindenburg were taken from us, nay worse: we Germans have learned from the war how many masters of strategy we possess; England has had to recognise how few Generals it has at its disposal. Apart from French it has none of Kitchener's stature. For England, he was the supreme commander. On the way to Russia, in order to give the Russian army the benefit of his advice, he fell victim to a stroke of fate that seems all the more tragic because it met him on an element that England declares it rules absolutely. On board a British warship he probably perished from a blow struck by the hated and despised German foe. As it happens, we had just received a tribute to Kitchener from the pen of one of our collaborators prompted by rumours telling of a journey by Kitchener to Russia. May this tribute to the British military leader characterise him once more and show us what England has lost in Kitchener.[31]

Had this story been echoed in other newspapers in Germany the *Leipziger Neuste Nachrichten* could indeed have claimed a scoop. But, beyond the cryptic nature of the penultimate sentence, that an obituary had been prepared in advance of Kitchener's visit to Russia, there is little else to insinuate a triumph of German strategic planning. Given the leaky nature of Russian security Kitchener's plans were indeed an open secret and probably known in Berlin, but the German naval staff could not possibly have known either the exact date of the journey or, more importantly, the route taken by the *Hampshire*, which was decided at the last minute. In that respect, the *Leipziger Neuste Nachrichten*'s report belongs to the realm of wishful thinking. Written on the occasion of Kitchener's Russian visit, the tribute might have been, but was never intended to be, an obituary. As it was, the 'tribute', written by one 'Dr Freiherr von Madan', was decidedly pro-Kitchener, hailing him as 'Lord Tommy Atkins', the creator of Britain's conscript armies. The only note of censure was an attack on Kitchener's Francophile tendencies which the author mistakenly attributed to Kitchener having a French mother.

What was surprising about the article was its timing. It appeared a day before the news broke in other German newspapers and on the same day as it dominated the London press. To some commentators this added weight to the theory that the Germans had planned Kitchener's death deliberately. Nothing could be further from the truth. Leipzig was an important publishing centre and the *Neuste Nachrichten* a leading newspaper with well-established contacts both at home and abroad. According to Walter Nicolai, the wartime head of the Newspaper Section attached to the German General Staff, and therefore responsible for all military and naval dealings with the press, German newspapers were permitted to print stories from London newspapers, picked up by German agents.[32] As the news of Kitchener's death had been announced in the London evening papers at lunchtime on 6 June there was ample opportunity to pass it to Germany for publication the following day. The same source also picked up other British items of news, such as the embargo on the export of certain raw materials, also announced in the British press on 6 June. Since October 1915 the German High Command had enjoyed direct control of German war reporting through its *Kriegespresseamt* (War Press Office) and it is logical to suppose that this censoring body gave the *Leipziger Neuste Nachrichten* permission to print its front-page story and the subsequent tribute to Kitchener.

During the first half of 1916 the Reichstag had given considerable time for debate about press censorship, which was extremely unpopular both with the Left and with newspaper proprietors. One of the reasons for its continuation centred on the U-boat war and Germany's relations with neutral countries, especially the United States of America, which was thought to be inclining more than ever toward the Allied side. On the one hand the *Kriegespresseamt* pursued a simple policy, which had been enshrined in a statement of March 1916, that unrestricted U-boat successes against merchant ships, particularly when neutral ships were involved.[33] The sinking of the *Lusitania* in May 1915 had provoked the first crisis: in proclaiming that feat the German press had incurred the wrath of an influential section of the American public who refused to accept the claim of the German Foreign Office that the liner was a legitimate naval target. In the intervening period the *Kriegespresseamt* had encouraged German newspapers to concentrate more on the strategic importance of submarine warfare and less on the exploits of individual commanders and their crews.

Also to be taken into account was the propaganda war over the Battle of Jutland, or the Battle of the Skagerrak as it was known in Germany. At the beginning of June the German press was hailing it as a German victory, citing the loss of a greater number of British ships and the failure of the Royal Navy to press home any tactical advantage. Had the sinking of the *Hampshire* been accepted as forming part of that victory it would have provided a particularly telling shot in the war of words between Germany and Britain. Not only was it a warship and therefore a potential target whose loss could be justified morally, but it fell victim to Scheer's submarine trap. But nothing was ever claimed elsewhere in the German press and the *Leipziger Neuste Nachrichten* was alone in making any allusion to a German naval or intelligence triumph.

In British political circles the news of Kitchener's death provoked a wide range of reactions. In a dramatic gesture to his Cabinet colleagues Lloyd George declared that Kitchener's blood was on their hands, although within days he was to modify his views with a more prosaic statement that Britain could now get on with the job of winning the war. Northcliffe, too, voiced that sentiment in private while his newspapers paid generous public tribute to the dead War Minister. Ian Hamilton and Churchill were sitting in the Athenaeum when the news was shouted out by newspaper boys in the streets below: both men, victims of the failure of Gallipoli, were unanimous that Kitchener had died at the right time in his life. Gradually that came to be the accepted view, that Kitchener was fortunate to die before his powers waned and his reputation was eclipsed by the tide of war.

15

THE KITCHENER LEGACY

The day after the disaster Frederick Sims and his fellow survivors were taken back to Scapa for a medical examination on the hospital ship *Soudan*, prior to giving evidence at a secret naval Court of Enquiry. Held on board the depot ship HMS *Blake* on 7 June the findings – in common with all internal investigations – were kept strictly confidential and have subsequently been the subject of much speculation. To those who fostered notions of the mystery of Kitchener's death the Admiralty's refusal to make public the findings merely intensified the rumours that surrounded the loss of the *Hampshire*. In fact there is no mystery attached to the report, neither does it contain evidence that was not made freely available in condensed form in a White Paper of 1926. Rather, the Admiralty's desire to keep the findings secret may have been prompted by the selective nature of the evidence taken by the Court of Enquiry and by its bare conclusions.

Based on the evidence of the signals that Jellicoe chose to make available, the findings charted the chain of orders that began with the selection of the *Hampshire* on 27 May to the final messages sent to her on 5 June. Then followed the evidence of the survivors, together with the narratives of their escape, which made it clear that the cruiser had struck a mine; and the final section dealt with the rescue and its aftermath.

In the beginning it had been thought that a stray mine had been the cause of the disaster, but following the discovery of Beitzen's minefield on 8 June the real reason could not be avoided. The findings concluded, therefore, that *Hampshire* had been accidentally sunk in an undiscovered, and therefore unswept, minefield and that Kitchener had gone down with the ship. No conclusions were reached about the provenance of the mines and no cognisance was taken of the three U-boat warnings that had arrived at Longhope on the day of *Hampshire*'s departure. Ten years later, when the government published its White Paper on the sinking of the *Hampshire*, the findings of the Court of Enquiry, with some embellishments, formed the basis of the Admiralty's conclusions.[1]

Jellicoe may well have signalled on 8 June that he could not 'adequately express the sorrow felt by me personally and by the officers and men of the Grand Fleet personally at the fact that so distinguished a soldier and so great a man should have lost his life whilst in a measure under the care of the Fleet'.[2] But from the selective presentation of evidence to the Court of Enquiry it was also clear that he was not prepared to accept too great a measure of the blame. In his own mind, at least, he must have been aware of the extent of his miscalculation, for when King George V visited Scapa on 15 June the defensive measures were particularly impressive. The King crossed from Scrabster to Scapa on board HMS *Oak*, the same destroyer that had conveyed Kitchener, but this time it was screened by sixteen torpedo-boat destroyers and three seaplanes. Before the crossing took place orders had been given to sweep all possible channels with the minesweeping flotillas being guarded by three sloops patrolling the approaches.[3] Although such measures were warranted, they stand in stark contrast to the navy's treatment of Kitchener.

Such was the Admiralty's desire to keep confidential the findings of the Court of Enquiry held on *Blake* that no part of it was made public, apart from a brief and imprecise summary issued to the press on 16 June. This was standard Admiralty practice, but even an approach from Britain's ally, Italy, refused to move the authorities. A few months later, on 11 October, the Italian naval attaché in London, Captain di Villeray, requested information about the sinking of the *Hampshire* so he could compare it to the sinking of the Italian cruiser *Leonardo da Vinci*, which had also fallen victim to a mine. The British response was

'No takers! Curiosity, I should think' and the Italians had to make do with a cursory, sixty-three word statement that stated vaguely the Admiralty had 'no definitive evidence' to pass on to their Allies.[4]

As the years passed the known existence of the Court of Enquiry and the mystery of its findings continued to excite curiosity. In a letter to *The Times* in 1926, Sir George Arthur claimed that 'early in 1920 the First Lord of the Admiralty (the late Lord Long) asked me to read the secret or unpublished report on the sinking of the *Hampshire* on the understanding that I would not divulge a word to anybody'.[5] Arthur turned down the invitation on the grounds that he was trying to uncover the truth and could not accept any restrictions. He was convinced that the whole story about the *Hampshire*'s loss had not yet been told and had already excited some comment by claiming in his official biography that Kitchener's death had been no accident:

> By an unhappy error of judgement an unswept channel was chosen for the passage of the cruiser; and Kitchener – the secret of whose journey had been betrayed – was to fall into the machinations of England's enemies.[6]

As Arthur had enjoyed a close relationship with Kitchener and had had access to official papers, many believed that he was making a serious point and that there was evidence of a plot to do away with Kitchener. In fact, even if Arthur been granted access to the unpublished report, he would have found little to support his fears. Without the evidence of the vital submarine sightings, Jellicoe's choice of the western route would indeed have appeared as 'an unhappy error of judgement', and not as a serious mistake. Of the notion that Kitchener's journey had been betrayed, Arthur was on less firm ground. The facts of Kitchener's mission were so widely known at such an early date that the Germans must have picked them up, but there is nothing to suggest that they acted upon their findings. *U-75* was at sea when it received its orders on 24 May, *Hampshire* was selected to undertake the voyage three days later on 27 May and her final sailing instructions were not ordered until the last minute on 5 June. From the evidence of the dates and from the sequence of Jellicoe's and Scheer's orders, there is no cause to believe that Kitchener had fallen 'into the machinations of England's enemies'; but of that, Arthur could not be sure.

The matter was not allowed to rest there. Arthur's allegations were raised in the House of Commons and this prompted talk among backbenchers about an official cover-up. Unfortunately, when questions were asked they were so closely identified with the idea of a 'Kitchener Mystery' that the First Lord of the Admiralty, W.C. Bridgeman, had little difficulty answering them. The most common conspiracy theory was that *Hampshire* had been sent to her doom through the intervention of spies – Irish or German – while she was refitting in Belfast in February 1916. According to these rumours, time-bombs had been placed on the cruiser, the perpetrators but not their handiwork had been discovered, and two naval ratings had subsequently been executed. Another story had it that a strongroom had been constructed during the refit to enable Kitchener to take with him to Russia £2 million-worth of gold in US five dollar pieces to bolster the Tsar's war effort. Bridgeman called such stories 'ridiculous and wicked', but his refusal to enlarge on the matter fuelled a controversy that could have been silenced by an examination of the facts.

The evidence of *Hampshire*'s log – which was locked from public view until 1967 – would have revealed that two ratings had been sent to Detention Barracks on 9 February 1916 while the ship was in Belfast.[7] It was a relatively minor disciplinary matter involving curiosity rather than criminal intention. One of the sailors had served as a gunner in the army before the war and when a new type of high-explosive shell arrived on board *Hampshire* he committed a naval offence by inspecting its fuse without prior authorisation. For this folly in tampering with a weapon of war, the two sailors had to be punished but the incident grew out of all proportion to become a tale of enemy sabotage. Even if the sailors had been saboteurs, it was straining credulity to claim that time-bombs could be placed on a warship so far in advance of a mission that had not even been planned. As for the strongroom, the idea is also ridiculous. No naval commander would risk a specially prepared ship in front-line action: between the refit in Belfast and the ill-fated voyage to Russia *Hampshire* had to run the gauntlet of submarine attack in northern waters, and play a significant role in the naval conflict at Jutland.

The final damning evidence that puts paid to stories about time-bombs and strongrooms – surprisingly, both had their followers well into the century[8] – comes from the underwater film of the *Hampshire*'s wreck taken by the American film-maker John R. Breckenridge in 1977 and 1983. On their first visit to the site he and his camera team found the remains to be 'in surprisingly good state of preservation ... what little footage we obtained on that visit definitely showed plates bent inward on the bows.'[9] The second visit confirmed those findings. In other words, there was no evidence of an internal explosion before the ship foundered and all the structural damage shows that the *Hampshire* was sunk after striking a mine (there were, of course, a number of explosions after the sinking, caused by the boilers and magazines blowing up). No gold was found by either expedition for the simple reason it was not there in the first place.

The conspiracy theorists were not alone, though, in voicing misgivings about foul play and a cover-up. Earlier, in 1921, Lord Alfred Douglas had suggested in his magazine, *Plain Words*, that *Hampshire* had been sunk by time-bombs placed on her by Sinn Fein agents in retaliation for Kitchener's recruiting policies in Ireland. His account contained wild rumours of over-inquisitive sailors being shot in the Tower of London, a hint of complicity by the naval authorities and the publication in Dublin of a republican newspaper announcing Kitchener's death on 5 June, before it had happened. Naturally, he had no evidence to back up his extraordinary revelations and the matter was allowed to drop until, in a later edition, he attacked Winston Churchill for falsifying the facts of the Battle of Jutland. For his extravagant claims Lord Alfred Douglas, at one time the friend and lover of the poet Oscar Wilde, was prosecuted and sentenced to six months' imprisonment.

Equally intemperate and equally vociferous in his claims was the journalist Arthur Vectis Freeman, who wrote under the pen name of Frank Power. Using his column in the *Sunday Referee*, he fought a vigorous press campaign beginning in November 1925, arguing that the Admiralty had deliberately sent Kitchener to his death and had then made little attempt to rescue the survivors. Spies, sabotage, the unsuitability of the *Hampshire* for the mission, leaving survivors to drown, all combined to present a picture that suggested criminal negligence on the part of the authorities. So irresponsible was his argument and so tendentious his claims that little attention was paid to him in official circles, but he did enjoy a huge popular following. As a result of his articles, the readership of *Sunday Referee* soared and public meetings organised to discuss the 'Kitchener Mystery' attracted large audiences. The hoax continued until the summer of 1926 when Power claimed that Kitchener's body had been washed ashore in Norway and would be returned in a special coffin. When it arrived in Britain the coffin was opened and found to be empty.[10]

In response to the clamour of people like Power and others, and to the questions in the House of Commons, Prime Minister Stanley Baldwin sanctioned the publication of a White Paper on the sinking of the *Hampshire*, which duly appeared in August 1926. Based largely on the findings of the Court of Enquiry held ten years earlier – namely, that *Hampshire* had struck a mine, that the existence of the minefield was unknown and that Jellicoe had been justified in his choice of route – the White Paper arrived at the following conclusions:

> … that the 'Hampshire' was a suitable ship to select for the conveyance of Lord Kitchener, and was in an entirely efficient condition; that her route was carefully selected by the Commander-in-Chief, and that his decision was a difficult one in the difficult circumstances of the moment; that the loss of the ship was not due to treachery but to her striking one or more moored mines laid by the U-75; that these mines were not laid with any knowledge of the 'Hampshire's' mission or any intention of destroying a particular vessel or person; that the only survivors from the 'Hampshire' were one warrant mechanician [sic] and eleven men, of whom the full names and details were published at the time; that there is no evidence that Lord Kitchener ever left the ship, and that none of the survivors saw any boat with occupants get clear of the ship.[11]

This is a reasonable précis of what occurred and bears out the facts that *Hampshire* was a sound choice for the journey, that its mission was kept secret at naval headquarters in Orkney and that she met her end on one of the mines laid by *U-75* as part of the German submarine offensive prior to Jutland. The White Paper also dealt summarily with all spy and sabotage stories and presented a clear account of the rescue operations, demonstrating that everything possible had been done by the naval and military authorities on Orkney to go to the aid of the survivors. On that level the loss of the *Hampshire* seemed to be due to an unlikely combination of mischances, prompting *The Times* to comment that the last word had been said on the subject:

> It is to be hoped that after this terrible recital of the facts, made with an obvious desire to lay the whole truth before the nation and before the world, the sensation-mongers will seek some other field. Further prowling about the Hampshire incident and the death of Lord Kitchener can only degrade them further in the public mind.[12]

But the whole truth had not been told. The official narrative in the White Paper is clear and precise and, based on the evidence of Jellicoe's signals, paints a reasonable picture of the events leading to the sailing of the *Hampshire* at 4.45 p.m. on Monday 5 June 1916. Using the evidence of Scheer's orders – by then available to the Admiralty – it was also able to state the reasons for the presence of a minefield off Marwick Head and the laying of the mines by *U-75*. The White Paper was, however, less candid in its explanation of the prevailing weather conditions and in its account of the submarine warnings.

According to the narrative, *Hampshire*'s loss was due more to happenstance than to any human error, 'Unconnected coincidences of exactly similar type occur, of course, frequently in the experience of almost every human being, but are apt to be overlooked except when, as in the case of the *Hampshire*, their consequences are momentous.' Such a conclusion would have been judicious but for the evidence of the weather and the messages about enemy submarine activity, both of which were available to naval headquarters on the afternoon of *Hampshire*'s departure. On the matter of the imminent change of weather, and the knowledge that the gale would back from the north-east to the north-west, the White Paper made no comment other than claiming that there had been an obvious risk in sending the cruiser by the eastabout route during a north-easterly gale.

The presence of a U-boat off the Pentland Skerries, reported on 3 June, was cited as another reason for abandoning the eastabout passage. Perversely, the White Paper does mention the first U-boat warning of 5 June from Cape Wrath, but not its successors, arguing that 'the information was not subsequently confirmed, and was probably erroneous'. The incident was introduced into the account to lend weight to Jellicoe's decision not to send *Hampshire* westwards into the Atlantic, past Cape Wrath, before joining the main mercantile route to Russia, but the statement is only half true. The message was repeated twice during the day, with confirmation of sightings by surface vessels, the armed yacht *024* and the armed trawler *1798*, arriving at Longhope in the late afternoon. Even though Jellicoe could not have known that mines had been laid, he possessed evidence that a U-boat was in the north-west triangle off Cape Wrath and therefore in a position to threaten any warship sailing to the west of Orkney. On that count alone Jellicoe must bear some of the blame for the loss of the *Hampshire*, although to put the matter in the context of the conflict he noted in February 1926 'there was always a risk in going to sea during the war.'[13]

By 1926, though, when the White Paper was published, the country was preoccupied with other matters and Baldwin's government was grappling with the problems of a receding economy, a General Strike and mass unemployment. Most politicians were prepared to let the matter drop, to accept the report and to leave the rumours to the scandal-mongers. As a safety measure, the findings of the Court of Enquiry, and the evidence of the submarine sightings, were restricted from public view until 1967.

The main protagonists in the story of the sinking of HMS *Hampshire* all met different fates. Asquith was deposed at the end of the year by Lloyd George; he eventually retired from public life in 1926 and died two years later. After a short spell as Secretary of State for War in succession to Kitchener, Lloyd George became Prime Minister of the Coalition government in Asquith's stead, but by 1922 his period of power was over. Between 1926 and 1931 he was leader of a much weakened Liberal Party and he died in 1945, aged eighty-two. It was he who put an end to Jellicoe's career. Created First Sea Lord in December, Jellicoe was sacked unceremoniously a year later, on Christmas Eve. Having refused to give total backing to a convoy system he clashed with Lloyd George and lived to see its implementation reduce British merchant shipping losses in 1918. For his services to the nation he was created Viscount Jellicoe of Scapa in 1918 and he received an earldom seven years later. As the man who, according to Churchill, could have lost the war in an afternoon, Jutland proved to be an incubus and his later years were clouded by controversy over his handling of the Grand Fleet during the battle. Between 1920 and 1924 he was Governor-General of New Zealand and he died in March 1936 not long after his friend, King George V.

The survivors from the *Hampshire* were sent to recuperate in naval hospitals at Rosyth and Portsmouth before being split up and posted to other ships. Frederick Sims ended the war bringing back Admiralty trawlers from Malta to Scotland. He left the navy in 1926 to work for London Trams and eventually became a driver with London Country Buses. Having retired to live in Hemel Hempstead, he died in 1991.

Ironically, the *Hampshire* was avenged by the same agent that had been the cause of her destruction. Mines. Kurt Beitzen was drowned in the West Channel after his U-boat, *U-102*, struck a British mine in September 1918; *U-75* met a similar end when she went down off Terschelling with the loss of all hands after entering a British minefield mistakenly on 13 December 1917.[14] *Hampshire* herself lies in forty-two fathoms of water off Marwick Head and the wreck has been much abused by the strength of the prevailing tides in the area. Breckenridge's expedition of 1983 brought back to the surface a number of items belonging to her, including a 50-ton propeller and shaft: these were ordered to be returned to the site by the Ministry of Defence as *Hampshire* is an official war grave. A proposal for an Admiralty salvage operation to the wreck was discussed in Parliament in November 1918 but rejected on account of the difficulties involved in diving at such depths and in such strong currents.

THE KITCHENER LEGACY

Today, Kitchener's death is marked in Orkney by a solitary tower that was dedicated in 1926; it stands on Marwick Head looking out to the spot where the *Hampshire* foundered. Some 300ft below, the seas crash on to the huge rocks that guard these formidable cliffs and even on a calm day it is possible to imagine the plight facing the survivors in the Carley rafts as they made for such an inhospitable shore. The monument was raised and paid for by the people of Orkney at a cost of £700 (£28,000 today) and is reached by a path leading from the road where the first naval and military patrols arrived at the scene of the disaster all those years ago. Over the years the fabric of the tower deteriorated but it was restored in time for the centenary of Kitchener's death in 2016 with assistance from the British Army and the US National Guard. Fittingly, given Kitchener's connection with the Royal Engineers, help was provided by 71 Engineer Regiment's 10 (Orkney) Field Troop. A memorial wall lists all the men who died on board the stricken cruiser.

For going to the assistance of the *Hampshire*'s crew the farming folk of Sandwick and Birsay received scant reward. A week after the incident Vice-Admiral F.E. Brock wrote to Jellicoe from Longhope suggesting that some acknowledgement should be made of the part played in the rescue by the Orcadians. Such recognition, he counselled, should not be money as the crofters were 'not of a class to which money could be sent; I am of the opinion that a letter of thanks would be much more highly prized, although the persons concerned are mostly poor'.[15]

A similar kind of parsimony almost befell the memory of Kitchener himself. An appeal for funds to complete the reconstruction of Broome Park was made by the Kitchener family to the new Chancellor of the Exchequer, Andrew Bonar Law, who turned it down on the grounds that funds for such luxuries could not be found in time of war. It was hinted that another approach could be made after the war was over but in a country fit for heroes nothing was done to save Kitchener's dream house until 1928 when the estate was broken up and Broome Park itself threatened with demolition. The magazine *Country Life* took up its cause and launched an appeal, which was read by a businessman, James Jell, who bought it and turned it into a country house hotel.

During the Second World War it served as the headquarters of a Canadian armoured regiment, The Fusiliers Mont-Royal, and in 1945 reverted to its peacetime role as The Broome Park Hotel. When Mr Jell retired in 1979 it was transformed into a time-share leisure complex and country club with a surrounding golf course.

In the immediate wake of Kitchener's death, pious promises were uttered that a national memorial would be built in his honour by a grateful nation once the war had ended. Although nothing came of such a grandiose scheme, The Lord Kitchener National Memorial Fund put in hand plans for a memorial chapel in Kitchener's honour, which was constructed in the north-west corner of St Paul's Cathedral in London. Lit by two windows in the north and west walls, the chapel consists of a simple, recumbent sculpture of Kitchener, designed and executed by Sir William Reid Dick. On either side stand the figures of the two soldier saints, St Michael and St George, and above the altar there is a Pietà. The chapel is also associated with the Royal Engineers, whose Roll of Honour is held within its walls, and the whole area is permeated by the spirit of sacrifice that characterised both Kitchener and the armies that rose at his call. It was dedicated in the late afternoon of 10 December 1925.

In all, the Fund, under the presidency of Queen Alexandra, had raised £250,000 by the end of 1918 and £30,000 was set aside for the construction of the memorial chapel and a further sum for a statue in Horse Guard's Parade. To commemorate Kitchener's connection with Sudan funds were made available for a Kitchener Medical School in Khartoum. Another area of support was a fund for disabled officers of the navy and army but the most lasting memorial established by the Fund's trustees was the Kitchener Scholars' scheme, which continues to this day. Like the Rhodes Scholarship system, it celebrates one man's service to his country and under its aegis, talented and public-spirited young people are offered generous scholarships to study at universities in this country and abroad.

However, even the name Kitchener has disappeared from the peerage. The first Earl died unmarried and childless and he was succeeded by his elder brother, Colonel Henry Kitchener, whose only son, Henry,

Viscount Broome, predeceased him in 1928. On his death in 1937 he was succeeded by his grandson, also Henry, as third Earl. The third Earl Kitchener died unmarried and childless in 2011 and the title therefore became extinct.[16] That was not quite the end of the matter. The Hon. Charles Kitchener, brother of the third Earl, had one daughter, Emma Joy Kitchener, who on the third Earl's death became the first Earl's heir general. She is married to the actor and screenwriter Julian, Lord Fellowes and on 9 May 2012 the Queen issued a Royal Warrant of Precedence allowing Lady Fellowes to enjoy 'the same title, rank, place, pre-eminence and precedence as a daughter of an Earl' as if her late father had survived his brother and therefore succeeded to the title.[17]

History, though, has been less than kind to Kitchener. Once the war was over he was attacked by French in his memoirs, *1914*, but the embittered field marshal paid so little attention to the truth that his wilder accusations were refuted easily. More serious damage was done by Lloyd George in his *War Memoirs,* which painted Kitchener as an archaic and taciturn monolith whose presence terrified his colleagues and disguised a multitude of shortcomings including incompetence and a refusal to delegate responsibility. Apart from his role in creating the New Armies, Lloyd George's Kitchener was a totem-like figure whose presence gave comfort to the nation in 1914, but by the following year had become ridiculous. In time that came to be the accepted view and 100 years after his death Kitchener's stock does not stand high. In a country that has slewed off and conveniently forgotten its imperial past his action-packed life seems to belong to another world – his cartographical adventures in Palestine, the campaign in the Sudan culminating in the victory at Omdurman, the sweeps and drives of the Boer War and the epic conflict between the *Mulki Lat* and the *Jangi Lat*. And to a generation groomed in the myth of honest soldiers being sacrificed by blundering generals, Kitchener became one of the guilty commanders who sent the generation of 1914 up the line to death, and the one who, because of the famous poster, became the best known.

Few reputations can have changed as dramatically as Kitchener's. The apotheosis of the Victorian hero and the symbol of his country's will to win, he was castigated by his colleagues after his death when he could not answer the charges brought against him. There is little doubt that he made many mistakes during the course of a long and varied life but many of the criticisms were born of ignorance or personal malice or a simple dislike of his personality.

Kitchener's preference for sharing his life and duties with handsome young ADCs have attracted comments that Kitchener was either a covert homosexual or a man whose homosexual instincts and activities have never been revealed. These include his shyness, his being ill-at-ease in the company of 'smart' women, his unmarried state and even his luxuriant moustache as evidence that he was a homosexual. Other straws take in his order that all his officers in the Sudan campaign should be single and his interest in the Boy Scout movement, and a number of wild rumours about his sexual preferences were in common currency in the years after his death. Gossip of that kind is still extant in the twenty-first century even though no scrap of evidence of homosexual activity has ever been produced, nor is it ever likely to be.[18] Kitchener's colleague, Lord Esher, concluded that the absence of evidence about his sexual interests 'leaves incomplete the story of his life or betrays a flaw in his nature' but any hint of homosexuality would certainly have been used against him by his enemies.[19] Throughout his life there were many who would have been pleased to see him fall from grace and it has to be remembered that homosexual acts were a crime until the passing of the Sexual Offences Act of 1967 and remained a court martial offence in the armed forces until 1994.

Although Kitchener as a boy was subject to a number of the factors that contemporary sexologists have taken to be ingredients in the formation of homosexuality in men – the adoration of his mother, the presence of a stern and domineering father, his narcissism and liking for female pursuits, for example – Kitchener was never averse to women. Apart from his early flirtation with Nellie Campbell among others, there is evidence aplenty in his correspondence with his sister Millie of the interest that Kitchener took in the opposite sex, including his 'Américaine' on the ship from Trieste to Alexandria whose husband had felt forced to protest. Kitchener always took care to mention female company at dinner parties to which he had been invited, especially if his partners were pretty, and he was also an inveterate matchmaker. 'Does the poor parson still enjoy celibacy?' he asked Millie of her brother-in-law's marriage prospects and he also took a good deal of interest in his brother Arthur's affairs. When an unsuitable match appeared in his brother's life he was not slow in offering well-meant advice: 'Get hold of some young woman with some tin,' he told Millie, 'and then let Arthur alone to do the rest.' As well as advice, Millie also received abundant dress material and instructions on what to make with it. 'I send you a Xmas present of some yellow silk knowing your fondness for gorgeous attire and your special weakness for the jaundiced hue,' he wrote to her from Cyprus in December 1878. 'They say there is more than enough for a dress. I hope I have not curtailed your skirts as I do like a good long dress. Don't you?'

Kitchener obviously did like women and he took no little pleasure in their company, but he felt it a great sadness that he was too unbending ever to enter into a completely satisfactory relationship. 'Your affectionate brother, unmarried and unlikely to be', became a familiar way of concluding his letters to Millie. That combination of curiosity, withdrawal and subsequent regret makes Kitchener conform, perhaps, to the pattern of the Victorian man to whom sexual relationships were something of a mystery. Without hard facts the most sensible conclusion is that arrived at by his biographer Philip Magnus, who suggested that Kitchener, like many other men of his period, particularly in the army, which imposes its own self-denying ordinances, conformed to the type that was naturally celibate.[20]

According to accounts of those who did not know him well, Kitchener possessed neither charm nor easy social graces: in their eyes he was also too imperious and too secretive for the good of the great offices he held. But to his innermost circle of friends he offered nothing but intimacy and an abiding loyalty. What he did possess in abundance was talent, a dogged determination and ambition. Not being endowed with personal wealth he had to rise in the world through his own devices and his early career speaks volumes for his resolve and abilities. It is on that score, surely, and not on the record of his psychological make-up, that Kitchener should be finally judged.

THE KITCHENER ENIGMA

In the years of Queen Victoria's apogee he emerged as one of the great builders of her Empire and through his exploits his countrymen were allowed to share, albeit vicariously, in the great enterprise of winning and maintaining Britain's imperial holdings. As a soldier he was responsible for bringing down the curtain on the last of the major Victorian colonial wars with his victory at Omdurman, yet within two years he was forced to lay plans for fighting and winning a modern war in South Africa. His diplomatic success in helping to bring the Boer War to a peaceful conclusion was no less impressive than the tact he had displayed four years earlier at Fashoda: in that respect, he presented a somewhat unusual figure to the world, that of the soldier who was also peacemaker and politician. As British Agent in Egypt – his spiritual home – he proved to be a capable and sincere proconsul, but when the call came to lead his own country in her hour of greatest need, he was equal to the task. Asquith's experiment of appointing a soldier to a political post was not altogether successful and gave rise to a number of unnecessary tensions in the British high command, but, given the difficulties Kitchener faced, having to fight a war on a previously unheard of scale, he turned a lifetime's experience to good advantage, insisting that Britain's first consideration should be the creation of a mass volunteer army with which to wage a lengthy war in Europe. As the nation's warlord, he then took steps to supply and arm the New Armies and to provide their leaders with a strategy that took into account the global nature of the conflict and the necessity of winning it on two Europeans fronts.

Kitchener was the only leader of any note from the warring nations to die on active service during the First World War, and even though his rivals had taken the first steps to remove him from office his unnecessary death was a loss that Britain could ill afford. When the waters closed around his neck that stormy June evening in 1916, the architect of Britain's war effort was going to his death before the completion of the edifice he had designed for Britain's eventual victory.

NOTES

Prologue

1 Maxwell, *Frank Maxwell VC*, 89
2 Grew, *Kitchener and Empire*, I, 13
3 Lloyd George, *War Memoirs*, II, 751
4 Sir Hedley Le Bas, 'Advertising for an Army', *Lord Kitchener Memorial Book*
5 The claim was made by Philip Magnus in *Kitchener*, 289, but in her autobiography *More Memories* (1933) Margot Asquith insisted that the comment was made by her daughter, Princess Elizabeth Bibesco
6 The phenomenon is discussed in James Taylor, *Your Country Needs You*, Glasgow, 2013 and is dismissed as 'an urban myth'
7 Esher, *Tragedy of Lord Kitchener*, xvi
8 Churchill, *My Early Life*, 176

Chapter 1

1 NA PRO 30/57/93, Kitchener Papers. Mrs Sharp to Sir George Arthur in response to requests for biographical material
2 J. Anthony Gaughan, *Listowel and its Vicinity*, Cork, 1973, 216
3 Ibid, 316
4 Magnus, *Kitchener*, 4
5 NA PRO 30/57/93, Kitchener Papers, Mrs Sharpe to Sir George Arthur
6 Magnus, *Kitchener*, 6
7 B. Beatty, *Kerry Memories*, Camborne, 1939, 26
8 NA PRO 30/57/93, Kitchener Papers, Mrs Sharpe to Sir George Arthur
9 Magnus, *Kitchener*, 6. This claim was disputed by the Kitchener family
10 Information from Mr John Savage, Tralee

11 Report on the Examination for Admission to the Royal Military Academy at Woolwich, held at the Royal Hospital, Chelsea on 3 January 1868, and following days, London 1868

Chapter 2

1   Arthur, *Life of Kitchener*, I, 6
2   Cambridge once remarked to a senior British officer who had ventured to offer his opinion, 'Brains! I don't believe in brains. You haven't any, I know, sir!'
3   Esher, *Tragedy of Lord Kitchener*, 192–193
4   Whitworth Porter, *History of the Corps of Royal Engineers*, London 1889, II, 185
5   NA PRO 30/57/93, Kitchener Papers, Colonel H.R. Williams to Sir George Arthur
6   Arthur, *Life of Kitchener*, I, 12
7   Walter Besant, *Twenty-one Years' Work in the Holy Land*, London, 1886, 2
8   Walter Besant, *Autobiography*, London, 1902, 152
9   Conder, *Tent-Work*, II, 164
10 Ibid, 195
11 Ibid, 196
12 Palestine Exploration Fund, Quarterly Statement, 1875, 198
13 H.H.K., 'A Visit to Sophia and the Heights of Kamerleh – Christmas 1877', *Blackwood's Magazine*, vol. 123, No. 1248, February 1878, 196
14 Michael Brander, *The Perfect Victorian Hero: The Life and Times of Samuel White Baker*, Edinburgh, 1982, 149
15 Besant, *Autobiography*, 127
16 Daiches, *Kitchener and Palestine*, 11
17 Palestine Exploration Fund, Quarterly Statement, 1877, 72
18 C.R. Low, *A Memoir of Lieutenant-General Sir Garnet Wolseley*, London, 1878, 280
19 Parliamentary Papers, 1880, Turkey, 4 and 23
20 The entire document is quoted in Arthur, *Life of Kitchener*, I, 44–46

Chapter 3

1   John Macdonald, 'Fellahin Soldiers, Old and New: A Reminiscence and a Moral', *Nineteenth Century*, vol. 44, 1898, 585
2   Arthur, *Life of Kitchener*, I, 50, note 2
3   Haggard, *Under Crescent and Star*, 24
4   NA PRO 30/57/102, Kitchener Papers, Bonte Elgood to Sir Philip Magnus
5   Arthur, *Life of Kitchener*, I, 60
6   Ibid, 56
7   *Pall Mall Gazette*, 9 January 1884
8   Kitchener to Besant, Archives of the Palestine Exploration Fund
9   NA PRO 30/57/4 Kitchener to Baring
10 Steevens, *Kitchener to Khartoum*, 9

NOTES

11 Magnus, *Kitchener*, 50
12 Hake, *Gordon Journals*, 360
13 NA PRO 30/57/4 Kitchener Papers, Kitchener to Baring, 31 August 1884
14 *The Times*, 7 October 1885
15 Hake, *Gordon Journals*, 92
16 Ibid, 362
17 Ibid, 395
18 Gleichen, *With the Camel Corps*, 78
19 Magnus, *Kitchener*, 61
20 Gleichen, *With the Camel Corps*, 243
21 Arthur, *Life of Kitchener*, I, 115
22 Ibid, 104–105
23 Ibid, 105
24 NA PRO 30/57/5, Kitchener Papers, Wolseley to Kitchener, 30 January 1885
25 Mrs J.W. Mackay, *A.M. Mackay*, London, 1890, 290
26 Kitchener's 'Notes on the Fall of Khartoum' are quoted in full in Arthur, *Life of Kitchener*, I, 116–124
27 The report is quoted in full in Arthur, *Life of Kitchener*, I 132–139
28 Ibid, 136
29 Grew, *Kitchener*, I, 117
30 NA PRO 30/57/5, Kitchener Papers, Kitchener to Wood, June, 1885

Chapter 4

1   Father Joseph Ohrwalder, *Ten Years Captivity in the Mahdi's Army*, London 1892; Rudolf Slatin, *Fire and Sword in the Sudan 1875–1895*, London, 1896
2   Magnus, *Kitchener*, 68
3   NA PRO30/57/8 Kitchener Papers, Zanzibar Boundary Commission 1885–1886
4   Ibid
5   *The Times*, 9 January 1888
6   *The Times*, 18 January 1888
7   Parliamentary Papers, Egypt, No. 1, 1889, 35
8   NA SP/A55, Salisbury Papers, Salisbury to Baring, 20 January 1888
9   Arthur, *Life of Kitchener*, I, 158
10 NA SP/A55 Salisbury Papers, Salisbury to Baring, 21 November 1890
11 Quoted in Thomas F.G. Coates, *Hector Macdonald*, London, 1900
12 Royle, *Death before Dishonour*, 81
13 Marlowe, *Cromer in Egypt*, 285
14 Cecil, *Leisure of an Egyptian Official*, 185
15 Cromer, *Modern Egypt*, II, 86-89
16 NA PRO 30/57/91 Kitchener Papers, Sir Reginald Wingate to Lord Midleton, 26 August 1916
17 'An Officer', *Sudan Campaign 1896–1899*, London, 1899, 72–73

18 Hector Macdonald, speech in Dingwall, May 1899, quoted in Coates, *Hector Macdonald*, 144
19 Marlowe, *Cromer in Egypt*, 154–155
20 NA FO 141/304, Kitchener to Cromer, 19 January 1894
21 Ibid, Rosebery to Cromer, 21 January 1894
22 NA PRO 30/57/10 Kitchener Papers, Rosebery to Kitchener
23 Mallet, *Life With Queen Victoria*, 99

Chapter 5

1 NA FO 633/7 Letters on Egyptian Affairs, Rosebery to Cromer, 22 April 1895
2 Bennett, *Downfall of the Dervishes*, 8
3 Milner, *England in Egypt*, 354
4 Mallet, *Life with Queen Victoria*, 99–100
5 Hamilton, *The Commander*, 100–104
6 Scudamore, *Sheaf of Memories*, 99
7 HHM SP/A 109/24 Cromer to Salisbury, 14 March 1896
8 Ibid, Cromer to Salisbury 15 March 1896
9 Magnus, *Kitchener*, 95
10 HHM SP/A 109/59 Cromer to Salisbury, 9 June 1896
11 Zulfo, *Karari*, 66
12 The most comprehensive account is Sandes, *Royal Engineers in Egypt and Sudan*
13 HHM SP/A 109/102 Cromer to Salisbury, 30 October 1896
14 NA PRO 30/57/10 Kitchener Papers, Kitchener to Grenfell, 14 October 1896
15 Quoted in Alford and Sword, *Egyptian Sudan*, 225
16 NA PRO 30/57/10 Kitchener Papers, Letters to Kitchener from Roberts and Wolseley, September 1898
17 Bennett, *Downfall of the Dervishes*, 70
18 Magnus, *Kitchener*, 134
19 R.G. Martin, *Lady Randolph Churchill*, London, 1971, II
20 Churchill, *River War*
21 NLS Acc 3155, Box 6, Haig Papers. Haig to his sister Henrietta, 1 April 1898
22 Ibid
23 Steevens, *With Kitchener to Khartoum*, 263
24 Churchill, *River War*, 137
25 NLS, Acc 3155 Haig Papers Box 6, Haig to Henrietta Haig
26 Cassar, *Kitchener*, 93

Chapter 6

1 Winston Churchill to Lady Randolph Churchill, 26 January 1899, quoted in Randolph S. Churchill, *Winston S. Churchill*, London, 1966, I, 424
2 Magnus, *Kitchener*, 136

NOTES

3 www.queenvictoriasjournals.org, Queen Victoria, Journal, 5 September 1898, vol. 108, 90
4 Burleigh, *Khartoum Campaign*, 254–255
5 NA FO 78/5050, Salisbury to Cromer, 3 September 1898
6 Watkins, *With Kitchener's Army*, 231
7 Smith-Dorrien, *Memories*, 126
8 Alfred Dreyfus, a Jewish officer in the French Army, had been accused in 1894 of passing secrets to the Germans and consequently imprisoned on Devil's Island off the coast of Guiana. Two years later fresh evidence showed that another officer, Major Esterhazy, was the real traitor but there was strong opposition and a violently anti-Semitic press campaign against reopening the Dreyfus case. Events came to a head in 1898, the year of Fashoda, with the publication of Emile Zola's famous letter, J'accuse, and the army and its officer corps were discredited in the country's eyes. Dreyfus's sentence was finally quashed in 1906.
9 *The Times*, 28 October 1898
10 Arthur, *Life of Kitchener*, I, 245
11 Wingate, *Not in the Limelight*, 21; Masters, *Nancy Astor*, 53
12 Steevens, *With Kitchener to Khartoum*, 50
13 Magnus, *Kitchener*, 149
14 Correlli Barnett, *Britain and Her Army*, London 1970, 480
15 C.O. Skinner, *Madame Sarah*, London, 1967, 287
16 Sir George Younghusband, *A Soldier's Memoirs*, London, 1917, 228
17 Gooch, *Boer War*, 54
18 Arthur, *Life of Kitchener*, I, 267

Chapter 7

1 Magnus, *Kitchener*, 171–172
2 Arthur, *Life of Kitchener*, I, 271
3 Quoted in Pakenham, *Boer War*, 319
4 Report of His Majesty's Commissioners on the War in South Africa, London, 1903, 23
5 Arthur, *Life of Kitchener*, I, 303
6 Pakenham, *Boer War*, 497
7 Maxwell, *Frank Maxwell VC*, 81–90
8 Maurice and Grant, *Official History*, II, 105
9 Amery, *Times History of the War in South Africa*, III, 423
10 Smith-Dorrien, *Memories*, 152
11 Magnus, *Kitchener*, 170
12 NA PRO 30/57/20 Kitchener Papers, Boer War: correspondence: Lord Roberts to Lord Kitchener
13 *Black and White Budget*, 8 December 1900
14 Judd and Surridge, *Boer War*, 232

15 NAM 7101/36/61 Roberts Papers, Kitchener to Roberts, 24 November 1901
16 NA PRO 57/22 Kitchener Papers, Kitchener to Brodrick, 28 December 1900
17 Ibid, Kitchener to Brodrick, 15 October 1901
18 Ibid, Kitchener to Brodrick, 22 March 1901
19 Frank Owen, *Tempestuous Journey: Lloyd George, His Life and Times*, London, 1954, 109
20 Headlam, *Milner Papers*, II, 166
21 Ibid, 184
22 Ibid, 326
23 Ibid, 364
24 J.C. Smuts, *Jan Christian Smuts*, London, 1952, 82–83
25 Niall Ferguson, *Empire: The Rise and Demise of the British World Order*, New York, 2003, 250
26 Pakenham, *Boer War*, 493–495
27 W.T. Stead, *Methods of Barbarism: The Case for Intervention*, London, 1901, 41
28 John Fisher, *That Miss Hobhouse: The Life of a Great Feminist*, London, 1971, 199
29 Rupert Hart-Davis, ed., *Siegfried Sassoon Diaries 1915–1918*, London, 1983, 247

Chapter 8

1 There is a good overview of this period in James Morris, *Pax Britannica: The Climax of an Empire*, London, 1968
2 *The Times*, 22 June 1897
3 Private information from Sir Philip Magnus-Allcroft
4 Ronaldshay, *Curzon*, II, 109
5 Dilks, *Curzon in India*, I, 217
6 NA PRO 30/57/26/8 Kitchener Papers, Lady Curzon to Kitchener, 9 December 1902
7 Dilks, *Curzon in India*, II, 24
8 Ronaldshay, *Curzon*, II, 251
9 NA PRO 30/57/28/5 Kitchener Papers, Kitchener to Roberts, 19 March 1903
10 Frank Richards, *Old Soldier Sahib*, London, 1936, 76
11 Ibid, 179
12 Dilks, *Curzon in India*, I, 213
13 There is a full account in King, *The Viceroy's Fall*
14 Ronaldshay, *Curzon*, II, 354
15 NA PRO 30/57/33, Kitchener Papers, Lady Curzon to Kitchener, undated, 1905
16 Ibid
17 Nigel Nicolson, *Mary Curzon*, London, 1979, 168–169
18 Ibid
19 Dilks, *Curzon in India*, II, 115
20 Magnus, *Kitchener*, 207
21 NA PRO 30/57/32, Kitchener Papers, Kitchener to Brodrick, 15 April 1904

NOTES

22 NA PRO 30/57/28/14–16, Kitchener Papers, Roberts to Kitchener, 18 June 1903
23 NA PRO 30/57/31, Kitchener Papers, Kitchener to Lady Salisbury, 25 January 1903
24 NA PRO 30/57/29 Kitchener Papers, Kitchener to Roberts, 6 May 1903
25 NA PRP 30/57/31/70 Kitchener Papers, Kitchener. 'Three essential principles of sound army administration in India', undated, 1904
26 Magnus, *Kitchener*, 220
27 Ibid, 223
28 *Spectator*, 2 September 1905, No. 4027, 310
29 NA PRO 30/57/37 and PRO 30/57/32/16, Kitchener Papers, Prince of Wales to Kitchener, 11 June 1906; Brodrick to Kitchener 30 August 1906
30 NA PRO 30/57/31/24, Kitchener Papers, Kitchener,' Memorandum to the British troops concerning venereal disease', October 1905
31 NA PRO 30/57/31/7, Kitchener Papers, Duchess of Portland to Kitchener, 11 January 1903
32 NA PRO 30/57/29/44 Kitchener Papers, Kitchener to Roberts, 7 July 1907
33 William Birdwood, *Reminiscences of the Residences of the Commanders-in-Chief in India*, Simla, 1930, 5–11
34 E.J. Buck, *Simla Past and Present*, Bombay, 1925, 255
35 Ibid, 234
36 Birdwood, *Reminiscences*, 18–19
37 NA PRO 30/57/108, Kitchener Papers, Slatin to Kitchener, 7 May 1912
38 Magnus, *Kitchener*, 229

Chapter 9

1 Wolpert, *Morley and India*, 77
2 Ibid, 86
3 Maurice, *Rawlinson*, 95–95
4 NA PRO 30/57/104, Kitchener Papers, King Edward VII to Kitchener, 1 August 1909
5 C.E. Callwell, ed., *The Autobiography of General Sir O'Moore Creagh*, London, 1924, 26
6 Cyril Pearl, *Morrison of Peking*, London, 1967, 200
7 Gilbert, *Rumbold*, 79
8 Ibid, 80
9 Kevin Fewster, ed., *Gallipoli Correspondent: The Frontline Diary of C.E.W. Bean*, London, 1983, 176–179
10 *Otago Daily Times*, 17 February 1910
11 NA PRO 30/57/39, Kitchener Papers, Kitchener to Sir Joseph Ward, 2 March 1910
12 Ibid, Kitchener's address to the Freemasons of New South Wales, March 1910
13 *New York Herald*, 20 April 1919

14 Esher, *Journals*, III, 3
15 Esher, *Tragedy of Lord Kitchener*, 26
16 Susan Mary Alsop, *Lady Sackville: A Biography*, London, 1978, 186–187
17 Victoria Glendinning, *Vita: The Life of Vita Sackville-West*, London, 1983, 69
18 *Country Life*, 11 November 1939, vol. LXXXVII, no. 2234, 498
19 NA PRO 30/57/106, Kitchener Papers, Lady Desborough to Kitchener, undated. June 1910
20 *The Times*, 17 July 1910
21 Mosley, *With Kitchener in Cairo*, 52
22 Ibid, 24
23 *The Times*, 21 July 1910
24 P.G. Elgood, *The Transit of Egypt*, London, 1928, 200
25 Storrs, *Orientations*, 122
26 *Glasgow Herald*, 9 July 1914
27 Winstone, *Diaries of Parker Pasha*, chapter 2
28 Storrs, *Orientations*, 177

Chapter 10

1 Hansard, Statement by Sir Edward Grey, HC Deb 03 August 1914 vol 65 cc1809–32
2 Storrs, *Orientations*, 146
3 NA PRO 30/57/76, Kitchener Papers, Asquith to Kitchener, 3 August 1914
4 An incident in March 1914 in which the commanding officers of the 3rd Cavalry Brigade, stationed at the Curragh, near Dublin, opted for resignation rather than be coerced to use force against the Ulster unionists. The Secretary of State for War, J.E.B. Seely, and the Chief of the Imperial General Staff, Sir John French, indicated that the officers would not be required to serve against the north. The Cabinet disagreed and Seely and French were forced to resign
5 J.A. Spender, *Life, Journalism and Politics*, London, 1927, II, 63
6 Simkin, *Kitchener's Army*, 35
7 Cassar, *Kitchener*, 170–177
8 Asquith, *Memories and Reflections*, II, 24
9 *The Times*, 5 August 1914
10 Brock, *Asquith Letters to Venetia Stanley*, 157
11 George Coppard, *With a Machine Gun to Cambrai*, London, 1969, 1
12 Simkins, *Kitchener's Army*, 39–40
13 Hansard, Secretary of State for War HL Deb 25 August 1914 vol 17 cc501–4
14 Simkin, *Kitchener's Army*, 24
15 Speech by Sir Stanley von Donop to the Kitchener Scholars Association, 5 December 1930
16 Ballard, *Kitchener*, 174–175
17 NA WO 106/50

NOTES

18 Edmonds, *Official History 1914*, I, 11
19 *Manchester Guardian*, 2 December 1907
20 Hansard, Secretary of State for War HL Deb 17 September 1914, vol 17 cc735–40
21 Brock, *Asquith Letters to Venetia Stanley*, 168
22 Haldane, *Autobiography*, 297
23 MacDonagh, *London during the Great War*, 51
24 Hansard, 'The Times and the Press Censor' HC Deb 31 August 1914 vol 66 cc454–511
25 Ernest Dunlop Swinton (1868–1951) worked at the War Office as Assistant Secretary to the War Council. Later in the war he became a proponent of the use of tanks, raising the Heavy Section (Tank) Machine Gun Corps in 1916. He was knighted in 1923 and retired from the army to become Chichele Professor of Military History at Oxford. Under the pseudonym of 'Ole Luk-Oie' he wrote stories of military adventure and prophecy, which were published under the title, *The Green Curve*
26 Howard Green, 'Kitchener's Army', *Army Quarterly*, April 1966. Vol. LXXXXII, no. 1, 88
27 Quoted in Alan Ereira, *The People's England*, London, 1981, 88–89
28 Riddell, *War Diary*, 50–52
29 Coppard, *With a Machine Gun*, 10
30 Callwell, *Wilson*, I, 178
31 Ibid, 159
32 Brock, *Asquith Letters to Venetia Stanley*, 306
33 Denis Gwynn, *The Life of John Redmond*, London, 1932, 366
34 *The Times*, 26 September 1914
35 NLI 15.201, Redmond Papers, Creedy to Redmond, 6 October 1915
36 NLI 15.261, Redmond Papers Memorandum by Redmond to Kitchener, 9 August 1915
37 Ibid, Memorandum by John Redmond after meeting with Kitchener at the War Office, 29 September 1915
38 Howard Green, 'Kitchener's Army', *Army Quarterly*, April 1966. Vol. LXXXXII, no. 1, 93
39 NA NATS 1/85 Monthly Recruiting Figures, September 1914–February 1915
40 *Punch*, 14 June 1916; *The Times*, 7 June 1916
41 Arthur, *Life of Kitchener*, III, 7
42 Esher, *Tragedy of Lord Kitchener*, 150; Hankey, *Supreme Command*, I, 221

Chapter 11

1 Hansard, Secretary of State for War, HL Deb, 17 September 1915 vol 17 cc735–40
2 Arthur, *Life of Lord Kitchener*, III, 74
3 Ibid, 256, note 1
4 Robertson, *Soldiers and Statesmen*, I, 41

5   Crow, *Man of Push and Go*, 71
6   Riddell, *War Diary*, 35–36
7   NA MUN 5/177/1200/21, Munitions Production, December 1914
8   Dewar, *Great Munitions Feat*, 126–127
9   NA MUN 5/62/322/8 Papers on Munitions Work Badges
10 Iain Mclean, *The Legend of Red Clydeside*, Edinburgh, 1999 (rev. ed.), xi–xxviii
11 Le Bas, *Kitchener Memorial Book*
12 Taylor, *Frances Stevenson Diary*, 7
13 NA PRO 30/57/82, Kitchener Papers, Kitchener to Asquith, undated (late September 1914)
14 NA WO 159/15 Major-General F.V. Wing to von Donop, 17 November 1914
15 Lloyd George, *War Memoirs*, I, 158
16 NA PRO 30/57/82, Kitchener Papers, Asquith to Kitchener, 8 April 1915
17 Riddell, *War Diary*, chapter III
18 Crow, *Man of Push and Go*, 111
19 See Lloyd George *War Memoirs* and the diaries of Frances Stevenson and A.J. Sylvester
20 Holmes, *Little Field Marshal*, 279
21 Ferris, *House of Northcliffe*, 197
22 *The Times*, 14 May 1915
23 NA WO 159/21, Note by the Secretary of State for War concerning the period August 1914–31 May 1915
24 *The Times*, 19 May 1915
25 *The Times*, 24 May 1915
26 NA PRO 30/57/59, Kitchener Papers, Esher to Kitchener, 19 May 1915
27 NA PRO 30/57/53, Kitchener Papers, Haig to FitzGerald, 24 May 1915
28 NA PRO 30/57/50 Kitchener Papers, Kitchener to French and French to Kitchener
29 Ibid
30 NA PRO 30/57/93, Kitchener Papers, Arthur Correspondence
31 NA PRO 30/57/106 Kitchener Papers, Margot Asquith to Kitchener, 18 August 1915
32 Churchill, *World Crisis*, II, 10
33 NA WO 159/21, Note by Secretary of State for War … 31 May 1915
34 Cross, *Life with Lloyd George*, 85
35 Crow, *Man of Push and Go*, 137–138
36 NA MUN 5/183/1300/130 Papers on Ammunition Output, June 1916

Chapter 12

1 NA PRO 30/57/50, Kitchener Papers, Kitchener to French, 2 January 1915
2 Roskill, *Hankey*, I, 172
3 Brock, *Asquith Letters*, 169

NOTES

4 NA CAB 3/2/1/44A 'Report of a Sub-committee appointed by the Prime Minister to reconsider the question of Oversea attack', 22 October 1908
5 NA PRO 30/57/77, Kitchener Papers, Grey to Kitchener, 21 October 1914
6 Brock, *Asquith Letters*, 281
7 NA PRO 30/57/51, Kitchener Papers, Rawlinson to Kitchener 25 November 1914
8 Edmonds, *Official History*, I, 444–445
9 NA PRO 30/57/49, Kitchener Papers, French to Kitchener, 14 November 1914
10 The exchange is contained NA PRO 30/57/49 and 50, Kitchener Papers
11 Ibid
12 NA FO 800/106 Kitchener to Grey, 1 September 1914
13 NA PRO 30/57/49, Kitchener Papers, French to Kitchener 13 October 1914
14 Holmes, *Little Field Marshal*, 254
15 French, *1914*, 332
16 NA FO 371/2095/55811 Kitchener to Grey for transmission to Buchanan, 4 October 1914
17 NA PRO 30/57/67, Kitchener Papers, Hanbury-Williams to Kitchener, 20 December 1914
18 NA WO 159/3 David Lloyd George 'Suggestions as to the Military Position', January 1915
19 NA CAB 22/1 Meeting of the War Council, 8 January 1915
20 NA PRO 30/57/50 Kitchener Papers, French to Kitchener, 3 January 1915
21 NA WO 106/1523, 'The Question of Engaging Forces Elsewhere than in the Western Theatre of war', 28 January 1915
22 NA CAB 42/1/42 Meeting of the War Council, 24 February 1915
23 Ibid
24 Hamilton, *Gallipoli Diary*, I, 2
25 The official account is C.F. Aspinall-Oglander, *Military Operations, Gallipoli*, 2 vols, London, 1929
26 NA CAB 19/31, Hamilton to Kitchener, 8 May 1915
27 NA PRO 30/57/67 Kitchener Papers, Kitchener to Hanbury-Williams, 12 May 1915
28 Ibid, 3 June 1915
29 Ibid, 21 June 1915
30 NA CAB 42/2/19, Meeting of the War Council, 14 May 1915
31 NA WO 159/7 Kitchener to Asquith, 17 August 1915
32 NA CAB 42/3/16, Meeting of Dardanelles Committee, 20 August 1915
33 NA WO 159/11, French to Kitchener, 6 July 1915

Chapter 13

1 NA WO 159/4 Kitchener to Colonel Phillips, 25 September 1915
2 Roskill, *Hankey*, I, 222

3 Arthur, *Life of Kitchener*, III, 185
4 Lloyd George, *War Memoirs*, I, 446
5 NA CAB 22/2, Cabinet Papers, Minutes, 9 October 1915
6 NA WO 159/4 Kitchener, Memorandum, 13 October 1915
7 Robertson, *Soldiers and Statesmen*, II, 97–99
8 NA PRO 30/57/91, Kitchener Papers, Birdwood to Arthur, 5 September 1916
9 NA PRO 30/57/76, Kitchener Papers, Asquith to Kitchener, 17 October 1915
10 NA PRO 30/57/106, Kitchener Papers, Margot Asquith to Kitchener, 18 August 1915
11 Taylor, *Stevenson Diary*, 72
12 Lloyd George, *War Memoirs*, I, 446–447
13 William Birdwood, 'Lord Kitchener at Gallipoli', Le Bas, *Kitchener Memorial Book*
14 Birdwood, *Khaki and Gown*, 280
15 NA PRO 30/57/66, Kitchener Papers, Kitchener to Asquith, 15 November 1915
16 NA CAB 22/3, Kitchener to Asquith, 22 November 1915
17 Roskill, *Hankey*, 237
18 NA PRO 30/57/67, Kitchener Papers, Hanbury-Williams to Kitchener, 10 December 1915
19 NA CAB 42/5.25 'The Future Military Policy at the Dardanelles', 29 November 1915
20 Robertson, *Soldiers and Statesmen*, I, 164
21 NA PRO 30/57/55, Kitchener Papers, Robertson to Kitchener, 5 December 1915
22 NA PRO 30/57/53 Kitchener Papers, Kitchener to Haig, 22 December 1915
23 Esher, *Tragedy of Lord Kitchener*, 189
24 NA PRO 30/57/53 Kitchener Papers, Kitchener to Haig, 22 December 1915
25 Churchill, *Lord Derby*, 209–210
26 Rodd, *Social and Diplomatic Memories*, 280
27 NA PRO 30/57/108 Kitchener Papers, Lady Desborough to Kitchener, 9 August 1915
28 Marquis de Chasseloup Laubat, 'Lord Kitchener as I knew Him', Le Bas, *Kitchener Memorial Book*
29 Hansard, Earl of Derby HL Deb 20 June 1916 vol 22 cc315–22
30 NA PRO 30/57/53, Kitchener Papers, Kitchener to Haig, 12 February 1916
31 Robertson, *Soldiers and Statesmen*, I, 255
32 NA PRO 30/57/67, Kitchener Papers, Hanbury-Williams to Kitchener, 28 February 1916

Chapter 14

1 Knox, *With the Russian Army*, II, 419
2 NA PRO 30/57/67, Kitchener Papers, Hanbury-Williams to Kitchener, 12 May 1916
3 NA PRO 30/57/85, Kitchener Papers, Kitchener to M. Sagaroff, 15 May 1916

NOTES

4. NA PRO 30/57/67, Kitchener Papers, Hanbury-Williams to Kitchener, 18 October 1914
5. Knox, *With the Russian Army*, II, 420
6. NA PRO 30/57/67, Kitchener Papers, Kitchener to Hanbury-Williams, 27 May 1916
7. Rodd, *Social and Diplomatic Memories*, III, 280
8. Arthur, *Life of Kitchener*, III, 327
9. NLS Acc 3155, Box 106, Haig Papers, Wigram to Haig, 4 June 1916
10. Arthur, *Life of Kitchener*, III, 353
11. Author's interview with Mr Fredrick Lot Sims, 13 February 1984. Subsequent quotations are from the same source.
12. Information about all ships listed from F.T. Jane, ed., *Fighting Ships*, London, 1905–1906
13. NA ADM 137/1992, 'Hampshire's Sailing Instructions', Iron Duke to Hampshire, 4 June 1916
14. BL Add MS 49031, Jellicoe Papers. Vol. XLIII (ff. 88) Jellicoe to Admiralty, 22 July 1916
15. Professor Alexander McAdie, 'Fate and a Forecast', *Harvard Graduate Magazine*, September 1923, 46
16. NA ADM 137/4069 Bruges to All Ships, 'Intercepted German Messages broadcast by W/T stations Nordeich, Wassen, Bruges etc relating to movements of British and Allied naval and merchant ships', n. 76, 30 May 1916
17. NA ADM 137/4105 Submarine Reports: Home Waters, 'Reports on Enemy Submarine Activity received in NID', 4 May–July 1916
18. Marder, *Dreadnought to Scapa Flow*, III, 148–154
19. Earlier reports gave *U-75*'s return as 3 June 1916 but this was corrected to 11 June 1916 in 'Original History Sheets of U-type German Submarines U-41–U-80', NA ADM 137/3913
20. NA ADM 137/4105, 'Submarine Reports' 1 June 1916
21. Ibid, 5 June 1916
22. Phillips, *Loss of HMS Hampshire*, 30
23. NA ADM 137/3621, Wesson's evidence, 'Court of Enquiry: Sinking of HMS Hampshire, Loss of Earl Kitchener of Khartoum'
24. *Orkney Herald*, 21 June 1916
25. Evidence of James Gaudie of Nether Skaill, Marwick, Orkney Sound Archive, OSA1, 'World War One', interview by Eric Marwick, Orkney Public Library, Kirkwall
26. Ibid, Evidence of Joe Angus, Stromness
27. NA ADM 53/ 66480 Log for HMS Unity, June 1916; NA ADM 53/67364, Log for HMS Victor, June 1916
28. Marder, *Dreadnought to Scapa Flow*, III, 192
29. All those points were made in a letter to *The Orcadian*, 25 August 1983
30. NA ADM 137/3904, Chief Censor, Admiralty, intercepted 20 June 1916, 'Papers concerning German Submarines U-60–U-90'

31 'Kitchener auf der Reise nach Russland ertrunken' *Leipziger Neuste Nachrichten*, nr. 7, 7 June 1916
32 Walter Nicolai, *Nachrichtendienst, Presse und Volkstimmung im Weltkrieg*, Berlin, 1920
33 Kurt Koszyk, *Deutsche Pressepolitik im Ersten Weltkrieg*, Dusseldorf, 1968, 200–206

Chapter 15

1 NA ADM 137/3261, Court of Enquiry: Sinking of HMS Hampshire, Loss of Earl Kitchener of Khartoum
2 Ibid, Jellicoe to Admiralty, 8 June 1916
3 NA ADM 137/1992, Grand Fleet Intelligence, vol. xxi, 18.1A and 18.11
4 NA ADM 1/8470/238, Precis of Enquiry
5 *The Times*, 10 February 1926
6 Arthur, *Life of Kitchener*, III, 354
7 NA ADM 53/43705, Copy of Log of HMS Hampshire, February 1916
8 *Daily Telegraph*, 10 August 1983
9 Letter to author from John R. Breckenridge, 7 September 1984
10 McCormick, *Mystery of Kitchener's Death*, 132–140
11 Great Britain, *The Loss of HMS Hampshire*, HMSO, 1926, 13–14
12 *The Times*, 10 August 1926
13 BL 1916–1926, Jellicoe Papers, vol. XLIII (ff. 88). Jellicoe to Bridgeman, 26 February 1926
14 NA ADM 137/3913, Original History Sheets of U Type German Submarines U-41–U-80
15 NA ADM 137/3261, Court of Enquiry: Sinking of HMS Hampshire, Loss of Earl Kitchener of Khartoum; Brock to Jellicoe, 12 June 1916
16 Obituary, *Daily Telegraph*, 23 December 2011
17 *London Gazette*, 23 May 2012, 9975
18 'A great British hero, rumours that he was gay – and conspiracy theories galore' Jeremy Paxman, *Daily Mail*, 15 November 2014
19 Esher, *Tragedy of Lord Kitchener*, 217
20 Magnus, *Kitchener*, 10

BIBLIOGRAPHY

Official Papers and Records

National Archives, Kew, Public Record Office (NA)

ADM 137 Admiralty: Historical Section: Records used for Official History, First World War
ADM 53 Admiralty, and Ministry of Defence, Navy Department: Ships' Logs
CAB 2–4 Committee of Imperial Defence and Standing Defence Sub-committee
CAB 19 Special Commissions to Enquire into the Operations of War in Mesopotamia (Hamilton Commission) and in the Dardanelles (Cromer and Pickford Commission): Records
CAB 22 War Council and successors: Minutes and Papers
FO 371 Foreign Office: Political Departments: General Correspondence 1906–1966
MUN 5 Ministry of Munitions, Munitions Council: Historical Records Branch
NATS 1 Ministry of National Service Records
PRO 30/57: Horatio Herbert Kitchener, 1st Earl Kitchener of Khartoum Papers
WO 106 War Office: Directorate of Military Operations and Military Intelligence, and predecessors: Correspondence and Papers
WO 159 War Office, Field Marshal Lord Kitchener, Secretary of State for War, Private Office Papers, 1914–1916; also known as Creedy Papers

National Army Museum (NAM)

Rawlinson Papers
Roberts Papers

National Library of Ireland (NLI)

Acc1154 and 2897 Redmond Papers

National Library of Scotland (NLS)

Acc. 3155 Haig Papers
Acc. 4736 Blackwood Papers
Acc. 10306 Haldane Papers

British Library (BL)

Add Ms 49031 Jellicoe Papers

Palestine Exploration Fund Archives, London (PEF)

www.pef.org.uk

Kitchener's letters to his sister Millie are in the possession of the family and have not been cited.

Newspapers and journals

Blackwood's Magazine
Daily Mail
Daily Telegraph
Glasgow Herald
Irish Times
Manchester Guardian
The Orcadian
Palestine Exploration Fund Quarterly Statements
Pall Mall Gazette
The Scotsman
The Times
Westminster Gazette

Secondary Sources

Alsop, Susan Mary, *Lady Sackville*, London, 1978
Arthur, Sir George, *General Sir John Maxwell*, London, 1932; *Not Worth Reading*, London, 1938
Asquith, H.H., *Memories and Reflections, 1852–1927*, vol. II: London, 1928
Asquith, Margot, *More Memories*, London, 1933
Birdwood, Field Marshal Lord, *Khaki and Gown: An Autobiography*, London, 1942
Blunt, W.S., *My Diaries*, London, 1919
Bonham-Carter, Mark, ed., *The Autobiography of Margot Asquith*, London, 1962
Bonham-Carter, Victor, *Soldier True: The Life and Times of Field-Marshal Sir William Robertson*, London, 1963
Brock, Michael and Eleanor, eds, *H.H. Asquith: Letters to Venetia Stanley*, London, 1982
Callwell, Sir C.E., *Experiences of a Dug-out, 1914–1918*, London, 1920; *Stray Recollections*, vol. II: London, 1923

BIBLIOGRAPHY

Churchill, Randolph, *Lord Derby: King of Lancashire*, London, 1959
Cross, Colin, ed., *Life with Lloyd George: The Diary of A.J. Sylvester*, London, 1975
Esher, Reginald Viscount, *Journals and Letters*, vols. I–IV: London, 1934–1938
Ferris, Paul, *The House of Northcliffe: The Harmsworths of Fleet Street*, London, 1971
Fisher, John, *That Miss Hobhouse*, London, 1971
French, The Hon. Gerald, *The Life of Field Marshal Sir John French*, London, 1931; *The Kitchener–French Dispute: A Last Word*, Glasgow, 1960
French, Field Marshal Sir John, *1914*: London, 1919
Gatacre, Beatrix, *The Story of the Life and Services of Sir W.F. Gatacre*, London, 1910
Gilbert, Martin, *Sir Horace Rumbold: Portrait of a Diplomat*, London, 1973; *Winston S. Churchill*, vols III and IV, Oxford 1971 and 1975
Grey of Falloden, Viscount, *Twenty-Five Years*, vol. II, London, 1929
Haldane, R.B., *An Autobiography*, London, 1929
Hamilton, Sir Ian, *The Commander: A Study of his Art*, London, 1957
Hamilton, Sir Ian B., *The Happy Warrior: The Life of General Sir Ian Hamilton*, London, 1966
Hankey, Lord, *The Supreme Command, 1914–1918*, vols. I–II, London, 1961
Holmes, Richard, *The Little Field Marshal: Sir John French*, London, 1981
James, David, *Lord Roberts*, London, 1954
James, Robert Rhodes, *Churchill: A Study in Failure, 1900–39*, London, 1970
Mallet, Victor, ed., *Life with Queen Victoria: Marie Mallet's Letters from Court, 1887–1901*, London, 1968
Masters, Antony, *Nancy Astor: A Life*, London, 1981
Maurice, Frederick, *The Life of Lord Rawlinson of Trent*, London, 1928
Maxwell, Charlotte, *Frank Maxwell, VC*, London, 1921
Mead, Gary, *The Good Soldier: The Biography of Douglas Haig*, London, 2007
Midleton, Earl of, *Records and Reactions, 1859–1939*, London, 1939
Rennell Rodd, Sir J., *Social and Diplomatic Memories, 1902–1919*, vol. III, London, 1925
Repington, C. a' Court, *Vestigia*, London, 1919
Richardson, Frank, *Mars without Venus: A Study of Some Homosexual Generals*, Edinburgh, 1981
Riddell, Lord, *War Diary*, London, 1933
Robertson, Sir William, *From Private to Field Marshal*, London, 1921; *Soldiers and Statesmen, 1914–1918*, vols I–II, London, 1926
Roskill, Stephen, *Hankey: Man of Secrets*, vol. I, London, 1970
Royle, Trevor, *Death Before Dishonour: The True Story of Fighting Mac*, Edinburgh, 1982
Scudamore, Frank, *A Sheaf of Memories*, London, 1925
Smith, Janet Adam, *John Buchan*, London, 1965
Smith-Dorrien, Sir Horace, *Memories of Forty-Eight Years' Service*, London, 1925
Spiers, E.M., *Haldane: An Army Reformer*, Edinburgh, 1980
Storrs, Sir Ronald, *Orientations*, London, 1937
Taylor, A.J.P., ed., *Frances Stevenson, Lloyd George: A Diary*, London, 1971
Terraine, John, *Douglas Haig: The Educated Soldier*, London, 1963

Kitchener Biographies and Books about Kitchener

Arthur, Sir George, *Life of Lord Kitchener*, vols. I–III, London, 1920
Ballard, C.R., *Kitchener*, London, 1930
Begbie, Harold, *Kitchener: Organiser of Victory*, New York, 1915
Cassar, G.H., *Kitchener: Architect of Victory*, London, 1977
De Watteville, H., *Lord Kitchener*, London, 1939
Esher, Reginald Viscount, *The Tragedy of Lord Kitchener*, London, 1921
Germains, V.W., *The Truth about Kitchener*, London, 1925
Grew, E.S., *Field Marshal Lord Kitchener: His Life and Work for the Empire*, vols. I–III, London, 1916
Groser, H.G., *Lord Kitchener: The Story of his Life*, London, 1916
Hodges, Arthur, *Lord Kitchener*, London, 1936
Le Bas, Sir Hedley, ed., *The Kitchener Memorial Book*, London, 1917
McCormick, Donald, *The Mystery of Lord Kitchener's Death*, London, 1959
Mackenzie, Donald A., *Lord Kitchener: The Story of His Life and Work*, London, 1916
Magnus, Sir Philip, *Kitchener: Portrait of an Imperialist*, London, 1958
Phillips, W.C., *The Loss of HMS Hampshire and the Death of Lord Kitchener*, London, 1930
Pollock, John, *Kitchener: The Road to Omudurman and the Saviour of the Nation*, London, 2001
Power, Frank, *The Kitchener Mystery*, London, 1926
Royle, Trevor, *The Kitchener Enigma*, London, 1985
Rye, James and Groser, H.G., *Kitchener in his own words*, New York, 1917
Warner, Philip, *Kitchener*, London, 1985
Wheeler, Harold F.G., *The Story of Lord Kitchener*, London, Harrap, 1916

Palestine

Conder, C.R., *Tent Work in Palestine*, vols. I–II, London, Palestine Exploration Fund, 1878
Daiches, Dr Samuel, *Lord Kitchener and His Work in Palestine*, London, 1915
Oliphant, Laurence, *The Land of Gilead: With Excursions in the Lebanon*, Edinburgh and London, 1880

Egypt

Blunt, W.S., *The Secret History of the English Occupation of Egypt*, London, 1907
Cecil, Lord Edward, *The Leisure of an Egyptian Official*, London, 1938
Cromer, Earl of, *Modern Egypt*, vols. I–II, London, 1908
Elgood. P.G., *The Transit of Egypt*, London, 1928
Gleichen, Count, *With the Camel Corps up the Nile*, London, 1888
Haggard, Andrew, *Under Crescent and Star*, Edinburgh and London, 1896
Lloyd, Lord, *Egypt since Cromer*, vol. I, London, 1933
Marlowe, John, *Cromer in Egypt*, London, 1970
Milner, Alfred, *England in Egypt*, London, 1892

Moseley, Sydney A., *With Kitchener in Cairo*, London, 1960
Newman, E.W. Polson, *Great Britain in Egypt*, London, 1928
Tulloch, Sir A.B., *Recollections of Forty Years' Service*, Edinburgh and London, 1903
Zetland, Marquis of, *Lord Cromer*, London, 1932

Sudan

Alford, H.S. and Sword, W.D., *The Egyptian Sudan: Its Loss and Recovery*, London 1898
Bennett, E.N., *The Downfall of the Dervishes*, London, 1898
Burleigh, Bennett, *Khartoum Campaign, 1898*, London, 1899
Chenevix–Trench, Charles, *Charley Gordon: An Eminent Victorian Re-assessed*, London, 1970
Churchill, Winston S., *The River War*, vols. I–II, London, 1899; *My Early Life*, London, 1930
Hake, A. Egmont, *The Journals of Major-General C. G. Gordon at Khartoum*, London 1885
Sandes, Lt-Col E.W.C., *The Royal Engineers in Egypt and the Sudan*, Chatham, 1937
Spiers, Edward M., ed., *Sudan: The Reconquest Reappraised*, London 1998
Steevens, G.W., *With Kitchener to Khartoum*, Edinburgh and London, 1989
Symons, Julian, *England's Pride: The Story of the Gordon Relief Expedition*, London, 1965
Watkins, Owen S., *With Kitchener's Army*, London, 1899
Warner, Philip, *Dervish: The Rise and Fall of an African Empire*, London, 1975
Wilson, Sir Charles W., *From Korti to Khartoum*, Edinburgh and London, 1886
Wingate, Reginald, *Mahdism and the Egyptian Sudan*, London, 1896
Wingate, Ronald, *Wingate of the Sudan*, London, 1955
Winstone, H.V.F., ed., *The Diaries of Parker Pasha*, London, 1983
Wright, Patricia, *Conflict on the Nile: The Fashoda Incident of 1898*, London, 1972
Ziegler, Philip, *Omdurman*: London, 1972
Zulfo, Ismat Hazan, *Karari*: London, 1980

South Africa and Boer War

Amery, L.S. ed., *The Times History of the War in South Africa, 1899–1902*, vols. I–VI: London, 1905–1909
Doyle, Arthur Conan, *The Great Boer War,* London, 1900
Farwell, Byron, *The Great Boer War*, London, 1977
Gooch, John, ed., *The Boer War: Direction, Experience and Image*, London, 2000
Headlam, Cecil, ed., *The Milner Papers*, vol. II, London, 1931
Judd, Denis and Surridge, Keith, *The Boer War*, London,
Kruger, Rayne, *Goodbye Dolly Gray*, London, Cassell, 1959
Maurice, F. M. and Grant, M. H., *Official History of the War in South Africa*, 4 vols, London, 1906–1910
Pakenham, Thomas, *The Boer War*, London, 1979

India

Dilks, David, *Curzon in India*, vols. I–III, London, 1969–70
Edwardes, Michael, *High Noon of Empire: India under Curzon,* London, 1965

King, Peter, *The Viceroy's Fall: How Kitchener destroyed Curzon*, London, 1986
Nicolson, Nigel, *Mary Curzon*, London, 1979
Ronaldshay, Lord, *The Life of Lord Curzon*, vol. II, London, 1929
Wolpert, Stanley, *Morley and India*, Berkeley, 1967
Zetland, Marquis of, *The Life of Lord Curzon*, vols. I–III, London, 1928

First World War

Adams, R.J.Q., *Arms and the Wizard: Lloyd George and Munitions*, London, 1974
Carlyon, L.A., *Gallipoli*, London, 2001
Cassar, G.H., *The French and the Dardanelles: A Study of Failure in the Conduct of War*, London, 1971; *Kitchener's War: British Strategy from 1914 to 1916*, Dulles, 2004
Dewar, G.A.B., *The Great Munitions Feat*, London, 1921
Edmonds, James E., General Editor, *History of the Great War, Based on Official Documents: Military Operations, France and Belgium*, 14 vols, London, 1922–1949
Fewster, Kevin, ed., *Gallipoli Correspondent: The Frontline Diary of C.E.W. Bean*, London, 1983
French, David, *British Economic and Strategic Planning, 1905–1915*, London, 1982
Germains, V.W., *The Kitchener Armies*, London, 1930
Gibson, R.H. and Prendergast, M., *The German Submarine War*, London, 1931
Gooch, John, *The Plans of War: The General Staff and British Military Strategy, 1900–1916*, London, 1974
Grant, R.M., *U-Boat Intelligence 1914–18*, London, 1969
Green, H., *The British Army in the First World War*, London, 1968
Guinn, Paul, *British Strategy and Politics, 1914 to 1918*, London, 1965
Holmes, Richard, *Tommy: The British Soldier on the Western Front*, London, 2004
James, Robert Rhodes, *Gallipoli*, London, 1965
James, Sir William, *The Eyes of the Navy: Biographical Study of Admiral Sir Reginald Hall*, London, 1955
Jellicoe, Viscount, *The Grand Fleet, 1914–1916*, London, 1916
Knox, A.F.W., *With the Russian Army*, vols. I–II, London, 1921
Liddell-Hart, B.H., *History of the First World War*, London, 1970 (rev. ed.)
Lloyd George, David, *War Memories*, vols. I–IV, London, 1933–36
MacDonagh, Michael, *In London During the Great War*, London, 1935
Mackay, Ruddock F., *Fisher of Kilverstone*, London, 1973
Marder, A.J., *From the Dreadnought to Scapa Flow*, vols. I–II, London, 1961, 1965
Marshall-Cornwallis, Sir James, *Haig as Military Commander*, London, 1973
Marwick, Arthur, *The Deluge: British Society and the First World War*, London, 1965
Maurice, Sir Frederick, *British Strategy*, London, 1929
Moorehead, Alan, *Gallipoli*, London, 1956
Messenger, Charles, *Call To Arms: The British Army 1914–18*, London, 2005
Neilson, Keith, *Strategy and Supply: Anglo-Russian Alliance 1914–1917*, London, 1984; *Britain and the Last Tsar: British Policy and Russia 1894–1917*, London, 1995
Nevakiki, Jukka, *Britain, France and the Arab Middle East, 1914–1920*, London, 1969

BIBLIOGRAPHY

Prior, Robin, *Gallipoli: The End of the Myth*, London, 2009
Repington, C. a' Court, *The First World War, 1914–1918*, London, 1921
Simkins, Peter, *Kitchener's Army: The Raising of the New Armies 1914–1916*, Manchester, 1988
Sheffield, Gary and Bourne, John, eds, *Douglas Haig: War Diaries and Letters 1914–1918*, London, 2005
Stevenson, David, *1914–1918: The History of the First World War*, London, 2004
Strachan, Hew, *The First World War*, vol I, Oxford, 2001
Swinton, Sir Ernest D., *Eye-witness*, London, 1932
Terraine, John, *Impacts of War*, London, 1970
Wallace, Edgar, *Kitchener's Armies and the Territorial Forces*, London, 1915

INDEX

Abbas, steamer, 61
Abbas Hilmi II, Khedive, 93, 94, 98, 217, 218, 300
Abdullah Ibn Husain, 225, 300
Abu Hamed, 97, 105, 106, 113
Abu Klea, 67
Adowa, 97
Afghanistan, 44, 140, 188
Alcester, Lord, 55
Aldershot, 33, 40, 146, 156
Alexandra, Queen, 376
Alexandretta, 299, 322
Alexandria, 35, 36, 52, 141, 217, 221, 225, 378
American Civil War, 51, 232, 234
Amery, L.S., 154, 157
Amiens, 242, 287, 288
Anatolia, 45–47, 61
Angus, Joe, 357–358
Antwerp, 292–293
Anzac forces, 209, 300, 305, 317, 321, 344
Arabi, Colonel, 51–52
Ari Burnu, 305
Armaments Output Committee, 265, 267
Army Council, 191, 254
Arnold-Foster, H.O., 186
Arras, 269, 286

Arthur, Sir George, 138, 157, 232, 254, 330, 343, 361, 368, 369
Ashanti Wars, 33, 43
Aspall Hall, 16, 22, 132
Asquith, H.H., 12, 201, 211, 229
  and outbreak of war, 229
  appoints Kitchener Secretary of State for War, 229–231
  and the Territorials, 240
  and Irish Home Rule, 247
  and Irish recruitment, 248–250
  and the wartime Cabinet, 254, 281–283
  relations with Kitchener, 255–256
  and security, 279
  and munition supplies, 257–261
  and Lloyd George's conflict with Kitchener, 275
  attitude to Kitchener, 276
  and domestic defence, 285–286
  and Wilson's attack on Kitchener, 287–289
  strategy in Europe, 291
  and Dardanelles campaign, 299–301
  forms a General Staff, 315
  warns Kitchener of intrigue against, 317–319
  sends Kitchener to the Dardanelles, 320

INDEX

reorganises the War Committee, 321
cuts back Kitchener's duties, 324–326
and the Kitchener–Robertson Pact, 328
and the Russian mission, 339
support fo rKitchener, 341–342
deposed, 373
Asquith, Margot, 13, 276, 318
Astor, Nancy, 132
Aswan, 84, 85, 177, 220
Atbara, 82, 110–115, 122, 152, 234
Aubers Ridge, 254, 269, 271–273, 305, 319
Australia, Kitchener visits, 206–209
Austro-Hungarian Empire, 297, 298, 306, 311, 313, 332, 337
Ayah Bay, 322
Azrak, Osman, 118

Baker, Hermione, 56
Baker, Sir Samuel White, 55
Baker, Valentine, 40, 55, 83
Baldwin, Stanley, 371
Balfour, Arthur, Kitchener meets, 137, 176
  takes over from Salisbury, 175
  and the Indian Military Member row, 184–190
  turns against Curzon, 191
  and munition supplies, 265
  on the War Council, 283
  joins new War Committee, 320
Balkans, 312–335
Ballard, General, 237
Ballygoghlan, 17–19, 22
Balmoral, 131, 223
Baring, Maurice, 336
Baring, Sir Evelyn, see Cromer, Lord
Barrow, Maj. Gen. Sir Edmund, 192
Beardmore, 260
Beatty, Lieutenant RN, 103
Beirut, 39, 45
Beitzen, Lt Cmdr Kurt, 351, 362, 374
Belgium, 228, 281, 287, 288, 293, 349
Bennett, Edward, 95, 112, 113, 122, 123

Bennett, Rev., 23
Bennett, Winifred, 270
Benson, Col G.E. 160
Berber, 58–61, 63, 67, 105, 107, 110, 112, 115
Bergendal, 155
Bernhardt, Sarah, 138
Bertie, Sir Francis, 291
Besant, Sir Walter, 34, 35, 38, 41, 57, 59
Biddulph, Maj. Gen. Sir Robert, 46, 47, 52
Birdwood, Lt Gen. Sir William, 137, 180, 181, 196–198, 284, 317, 321, 322
Birrell, Augustine, 251
Birsay, 355–359, 372
Blair, Capt. James, 295
Blake, HMS, 366–367
Bloemfontein, 146, 149–151, 154
Board of Trade, 230, 262, 296
Boer War, 11, 138, 143–174
Booth, George, 265, 280
Bordein, steamer, 63
Botha, Louis, 155, 162–168, 172
Breckenridge, John R., 8, 370
Breslau, 299
Bridgeman, W.C., 369
Brindle, Father, 125
British Expeditionary Force (BEF), mobilisation, 232–234
Broadwood, Col R.G., 114, 147, 156
Brock, Vice-Admiral, 375
Brodrick, St John, 157–159, 161, 162, 168, 176, 186, 188–192, 194
Brooke, Maj. Victor, 180, 201, 330
Broome Park, 11, 212–216, 223, 230. 242, 375–376
Buchan, John, 273
Buchanan, George, 295
Buckingham Palace, 225, 274
Bulgaria, 38, 302, 303, 307, 312, 313, 316
Buller, Gen. Sir Redvers, 43, 66–70, 139–143, 149, 153–157
Burger, Schalk, 165
Burleigh, Bennett, 112

Burnaby, Col Frederick, 65
Byng, Gen. Sir Julian, 156, 321

Cairo, 51, 53–60, 74, 81–86, 89, 96, 108, 215–229, 324
Calcutta, 196
Cambodia, HMS, 358
Cambridge, Field Marshal Duke of, 30–31, 105, 169
Cammell Laird, 260
Campbell-Bannerman, Henry, 173
Campbell, Eleanor, 27, 378
Canterbury, NZ, 209
Cape Helles, 322, 326, 328
Cape Town, 143, 168, 172
Capernaum, 42
Carden, Rear Admiral Sir Sackville, 300–301
Cardwell, Edward, 43
Carson, Sir Edward, 247–248, 252, 314–316
Cator, Lt, 106
Cavan, Lord, 251
Caxton Advertising Agency, 12, 241
Cecil family, 82
Cecil, Lady Edward, 163
Cecil, Lord Edward, 86, 96, 129, 148, 220
Chamberlain, Joseph, 164–167
Chanzy, Gen., 30
Chasseloup Laubat, Marquis de, 235, 331
Château du Grand Clos, 23–24
Chatham, 31–33
Chermside, H.C., 26
Chevallier, Henry Elliott, 16
Chevallier, John, 16
Chevallier, Temple Fiske, 16
Chevallier, Temple, 16
Chilcot family, 27
China, Kitchener visits, 207–208
Churchill, Sir Winston, 12, 264, 289, 309, 331
  and the reconquest of Sudan, 113–114, 122, 229

Gallipoli campaign, 282, 298–301, 308
loses office, 275–276
munition supplies, 277
and domestic defence, 285
and the Kitchener/French conflict, 292, 294
in Antwerp, 293
and Kitchener's death, 365
Lord Alfred Douglas attacks, 370
on Jellicoe, 374
Colenso, 139
Colley, Gen. Sir George, 43
Collis, Maurice, 132
Colvile, Lt Gen. Sir Henry, 147
Colville, Stanley, Lieutenant RN, 103
Committee of Imperial Defence, 188, 205, 215, 283
Conder, Claud Reignier, 25–26, 34–37, 41
Congress of Berlin, 43
Connaught, Duke of, Prince Arthur, 27, 169, 205, 210, 274
Constantine, King, 314, 322, 323
Constantinople, 35, 38–40, 200, 297–298, 301, 329
Coppard, George, 233, 245
Cork, 23, 74
Coventry Ordnance Works, 260
Cowans, Gen. Sir James, 254
Cowper, Lady, 137
Cranborne, Lady Cicely Alice, 137, 140, 147, 154, 158, 162, 176, 183–187
Creagh, Gen, Sir O'Moore, 206
Creedy, Herbert, 232, 250, 343
Crewe, Lord, 320
Crichton-Stuart, Lord Colum, 220
Cromer, 1st Earl of (Sir Evelyn Baring), 92–95, 98–110, 124–129, 134–138, 215–218
  appointed British Agent in Egypt, 53
  on Gordon, 58
  and the relief of Khartoum, 60–62
  and Kitchener at Suakin, 79–82

INDEX

and French incursions into the
  Upper Nile, 127–129
and the reconquest of Sudan, 86, 92,
  95, 97, 104
as autocratic ruler in Egypt, 218
admiration for Kitchener, 86–89
and Kitchener's Governorship of
  Sudan, 133–135
to leave Egypt, 203
garden parties, 223
Cronje, General Piet, 149–152, 154
Cross, Harry, 112
Crotta House, 19, 22, 23
Curzon, Lord George
  background, 178–179
  Kitchener meets, 137
  wants Kitchener as C-in-C in India, 158
  relations with Kitchener, 163–164
  quarrel with Kitchener, 179–193,
    266–267
  and the Military Member row,
    181–184, 190
  army's attitude to, 182–183
  sense of justice, 182
  Kitchener works against, 192–194
  resigns, 192
  leaves India, 193
  First World War, 317–318, 325
Curzon, Lady Mary, 177–178, 186, 193
Cyprus, 43–48
Cyprus Museum, 47

Daiches, Samuel, 42
Dal, gunboat, 129
Dalhousie, Lord, 198
Dardanelles Committee, 308–309,
  313–315
Dartmouth, HMS, 321
Davies, Francis, 321
Dawkins, Clinton Sir, 178
Dawnay, Capt. Guy, 317
Dawson, Geoffrey, 271
De La Rey, Koos, 166

De Robeck, Rear-Admiral Sir John, 301
De Wet, Christian, 150, 152, 153, 155,
  161, 166, 173
Deakin, Alfred, 208
Debbeh, 62, 64
Derby Scheme, 252–253
Derby, Lord, 11, 259, 329
Desborough, Lady (Ettie Grenfell), 214,
  330–331
Desborough, Lord (William Henry
  Grenfell), 73–74
Dessau, 199
Dickinson, Rebecca, 40
Digna, Osman, 57, 76–80, 110
Disraeli, Benjamin, 46, 51
Donaldson, Sir Frederick, 339–340
Dongola, 53, 59–61, 67–71, 102–104
Douglas, Lord Alfred, 370
Du Maurier, Guy, 285
Dublin, 17, 42, 136, 216, 249, 339, 370
Dundee, South Africa, 143
Dunedin, 24, 209
Dunottar Castle, SS, 141–142
Durban, 143

Ed Debba, 61, 104
ed Din, Sheik, 118
Edward VII, King, 183, 203, 205, 211
Egypt, Kitchener with the Egyptian Army,
  50–71
  Kitchener as Inspector-General of
    police in, 85–86
  Kitchener becomes Sirdar, 86
  Britain's total control of, 94
  reconquest of Sudan, 95–121
  and government of the Sudan, 125,
    133
  Kitchener as pro-consul, 215–226
Elgood, P.G., 219
Ellershaw, Brig. Gen. W., 338–340
Elles, Sir Edmund, 182–184, 189–191
Elliott, Mary, 17
Elswick, 285

405

Empress, SS, 130
Encounter, HMS, 208
Esher, Lord, 13, 31, 158, 211, 256, 274–275, 319, 327, 378
Ethiopia, 82, 97, 130

Fashoda incident, 127–130
Feldmarschall, 214
Fellowes, Julian, Lord, 377
Firket, 99–103
Fisher, Admiral Sir John, 272, 283, 301
FitzGerald, Col Oswald, 148, 201, 216, 220, 232, 330, 356, 359
Flying Kestrel, 358–359
Foch, General, 293
France, and Zanzibar Boundary Commission, 74–76
  in east Africa and Congo, 82
  Fashoda Incident, 127–130
  First World War, 286–295, 309–311, 332–334
  and the Balkans, 312–314
Franco-Prussian War, 29–31
Franz Ferdinand, Archduke, 227
Freeman, Arthur Vectis (Frank Power), 370
French, Field Marshal Sir John
  Boer War, 150–156
  outbreak of First World War and length of war, 245
  and use of the New Armies, 245–246
  and the shortage of munitions, 258–259
  Aubers Ridge, 269
  attacks on Kitchener, 270–275
  strategy, 281, 288, 296, 310
  attitude to Kitchener, 291–293
  and the Dardanelles campaign, 309–312
  commands home forces, 330
Frost, George Rev., 24

Galatea, HMS, 352
Gallipoli campaign, 301–326
Gatacre, Maj. Gen. W.F., 108, 110, 114, 143, 145, 147
Gaudie, James, 357
Geddes, Sir Eric, 278
Gedid Wells, 136
George V, King, 199, 214, 223, 274, 325, 367
Germany
  and Zanzibar Boundary Commission, 74–76
  in east Africa, 97
  builds up navy, 175
  First World War, 227–380
Gilinski, Gen., 335
Giret, 290
Gladstone, William Ewart, 39, 50–53, 57–62, 69, 87, 178
Glasgow, 244, 263
Gleichen, Count, 64, 66
Goeben, 299
Gold Coast, 33–34
Gonne, Maud, 252
Gordon, Maj. Gen. Charles George, 57–72, 77, 79, 81–84, 92, 111
Gordon, W.S. 'Monkey', 116
Gorst, Sir Eldon, 134, 203, 215–218, 221, 223
Grant, Lt S.G., 47
Grant, Gen. Ulysses S., 234
Granville, Lord, 52
Greaves, Brig., Gen. George Richard, 32, 43
Greece, 48, 297, 302–303, 312, 322
Grenfell, Francis Wallis, Field Marshal Lord, 71, 77, 79, 83–86, 107–108
Grenfell, Julian, 11, 330
Grey, Sir Edward, 215–218, 221, 228–230, 255, 293, 320
Guest, Capt. Frederick, 270
Gunsborough Villa, 15, 17, 22

INDEX

Haifa, 37, 38
Haig, Doublas, Field Marshal Earl, and the reconquest of Sudan, 114–116
   Boer War, 147, 150
   and the Territorial Force, 239
   and Repington, 270–271
   and attacks on Kitchener, 274
   First World War, 284, 315, 317, 321, 328, 331–333
Haldane, R.B., 204–206, 211–212, 230, 238–240, 264, 275, 286
Hall, Capt. W.R., 349
Hamilton, Lord George, 179
Hamilton, Maj. Gen. Hubert, 180, 330
Hamilton, Gen. Sir Ian
   Boer War, 161–167
   observes the Russo-Japanese War, 194
   invasion defences, 286
   offered as replacement for French, 293
   Gallipoli campaign, 304–317
   and Kitchener's death, 365
Hampshire, HMS, 340, 343–375
Hanbury-Williams, Maj. Gen. John, 295, 306, 307, 310
Handub, 79, 80
Hankey, Sir Maurice, 284, 286, 314–316, 325, 335–340, 325–326
Hannay, Col Ormelie, 150–153
Hardinge, Sir Charles, 211
Harris, Sir Charles, 284
Hartington, Lord, 138
Harvey family, 357
Harvey, Sir Paul, 220
Hatfield House, 82, 131, 137–138, 163, 176–178, 197, 213, 334
Henderson, Arthur, 12, 263
Herbert, Sir Ivor, 341
Hermonius, Gen., 336
Hertzog, Barry, 166
Hicks-Beach, Sir Michael, 105
Hicks, Col William, 53, 56, 57
Hobhouse, Emily, 172

Hood, H. L. A. Lieutenant RN, 103
Howard, Hubert, 113, 123
Huguet, General, 291
Hunter, Gen. Sir Archibald, 90, 106, 110, 112, 126, 156, 245

Indian Army, 178–195
Ireland
   Kitchener's boyhood in, 15–22, 212
   Kitchener works on barracks in Cork, 74
   Home Rule for, 319–320
   recruiting in, 247–252
Irish Volunteers, 248, 249
Iron Duke, HMS, 345–347, 353, 359
Isis, HMS, 141
Ismail Pasha, Khedive, 50
Italy, activities in Ethiopia, 82, 97

Jackson, Admiral, 360
Jakdul, 64, 66
Jameson, Leander, Starr, 141
Japan
   Kitchener visits, 207, 208
Jason II, HMS, 358
Java, Kitchener visits, 208
Jebel Royan, 116
Jell, James, 375, 376
Jellicoe, Admiral Sir John, 340, 345, 347, 349, 351, 353, 360, 367, 370, 373–374
Jerusalem, 35–36
Joffre, Field Marshal, 287–295, 302, 309–312, 316, 331–333
Johannesburg, 154, 160, 168, 171
Joubert, Pieter, 154

Kaileys, Dr, 199
Karmerleh, 39, 40
Kassala, 82, 97, 107
Kastamonu, 45
Kelly-Kenny, Lt. Gen. Thomas, 151–153
Kennedy, Lord John, 47

Kenya, 76, 213–214
Keppel, Colin, Lt RN, 103
Kerma, 102–103
Kerreri, 110, 116–121, 124
Khartoum, Gordon besieged in, 57–66
   recaptured, 124–126
   reconstruction, 135–138
   Kitchener revisits, 177
   memorial to Kitchener, 376
Kilflynn, 19
Kimberley, 143, 149–151, 292
Kimberley, HMS, 352
Kipling, Lockwood, 197
Kipling, Rudyard, 185
Kirbekan, 67
Kirk, Sir John, 75
Kirkwall, 358, 359
Kitchener, Arthur (Kitchener's brother), 16, 23, 92
Kitchener, Hon. Charles, 377
Kitchener, Elizabeth, 15
Kitchener, Emma (Kitchener's stepmother), 24
Kitchener, Emma Joy, 377
Kitchener, Frances Ann 'Fanny' (Kitchener's mother), 16
Kitchener, Frances Emily Jane 'Millie' (Kitchener's sister) *see* Parker, Millie
Kitchener, Francis (Kitchener's cousin), 20, 24
Kitchener Frederick Walter (Kitchener's brother), 16, 23, 24, 85, 91, 99, 136, 148
Kitchener, Henry Elliott Chevallier (Kitchener's brother), 16
Kitchener, Col Henry Horatio (Kitchener's father), 16–21, 24, 29, 33, 38, 41, 92
Kitchener, Horatio Herbert, Field Marshal Earl
   boyhood
      family background, 15–17
      birth, 15
      in Ireland, 17–23
      discipline, 19–20
      education, 20
      estate work, 20
      in Switzerland, 23–24
      and his mother's death, 23
      at military academy, 25–28
   early career
      obtains a commission, 29
      Franco-Prussian War, 29–31
      at School of Military Engineering, 31
      shows promise, 32
      tour of Austria–Hungary, 32–33
      posted to Aldershot, 33
      surveys the Levant, 34–36
      incident at Safed, 37
      first command, 38
      survey of Cyprus, 43–46
      military vice-consul in Kastamonu, 45
      introduced to imperial administration, 46
   with the Egyptian Army
      tries to get post in, 52–53
      posted to Egypt, 53
      leadership, 54
      selects new cavalry uniforms, 54–55
      social life in Cairo, 55, 56
      liking for Cairo, 55
      disliked in, 55
      gathers intelligence about Sudan, 57–62
      love of the desert, 59–60
      contact with Gordon, 60
      and relief of Gordon, 62
      Gordon on, 63
      and death of Gordon, 66
      on the fall of Khartoum, 67–68
      returns home, 71
      and public acclaim, 72–74

INDEX

resentment against, 78, 86–87
reforms Egyptian Army, 88–91
economic measures, 92
Abbas Hilmi criticises, 93–94
in Sudan
   appointed Governor General to Eastern Sudan, 76
   attack on Suakin, 79–82
   wounded, 81–82
   criticism of, 86
   and revenge for Gordon, 81
   battle of Toski, 83–85
   becomes Sirdar, 86
   staff, 89–90
and the reconquest of Sudan
   Kitchener to lead expedition, 97–98
   supplies, 99–100
   builds railway, 100
   attacks Firket, 100
   uses gunboats, 102
   takes Kerma, 103
   advance on Dongola, 103–104
   lack of funds, 104
   seeks support in London, 105
   fears he may lose overall control, 107
   weapons available to, 109
   Atbara engagement, 110–111
   public acclamation, 111
   criticism, of 111–112
   treatment of Mahmud, 112
   and the press corps, 112–113
   captures Omdurman, 95–121
   and treatment of the wounded, 122
   enters Khartoum, 124–125
   destroys the Mahdi's tomb, 126
   and the Mahdi's body, 126–127
   and the appearance of the French at Fashoda, 127–130
   reception back home, 130–132
   appointed Governor General, 133
   reconstruction of Khartoum, 135–137
Boer War
   appointed Roberts's Chief of Staff, 139
   reorganises the transport system, 142–145
   little regard for army in, 142
   staff, 147
   attack on Paardeberg, 151–154
   criticism of, 154, 171–173
   takes over British Army in, 156
   wants end of war, 157–158
   scorched earth methods, 159–160
   sets up internment camps, 159
   use of blockhouses, 161, 168
   and drive policies, 161
   peace negotiations, 162–167
   returns to England, 168–170
C-in-C in India
   seeks appointment as, 136
   leaves for India, 177
   relations with Curzon, 177–192
   quarrel with Curzon, 179–193, 266–267
   and the Military Member, 181–184, 190
   army's reaction to, 182–183
   works behind Curzon's back, 184
   founds a Staff College, 194
   recreation, 197
   reorganises Indian divisions, 195
   achievements in, 194–195
   riding accident, 198–199
   given two-year extension, 199
   loses interest in, 200
   staff, 200–201
   relations with Minto, 202
   wishes to become Viceroy, 203
   leaves India, 206–210
as pro-consul in Egypt
   appointment, 215–218
   relations with the Khedive, 217

Italian–Turkish war, 218–219
staff, 219–220
irrigation and agriculture reforms, 220–223
plots against, 225
liberalisation, 222
regal style in, 223
and power struggle in Ottoman Empire, 224
naval defence of the Mediterranean, 224–225
leaves Egypt, 225

First World War
outbreak of war, 227–230
appointed Secretary of State for War, 231–232
recruitment, 233
and conscription, 235–236
recruiting poster, 12–13, 241
discusses war with MPs, 341–342
and length of the war, 234
size of army required, 233
created the 'New Armies', 235
and newspaper reporting, 242–243
Pals battalions, 244
and Lloyd George's call for special treatment for Welsh, 246–247
Irish recruiting, 247–251
supplies, 243
in Cabinet, 245–247
relations with Asquith, 255
and security 255
munitions, 258–259
enlists support of labour force, 262–263
and the Shells Committee, 264
conflict with Lloyd George, 264
attempts to remove from office, 270–275
reconfirmed as Secretary for State for War, 275
attitude to machine guns, 278–280
strategy, 281–311
home defence, 284–286
Western Front strategy, 286–294
French's attitude to, 290–291
Russian position, 294–311
Gallipoli campaign, 282, 298–301, 308
and the Balkans, 312–335
accepts a General Staff, 315
low standing, 317–318
visit to the Dardanelles, 320–321
attempts to replace, 319, 324
offers his resignation, 327
and the Pact with Robertson, 328
exhaustion, 329
death of friends, 330–331
continuing public support, 331
enthusiastic about tanks and aircraft, 334
and events in Russia, 335
move to reduce salary of, 341

death
mission to Russia, 336–365
accepts invitations, 338–340
lack of security, 338, 364
travel arrangements, 340–343
joins the Hampshire, 349
weather for the trip, 348
known U-boat activity, 349–352
sets sail, 353
Hampshire sunk, 354–356
search for, 358–359
death announced, 360–361
press reports in Germany, 362–363
reactions to the news, 364–365
Court of Inquiry, 366
claims that death was no accident, 368–372
national memorial proposed, 376
change in reputation after his death, 377–380

INDEX

character
- acquisitiveness, 132–133, 197, 225
- aloofness, 21, 86, 88
- ambition, 179
- appearance, 13–14, 20–21, 47, 133, 137, 197, 284
- boyhood character, 21
- breakdowns, 24, 108, 160
- as a chain-smoker, 219
- cruelty, 96
- and female company, 27
- friendships, 74
- grim humour, 81
- horse-riding ability, 47
- incapacity for delegation, 117
- leadership, 54, 100
- linguistic ability, 29, 60
- loneliness, 201
- meanness, 228
- and religion, 26, 32
- sensitivity, 13, 126
- sulkiness, 55
- vanity, 13
- and women, 207–208, 378–379

private life
- buys Broome Park, 212–214
- buys estate in Kenya, 214
- collects porcelain, 11, 47, 86, 132, 207
- confidantes, 137
- created a peer, 131
- family relations, 97, 148, 224
- and female company, 36, 56, 137–138
- financial affairs, 170
- and Hermione Baker, 56
- homosexuality, alleged, 201, 378
- illnesses, 28, 36
- interest in Freemasonry, 210
- interest in photography, 33, 36
- interest in the Levant, 26
- learns to relax and enjoy life, 196
- liking for Arab dress, 41–42
- love of France, 24
- and marriage, 88, 177
- out of sympathy with the times, 223–224
- *Photographs of Biblical Sites*, 38
- relations with his father, 29–30
- social life in India, 179, 200
- writings for *Blackwood's Magazine*, 39

Kitchener, Kawara (Kitchener's sister), 24
Kitchener, Thomas, 15
Kitchener, William (Kitchener's grandfather), 15, 16
Kitchener Medical School, Khartoum, 376
Klip Drift, 150, 151, 292
Knole, 212–213
Knowles, Gen., 98
Knox, Col A.F.W., 295, 336–338
Kordofan, 136
Korosko, 59, 84
Kosheh, 102, 105
Kruger, Paul, 141, 154
Kut, 326

Ladysmith, 143, 149, 154–157
Lansdowne, Lord, 23, 140, 158, 165, 253
Lanzerac, Gen., 288, 289
Lauder, Harry, 241
Laval, 30
Law, Andrew Bonar, 12, 270, 275, 320, 375
Lawson, Henry, 30
Le Bas, Sir Hedley, 12, 242
Le Cateau, 274, 288, 290
Lee, Gen., 234
Leete, Alfred, 11–13
Leiter, Daisy, 177, 185
Leiter, Levy Z., 177
Lewis, Lt Col D.F., 118
Lichnowsky, Prince, 229
Liverpool, 44, 244
Lloyd George, David, 11, 170
- Boer War, 163

411

and Welsh recruits, 246–247
and security, 255
munition supplies, 259, 263–267
quarrels with Kitchener, 270–275
and supply of machine guns, 278–280
on Kitchener, 280
strategy in the Balkans, 297–320
and Kitchener's attitude, 310–311
calls for conscription, 235, 253
and the Russian mission, 336–338
and Kitchener's death, 365
becomes Prime Minister, 373
on Kitchener in his memoirs, 377
London, Chatham and Dover Railway, 130, 214
Long, Lord, 368
Loos, 254, 310, 311, 314, 319
Lucas, Lord, 264
Ludendorff, Gen., 326
Lyttelton, Gen. Sir Neville, 114, 146

MacBride, John, 252
Macdonald, Maj. Gen. Sir Hector, 83, 90, 102, 119–120, 147, 153, 156
MacDonnell, Sir Schomberg, 181
MacEniry, Sean, 18
Mackay, Alexander, 69–70
Mackensen, Field Marshal August von, 306
Madan, Freiherr von, 364
Mafeking, 143, 154
Magdeburg, 349
Magersfontein, 145, 149, 150
Magnus, Sir Philip, 8, 371
Maher Pasha, 93, 94
Mahmud, Emir, 110–112
Majuba Hill, 141, 154
Mallet, Marie, 96
Mallow, 250
Malta, 204, 345
Manchuria, 207
Marker, Col R.J., 148, 180, 185, 190–193, 200, 330

Markham, Sir Arthur, 242
Marne, 290. 292
Mary, Queen, 223
Maubeuge, 287–290
Maxwell, Brig. Gen. Frank Aylmer 'The Brat', 10, 147–149, 197–200
Maxwell, Maj. Sir John, 156, 300
Mayberry, 349, 353
McKenna, Reginald, 264, 283, 320, 337, 339
McMahon, Sir Henry, 324
McPherson, Lt, 339, 340
Melba, Nellie, 138
Melbourne, 208, 209
Merowe, 104
Metemma, 64–66, 105, 110
Methuen, Lt Gen. Lord, 143, 150, 160
Millerand, A., 291, 293
Milner, Sir Alfred, 91, 96, 160–171, 216
Minto, Lord, 192, 202–206
Moltke, Helmut von, 289, 290
Mombasa, 214
Monro, Gen., Sir Charles, 317, 321, 324, 326
Mons, 242, 258, 289, 290
Montagu-Stuart-Wortley, Edward, 114
Montagu, Edwin, 284
Moore, Arthur, 242
Moreton, Lady Jane, 73
Moreton, Sir Richard, 73
Morley, John, 125, 197, 200, 202–206, 211
Morrison, George, 207
Mosul, 48
Mount Stewart, 176
Mudros, 321, 323
Muhoroni, 214
Munitions, Ministry of, 268, 275, 277, 279, 321, 340
Munitios Committee, 265, 267
Murdoch, Keith, 317
Murmansk, 337, 347
Murray, Gen. Sir Archibald, 284, 294

INDEX

Nablus, 42
Namur, 289
Napolien III, Emperor, 30
National Shells Factories, 268
Naval Intelligence Department (NID), 349
Neilson, Capt. J.F., 295, 339
Neufeld, Charles, 72, 123
Neuve Chapelle, 10, 254, 269, 305, 319
New York, 210
New Zealand, Kitchener visits, 206–210
Nicholas II, Tsar, 297, 306, 326, 338
Nicolai, Walter, 364
Nicosia, 43, 46, 47
North London Association of Boy Scouts, 214
Northcliffe, Lord, 230, 255, 270, 273–276, 365
Northward, 358
Noyon, 310
Nubar Pasha, 55, 94

O'Beirne, H.J., 340, 343
Oak, HMS, 343, 345, 367
Ohrwalder, Joseph, 72
Oku, 352
Olifant's Nek, 155
Omdurman, 95–121
Ordnance Board, 259, 260
Orotava, SS, 168–169
Osborne, 71
Osprey, 55

Paardeberg, 151, 154, 173, 234, 244, 292, 331
Page, Walter, 255
Palestine Exploration Fund, 34–36, 41, 45, 56
Palmer, Sir Elwin, 107
Palmer, Gen. Sir Power, 181, 182
Panshanger, 137–138, 176, 283
Parker, Alfred Chevallier 'Wallier', 97, 135, 224
Parker, Frances (niece), 223–224

Parker, Harry, 24, 97
Parker, Millie (Frances Emily Kitchener), 16, 24
   Kitchener's letters to, 11, 26, 27, 33, 36, 39, 45, 54–56, 60, 64, 68, 74, 76, 84, 86, 88, 97, 136
   helps Kitchener in Sudan, 77
   lives in New Zealand, 88, 92
   help from Kitchener, 96
   and Kitchener's visit to New Zealand, 209
   and Kitchener's death, 361
Parliamentary Recruiting Committee (PRC), 12, 240
Parnell, Charles Stewart, 341
Parsons, Sir Lawrence, 250–251
Pease, Jack, 283
Pétain, Marshal, 333
Peters, Karl, 75
Petrograd, 303, 307, 310, 325, 336–340
Phillips, Colonel George Fraser, 313
Phillips, William Charles, 354
Port Said, 94, 223
Portland, Lady, 196
Pretoria, 141, 154, 155, 165–167, 174
Prinsloo, Gen., 156
Pritchard, Lt, 119–120

Queen Elizabeth, HMS, 299
Quetta, 194

Ralli Pandeli, 73–74, 97, 131, 142, 146, 177, 216
Ramdam, 150
Rawlinson, General Sir Henry, 139, 147, 156, 204, 274, 284, 286, 293
Redmond, John, 247–252
Renshaw, Sir Arthur, 170
Renzo, 358
Repington, Col Charles a Court, 270–275
Rheims, 298, 333
Rhodes, Cecil, 141–142

Rhodes, Frnakie, 112
Richards, Frank, 182
Richardson, Sir George, 248
Riddell, Sir George, 260, 266
Ridley, C.P., 150
Roberts, Field Marshal Lord 'Bobs'
   Boer War, 143–155
      'Black Week', 139, 176
      attack on Paardeberg, 151–154
      pulls Kitchener out of the field, 154
      returns home, 155
      considers war over, 156
      increases funds, 157
      sends Hamilton to report on Kitchener, 161
   other aspects
      background, 11
      character, 139, 140
      and the reconquest of Sudan, 111
      Kitchener meets, 131, 136
      made Commander-in-Chief, 137
      and Kitchener in India, 158, 181, 184, 187–189
      and conscription, 235–236
      and the Territorial Forces, 236
      death, 330
Roberts, Freddy, 139
Roberts, Lady, 196
Robertson, General Sir William, 259, 294, 321, 325, 327–328, 332–334
Robinson, Henry Crabb, 15
Rodd, Sir Rennell, 324, 329
Rodino, 352
Rogerson, Charles, Leading Seaman, 356
Romania, 297, 302, 303
Rosebery, 5th Earl of, 76, 94, 95
Rothley Temple, 24
Rothschild, Alfred, 199
Rothschilds, 51
Royal Aircraft Establishment, 260
Royal Arsenal, Woolwich, 25, 260–261
Royal Military Academy, Woolwich, 25
Rumbold, Horace, 207

Runciman, Walter, 230, 262, 264
Rundle, Gen. Sir Leslie, 28, 58, 89, 92, 156
Russia, First World War, 232–311, 335–341
Russian Supply Committee, 337

Sackville, Lady Victoria, 212
Sackville-West, Vita, 213
Safed, 37
St Mihiel, 333
Salisbury, 3rd Marquess, 80
   background, 82
   appoints Kitchener Adjutant-General to Grenfell, 82
   and European expansion in east and central Africa, 83
   and Kitchener's appointment as Sirdar, 86–87
   and the reconquest of Sudan, 95, 97–100, 105–108, 125
   Kitchener's governorship of Sudan, 131–134
   and the Boer War, 139, 155, 158
   retires, 175
Salonika, 297, 313, 316, 322, 324–326, 334–335
Sandwick, 356, 375
Sarrail, General Maurice, 316
Savage family, 23
Savill, Capt. H.J., 344–348, 353–355
Scapa Flow, 340, 343, 353
Scheer, Admiral, 344, 350–352, 362, 365, 368, 372
Schlieffen Plan, 288, 290
School of Military Engineering, Chatham, 31
Scott, C.P., 126
Scott, John, 91
Scrabster, 343, 345, 367
Searanger, 352
Seely, Col, 215, 230
Serbia, 225–228, 296–297, 301, 311–316, 334–335

INDEX

Seymour, Sir Beauchamp, 52
Sharpe, Mrs, 18, 19
Shells, Committee, 264
Simla, 179, 180, 185, 186, 193–198, 206, 213
Simmons, Maj. Gen. Sir Lintorn, 25
Sims, Frederick 344, 353–357, 366, 374
Sinai, 57, 224–225
Singh, Sardar Ram, 197
Slatin, Sir Rudolf Pasha, 72, 109, 116, 199
Smith-Dorrien, Gen. Horace, 123, 129, 147, 153, 284, 290
Smith, Col Holled, 82
Smith, F.E., 242
Smuts, Jan, 155. 160, 166, 167
Snowdon, villa in Simla, 179, 196–198
Solomon, Sir Richard, 166
Somme, 244, 277, 328, 332
South Africa, see Boer War
Southampton, 169
Spion Kop, 149
Stanley, Venitia, 232, 255, 286
Starling, HMS, 81
Stead, W.T., 58
Steevens, G.W., 59, 113, 118, 133
Stevenson, Frances, 320
Stewart, Brig. Gen. Sir Herbert, 64–65
Stewart, Col Herbert, 61–63
Stopford, Lieutenant General Sir Frederick, 317
Stormberg, 139, 145
Storrs, Ronald, 219–220, 226, 229
Stromness, 357–360
Stuart, Sir Nicholas, 15
Suakin, 57, 59, 69, 76–82, 96–99, 133, 207
Sudan, Mahdist unrest, 52–55, 57
    Gordon sent to Khartoum, 58
    Kitchener gathers intelligence about, 60
    Gordon besieged, 60–64
    Gordon's death, 66
    Gladstone evacuates, 69

    Kitchener appointed Governor General to Eastern Sudan, 76
    attack at Suakin, 78–80
    reconquest, 95–12
    enters the Empire, 125
    government by Egypt, 134
Suez Canal, 75, 204, 224, 299, 300, 322
Sullivan, Jamesy, 21
Suvla Bay, 308, 312, 317, 322, 326
Swinton, Col Ernest, 243, 334
Syria, 26, 322, 323, 329

Tahiti, 210
Taplow Court, 73, 227
Tatar Bazardjik, 39
Taylor, Lt Col, 53–55
Tel-el-Kebir, 52
Tennant, H.J., 251, 341
Territorial Forces, 285–286
Tewfik, Khedive, 51
Thomas, Col Owen, 247
Thurso, 343, 345
Tokar, 85
Tokyo, 207
Tor Point, 349, 354
Toski, 83–86
Transvaal, see Boer War
Trident, HMS, 352
Triple Alliance, 97
Turkey, 38–39, 45, 50, 219, 225, 297–303, 316, 322
Tyrwhitt-Drake, Charles, 34

United States, Kitchener visits, 210
Unity, HMS, 349, 354, 358
Uskub, 316

Vaal Krantz, 149, 166
Venizelos, E., 313–314
Verdun, 290, 333
Vereeniging, 166–168, 173
Vickers, 260
Victor, HMS, 349, 354, 358

Victor Emmanuel, King of Italy, 324
Victoria, Queen
   and Valentine Baker's promotion, 55–56
   and Gordon's death, 66
   Kitchener presented to, 71
   and Kitchener's wound at Suakin, 81
   Kitchener's first visit to Windsor, 94
   and the recapture of Khartoum, 124
   Kitchener's treatment of the Mahdi's body, 126–127
   death, 175
Vienna, 32–33, 93, 228
Villeray, Capt. di, 367
Villiers, Fred, 112
Viviani, René, 191
Von Donop, Maj. Gen. Sir Stanley, 254, 259, 261, 264, 266

Wad Bishara, Emir, 103–104
Wad-el-Nejumi, 83–84
Wadi Halfa, 69, 83–85, 89, 99, 105–107, 127
Walker, Capt. F.M., 358
Walker, Major General Sir Frederick, 93
Walmer Castle, SS, 169, 294
Walters, Catherine, 'Skittles', 137
Waltham Abbey, 260
Wantage, Lady, 232
War Committee, 317, 320–324, 332–334, 339
War Council, 245, 282–284, 296–303, 308, 327
War Office 261–270, 273–280, 284–286, 332–340, 360
War Supplies Committee, 265
Ward, Sir Joseph, 209–210
Waterval Drift, 150
Watkins, O.S., 126
Watson, Maj., 97–98
Watson, Rev., 125
Wauchope, Gen. Andrew, 114, 125, 145
Wesson, Wilfred, 356
West Point, 210
Western, Walter, 212

White, General Sir George, 143, 157
Whittingehame, 176
Wilhelm II, Kaiser, 214, 225, 314
Wilkins, Rev., 125
Willcocks, Sir William, 220
William III, King of England, 15
Williams, Captain H.R., 32
Wilson, Col Sir Charles, 44, 45, 61, 65–66
Wilson, Gen. Sir Henry, 246, 287–293
Wing, Maj. Gen. F.V., 264
Wingate, Gen. Sir Reginald, 57, 89, 103, 106–110, 127, 136–139, 225
Wintour, U.F., 296
Witwatersrand, 141
Wodehouse, Col Josceline, 84, 86
Wolfe-Murray, General Sir James, 283–284
Wolseley, Field Marshal Lord
   Ashanti War, 33–34
   in Cyprus, 43–46
   in Egypt, 52
   sent to relieve Gordon, 60–64
   support for Kitchener, 78, 98
   and the reconquest of Sudan, 111, 131
   Roberts succeeds, 137
Wolseley, Lady, 48
Wood, Gen. Sir Evelyn
   with Wolseley in Ashanti War, 43
   Kitchener joins in Egypt, 53–57
   as Sirdar, 56
   sends Kitchener to collect intelligence of Sudan, 57
   opinion of Kitchener, 60
   Grenfell succeeds, 71
   notes Haig, 114–115
Wynford Park, 176

Yakub, 118–119
York, Duke of, 137
Younghusband, Sir George, 139
Ypres, 254, 292–294

Zafir, gunboat, 102, 109
Zanzibar Boundary Commission, 74–76
Zeebrugge, 298